W9-CRY-391

Countryside Planning

Countryside Planning

New Approaches to Management and Conservation

Edited by

Kevin Bishop and Adrian Phillips

London • Sterling, VA

First published by Earthscan in the UK and USA in 2004

A catalogue record for this book is available from the British Library

ISBN: 1-85383-849-7 paperback
     1-84407-059-X hardback

Typesetting by MapSet Ltd, Gateshead, UK
Printed and bound in the UK by Creative Print and Design (Wales), Ebbw Vale
Cover design by Danny Gillespie

For a full list of publications please contact:

Earthscan
8–12 Camden High Street
London, NW1 0JH, UK
Tel: +44 (0)20 7387 8558
Fax: +44 (0)20 7387 8998
Email: earthinfo@earthscan.co.uk
Web: **www.earthscan.co.uk**

22883 Quicksilver Drive, Sterling, VA 20166-2012, USA

A catalogue record for this book is available from the British Library

Library of Congress Cataloging-in-Publication Data

Countryside planning : new approaches to management and conservation / edited by
Kevin Bishop and Adrian Phillips.
    p. cm.
Includes bibliographical references and index.
    ISBN 1-84407-059-X (hc) – ISBN 1-85383-849-7 (pb)
     1. Regional planning. 2. Regional planning–Environmental aspects. I. Bishop,
    Kevin, 1966- II. Phillips, Adrian.

HT391.C68 2003
307.1'2–dc21

2003012568

Earthscan publishes in association with WWF-UK and the International Institute for
Environment and Development

Contents

List of Tables, Figures and Boxes   *ix*
List of Contributors   *xi*
List of Acronyms and Abbreviations   *xiv*
Preface   *xvii*

1 Then and Now: Planning for Countryside Conservation
Kevin Bishop and Adrian Phillips   1
Introduction   1
Defining countryside conservation and planning   2
Then: a lasting legacy   3
Now: a new era?   6
An outline   9

PART 1: THE INTERNATIONAL CONTEXT FOR COUNTRYSIDE PLANNING AND MANAGEMENT

2 From Sandy to Rio: The Development of Biodiversity Action Planning
Kevin Bishop and Richard Cowell   19
The road to Rio   20
The road from Rio   24
Re-framing the agenda   28
Conclusions   33

3 European Frameworks for Nature Conservation: The Case of the Birds and Habitats Directives
Dave Burges   37
The birds and habitats directives   37
Delivery mechanisms   42
Impact on the British planning system and wider countryside policy
frameworks   44
The changing context   45
Conclusions   47

4   **Our Landscape from a Wider Perspective**
     Adrian Phillips and Roger Clarke   49
     Landscape – an elusive concept for international policy   49
     Cultural landscapes and the world heritage convention   54
     Protected landscapes   55
     European landscape convention   58
     Recent developments in the European Union   61
     The implications for the UK   62

5   **Policy Context for Community Involvement in**
     Countryside Planning
     Diane Warburton   68
     Global and European drivers towards sustainable development,
     human rights and environmental policy   71
     The UK response   73
     Conclusions   83

PART 2: NEW CONCEPTS AND TOOLS

6   **The Natural Area Experience**
     Keith Porter   91
     New solutions to old problems   91
     New needs and drivers   94
     Developing the framework   96
     Natural areas in practice   100
     Where next?   103
     Conclusions   105

7   **The Assessment of Countryside and Landscape Character in**
     England: An Overview
     Carys Swanwick   109
     The evolution of countryside and landscape character assessment   110
     Making judgements based on countryside and landscape character   116
     Practical applications of landscape character assessment   120
     Current and future issues   122

8   **Policies and Priorities for Ireland's Landscapes**
     Michael Starrett   125
     The heritage council   125
     The first steps   126
     The pilot landscape characterization – County Clare   129
     The next steps   137
     Conclusions   139

9   **Development and Application of Landscape Assessment
      Guidelines in Ireland: Case Studies using Forestry and
      Wind Farm Developments**
      Art McCormack and Tomás O'Leary   141
      Irish landscape assessment guidelines   142
      Case study 1: landscape assessment in the planning and design of
      forestry   146
      Case study 2: landscape assessment in the planning and design of
      wind farms   150
      Conclusions   151

10   **Historic Landscape Characterization**
      Lesley Macinnes   155
      Background   155
      Historic landscape characterization   156
      The application of HLC   163
      Conclusions   166

11   **Connecting the Pieces: Scotland's Integrated Approach to the
      Natural Heritage**
      Roger Crofts   170
      The overall philosophy   171
      Basic structure of approach   173
      What are the benefits – actual and expected?   177
      Conclusions   185

12   ***LANDMAP*: A Tool to Aid Sustainable Development**
      Rob Owen and David Eagar   188
      Organizational change   188
      How the method was developed   190
      The *LANDMAP* method   191
      Where next – towards sustainability?   198

PART 3: FROM THEORY TO PRACTICE

13   **Applications of Landscape Character Assessment**
      Julie Martin   203
      Range of applications   203
      Character assessment and planning   205
      Character assessment and land management   214
      Character assessment and other strategic initiatives   216
      Towards good practice   219

14   **The Link Between Landscape, Biodiversity and Development
     Plans: A Move Towards 'Positive Planning'?**
     Kevin Bishop and Richard Bate   222
     The policy context for positive planning   222
     Research method   224
     Development of Regulation 37 policies   224
     Policies promoting/enhancing biodiversity   231
     Implementing positive planning policies   233
     Conclusions   234

15   **A New Way of Valuing Land in the Countryside: Are We Lost
     Without a Map?**
     Jo Milling   237
     Links to the statutory land use planning system   238
     Effectiveness of the new approaches   239
     Community involvement   246
     Conclusions   248

16   **Community Involvement in Countryside Planning in Practice**
     Diane Warburton   250
     Frameworks for analysing levels of community involvement   251
     Examples of community involvement in countryside planning   253
     Overall strands and themes   264
     Conclusions   268

Index   271

List of Tables, Figures and Boxes

TABLES

9.1 Forest landscape planning and design criteria and factors   147
9.2 Proposed implications of the five sensitivity classes for wind farm
       development in County Cork   152
14.1 Factors influencing the decision to include a Regulation 37 policy in
       development plans   225
14.2 Factors influencing the decision to include a Regulation 37 policy
       in development plans   226
14.3 Implementation mechanisms for positive planning policies   233

FIGURES

(Plates located in centre pages)

1.1 The countryside planner's bookshelf   2
1.2 The countryside planner's toolkit   3
2.1 Spatial hierarchy of biodiversity action planning in the UK   29
6.1 Oxfordshire Midvale Ridge Natural Area showing known fen locations
       and those 'discovered' through application of predictive search   93
6.2 Chilterns Natural Area showing National Nature Reserves and
       Sites of Special Scientific Interest   93
6.3 The Yorkshire Dales Natural Area   94
6.4 The Natural Areas framework, 2002   plate
6.5 Vision map of the Alde project area   plate
6.6 A 'layered' approach to data integration   106
8.1 Preliminary landscape character types in County Clare   plate
9.1 Model for the identification of landscape character areas   143
9.2 Model proposed for strategic forest landscape planning and design   147
9.3 Suggested landscape character types in County Cork for wind farm
       planning and design   plate
9.4 Suggested landscape sensitivity classification of County Cork for
       wind farm planning and design   plate
11.1 Systematic diagram of Natural Heritage Units   175
11.2 Natural Heritage Units of Scotland   plate
15.1 Development at the Hedgerows, Leigh on Mendip   plate
15.2 Development at Townsend Farm, Leigh on Mendip   plate
16.1 Arnstein's ladder of participation   251

BOXES

2.1 Specific aims of RSPB action plans   24
2.2 Key elements of the Biodiversity Challenge approach   26
3.1 The EU Birds and Habitats Directives   38
3.2 European Court of Justice decisions under the EU Birds Directive   40
4.1 IUCN protected area management categories   56
4.2 Main provisions of the European Landscape Convention   61
4.3 The Oxford Landscape Declaration   64
6.1 Examples of approaches explored in devising the Natural Areas
     framework   97
6.2 Variables used to establish the Countryside Character Map   100
6.3 Key functions of Lifescapes   105
7.1 The evolution of Landscape Character Assessment   114
7.2 Main steps in Landscape Character Assessment   117
8.1 Technical explanation of the statistical approach   134
8.2 Technical explanation of the expert analysis   136
8.3 Summary of recommendations on landscape policy by the Heritage
     Council   138
11.1 Timetable for the Futures Programme   173
11.2 Stages in the definition of Natural Heritage Futures Units   174
11.3 Defining visions for the natural heritage   178
12.1 Wales Landscape Partnership Group   189
12.2 Local information user groups   193
12.3 Role of the Aspect Specialist   195
12.4 Potential uses of *LANDMAP Information*   198
13.1 The range of Landscape Character Assessment Applications   204
13.2 Landscape policy in the Hart District local plan   205
13.3 Landscape policy in the Staffordshire structure plan   206
13.4 Good practice in formulating development plan landscape policy   208
13.5 Criteria for establishing landscape sensitivity to wind farm
      development   209
13.6 Locating new housing development in South Hams District   210
13.7 Countryside Design Summary for West Lindsey District   211
13.8 The Hampshire landscape strategy   212
13.9 Identifying planting areas in the National Forest   213
13.10 Traffic Appraisal and Impact Monitoring System (TAIMS)   217
13.11 Landscapes working for the Vale of Glamorgan   218
14.1 West Lancashire Local Plan (Adopted) 1999   227
14.2 Devon Structure Plan First Review 1995–2011 (Adopted) 1999   229
14.3 Leicestershire, Leicester and Rutland Structure Plan 1991–2011   232
15.1 Landscape character area descriptions   239
15.1 Village Design Statement for Leigh on Mendip   243

List of Contributors

Richard Bate is a planning and environment consultant specializing in the development of national policy and its local application. He has worked extensively on the promotion of ecological, rural and affordable housing, particularly in the voluntary sector. He is the specialist adviser on planning to the House of Commons through its Select Committees shadowing the former Department of the Environment, Transport and the Regions (DETR) and now the Office of the Deputy Prime Minister (ODPM).

Kevin Bishop is a geographer and planner. He is Head of Environment and Regeneration at the Welsh Local Government Association and prior to this was Head of the Environmental Planning Research Unit at Cardiff University. He has research and policy interests in protected areas, countryside planning and management and sustainable development.

Dave Burges is currently Head of WWF-UK's European Programme. He joined WWF-UK in 2000, working initially on Natura 2000 issues and later leading the Future Landscapes Team which focused on integrated land use management. Prior to this, Dave worked for many years at the RSPB (Royal Society for the Protection of Birds), latterly as a Conservation Officer in the South East England Regional Office.

Roger Clarke is Chief Executive of the Youth Hostels Association (YHA) (England and Wales). Prior to joining the YHA he was a Director at the Countryside Agency. While working at the Countryside Agency he took the policy lead on landscape and protected area issues.

Richard Cowell is a lecturer in the Department of City and Regional Planning, Cardiff University. He is a co-author (with Susan Owens) of *Land and Limits: Interpreting Sustainability in the Planning Process* (Routledge, 2002) and has written widely on the interface between land use planning, sustainable development and environmental politics. His current research embraces the role of evaluation and audit tools in promoting sustainable development (such as Best Value and environmental footprinting), and the role of community strategies in delivering joined-up and participatory governance.

Roger Crofts trained as a geographer and spent his early career researching the geomorphology of coastal and mountain systems. He worked in government at the Scottish Office as an adviser on development in Scotland. He was Chief Executive of Scottish Natural Heritage from 1992 to 2002. He is actively involved in IUCN (the World Conservation Union) in the UK and Europe.

David Eagar trained as a geographer, landscape scientist and planner, and has worked extensively in countryside planning and management in England and Wales. He was senior landscape policy officer for the Countryside Council for Wales, where he helped devise, and later managed, the *LANDMAP Information System*. David worked as a planner for Hampshire, Norfolk and Gwynedd county councils, rejoining the Countryside Commission in 1985. There he initiated the Warwickshire Landscapes Project that begat the character method of landscape assessment.

Lesley Macinnes is a Principal Inspector of Ancient Monuments, with particular responsibility for landscape, environment and sustainability. Her archaeological research interests lie in the Iron Age and native settlements of the Roman period, about which she has written several papers and co-edited a volume, and in the study of cropmarks. She is also interested in cultural resource management, both generally and in the particular issues affecting archaeology in the modern environment, and has written several papers and co-edited a book in this field.

Julie Martin is a geographer, landscape architect and planner. She has more than 20 years' experience of assessing the impacts of major developments within sensitive rural environments, as well as advising government agencies and local authorities on conservation and sustainable development policy. She was the author of *Landscape Assessment Guidance* (Countryside Commission, 1993) and technical editor of the *Guidelines for Landscape and Visual Impact Assessment* (Landscape Institute and Institute of Environmental Assessment, 1994). She is coordinator of the Countryside Agency's Countryside Character Network and has played a pioneering role in landscape planning initiatives in England, Scotland, Northern Ireland and Ireland.

Art McCormack is a senior researcher in the Faculty of Agriculture at NUI Dublin and a Principal of MosArt Landscape Architecture and Research based in County Wicklow. His academic research and private practice over the past decade has focused upon such fields as landscape characterization, development of landscape related guidelines, and assessment of public attitudes towards landscape change.

Jo Milling is a planning and environmental Policy Officer at Mendip District Council. She has 15 years' experience of local government policy-making. She has experience in environmental assessment, landscape assessment, community participation, planning policy and community strategy and led the environmental input to the recently adopted Mendip District Local Plan. She lives and works in rural north-east Somerset.

Tomás O'Leary is a senior researcher in the Faculty of Agriculture at NUI Dublin and a Principal of MosArt Landscape Architecture and Research based in County Wicklow. His academic research and private practice over the past decade has focused upon such fields as landscape characterization, development of landscape related guidelines, and assessment of public attitudes towards landscape change.

Adrian Phillips was Director General of the Countryside Commission between 1981 and 1992. He held a part-time Chair at Cardiff University from then until 2001. He was a trustee for the World Wide Fund For Nature (WWF) and is currently Chair of the Campaign to Protect Rural England's Policy Committee and of WWF's Programme Committee. He lives in rural Gloucestershire, enjoys walking and tries to grow more of his own vegetables.

Rob Owen is Head of Communication and Interpretation for the Countryside Council for Wales. His background is in countryside planning. He was actively involved in the initial development of *LANDMAP* prior to his secondment to the Wales European Centre for two years.

Keith Porter has worked for English Nature and the former Nature Conservancy Council since 1985 and is currently the Environmental Information Manager. He was closely involved in the development of the Natural Areas approach. He has had a life-long fascination with natural history, culminating in a strong interest in insects. This remains a 'hobby', when time permits.

Michael Starrett is a graduate ecologist and biologist with a postgraduate qualification in education. He has worked in the area of protected area management since 1979. He has been the Chief Executive of the Heritage Council (Ireland) since 1996. The Heritage Council proposes policy to the Irish government on aspects of both the natural and cultural heritage.

Carys Swanwick has been Head of the Department of Landscape at the University of Sheffield since 1995. Prior to that she was a Principal and Director of Land Use Consultants and has 28 years' experience of landscape and environmental planning. She has specialized in the field of landscape assessment and has been instrumental in developing approaches both through practical projects and by preparing advice and guidance. She led the New Map Consortium which piloted the English approach to character assessment at the national and regional scales and is the author, with Land Use Consultants, of the Countryside Agency and Scottish Natural Heritage guidance on Landscape Character Assessment.

Diane Warburton is an independent researcher and writer on participation and sustainable development. She is an honorary fellow of the University of Brighton, a founding co-partner of Shared Practice (www.sharedpractice.org.uk) and a member of InterAct (specializing in evaluating participation). Her publications include *Community and Sustainable Development: Participation in the Future* (Earthscan, 1998) and *From Here to Sustainability* (with Ian Christie) for the Real World Coalition (Earthscan, 2001).

List of Acronyms and Abbreviations

ACRE	Action with Communities in Rural England
AONB	Area of Outstanding Natural Beauty
ASSI	Areas of Special Scientific Interest
BAP	biodiversity action plan
BSE	Bovine Spongiform Encephalopathy
BTCV	British Trust for Conservation Volunteers
CAP	Common Agricultural Policy
CBD	(United Nations) Convention on Biological Diversity
CCW	Countryside Council for Wales
CDP	Community Development Projects
CDS	Countryside Design Summaries
CEC	Commission of the European Communities
CLCA	County Landscape Character Assessment (Ireland)
CLRAE	Congress of Local and Regional Authorities
COE	Council of Europe
CPRE	Campaign to Protect Rural England (formerly the Council for the Protection of Rural England)
CSS	Countryside Stewardship Scheme
DAHGI	Department of Arts, Heritage, Gaeltacht and the Islands
DCMS	Department of Culture, Media and Sport
DEFRA	Department of the Environment, Food and Rural Affairs
DOE&LG	Department of the Environment and Local Government (Ireland)
ECJ	European Court of Justice
EECONET	European Ecological Network
EIA	environmental impact assessment
EIS	environmental impact statement
ELC	European Landscape Convention
ESA	Environmentally Sensitive Areas
ESRC	Economic and Social Research Council
FIPS	Forestry Inventory Planning System (Ireland)
FMD	Foot and Mouth Disease
FWAG	Farming and Wildlife Advisory Group
GDO	General Development Order
GIS	Geographical Information System
GM	genetically modified
HLA	Historic Land Use Assessment
HLC	Historic Landscape Characterization
HS	Historic Scotland

ICPL	International Centre for Protected Landscapes
IFS	Indicative Forestry Strategy
IUCN	World Conservation Union
JNCC	Joint Nature Conservation Committee
LA21	Local Agenda 21
LBAP	Local Biodiversity Action Plans
LCA	Landscape Character Assessment
LEAP	Local Environment Agency Plans
LGA	Local Government Association
LGMB	Local Government Management Board
LPA	local planning authority
MAFF	Ministry for Agriculture, Fisheries and Food
MRTPI	Member of the Royal Town Planning Institute
NCC	Nature Conservancy Council
NEST	NVCO Environment Support Team
NGO	non-governmental organization
NHZ	Natural Heritage Zone
NVC	National Vegetation Community
NVCO	National Council for Voluntary Organisations
PEBLDS	Pan-European Biological and Landscape Diversity Strategy
QoL	Quality of Life
RCAHMS	Royal Commission on the Ancient and Historical Monuments of Scotland
RCAHMW	Royal Commission on the Ancient and Historical Monuments of Wales
RCC	rural community council
RDC	Rural Development Commission
RCEP	Royal Commission on Environmental Pollution
RSPB	Royal Society for the Protection of Birds
RTPI	Royal Town Planning Institute
SAC	Special Area for Conservation
SCAN	Sustainable Communities Action Network
SDU	Sustainable Development Unit
SEU	Social Exclusion Unit
SMRs	sites and monuments records
SNH	Scottish Natural Heritage
SPA	Special Protection Area
SPG	Supplementary Planning Guidance
SPNR	Society for the Promotion of Nature Reserves
SSSI	Site of Special Scientific Interest
TAIMS	Traffic Appraisal and Impact Monitoring System
UKBAP	UK Biodiversity Action Plan
UNCED	United Nations Conference on Environment and Development
UNEP	United Nations Environment Programme
UNCHE	UN Conference on the Human Environment
VDS	Village Design Statements

UNEP WCMC	United Nations Environment Programme World Conservation Monitoring Centre
WCPA	World Commission on Protected Areas
WDA	Welsh Development Agency
WLPG	Wales Landscape Partnership Group
WRI	World Resources Institute
WTO	World Trade Organization
WWF	World Wide Fund For Nature

Preface

The origins of this book lie in an Economic and Social Research Council (ESRC) sponsored seminar series exploring the linkages between society, sustainability and planning and, in particular, in a well-attended seminar held in Cardiff in May 2000 on the theme of new approaches to countryside planning and management. Many of the chapters derive from contributions made at that seminar, though others were added for the sake of completeness.

The result is a volume of essays which explores the new frameworks for planning and managing the countryside and its natural values, reviews the new tools being developed to guide the identification, protection and management of land with environmental value in the countryside, and assesses the value of these new approaches through several case studies. We did not realize when we began writing and editing this book how topical its subject matter would become; but at no time in recent history has the future of the countryside been the subject of such profound uncertainty and anguished debate. It is now clear that we are at a watershed: the future of the countryside is bound to be very different from its recent past. Many groups and professions are now engaged in a discussion about shaping the future direction of countryside policy and practice. We hope that this volume will contribute to their endeavours.

We believe that the strength of this book lies in the diversity of the contributions and their individual subject expertise. However, as with many edited volumes, such diversity presents the challenge of how to bring together a large number of disparate contributions so that they cohere into a publication that hangs together. As editors, we trust that this has been achieved. The collective experience and expertise of the individual contributors far outweighs the thoughts and analysis that we as editors can bring to this topic. Our aim has been to ensure that the individual contributions are clear in their description and analysis; and that the story told in this volume as a whole adds up to more than the sum of its many individual parts.

Our first note of thanks must be to the ESRC for their financial assistance for the seminar that gave birth to the book. However, our greatest debt of gratitude is to the individual contributors for their chapters, sometimes written under considerable pressure whilst they attempted to balance this extra task with their full-time responsibilities in key roles within public, private and voluntary bodies. We would also like to thank the colleagues, friends, partners and families of our contributors for their patience and support.

The staff at Earthscan, notably Pascale Mettam who commissioned the book and Tamsin Langrishe who inherited the project, have been both supportive and patient. Our thanks also to Janice Edwards and Alex Farr in the

Department of City and Regional Planning for their assistance with the illustrations. Our final thanks must be to our respective families for their tolerance whilst we worked on this project. Also an apology to James and particularly Thomas who thought that their Dad was working on a Bob the Builder style blockbuster. We will never again underestimate the effort involved in editing a book!

Chapter 1

Then and Now: Planning for Countryside Conservation

Kevin Bishop and Adrian Phillips

INTRODUCTION

Not since the Corn Law debates of the 19th century has the countryside been such a focus of political and public attention. Fundamental attitudes and assumptions that have underpinned policy in this field for more than half a century have been challenged. In recent years, a watershed has arrived: we can be sure that the future for the countryside will not be a continuation of past trends.

New tools are therefore needed to help us plan and manage the countryside at a time of unprecedented change. This is what this book is about, and in particular about the various approaches being developed to promote environmental concerns. Its main aim, therefore, is to review experience within the UK and Ireland in shaping what the Performance and Innovation Unit of the Cabinet Office has called a 'a new national framework for protecting land of environmental value in the countryside' (1999, p78).

The book's more detailed aims are to:

- examine the impact of new international and European frameworks for planning and managing the countryside and its natural values;
- review the range of new tools for the identification, protection and management of land with environmental value in the countryside;
- assess the value of these new approaches through a range of case studies; and
- draw conclusions on a new approach to countryside planning.

To set the scene, this introductory chapter outlines what we mean by the terms 'countryside conservation' and 'planning', looks back at how the countryside has been planned and managed over the last 50 years, compares this with the situation now and then identifies the key themes addressed in this book.

Figure 1.1 *The countryside planner's bookshelf*

DEFINING COUNTRYSIDE CONSERVATION AND PLANNING

In reality, there is no single system of 'countryside planning' in the UK but rather a number of separate systems and initiatives which represent an ad hoc policy response to different issues that have arisen over time. Despite the introduction of a 'comprehensive' system of town and country planning in 1947, planners (in a statutory sense) have played a limited role in rural land use – often being mere bystanders to the changes in landscape and loss of ecological resources that have occurred. Whilst relatively minor built development has been subject to the full rigour of planning control, major agents of landscape change, such as afforestation schemes and agricultural improvements, have been allowed to proceed outside the planning system. In reality, economic forces driving land management have shaped the countryside far more than has town and country planning.

That is why our definition of countryside conservation and planning is not focused only on the statutory system of town and country planning – and the term 'planner' means more here than those professionals entitled to use the initials 'MRTPI' (Member of the Royal Town Planning Institute). Rather, we are concerned with how society plans and manages the natural and cultural heritage of the countryside in its widest sense. Thus defined, there has been a profusion of countryside plans and strategies aimed at conserving the countryside. As illustrated in Figure 1.1, the countryside planner's bookshelf is now sagging under the weight of such documents. Moreover, a veritable toolkit of countryside planning processes has been devised to help identify, conserve and manage the natural and cultural heritage to help the planner in his or her work (see Figure 1.2).

The focus of this book is on these new frameworks and processes for countryside conservation and planning. In particular, these include:

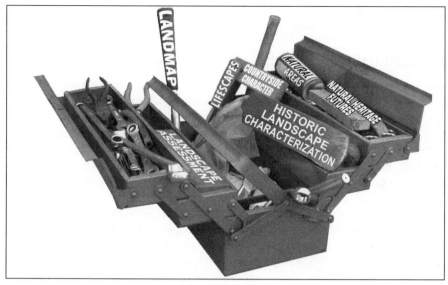

Figure 1.2 *The countryside planner's toolkit*

- methodologies to describe landscape character and natural qualities;
- historic landscape assessments;
- a national to local system of biodiversity action plans; and
- ways of involving local communities in the protection and enhancement of their own environments.

But despite these innovations, the current framework for rural policy still bears the imprint, in part, of the thinking of the 1940s. Therefore, before discussing the key themes addressed in the book in further detail, we briefly recall the origins of countryside planning and management, and how attitudes and policy have changed over the past 50 years.

THEN: A LASTING LEGACY

The prevailing view of the 1940s was clearly captured in the Scott Committee (1942) *Report on Land Utilisation in Rural Areas.* This held that a healthy farming industry was a sine qua non for national food policy, landscape protection and the revival of the rural economy (Cherry and Rogers, 1996). For half a century, this assumption dominated countryside planning and management. The approach that it gave rise to was characterized by the following themes, each of which is explored below:

- agricultural fundamentalism;
- containment planning;
- site specific conservation;
- functional divergence;

- domestic drivers;
- community consultation.

Agricultural Fundamentalism

In the early years after World War II, there was a clear view of what the countryside was for and what should be done to realize this vision. There was a general determination amongst politicians and policy-makers to develop further the 'Dig for Victory' approach to agriculture which had served Britain so well during wartime. Agriculture was seen as the primary function of rural areas and the role of farmers was to ensure food security. The role of government was to support agriculture and provide a policy framework that encouraged food production and provided a favourable environment for farmers to achieve this. Successive governments intervened in the agriculture sector in order to foster and promote domestic food production through price support, production subsidies, scientific research and special treatment for farmers within the land use planning and taxation systems. Though it took a different form after the UK joined the Common Market (now the European Union – EU), production-focused support continued, and was indeed reinforced, under the Common Agricultural Policy (CAP). This philosophy of what the late Gerald Wibberley called 'agricultural fundamentalism' only began to be seriously challenged in the 1980s, perhaps most dramatically with the arrival of milk quotas in 1984. But, despite more than ten years of continual reform to the CAP and national agricultural policy, some of the framework developed immediately after World War II remains intact (Performance and Innovation Unit, 1999; Policy Commission on the Future of Farming and Food, 2002).

Containment Planning

During the inter-war years, Britain took tentative steps towards establishing a town and country planning system, but in reality progress was slow and piecemeal. The major impetus for a national land use planning system came from a trilogy of wartime reports – Barlow (1940), Scott (1942) and Uthwatt (1942). All three reports took the view that a land use planning system should have as one of its primary duties the protection of agricultural land. The seminal influence of the Scott Committee has already been noted. It considered that planning should be about protecting farmland, and farming should have a prior claim to land use unless competing uses could prove otherwise. Such thinking was embodied in the Town and Country Planning Act 1947, which was largely designed to protect the countryside and agricultural land from urban encroachment. The planning system not only sought to contain urban development in order to safeguard agricultural land, it also imposed minimal controls on agricultural and forestry enterprises. The use of land and buildings for agriculture and forestry was (and remains) excluded from the definition of development contained in the 1947 and all subsequent planning acts; hence there is no need to obtain planning permission for agriculture or forestry operations. Also, most building or engineering operations carried out for agriculture or forestry purposes are classified as permitted development under the General Development Order (GDO) Schedule 2. Though some limited erosion of this freedom has taken place over the years, successive governments have resisted pressure from amenity and conservation interests to extend planning controls over a variety of farming and forestry activities. Indeed, strong protection of agricultural land has been the bedrock of national planning policy in the UK for over 50 years (Green Balance, 2000). In so far as the planning system has protected the rural heritage, it has been primarily achieved incidentally, through the protection of the best, most versatile agricultural land from urban development. Since the formal planning system has played such a limited role in protecting the landscape, nature and the historic heritage within the farmed and forested countryside, a range of alternative non-statutory and often innovative approaches have evolved.

Site Specific Conservation

Conservation was an important part of the post-war vision of building a 'Better Britain'. The National Parks and Access to the Countryside Act 1949 marked the culmination of decades of argument and lobbying about the need for conservation of the countryside. Under the Act, conservation efforts were to be focused on the designation and notification of protected areas – special places identified as such because of their scientific or amenity value. For example, the newly established Nature Conservancy was charged with notifying owners and appropriate authorities of the value of 'any area of land of special interest by reason of its flora, fauna, geological or physiographical features' and from this the SSSI (Sites of Special Scientific Interest) 'system' was established. Similarly, the National Parks Commission was charged with designating National Parks and Areas of Outstanding Natural Beauty (AONBs).

The distinction between protected and unprotected places has been fundamental to policy-making and much of the thinking about conservation in the UK over the last 50 years (Bishop et al, 1995; Adams, 2003). For many years, most people probably thought that conservation was something that took place only within protected areas.

Functional Divergence

The network of nature conservation bodies, environmental groups and countryside lobbies that developed in Britain during the first part of the 20th century was united in its concern about unregulated urban encroachment and the need for protected areas. However, these groups held different views on the purpose and function of such areas. For example, the arguments of bodies such as the Society for the Promotion of Nature Reserves and the Council for the Protection of Rural England (now Campaign to Protect Rural England) was reflected in the Huxley and Hobhouse Committees' reports of 1947 on nature conservation and National Parks respectively (Hobhouse Committee, 1947; Huxley Committee, 1947). Whilst the two committees struggled for a short while to develop a unified approach, it was not long before the Huxley Committee opted to follow its own separate route. So, when Hobhouse argued aesthetics, Huxley argued science; where Hobhouse had access and public benefit in mind,

Huxley had study and learning; where Hobhouse saw local authorities, working through the town and country planning system, as the chief deliverers of countryside protection and enjoyment, Huxley wanted hands-on ownership and the management of nature reserves by scientists (Phillips, 1995). The National Parks and Access to the Countryside Act 1949 incorporated these differences into legislation. By the end of 1949, the 'great divide' that would last for 40 years or so was in place, with National Parks and countryside work separated institutionally from that on the conservation of nature – and both quite separate from historic heritage protection. Henceforth, landscape, nature and historic heritage were to be pursued as separate policy areas (Gay and Phillips, 2000).

Domestic Drivers

Whilst those lobbying for the establishment of National Parks drew some inspiration from the experience of countries such as the US, in general the values, beliefs and approaches upon which post-war policy was based were largely domestic. There was very little influence from beyond these shores and certainly no significant international drivers to 'push' or 'pull' domestic policy until the 1980s (the first nature conservation treaty to affect the UK significantly, the Berne Convention, was adopted in 1979, which was also the year in which the Birds Directive took effect).

On the other hand the context used in post-war legislation, and subsequently, was not particularly sensitive to national differences within Great Britain. Thus the National Parks and Access to the Countryside Act 1949 provided for a common system of nature conservation for Great Britain and a common system of landscape protection for England and Wales. Whilst Northern Ireland developed its own legislative frameworks, these mirrored the approach across the Irish Sea.

Community Consultation

Concepts of community engagement, enablement and participation were conspicuously absent from the thinking behind the post-war policy framework that shaped the UK's approach to countryside conservation and planning. The model developed was one of top-down, paternalistic delivery with community involvement often restricted to a limited form of consultation under the formal planning system.

NOW: A NEW ERA?

A comparison of the legacy of the 1940s with the current context suggests that a critical point has been arrived at in terms of how we plan and manage the countryside. The consensus that characterized the approach of successive UK governments to the countryside has broken down.

First, and perhaps foremost, the predominance of agriculture has been challenged and notions of 'agricultural fundamentalism' potentially consigned to history – though as some anguished comments from farmers' interests during the recent epidemic of Foot and Mouth Disease (FMD) show, it retains a near-mythical following in some quarters. The evidence of damage to landscape, wildlife and historic heritage brought about by modern agricultural practices challenged the thinking of the 1940s; it suggested that the price paid by society for farming's privileged position was too high. However, history will probably confirm that domestic food scares (such as BSE – Bovine Spongiform Encephalopathy) and the FMD epidemic of 2001 were the key national events in bringing about insistent calls for changes in agricultural policy. Meanwhile, at the European level the cost of the CAP, and especially of the planned EU expansion, are driving the search for CAP reform; while globally the move for change comes from pressures to liberalize trade in agricultural products. The discussion is now about how to ensure that farmers are rewarded for positive management of the countryside in an environmentally responsible way rather than being subsidized to produce food (Policy Commission on the Future of Food and Farming , 2002). The minority view expressed by Professor Dennison in an appendix to the Scott Committee report (1942) has achieved respectability at last. Furthermore, the debate is not just about what we should be conserving in the countryside but also about what to restore and enhance. Thus there is now a need for planning processes that can identify the character of different areas and guide how that character could be enhanced.

The purposes of town and country planning have had to absorb some important new influences in recent years, perhaps the most relevant to our account being the concept of sustainable development. The focus on urban containment remains, but the sustainable development agenda highlights the importance of comprehensive and environmentally informed planning systems (Owens and Cowell, 2001). More particularly, there is a desire to replace the old orthodoxy of protecting the best and most versatile agricultural land with a new set of environmental values that better reflects the character of the countryside. The new approaches to countryside conservation and planning reviewed in this book help to identify such values. They should provide the basis for environment-based rather than agriculture-led planning of the countryside.

Although there is still a practical focus on site-based nature conservation, it is now widely understood that conservation needs to move beyond protected areas to embrace the whole landscape. Protected areas do not exist in a vacuum: their ecology, and thus their integrity, are influenced not just by internal management but also by wider processes beyond their boundaries. The practice of nature conservation has been evolving in the following ways (Bishop et al, 1995):

- from the protection of species towards the protection of their habitats;
- from the protection of species and habitats towards placing their conservation within the protection of the natural processes upon which they depend;
- from self-contained nature conservation towards its integration into the planning and management of the terrestrial and marine environment as a whole, and into each economic sector;

- from isolated local and national initiatives towards contributions to international programmes, guided by internationally agreed criteria; and
- from a concern with scientific and aesthetic qualities towards a recognition of the importance of biodiversity (ie ecosystems, species and the variety within species) as a component of sustainable development.

Similar trends in thinking can also be detected in the sphere of landscape conservation (Bishop et al, 1995):

- from an almost exclusive concern with the protection of the 'best' towards an interest in (a) the diversity of the entire landscape, and (b) local distinctiveness;
- from a concern with 'protection' towards more interest in creative conservation, both to restore lost features and to create new ones; and
- from an essentially aesthetic approach towards a deeper appreciation of the ecological, historical and cultural values of landscape and the ways in which these are interwoven.

Many of the new countryside planning processes are based on the concept of landscape ecology and the need to develop a landscape-scale perspective to the conservation of the natural heritage (Adams, 2003). They provide the potential for innovative thinking about how to connect protected areas and link them to the wider countryside, rather than viewing them as 'islands' of conservation.

There have also been important developments in the integration of the previously separate components of conservation: joining together landscape, nature and historic dimensions of the countryside and breaking down the functional divisions that have characterized British conservation since the 1940s. The 'great divide' between landscape and nature conservation agencies was, in structural terms, ended in Wales and Scotland with the establishment of new integrated agencies – the Countryside Council for Wales in 1991 and Scottish Natural Heritage in 1992. The appreciation of the historic dimensions of the countryside has also matured: in particular, archaeologists and historians now lay much more emphasis on the links between heritage and nature conservation, promoting archaeology as a 'green' topic which contributes 'time-depth' to understanding the environment (Macinnes and Wickham-Jones, 1992).

Conservation is no longer only about nature, landscapes or history – it is also increasingly about people. If conservation is to be effective and sustainable in the long-term, then it must re-connect with people and the local economy. As is now widely understood (though not always acted on in practice), planners have to do more than merely consult people on pre-determined plans; they need to involve them in the formulation and implementation of plans and projects. It is becoming much more common for policy initiatives related to countryside conservation or planning to involve some form of community participation. Indeed, involving local people in decision-making and delivery is often seen as key to strategies for enhancing and sustaining the rural environment.

Another important factor has been devolution. The changes that followed the abolition of the former Nature Conservancy Council in 1991, and in particular the establishment of separate conservation agencies in Scotland and Wales, were reinforced by the devolution agenda of the Labour government elected in 1997. This led to the setting up of separate legislatures in both countries and in Northern Ireland. The significance of this development is very apparent in those chapters of this book that show how each country is now adopting its own approach to planning and managing its countryside. Devolution has led to divergence and diversity. It is in this context that it seems particularly appropriate to also include the experience of Ireland, which is probably now only marginally more distinctive from the English approach than that of the 'peripheral' countries of the UK.

Finally, globalization has also affected the practice of countryside conservation just as it has the face of retailing or manufacturing (Marsden et al, 1993). Despite the protection still afforded by the CAP, global markets increasingly affect rural land use in the UK as trade liberalization is promoted by the World Trade Organization (WTO). The environmental movement has itself been 'globalized': there are now global pressures for environmental protection and international frameworks (such as conventions) to secure this. In countryside protection, as in everything else, the UK no longer exists in 'splendid isolation'. More and more, countryside, environmental and conservation policy is made not only in the UK but also in Brussels and globally – and the flow of ideas is now as international in the conservation sector as it is in many others. The result is a very creative period in countryside conservation and planning which we hope this book helps to reveal and record.

AN OUTLINE

The book is divided into three parts. Part 1 looks at the wider context for countryside planning and discusses some of the key drivers behind the new approaches. By reference to experience in England, Ireland, Scotland and Wales, Part 2 examines in detail a range of the new approaches to countryside planning, the thinking behind these, their proposed and actual uses and their effectiveness. Part 3 explores, through the use of several case studies, the practical use of these new approaches.

Whilst the tendency may be to look at international policy drivers as part of a top-down process, this simplifies what is often a complex policy network. In Chapter 2, Kevin Bishop and Richard Cowell focus on the impact on the UK of the United Nations Convention on Biological Diversity (CBD) and, in particular, the development of biodiversity action planning. The analysis presented demonstrates the key role of certain environmental non-governmental organizations (NGOs) in influencing the UK's position on the drafting of the CBD and its subsequent implementation. Unlike most other international conventions and agreements relating to biodiversity, the CBD does not introduce its own category of protected area; it is focused on 'process' rather than 'product'. The authors trace the way in which environmental groups, such as the Royal Society for the Protection of Birds (RSPB), used this opportunity to develop a new system of biodiversity action planning in the UK. This in turn has helped such groups acquire resources and increase their political influence. It is a complex story of policy networks – of who promoted biodiversity action plans (BAPs), to whom, in what areas and with what results – and of policy learning, rather than simply a tale of policy implementation.

In contrast to the framework approach of the CBD, the focus of the 1992 EU Birds and Habitats Directives is clearly on product. The Habitats Directive provides for the designation of 'Special Areas for Conservation' (SACs) which are to form part of a trans-European network of sites called 'Natura 2000'. Special Protection Areas (SPAs), declared under the earlier Birds Directive, will also be part of this network. In Chapter 3, Dave Burges explores the impact of these directives on the British planning system and wider countryside policy frameworks. He notes that, to date, their effect has often been to reinforce site-based nature conservation and that the thinking about how such sites can be connected and, in turn, linked to the wider countryside has been secondary. The analysis presented in Chapter 3 highlights the way in which nature conservation has been 'Europeanized' with decision-making for SACs and SPAs centralized in Brussels in cases of 'overriding public interest'.

Chapter 4, by Adrian Phillips and Roger Clarke, is concerned with a new development: the harnessing of landscape as an international policy instrument, and the impact of this on conservation and land use policy and practice in the UK. It considers two significant, parallel and related developments: how landscape has become a source of international attention, notably through the World Heritage and European Landscape Conventions; and how landscape has emerged both as a precious resource in its own right and as a means of achieving sustainable development. The central argument is that landscape policy is now becoming an international driver, shaping environmental and rural policy within the UK. This influence may become even more pronounced if the UK signs the European Landscape Convention (ELC).

Countryside conservation can never succeed without the active engagement of people. This is the central tenet of Diane Warburton in Chapter 5, who reviews the European and global drivers for community involvement in countryside planning, such as Agenda 21, and analyses the UK response. Community involvement should not be a box in a flow chart for a countryside planning process, but rather it is a profound challenge for policy-makers. The need is to ensure local participation, and the key words to guide a community-based approach are: listening, honesty and partnership.

As Chapters 2 to 5 illustrate, there is a diversity of approach from the rigid requirements of the Birds and Habitats Directives to the looser framework of the ELC. These evolving frameworks have offered a new language to conservation circles (witness the business-derived terminology of biodiversity action planning) and new concepts, such as ecological corridors. They also introduce the concept of accountability to higher levels (eg through the formal decision-making procedures of the Habitats Directive or the national reporting requirements of the CBD). Yet these international agreements, conventions and European directives have grown in an ad hoc way. As a result, it is often left to the national or even sub-national level to achieve integration between them.

Part 2 contains a set of chapters that explore in detail some of the new approaches to countryside and nature conservation that have been developed in the countries of the UK and in Ireland, the thinking behind these policy initiatives, their proposed and actual uses and their effectiveness.

In 1992, English Nature began to look for a rational framework that would bring together species and habitat targets at a landscape scale. The result was a biogeographic framework termed 'Natural Areas'. Keith Porter in Chapter 6 provides an analysis of why Natural Areas were developed, how this was done and how English Nature and others have used the framework. He reports on how a nature conservation agency is recognizing that biodiversity targets cannot be achieved through a narrow focus on species, habitats and natural features and site-based conservation alone. The Natural Areas framework, and the associated 'Lifescapes' initiative, are an attempt to link the various aspects of heritage – natural and cultural – and communicate these to the partners that English Nature needs to work with to deliver its own objectives in relation to nature conservation.

In the last five years, the concept of 'countryside character' has become central to a wide range of activities in landscape and environmental planning and management in England. It is largely, but not completely, synonymous with the term 'landscape character'. Both focus on the use of character as a framework for decision-making on environmental issues. There are two main differences: countryside character is a broader, integrating concept that draws together landscape, wildlife and archaeological and historical aspects of the countryside, and focuses largely on the rural environment; landscape character is concerned with all types of landscape, in both town and country. In Chapter 7, Carys Swanwick provides an overview of approaches to the assessment of countryside and landscape character in England. She explores the evolution of thinking about countryside and landscape character from its origins in earlier work on landscape evaluation and landscape assessment, and examines the way that methods for assessing character have developed and been applied in a wide range of practical situations. She also considers the links that exist between this approach and other emerging tools that have been developed to assist with planning for sustainable development (such as Village Design Statements and Quality of Life Capital). Carys Swanwick concludes by calling for research into the value of this approach in the decision-making arena.

Chapters 8 and 9 deal with the development of landscape characterization and assessment methodologies in Ireland. Michael Starrett in Chapter 8 describes the work of the Heritage Council which, unlike similar advisory bodies in the UK, has a remit that embraces most aspects of Ireland's natural and cultural heritage. There is no separation of responsibility for the built and natural heritage, as there is, for example, between the duties of Scottish Natural Heritage (SNH) and of Historic Scotland (although Chapter 11 shows how SNH is working to overcome this separation), or between those of English Heritage and English Nature. Only the Heritage Lottery Fund in the UK has a comparably broad remit. The European Landscape Convention and the EUROPARC network were important 'pull factors' in the approach developed by the Heritage Council. Concerns that planning authorities and development agencies might act in an ad hoc and ill-informed way without standardized landscape character were important 'push factors'. Building upon work undertaken in England, the Heritage Council has pioneered an integrated approach to landscape characterization that it is now hoping will be adopted throughout Ireland.

In parallel with the work of the Heritage Council, the Irish Forest Service and Department of the Environment and Local Government have funded research to develop a landscape assessment methodology, described by Art McCormack and Tomás O'Leary in Chapter 9. They detail the approach adopted in developing the Irish Landscape Assessment Guidelines and evaluate their application through case studies concerned with afforestation and wind farm developments.

Standard approaches to Landscape Character Assessment (such as those reviewed in Chapter 7) tend to understate the complex ways in which humans impact on the appearance of the landscape and the length of time over which this influence has occurred. By focusing on the more recent past and highly visible historic features, the more subtle connections between vegetation cover, land use and human history may be under-played in the landscape characterization process. A desire to ensure that historical influences are properly reflected in such processes has led to the development of different techniques for historic landscape characterization. Lesley Macinnes reports in Chapter 10 on the evolution of historic landscape characterization in Great Britain and beyond, and provides a preliminary evaluation of its application.

Chapters 11 and 12 detail the new approaches to countryside conservation and planning being developed in Scotland and Wales respectively. In Scotland, Scottish Natural Heritage (SNH) started work in the mid-1990s on what was then called the 'Natural Heritage Zonal Programme' with the aim of developing an integrated approach to wildlife, landform and landscape protection and management. As made clear by Roger Crofts in Chapter 11, the objectives of this initiative derived in part from international thinking about the need to take a holistic approach to environmental protection, but also from a practical wish to demonstrate that SNH was delivering on its new integrated remit. Although he makes the point that it is still too early fully to evaluate the impact of the programme (now called 'Natural Heritage Futures'), Roger Crofts shows that the initiative has played an important part in developing the culture of a new organization.

In contrast to the initiatives in England, Scotland and Ireland, the *LANDMAP* approach developed in Wales is based on collaboration rather than an exclusively agency-led programme, and is described in Chapter 12 by Rob Owen and David Eager. Thus, whilst the Countryside Council for Wales has played an important role in developing the *LANDMAP* methodology, it has done so through the Wales Landscape Partnership which involves the National Assembly for Wales, the Welsh Development Agency and local authorities. The methodology is also very different from that used in other countries in that it attempts to combine natural, cultural and historical information and has been implemented at a local authority level rather than through a national initiative.

It is possible to discern a number of common themes from the chapters in Part 2:

- Many of the new approaches would not be possible without recent developments in technology. The widespread use of geographical information systems has facilitated the analysis of different data sets and allowed for the ready identification of different character areas. Future technological developments (web-based mapping and improved three-dimensional modelling) should further improve the user-friendliness of these programmes, enable the handling of data from more diverse sources and extend the range of potential uses.
- They are all area-based methodologies rather than being site-specific. Consciously or unconsciously, they adopt a landscape-scale approach.
- The approaches are forward-looking and often developed to influence the programmes and practices of third party organizations (eg government departments, local planning authorities, landowners).
- There is a country divergence, with each part of the UK (and Ireland too) developing different approaches. The consistency of approach that historically characterized British conservation has disappeared.

There are also two important differences between the new approaches to countryside conservation and planning:

- Some have been more successful at integration than others. *LANDMAP*, for example, attempts to integrate scenic, sensory, earth science, biodiversity, historical and cultural information, whilst in England, the Natural Areas and Countryside Character initiatives have remained as distinct processes.
- There are important differences in terms of orientation. Most approaches are country-wide and top-down in the sense that the 'product' has been developed in the relevant countryside agency and then made available for wider use, but *LANDMAP* is more bottom-up. The *LANDMAP* methodology was developed through the Wales Landscape Partnership Group but then implemented by individual local authorities independently. Thus, at the time of writing, there was no national *LANDMAP* dataset for Wales.

Part 3 of the book explores, through case studies, the use of these new approaches. Whilst the choice of case studies is necessarily selective, the analysis of a number of common issues can be discerned. Julie Martin in Chapter 13 describes how the national work on Landscape Character Assessment (LCA) has been taken up at local level, not only by official bodies but also land managers, consultants and community groups. The potential application of the approach in the areas of development control, impact analysis and land management is considered. She concludes that, whilst there is still much work to do to refine the approach, the greater need now is to promote good practice.

In Chapter 14, Kevin Bishop and Richard Bate find that there has been little integration between local BAPs and the statutory town and country planning system. There are also issues of consistency of approach within and across government departments – for example, the conflicting advice being given to local planning authorities by central government and regional government offices on the requirements of Article 10 of the Habitats Directive. Yet in other areas the influence would appear quite profound – for example BAP targets are being used in the regional chapters of the England Rural Development Plan and in guiding the distribution of Lottery funding (see Chapter 2).

As Jo Milling makes clear in Chapter 15, the nature of the influence often depends upon the commitment of one or more key individuals and a willingness on their part to experiment and take risks. It is also clear that new initiatives in countryside planning and management call for greater collaboration between and within local government departments than has been usual in the past.

Finally, in Chapter 16, Diane Warburton's overview looks at a range of recent initiatives in which community participation is central, including Parish Appraisals, Village Design Statements and Countryside Design Summaries. She concludes that often the value of many of the new approaches to community participation lies as much in the process as in the product. Indeed, many of the approaches discussed in this book involve a learning experience for all involved.

All the approaches described in Part 3 are still in their infancy and the analysis is inevitably incomplete and partial. Moreover, there is an unavoidable time lag between development and implementation. Whilst there has therefore, as yet, been no time for a proper evaluation of the new approaches to countryside conservation and planning, there is a need for such an exercise to be undertaken soon. It should also consider wider questions about whether it is possible to 'plan for nature', how such approaches should influence economic development, and what scope there is for knowledge transfer between different parts of the UK and Ireland.

In conclusion, this book identifies the global drivers, the attempts at joined-up thinking and the local action that are all features of countryside planning and management in Britain and Ireland at a historic point of time. The legacy of the post-war settlement for the countryside is passing into history. A new context is emerging: it is to be hoped that the tools that are now being fashioned will help realize the vision of the Policy Commission on the Future of Food and Farming of a '... countryside that is varied and attractive ... [and that] has regained its diversity and regional character' (2002, p11).

REFERENCES

Adams, W (2003) *Future Nature: A vision for nature conservation*, revised edition, Earthscan, London

Barlow Report (1940) *Report of the Royal Commission on the Distribution of Industrial Population*, Cmd 6153, HMSO, London

Bishop, K, Phillips, A and Warren, L (1995) 'Protected for Ever? Factors shaping the future of protected areas policy', *Land Use Policy*, vol 12(4), pp291–305

Cherry, G E and Rogers, A (1996) *Rural Change and Planning: England and Wales in the Twentieth Century*, E & F N Spon, London

Gay, H and Phillips, A (2000) 'Natural and Cultural Heritage: Exploring the relationships', *ECOS*, vol 22(1), pp28–35

Green Balance (2000) *Valuing the Land: Planning for the best and most versatile agricultural land*, Council for the Protection of Rural England, London

Hobhouse Committee (1947) *Report of the National Parks Committee (England and Wales)*, Cmd 7121, HMSO, London

Huxley Committee (1947) *Conservation of Nature in England and Wales*, Cmd 7122, HMSO, London

Macinnes, L and Wickham-Jones, C (eds) (1992) *All Natural Things: Archaeology and the green debate*, Oxbow Books, Oxford

Marsden, T, Murdoch, J, Lowe, P, Munton, R and Flynn, A (1993) *Constructing the Countryside*, UCL Press, London

Owens, S and Cowell, R (2001) *Land and Limits: Interpreting sustainability in the planning process*, Routledge, London

Performance and Innovation Unit (1999) *Rural Economies*, TSO, London

Phillips, A (1995) 'The Merits of Merger: A history and the issues' in Bishop, K (ed) *Merits of Merger*, Environmental and Countryside Planning Unit, Department of City and Regional Planning, Cardiff University, Cardiff, pp3–11

Policy Commission on the Future of Food and Farming (2002) *Farming and Food: A sustainable future*, Cabinet Office, London

Scott Committee (1942) *Report of the Committee on Land Utilization in Rural Areas*, Cmd 6378, HMSO, London

Uthwatt Report (1942) *Expert Committee on Compensation and Betterment, Final Report*, Cmd 6386, HMSO, London

Part 1

The International Context for Countryside Planning and Management

Chapter 2

From Sandy to Rio: The Development of Biodiversity Action Planning

Kevin Bishop and Richard Cowell

This chapter focuses on the impact on the UK of the United Nations Convention on Biological Diversity (CBD) and, in particular, on the development of biodiversity action planning. The UK government's signature of the CBD at the Earth Summit in Rio de Janeiro in 1992 can be seen as a landmark measure that has had a significant impact on UK policy (House of Commons Environment, Transport and Regional Affairs Committee, 2000). Since the signing of the CBD by the UK, and its subsequent coming into force, the language of nature conservation in this country has shifted significantly, as the new concern for 'biodiversity' began to change the way people thought about conservation (Adams, 1996). Biodiversity action plans (BAPs) – combining species and habitat targets, with agendas of action to achieve them – have emerged to become a widely utilized tool of environmental planning in the UK.

Whilst the tendency may be to look at the CBD as a top-down global driver that has provided the framework for biodiversity action planning in the UK, it will be argued that this perspective ignores a more complex picture whereby 'domestic thinking' (and, in particular, the changing strategies of certain environmental groups) helped influence the UK's position on the drafting of the CBD and its subsequent implementation. In the context of a governing culture generally resistant to the idea of environmental targets, BAPs have been mobilized skilfully by conservation NGOs at a variety of spatial scales. As a consequence, BAPs now form an important source of guidance, objectives and targets for land use planning, the distribution of lottery grants and the allocation of agri-environment funding. This chapter examines how the BAP concept was developed in the UK. It is a story of policy networks (of who promoted BAPs, to whom, in what areas and with what capacity to bring pressure to bear) and of policy learning. In particular, is there something about the managerialist language of BAPs, with their claim to a strongly rational approach to planning, that enabled them to acquire support from particular quarters? To address these issues, it is necessary first to understand how the mandate behind BAPs was pieced together in international arenas.

THE ROAD TO RIO

Work on what was to become the CBD formally commenced in 1987 when the Governing Council of the United Nations Environment Programme (UNEP) established an ad hoc working group to investigate the '… desirability and possible form of an umbrella convention to rationalise current activities in this field [biological diversity], and to address other areas which might fall under such a convention' (UNEP Governing Council Resolution 14/26 (1987), cited in Glowka et al, 1994). This resolution was, in part, a response to: work by the IUCN's Commission on Environmental Law that had coordinated the production of draft articles for inclusion in a new global treaty on biodiversity; the proposal contained in *Our Common Future* (World Commission on Environment and Development, 1987) for a species protection convention; and calls by the US for an initiative to develop a global convention on biological diversity.

The ad hoc working group concluded that existing conventions were piecemeal in their coverage. They either covered only internationally important natural sites (the World Heritage Convention), the specific threat of trade in endangered species (CITES), a specific ecosystem type (such as the Ramsar Convention on Wetlands of International Importance) or a group of species (such as the Migratory Species Convention). Even when taken as a whole, these treaties were clearly failing to ensure the global conservation of biodiversity. Nor did they respond well to the broader agendas of sustainable development advocated by the *World Conservation Strategy* (IUCN, UNEP and WWF, 1980), *Caring for the Earth* (IUCN, UNEP and WWF, 1991) and the *Global Biodiversity Strategy* (WRI, IUCN and UNEP, 1992). These reports shifted the ethos of conservation from a largely scientific basis and linked it to ethics, development aims, economic benefits and human survival. The UNEP-appointed working group determined that the concept of preparing an umbrella convention that would absorb or consolidate existing conventions would be practically impossible. Instead, they proposed a framework convention that would build upon existing conventions by providing overall goals and policies for the conservation of biodiversity.

At its 15th meeting, held in May 1989, UNEP's Governing Council authorized the Executive Director to start work on an international legal instrument for the conservation of the biological diversity of the planet. This would address social and economic issues and the use of genetic resources in biotechnology development as well as more 'traditional' conservation issues (Decision 18/12). The instrument was to be formally negotiated by another ad hoc working group, in this case composed of technical and legal experts.

As with the negotiation of all international treaties, progress was slow and negotiation difficult, with issues of power and control over conservation resources very much to the fore. The UK delegation was briefed from an early stage to propose national conservation strategies as a basis for national action to achieve global aims (McConnell, 1996). The preparation of such strategies, plans or programmes was seen as a relatively neutral, essentially procedural requirement but one that would foster a comprehensive national-level process for the conservation of biodiversity. This position did not always meet with universal support. For example, the French were keen to support top-down action that would enable supranational decisions to be taken, whilst many of the G77 developing nations were initially suspicious of UK-led proposals, fearing a post-imperialist conspiracy to dictate and impose actions in the developing world. Importantly, the UK government's position on 'national action as the basis for global agreement' (McConnell, 1996, p9) brought together traditional concern for solutions that preserved national sovereignty and new thinking amongst certain environmental groups in the UK who were attempting to develop a more rational and planned approach to nature conservation.

This confluence of agendas occurred largely because, unlike previous global agreements, UK environmental groups were given a role in the negotiation process. The UK delegation to the first preparatory conference for UNCED (United Nations Conference on Environment and Development – the 1992 Earth Summit) included a representative from an NGO. This innovation effectively opened up the negotiation process and it was reinforced by domestic manoeuvres, notably the establishment of the UK Advisory Group on Biological Diversity in May 1991. This group was borne out of necessity: the Department of the Environment (DoE) was leading on the UK's input to UNCED and this was placing severe burdens on civil servants (McConnell, 1996). The advisory group was established to try and streamline the consultation process; to keep interest groups informed about negotiations; to take account of their views; and to attempt to develop consensus on a UK position (McConnell, 1996). It brought together different government departments (Ministry for Agriculture, Fisheries and Food (MAFF), Overseas Development Administration, DoE, Department of Trade and Industry and Foreign and Commonwealth Office) with representatives of environmental NGOs (RSPB, WWF and Wildlife Link), business, academia, and learned institutions such as Kew Gardens and the Natural History Museum. The establishment of the advisory group and invitations to some UK environmental NGOs to participate in the drafting of the CBD gave such groups unprecedented access to policy-making networks both within the UK and at a UN level. Indeed, such an emphasis on treating NGOs as partners for sustainable development was a characteristic common to the UNCED process as a whole.

Negotiations on the CBD went 'to the wire' and it is unlikely that agreement would have been reached but for the imposed deadline of UNCED (Glowka et al, 1994). The CBD was eventually agreed on the final day of the final scheduled negotiating session and a record number of over 150 countries signed it at the Earth Summit in Rio de Janeiro. The treaty has been described as a landmark as it takes a comprehensive rather than a sectoral approach to the conservation of biodiversity (Glowka et al, 1994). But a key feature of the CBD is the retention of decision-making powers at the national level. Unlike some other conservation treaties, there are no CBD lists of species to be protected or protected areas to be established. Article 6 requires each signatory to develop national strategies, plans or programmes for the conservation of biodiversity and sustainable use of biological resources and to integrate the conservation and sustainable use of biological diversity into relevant sectoral or cross-sectoral plans, programmes and policies as well as national decision-making.

The focus on national-level action and priority setting was a practical response to the concerns regarding ecological colonialism expressed by developing countries about international mechanisms, but it was also regarded as desirable for the following reasons:

- The national and sub-national level was seen as the optimum spatial level for biodiversity to be conserved and biological resources managed.
- States are more likely to adhere to priorities developed at a national level than to 'imposed' global targets.
- The complex nature of biodiversity conservation and management lends itself to national- and local-level action rather than top-down global decisions (Glowka et al, 1994).

For the environmental NGOs involved in shaping the UK's position during the UNCED process, their international efforts reaped domestic dividends: the CBD has provided a crucial lever for lobbying and shaping a national plan for biodiversity. The next step of the story is to explain how the strategies of conservation groups came to converge with international diplomacy in the concept of BAPs.

From Preservation to Positive Action

The history and practice of nature conservation in the UK is inextricably linked to the development of the voluntary organizations who both lobbied for government action and undertook practical measures to safeguard nature. The idea of nature conservation, first promoted by groups such as the Selbourne Society for the Preservation of Birds, Plants and Pleasant Places and the Society for the Promotion of Nature Reserves (SPNR) has a long history. It is based largely on the desirability of preserving in perpetuity sites suitable for nature reserves. At least until recently, the language was of preservation and the focus was substantially on special sites, a mode of operation that was transferred into the statutory system of protection. Indeed, the first official report on countryside conservation in Great Britain contained recommendations to establish 'nature sanctuaries' (National Park Commission, 1931). The designation of protected areas was formally enshrined in the National Parks and Access to the Countryside Act 1949, and the newly established government body the Nature Conservancy began to establish a pattern of post-war conservation based on the designation and notification of National Nature Reserves and Sites of Special Scientific Interest.

However, whilst the number of protected areas increased and the voluntary conservation movement continued to expand, nature continued to retreat. Despite attempts to strengthen the machinery of protection (witness the Wildlife and Countryside Act 1981 and the Wildlife and Countryside (Amendment) Act 1985), the rate of damage to and destruction of the nature resource continued unabated and, in certain instances, actually increased. The scale of the problem demonstrated the weakness of traditional site-based nature conservation measures: they were insufficient to preserve features of interest within the sites, especially where impacted by wider ecological and economic processes extending far beyond the site itself; they also neglected the ecological value of the wider (ie undesignated) countryside. These systemic weaknesses, coupled with the institutional deficiencies of leaving responsibility for conservation to special interest statutory bodies, served to underline the need for new thinking.

This need was recognized by certain of the voluntary conservation groups, notably the RSPB. In the 1980s, groups such as the RSPB underwent an organizational step change. An increase in members, attendant on widening public concerns for the environment, generated additional revenue: the RSPB had an annual budget in excess of £30 million by the beginning of the 1990s. Although benefiting from increased resources, there was growing recognition that the organization needed to target its resources more effectively if it was to achieve its stated aim of conserving wild birds and the wider environment on which they depended. Part of this involved employing staff in fields such as economics and policy advice; part of it involved applying a focused rationality to their own conservation agenda. Meanwhile, the production of *Red Data Birds in Britain* (Batten et al, 1990) provided, as one official put it, 'an internal bible', which effectively established bird-species conservation priorities. Priority species were considered to be those that bred or wintered in Britain in internationally important numbers, had localized breeding or wintering populations, were rare breeders or had declined by more than 50 per cent since 1960. Having established conservation priorities (in terms of species and the habitats that supported them), the RSPB developed an internal system of action plans to convert the priorities into practical effect (Porter et al, 1994). The action plans were strategic in nature, covered a five to ten year time span, and identified a measurable conservation objective. This was a desired end-point in terms of the numbers, range and/or productivity of a given species; the extent and quality of the habitat; or the areal extent and quality of sites (Porter et al, 1994). Within the RSPB, the action plans were used initially to frame the development of annual work programmes. As such, they represented a new approach that was more business-like. The focus on outcomes (in terms of targets) and specific actions to achieve these targets had clear parallels with the language of business plans. Moreover, the specific aims of the action plans developed by the RSPB (see Box 2.1), whilst focused on the conservation of wild birds and the habitats that sustain them, took the RSPB into a whole ecosystem approach and underlined the importance of partnership working.

Work on species action plans for birds began in 1989 and by April 1994 plans had been completed for 50 of the 118 Red Data bird species. In addition, habitat action plans had been prepared for lowland wet grassland, lowland heathland, Caledonian pine forest, lowland peat bogs and marine habitats. The RSPB was joined in this task by the Joint Nature Conservation Committee (JNCC), the statutory conservation agencies and the Wildfowl and Wetlands

---

BOX 2.1 SPECIFIC AIMS OF RSPB ACTION PLANS

- 'Prevent loss of any regular breeding or wintering species due to human activities.
- Achieve a measurable increase in the numbers, ranges and productivity of bittern, red kite, white-tailed eagle, hen harrier, capercaille, grey partridge, corncrake, stone curlew, redshank, chough, cirl bunting. These species were selected as being threatened in their own right or being 'indicator' species of threatened or degraded habitat.
- Achieve the number and range of targets set in Species Action Plans for other Red Data Book birds.
- Improve the extent and condition of lowland wet grassland, reedbeds, lowland heath, Caledonian pine forest, dry grassland (as occurring in Breckland) and deciduous woodland.
- Slow the rate of deterioration and loss of upland heaths and mires, lowland peat, and estuarine habitats.
- Prevent the loss of and limit the damage to internationally and nationally important bird sites.
- Maintain and, where appropriate, enhance the numbers and ranges of common bird species.
- Improve the wildlife value of the wider countryside and marine environment.'

Source: Porter et al, 1994, pp6–7

Trust. What started off as a managerial prioritization process for the RSPB began to influence UK thinking on the CBD through the RSPB's involvement in the Advisory Group for Biodiversity discussed above.

The benefits of a convention that supported and required national strategies, plans or programmes for biodiversity conservation were obvious to the RSPB and the other NGOs, such as WWF, Plantlife and Butterfly Conservation, that had come to be persuaded of the merits of the action planning approach. It would require the UK government to clarify its biological objectives for the environment, and provide an opportunity to promote an objective-led approach to the conservation of biodiversity (Wynne et al, 1995a). But the challenge was significant: after all, the government's own white paper on the environment, *This Common Inheritance* (H M Government, 1991), richly illustrated a deep-rooted political and administrative aversion to setting targets in the environmental field. Nevertheless, the concept of biodiversity action planning, initially viewed with scepticism, has become the language of nature conservation, and has managed to insinuate itself into the state's governing machinery. In so doing, the NGOs promoting the concept ceased to be 'outsiders' and became instead part of the governing policy network for biodiversity action planning.

THE ROAD FROM RIO

The CBD was signed in Rio de Janeiro by the UK Prime Minister, John Major, triggering a series of changes to conservation policy and practice that are still unfolding. Shortly after the Earth Summit, the Prime Minister wrote to leaders of all European Union (then Community) and G7 countries proposing an eight-point action plan to follow-up the agreements signed at Rio de Janeiro. Included on this list was a commitment to publish a plan for action on biodiversity and to establish the basis for ratification of the CBD. The DoE began work on a national biodiversity plan for the UK almost immediately. This process was initially 'closed': the DoE declined offers from the RSPB and other NGOs to assist in the process, stating that they would be consulted in due course.

In May 1993, the JNCC organized a meeting at the Royal Geographical Society to discuss the format, purpose and content of the plan. This event provided an opportunity for the RSPB and other NGOs to press for an objective-led approach to the conservation of biodiversity. There was concern that early drafts of the plan prepared by the DoE were not a plan at all, but were redolent of the style of *This Common Inheritance*: more, as one NGO official satirized it:

> *an essay extolling the wonders and virtues of the English countryside ... how wonderfully important biodiversity was [and how] it was terribly important that we carried on with the policies that we'd adopted ever since 1981* (pers comm).

The RSPB and other NGOs lobbied for the adoption of an objective-led approach and used their own experience with species action plans as a model. Despite some interest in this approach, the government remained largely sceptical, claiming that whilst it might work for birds it would not be possible for invertebrates or plants. The government's conservation agencies were also initially sceptical about the use of targets for biodiversity – a concern that seems to have been based on fear of the potential ramifications of not meeting such targets, the realization of which was not wholly within their control. This scepticism and, in some instances hostility, prompted certain environmental groups to start work on their own UK BAP in the summer of 1993 – to test the efficacy of an objective-led approach across a range of different taxa (Wynne et al, 1995a).

Thus two parallel processes were set in motion: the DoE was leading on the preparation of the official UK BAP, whilst six environmental groups (Butterfly Conservation, Friends of the Earth, Plantlife, the RSPB, the WWF and the Wildlife Trusts) were collaborating on the preparation of their own version. These processes did not take place in complete isolation from each other: material was fed across from the NGO initiative to government officials, and vice versa. However, the government remained reluctant to use the advent of a UK BAP 'merely' to set in motion a new planning process. At this stage the NGO alliance working on the objective-led approach decided to publicize their thinking. *Biodiversity Challenge: An agenda for conservation in the UK* (Wynne et al, 1993) was published in December 1993 and set out the basis of a process for planning to conserve biodiversity in the UK. The central focus was outcomes – ie what needs to be achieved for individual species, in terms of numbers and ranges, and for habitats, in terms of extent and quality (Wynne et al, 1993).

The key elements of the 'Biodiversity Challenge' approach are illustrated in Box 2.2. An initial audit of biodiversity was seen as necessary to ensure that

---

**BOX 2.2 KEY ELEMENTS OF THE BIODIVERSITY
CHALLENGE APPROACH**

1   An audit of biodiversity (what do we have?)
2   A goal, objectives and measurable species and habitat targets (what do we want?)
3   Priorities (where should we start?)
4   Implementation of a plan for action (what should we do?)
5   Monitoring and review arrangements (what have we done? did it work?)

Source: Wynne et al, 1995b, p15

---

policy decisions and actions would be based on sound information and knowledge. The audit process would also provide a baseline against which to monitor and assess biodiversity action planning itself. The document contained an overall goal for UK biodiversity action, broader conservation objectives and detailed targets for species and habitats: 530 species targets and 16 habitat targets were presented as examples. It argued that priorities should be established according to the criteria adopted in the Red Data Books namely: priority to the conservation of those internationally important species and habitats that are present in the UK, and to species and habitats that are threatened. A key part of the new approach was the production of detailed action plans for all priority species and habitats, following the model of the RSPB's internal action plans, which they had been developing since the late 1980s. These action plans should include a brief analysis of threats, a statement of biological objectives, broad policies and a plan for action. Although Biodiversity Challenge did not include costings, it was envisaged that the individual action plans would be fully costed. The final element of the approach outlined in Biodiversity Challenge was 'monitoring and review'. This would address such questions as whether conservation targets were being met, whether the conservation targets were the correct ones, and whether priorities for action had changed. The results of this exercise would then inform what was seen as a continual, cyclical process of plan–manage–monitor.

The official action plan – *Biodiversity: The UK Action Plan* (H M Government, 1994) – was formally published in January 1994 as part of the UK's follow-up to the agreements reached at the Earth Summit. Whilst *The UK Action Plan* did not adopt the objective-led approach being proposed by the Biodiversity Challenge group it did show some evidence of NGO input:

- The overall goal and objective of both documents were similar in focus, if not wording. They were both aimed at no further net loss of biodiversity.
- The need for conservation targets was recognized in *The UK Action Plan*. Late in the drafting stage, following continued lobbying by the Biodiversity Challenge group, civil servants inserted a list of 59 steps or action points to conserve and, where practicable, enhance wild species and wildlife habitats. Number 33 in this list was a commitment to produce action plans for threatened species; a priority similar to that advocated in *Biodiversity Challenge*.

- Both documents emphasized the need for an integrated approach to biodiversity conservation. This was underlined by the fact that *The UK Action Plan* was a Command Paper and presented to Parliament by the Secretaries of State for Environment, Foreign and Commonwealth Affairs, Transport, Defence, National Heritage, Employment, Scotland, Northern Ireland and Wales, the President of the Board of Trade, the Chancellor of the Exchequer, Chancellor of the Duchy of Lancaster, the Minister for Agriculture, Fisheries and Food and the Minister for Overseas Development. Thus it had common ownership and could not be portrayed as an initiative of the DoE – even the Treasury had signed up to the concept of costed action plans for conservation with detailed targets.

Through its commitment to produce action plans for threatened species in priority order, *The UK Action Plan* provided an important entry point for continued lobbying by the Biodiversity Challenge group. The action plan contained a commitment to establish a Biodiversity Action Plan Steering Group, comprising representatives from relevant government departments, the statutory conservation agencies, NGOs and nominees from academic institutions and local government. The establishment of this group moved the NGOs closer to the heart of the policy process. Even though the steering group was to be advisory, the government would be honour-bound to respond to its views and recommendations. Moreover, the group was set a specific brief to:

- develop a range of specific costed targets for key species and habitats for the years 2000 and 2010 to be published in 1995;
- make recommendations designed to improve the accessibility and coordination of existing biological datasets, and to provide common standards for future recording;
- prepare and implement a campaign to increase public awareness and involvement in conserving UK biodiversity; and
- establish a review process for the delivery of the 59 action points listed in The UK Action Plan.

In January 1995 the Biodiversity Challenge group published a second edition of *Biodiversity Challenge: An agenda for conservation in the UK* (Wynne et al, 1995b). This was a more detailed version of the first report aimed at informing the implementation of the UK action plan. The document provided more detail on the objective-led approach that the group wished to see the UK adopt. It contained detailed examples of species and habitat action plans, and it began to address the issue of costing biodiversity targets. Rather than re-invent the wheel, the Biodiversity Action Plan Steering Group decided to contract the Biodiversity Challenge group to draft the species and habitat action plans that it was directed to prepare by the government. Thus the role of the NGOs was inverted. While normally commenting on and attempting to strengthen documents prepared by government, the NGOs were now placed in the position of actually drafting the documents and trying to prevent them from being weakened (Tydeman, 1995).

Whilst the template for BAPs outlined in the two Biodiversity Challenge reports (Wynne et al, 1993, 1995b) was largely accepted, the costing element still caused concern within certain government departments (notably MAFF, the Scottish Office and HM Treasury). The action plan process, if implemented, would require a change in policy and increased expenditure – both challenging propositions to a government keen to control public expenditure.

The Biodiversity Steering Group published its report in two volumes: the first, *Meeting the Rio Challenge* (UK Biodiversity Action Plan Steering Group, 1995a), set out criteria for the selection of species and habitat types of conservation concern and the second volume contained costed action plans for 116 priority species and 14 priority habitats (UK Biodiversity Action Plan Steering Group, 1995b). These plans, and the approach that they adopted, were endorsed by the UK government in its response (H M Government, 1996). By October 1999 a total of 391 species and 45 habitat action plans were in place (UK Biodiversity Steering Group, 2001). The government also established the UK Biodiversity Group as a successor to the steering group and charged it with producing a report evaluating progress every five years.

RE-FRAMING THE AGENDA

Diffusion and Profusion

As illustrated in Figure 2.1, the BAP process has developed to encompass a variety of spatial scales and different formats. At a country level, country biodiversity steering groups have been established and they have identified their own priorities and programmes within the context of the UK BAP (see Figure 2.1). In Scotland, a Scottish Biodiversity Group was set up in 1996, with representatives from departments of the Scottish Executive, farming and land-owning groups, conservation NGOs as well as the scientific community (Ekos Ltd, 2001, p6). Several of the English regions have prepared regional BAPs.

The official backing given to the BAP process has also galvanized significant practical action at a local level. The UK Biodiversity Action Plan Steering Group (1995a, 1995b) proposed the preparation of Local Biodiversity Action Plans (LBAPs) as a means of ensuring that national targets would be translated into local action, by linking together stakeholders from a variety of sectors and encouraging participation. Driven by the statutory mandate given to the BAP process, these LBAPs have proved highly influential in extending the local networks of conservation bodies, and in refocusing them around an action planning process (Selman and Wragg, 1999a). In terms of the actual process, Selman and Wragg (1999b, p335) describe how the 'UK BAP has been cascaded down to county level through a process initially entailing the production of Biodiversity Challenge documents … outlining locally important habitats and species towards which conservation priority should be directed'. In converting conservation priorities into objectives and strategies for each prioritized species and habitat, the LBAP process echoes strongly the rational planning approach of the UK BAP at the local level. There are now over 160 LBAPs across Great

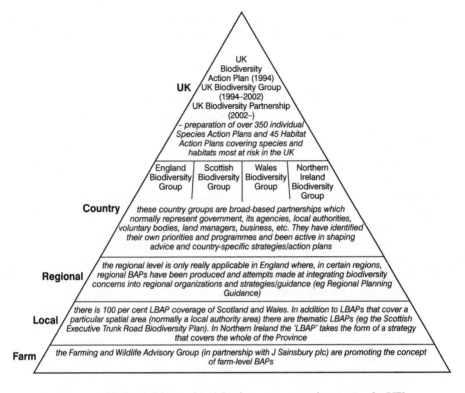

Figure 2.1 *Spatial hierarchy of biodiversity action planning in the UK*

Britain with an advisory target of 100 per cent coverage (UK Biodiversity Group, 2001).

Other organizations, too, have taken up the BAP agenda. A joint initiative between FWAG (the Farming and Wildlife Advisory Group) and J Sainsbury PLC has extended the concept of biodiversity action planning to individual farms (Sainsbury's, 1997). The BAP process has also been adopted by individual companies (the Wessex Water Biodiversity Action Plan, for example) and for specific sectors. The Scottish Executive has prepared a Trunk Road BAP and Dumfries and Galloway have developed their own Roads BAP.

The momentum is such that, since 1995, one can say that the BAP has provided the dominant framework within which nature conservation has been pursued in the UK (Parliamentary Office of Science and Technology, 2000). Despite a governing culture generally resistant to the idea of environmental targets, the government has accepted the concept of objective-led conservation plans. Thus in the Countryside and Rights of Way Act 2000, it introduced a new duty on government ministers and departments, and the National Assembly for Wales, to have regard to the purpose of the conservation of biological diversity in the exercise of their functions – a duty explicitly related to the obligations of the CBD. The Act also supports the biodiversity action planning process by requiring the Secretary of State and the National Assembly for Wales to maintain and publish lists of 'living organisms', that is species and habitat types which are of principal importance for the conservation of biodiversity. They must also take steps to further their conservation and to promote the taking of such steps by others.

This new approach involves the widening and deepening of partnership working for the conservation of biodiversity in the UK (Selman and Wragg, 1999b). It signals a departure from the traditional approach to conservation which saw it as a responsibility of relatively few, specialized organizations (primarily the statutory conservation agencies). The BAP process has seen the conservation NGOs become fully involved in the development of policy and there have also been moves to involve industry and commerce. For example, the UK Biodiversity Action Plan Steering Group introduced the notion of 'species champions' who are prepared to fund or support conservation work on particular species. Under this scheme, several species action plans have attracted support from corporations, ranging from ICI's support for the Large Blue Butterfly to Tesco's support for the Skylark. It is estimated that these 'species champions' have contributed over £1.4 million to the biodiversity action planning process (UK Biodiversity Steering Group, 2001) albeit that their support is limited to just 6 per cent of the priority species (Avery et al, 2001). The partnership approach is clearly witnessed in the steering groups established to guide and oversee the species and habitat action plans. From a survey of 191 species and habitat action plans, it was found that 243 different organizations were involved in their production and implementation (UK Biodiversity Steering Group, 2001).

After five years, the BAP process was subject to an official review, *Sustaining the Variety of Life: Five Years of the UK Biodiversity Action Plan* (UK Biodiversity Steering Group, 2001) and a separate evaluation by the Biodiversity Challenge group: *Biodiversity Counts: Delivering a Better Quality of Life* (Avery et al, 2001). The UK Biodiversity Group argued that the process had resulted in significant achievements in terms of the actual preparation of species and habitat action plans, the partnerships being formed to develop and implement these action plans and the establishment of support frameworks such as the National Biodiversity Network (UK Biodiversity Steering Group, 2001). Such achievements may hide a more profound impact. The promotion of biodiversity action planning is changing the way in which certain NGOs operate and their position in the policy process. It is part of a series of forces that are reconstituting NGOs, such as the Wildlife Trusts, from being guardians of nature, in the face of a not always cooperative state, to becoming agents for delivering the conservation of biodiversity. The Wildlife Trusts have been particularly successful in using BAP targets to help justify support for practical conservation projects funded by the National Lottery (Bishop, Norton and Phillips, 1999). BAP targets also represent, in theory at least, a more rational approach to resource allocation which, remarkably, has been able to travel between policy silos. The new wave of rural development plans in the UK all make reference to BAP targets in relation to agri-environment schemes. For example, the Rural Stewardship Scheme in Scotland applies a new system for ranking applications based on the contributions that farmers' actions will make to national and local BAP targets (Abernethy, 2000; UK Biodiversity Steering Group, 2001).

Lines of Resistance

Overall, the BAP process has generated a significant degree of support from a wide range of organizations: public, private and voluntary sector. The core environmental groups involved feel that, 'for the first time, we now have a common agenda for action backed by government, agreed by all major partners and which responds to international obligations' (The Wildlife Trusts, 2000, p58). That is not to say that biodiversity action planning has been immune from criticism. Indeed, both official (UK Biodiversity Steering Group, 2001) and unofficial evaluations (Avery et al, 2001) of the first five years identified a potential implementation deficit and emphasized the need to ensure plans turn into action.

More fundamental criticisms have been levelled at the extent to which BAPs now dominate the conservation agenda, excluding other legitimate interests. It has been argued that 'the BAP represents a species-centred view of nature conservation more appropriate to the wilds of Brazil or Botswana than a long-farmed environment like Britain. It has shown huge appetite for resources, and has generated more bureaucracy than conservation' (Marren, 2000, p43). For some, biodiversity action planning has emphasized process over product: 'many of the species action plans seem to be written to a bureaucratic formula, dare one say by someone not necessarily well-acquainted with the plant or beast in the spotlight (Marren, 2000, p44). There is a concern that the process of preparing BAPs has diverted resources and effort away from practical conservation, generating a mass of detail that can result in confusion rather than clarity (Green, 2000; Marren, 2000).

Broader dilemmas arise from the practicality and cultural politics of seeking to 'plan for nature'. Rooted in the very language of BAPs is a belief that nature is something that can be regulated to achieve precise, human objectives. This perspective rather marginalizes the view that the value of the natural world lies, in part, in its capacity to 'function outside human planning' (Adams 1996, p173; Evans, 1996). A related concern is that the ethics underpinning BAPs are anthropocentric and selective (Green, 2000; Marren, 2000): rationalizing conservation based on the contribution species and habitats can make to human life rather than any moral duty we may have to nature. Equally significant is the difficulty – which varies between species and habitats – in steering complex ecosystems and social processes to deliver specific outcomes over time, one of the qualms raised in early debates about the Biodiversity Challenge approach. Green (2000) argues that the BAP process is stuck in a dated, interventionist, hierarchical and isolationist approach to conservation that ignores recent moves in ecological science away from a balance of nature towards a more fluid state where ecosystems are in constant flux.

Such isolated voices have scarcely affected the momentum of BAP activity, and in any case it would be countered that the BAP targets are merely desirable aspirations, not something over which the parties involved should be held to account. But this rather belies the diligence with which environmental groups have sought the institutionalization of BAP processes and species targets across government. Selman and Wragg (1999a) observed how the imperative of biodiversity action is proving a strong basis for spontaneous cooperation between different interests, but expressed concern about the fragility of these alliances in the face of failure to achieve targets, especially given the demands of time and resources that the BAP process entails and, at the LBAP level, the lack of statutory mandate.

Questions might also be asked about the politics of integration: whose agenda is being aligned with whose? Research suggests that only halting progress is being made in integrating LBAP objectives into land use plans (Selman and Wragg 1999a; Ekos Limited, 2001), albeit that there is greater uncertainty facing their relationship with Local Agenda 21, and community strategies and plans (Ekos Limited, 2001). The 'successful' alignment of formerly conflicting interests raises challenges of its own. Outside the conservation community, the popularity of the BAP process seems most strikingly apparent with just those policy or economic sectors that have the greatest need to legitimize the land use impacts of their own activities – the MoD, transport and mining departments. Selman and Wragg (1999a) identified familiar concerns among conservation groups that consensual joint working with industry around LBAPs may compromise their ability to object to undesirable proposals. In so far as LBAPs are being rolled out through partnerships and consensus, one might soon detect limits in conservation terms to what this mode of governance can achieve.

Returning to the five-year reviews of the BAP process, this has yet to form a major line of concern. Indeed, both *Sustaining the Variety of Life* (UK Biodiversity Group, 2001) and *Biodiversity Counts* (Avery at al, 2001) would seem to shift the emphasis away from the initial focus on habitat and species action plans towards implementation. Both of these documents identify the need to ensure that the process becomes more dynamic in terms of practical action and more participatory. An important aspect of this is that biodiversity itself, 'is not, as yet, a well understood concept within local authorities or the wider public' (Ekos Limited 2001, p4), with the risk that BAP activity is 'divorced from real-life' and can act as a barrier to the engagement of society at large in biodiversity conservation (Sergeant, 2000). This new phase in the UK BAP process relates to current international thinking: the 1998 Meeting of the Parties to the CBD recognized that conservation involves societal choices and thus needs to involve all relevant sectors. A good example of this new emphasis on participation is the funding of new facilitator posts within such organizations as the RSPB and the Natural History Museum. The aim of these posts is to harness the support of amateur naturalists who, it is argued, are disengaged from the official BAP process. From a policy perspective, the attempts to broaden participation and engage new stakeholders should assist policy implementation and delivery. It may also be seen as further evidence that the role of science, as delivered by 'experts' who are considered above challenge, is becoming less influential as a legitimate basis for public actions.

Yet there are inherent conflicts or problems, the first being that calls for wider, more meaningful participation must be rationalized with the delivery of species and habitats defined according to national criteria. By and large, the first five years of the UK BAP process measured conservation need in terms of rarity and threat to extinction at the expense of the more common species and habitats. This tension has played itself out in different ways in different locations. Selman and Wragg (1999b) explain how, in Oxfordshire, the process of translating national targets into local action plans was conducted predominantly by professionals; consultation was perceived to be limited, and partners sought to balance the selection of target species on the grounds of rarity and threat with the case for selecting 'more charismatic' species with a perceived capacity to engage a wider public. In Buckinghamshire, wider public input to LBAP development was sought. A second issue is that, in some local authorities across Scotland, it is believed that the scope for achieving greater integration between LBAPs and development plans would be enhanced by a greater statutory impetus from central government (Ekos Limited, 2001). Limits to spontaneous local cooperation might by addressed by more, rather than less, central direction.

CONCLUSIONS

Over the last 20 years the UK government has adopted a large number of international conventions and agreements relating to biodiversity. Of these, the House of Commons Environment, Transport and Regional Affairs Committee identified the CBD (1992) and the European Community Birds and Habitats Directives (1979 and 1992) as the key landmark measures that dictate the shape of current UK policy on biodiversity. Unlike most other international conventions and agreements relating to biodiversity or the Birds and Habitats Directives (see Chapter 3), the CBD does not require the designation of protected areas; it is focused on process rather than 'product'. In the UK, the CBD has led to a new system of biodiversity action planning. Conservation groups such as the RSPB have successfully used the CBD, and the mechanism of BAPs, to acquire resources and political clout. The business-like language of BAPs has managed to secure the attention of politicians and decision-makers in a way that traditional 'nature conservation' never did. A key feature of this new approach has been the widening and deepening of partnership working, with the conservation NGOs becoming more fully involved in the development of policy and its subsequent implementation.

The realization of BAPs raises much broader questions for nature conservation, for conservation groups and for notions of nature in general. The insinuation of BAPs into government policy entails simultaneously the creation of alliances between various actors and the issue of institutional linkages between BAPs and other strategy building exercises. Hence BAPs provide a context in which to further understand the processes of policy integration and the extent to which the practice of integration is almost always asymmetric, with one agency or objective becoming subservient to another. Looking at horizontal integration, the issue is how far – due to their national policy status, powerful managerial logic, or networks of local partnerships – BAPs can influence the design and content of statutory development plans and other non-statutory environmental plans (eg Local Environment Agency Plans). It is also unclear so far whether BAPs really make an impact on the core objectives of corporate or governmental organizations involved in the BAP process, or whether it leads to no more than symbolic compliance. The determination of BAP objectives also raises important questions about vertical integration – the linkages between global ecological concerns and local action. These questions concern such matters as the role of science-based and local knowledge in the formation of alliances and in the transmission of policy goals through different policy and corporate arenas.

The fact that BAPs, with their detailed structure of targets and timetables, appear to have found acceptance in several branches of policy-making demands closer inspection since, broadly-speaking, central government has continued successfully to resist the institution of targets in what it perceives as sensitive policy areas – traffic reduction being a prominent example. Part of this stems from the fact that a real effort to achieve targets can mean confronting the divisive issue of environmental limits; that to sustain a specified level of habitat or population, development will sometimes need to be regulated or even forbidden altogether. Yet the consensual, partnership-based ethos of BAP activity tends to retreat into a managerialist logic rather than confront such issues. It is possible that the capacity of BAPs to negotiate environmental limits – and with it to renegotiate interests in nature conservation – has yet to be fully tested.

REFERENCES

Abernethy, V (2000) 'Local BAPs in Scotland – What difference have they made?', *ECOS*, vol 21(2), pp21–23

Adams, W (1996) *Future Nature: A Vision for Nature Conservation*, Earthscan and the British Association of Nature Conservationists, London

Avery, M, Bourn, N, Davis, R, Everitt, J, Halahan, R, Harper, M, Parsons, M, Phillips, M, Sands, T, Williams, G and Wynde, R (2001) *Biodiversity Counts: Delivering a Better Quality of Life*, Royal Society for the Protection of Birds, Sandy

Batten, L, Bibby, C, Clement, P, Elliott, G and Porter R (1990) *Red Data Birds in Britain*, T and A D Poyser, London

Bishop, K, Norton, A and Phillips, A (1999) 'He Who Pays the Piper – the impact of the National Lottery on countryside conservation policy', *ECOS*, vol 20(3/4), pp20–29

Ekos Limited (2001) *The Influence of Local Biodiversity Action Plans on the Unitary Authority LA21 Process and Community Planning*, Scottish Executive Central Research Unit, Edinburgh

Evans, P (1996) 'Biodiversity: Nature for Nerds?', *ECOS*, vol 17(2), pp7–12

Glowka, L, Burhenne-Guilmin, F, Synge, H, McNeely, J and Gundling, L (1994) *A Guide to the Convention on Biological Diversity*, Environmental Policy and Law Paper No 30, IUCN Environmental Law Centre, The World Conservation Union, Gland

Green, M (2000) 'Human Nature', *ECOS*, vol 21(2), pp47–52

H M Government (1991) *This Common Inheritance: Britain's Environmental Strategy*, Cmd 1200, Her Majesty's Stationery Office, London

H M Government (1994) *Biodiversity: The UK Action Plan*, Cm 2428, Her Majesty's Stationery Office, London

H M Government (1996) *The Government's Response to the UK Steering Group Report*, Cmd 3260, Her Majesty's Stationery Office, London

House of Commons Environment, Transport and Regional Affairs Committee (2000) *UK Biodiversity: Report and Proceedings of the Committee*, House of Commons Paper HC 441, The Stationery Office, London

IUCN, UNEP and WWF (1980) *World Conservation Strategy: Living Resource Conservation for Sustainable Development*, International Union for Conservation of Nature and Natural Resources, United Nations Environment Programme and World Wildlife Fund, Gland

IUCN, UNEP and WWF (1991) *Caring for the Earth: A Strategy for Sustainable Living*, The World Conservation Union, United Nations Environment Programme and World Wide Fund for Nature, Gland

Marren, P (2000) 'Did the Bittern Read the BAP?', *ECOS*, vol 21(2), pp43–47

McConnell, F (1996) *The Biodiversity Convention: A Negotiating History*, Kluwer Law International, London

National Park Commission (1931) *Report of the National Park Committee*, Cmd 3851, Her Majesty's Stationery Office, London

Parliamentary Office of Science and Technology (2000) Briefing Note for the House of Commons Environment, Transport and Regional Affairs Committee, pp 1ii–1xiii in House of Commons Environment, Transport and Regional Affairs Committee, *UK Biodiversity: Report and Proceedings of the Committee*, House of Commons Paper HC 441, the Stationery Office, London

Porter, R, Wynne, G, Avery, M, Thomas, G and Williams, G (1994) 'Into the Future: The RSPB's conservation priorities for the UK', *RSPB Conservation Review*, No 8, pp5–9

Sainsbury's (1997) *Biodiversity on the Farm*, Sainsbury's, London

Selman, P and Wragg, A (1999a) 'Networks of Co-operation and Knowledge in 'Wider Countryside Planning', *Journal of Environmental Planning and Management*, vol 42(5), pp 649–669

Selman, P and Wragg, A (1999b) 'Local Sustainability Planning: From interest-driven networks to vision-driven super networks?', *Planning Practice and Research*, vol 14(3), pp329–340

Serjeant, T (2000) 'Getting Biodiversity into Local Agenda 21', *ECOS*, vol 21(2), pp32–36

The Wildlife Trusts (2000) 'Memorandum of Evidence Submitted to the House of Commons Environment, Transport and Regional Affairs Committee Inquiry into UK Biodiversity', in House of Commons Environment, Transport and Regional Affairs Committee, *UK Biodiversity: Memoranda Relating to the Inquiry Submitted to the Environment Sub-committee*, House of Commons Paper HC 441-II, The Stationery Office, London, pp58-66

Tydeman, C (1995) 'Biodiversity on Target?', *ECOS*, vol 16(3/4), pp10–13

UK Biodiversity Action Plan Steering Group (1995a) *Biodiversity: The UK Steering Group Report Volume 1: Meeting the Rio Challenge*, Her Majesty's Stationery Office, London

UK Biodiversity Action Plan Steering Group (1995b) *Biodiversity: The UK Steering Group Report Volume 2: Action Plans*, Her Majesty's Stationery Office, London

UK Biodiversity Steering Group (2001) *Sustaining the Variety of Life: 5 Years of the UK Biodiversity Action Plan*, Report of the UK Biodiversity Group to the UK Government, the Scottish Executive, the National Assembly for Wales and the Northern Ireland Executive, Department of the Environment, Transport and the Regions, London

World Commission on Environment and Development (1987) *Our Common Future*, Oxford University Press, Oxford

WRI, IUCN and UNEP (1992) *Global Biodiversity Strategy: Guidelines for Action to Save, Study and Use Earth's Biotic Wealth Sustainably and Equitably*, World Resources Institute, World Conservation Union and United Nations Environment Programme, Gland

Wynne, G, Avery, M, Campbell, L, Gubbay, S, Hawkswell, S, Juniper, T, King, M, Newbery, P, Smart, J, Steel, C, Stones, T, Stubbs, A, Taylor, J, Tydeman, C and Wynde, R (1993) *Biodiversity Challenge: An Agenda for Conservation in the UK*, Royal Society for the Protection of Birds, Sandy

Wynne, G, Avery, M, Hawkswell, S, Juniper, T, King, M, Smart, J, Steel, C, Stones, T, Stubbs, A, Taylor, J and Tydeman, C (1995a) 'The Road from Rio: Action for biodiversity', *RSPB Conservation Review*, No 9, pp14–19

Wynne, G, Avery, M, Campbell, L, Gubbay, S, Hawkswell, S, Juniper, T, King, M, Newbery, P, Smart, J, Steel, C, Stones, T, Stubbs, A, Taylor, J, Tydeman, C and Wynde, R (1995b) *Biodiversity Challenge: An Agenda for Conservation in the UK*, 2nd edition, Royal Society for the Protection of Birds, Sandy

Chapter 3

European Frameworks for Nature Conservation: The Case of the Birds and Habitats Directives

Dave Burges

This chapter will focus on the requirements of the Birds and Habitats Directives. It will identify the significant (and, in the UK, the novel) thinking that these European frameworks introduce by emphasizing the move away from a narrow concentration on protected areas, and the development of spatial planning, which links land use and land management. Such thinking is also reflected in other Europe-wide initiatives. These developments have important implications for countryside planning in the UK.

THE BIRDS AND HABITATS DIRECTIVES

Looking back from the present, it seems increasingly difficult to recall a time when the UK was without a European obligation to protect wildlife and wildlife habitats. The European Union Directive on the Conservation of Wild Birds (Birds Directive) (Commission of the European Communities, 1979) has in fact been in force since 1979; and the European Union Directive on the Conservation of Natural Habitats and of Wild Fauna and Flora (Habitats Directive) (CEC, 1992) has been at the centre of the EU's nature conservation efforts for ten years (see Box 3.1).

Nevertheless, despite the impact that both directives have had in nature conservation planning and decision-making, neither has been fully implemented in any EU member state. Indeed the process of identifying and designating Special Protection Areas (SPAs) and Special Areas for Conservation (SACs) under the Birds and Habitats Directives respectively is still underway, with no clear indication of when either will be completed – finally delivering the *Natura 2000* Network of protected areas underpinned by Article 3 of the Habitats Directive.

BOX 3.1 THE EU BIRDS AND HABITATS DIRECTIVES

The European Directives on the Conservation of Wild Birds (79/409/EEC) – the Birds Directive – and the Conservation of Natural Habitats and of Wild Fauna and Flora (92/43/EEC) – the Habitats Directive – are the two key instruments of European Union nature conservation policy.

In essence the Birds Directive, which came into force in 1979, aims to protect rare and vulnerable bird species, listed in Annex 1 of the Directive, principally by means of the designation by member states of Special Protection Areas (SPAs). It also requires member states to establish a more 'general system of protection for all species' with respect to killing or capture, destruction of nests or eggs and disturbance. Certain species may still be hunted under defined criteria.

The Habitats Directive of 1992 aims, amongst other things, to complement the Birds Directive for identified priority habitats, flora and fauna other than birds. One of the principal mechanisms is the designation of Special Areas of Conservation (SACs) by member states. In contrast to the Birds Directive process where the selection of SPAs is largely a national decision, the final selection of SACs is 'moderated' by the European Commission (EC). Like the Birds Directive, it also establishes additional protection measures for certain species outside SACs.

Both SPAs and SACs contribute to the *Natura 2000* Network of protected areas across the community, which is subject to strict legislation designed to protect the sites against damaging developments. Both Directives also require Member States to address the 'wider countryside' within which the *Natura 2000* sites sit.

Since the Birds and Habitats Directives are often spoken of in one breath, it might be assumed that they are broadly similar instruments. It is true that both have their origins in the Convention on the Conservation of European Wildlife and Natural Habitats (the Berne Convention), ratified by the UK in 1982, which places obligations on all European states to protect endangered flora and fauna and the habitats that support them. However, the apparent focus of both directives on protected areas conceals important differences: both are products of their time, and whilst separated by only 12 years, the latter at least aims to be much more wide-ranging.

The Birds Directive focused on the need for protected areas for birds (SPAs), sought to ensure the protection of listed species outside these areas and aimed to control the hunting of protected quarry species. It therefore recognized that the conservation of rare, declining and migratory bird species depended on concerted action across the EU. However the directive also noted, in so many words, that birds were a good indicator of environmental health and constituted a common heritage, themes which were to recur in the Habitats Directive. Critically, it recognized – although the terms were not in common use at the time – the need for the conservation of biodiversity through protected area networks and beyond, and the need for sustainable development. The directive also includes measures to control the introduction of alien species, and recognizes the importance on ongoing research in delivering its conservation objectives.

In delivering these objectives, the Birds Directive notes in Article 2 that 'Member States shall take the requisite measures to maintain the population of the species referred to in Article 1 at a level which corresponds in particular to ecological, scientific and cultural requirements, while taking account of economic and recreational requirements, or to adapt the population of these species to that level'. It could be argued that this text is a forerunner of two concepts, both of which are set out in the Habitats Directive: 'favourable conservation status' and sustainable development. In practice, the application of Article 2 has proved to be rather more difficult, and perhaps even more so since the adoption of the second directive.

Articles 3 and 4 form the heart of the Birds Directive, requiring (in Article 3) member states to 'preserve, maintain or re-establish a sufficient diversity and area of habitats for all the species of birds referred to in Article'. Whilst a key element of Article 4 is the need for protected area designation, it could reasonably be argued that the above also requires a wider countryside approach.

This would in theory provide the matrix within which SPAs sit, as the 'special conservation measures' for the species listed in Annex 1 to the directive. The extent to which the former has been delivered in the UK may be arguable, although successive governments would no doubt claim that the increasing range and scope of agri-environment measures flowing from reform to date of the Common Agricultural Policy (CAP) help to address this requirement. In any event, rather more attention has been focused on the classification of 'the most suitable territories in number and size as special protection areas for the conservation of these species'. The SPA designation process is still underway for terrestrial sites throughout the EU. Giving effect to this part of the Birds Directive in the marine environment is proving still more problematic and time consuming, an experience which is also evident with the Habitats Directive.

Article 4(4) of the Birds Directive comprises just two sentences: '... Member States shall take appropriate steps to avoid pollution or deterioration of habitats or any disturbances affecting the birds, in so far as these would be significant having regard to the objectives of this Article. Outside these protection areas, Member States shall also strive to avoid pollution or deterioration of habitats'. Whilst, therefore, the directive intended that protected areas be considered in a wider framework, the focus has in fact been rather narrower. This has been controversial and the debates over the interpretation of the directive have thrown up significant European case law. The Leybucht Dykes, Santona Marshes and Lappel Bank cases are still widely quoted and have in turn shaped policy and practice across the EU (see Box 3.2).[1,2,3]

However, it was the introduction of the Habitats Directive that really brought about a step change in the level and complexity of debate surrounding EU nature conservation policy and practice. This applies both to the selection processes for protected areas, and to the measures designed to protect those sites. It is particularly relevant that the first two sentences of Article 4(4) of the Birds Directive, quoted above, are subsumed by four paragraphs in Article 6 of the Habitats Directive, which consider the treatment of plans or projects affecting all Natura 2000 sites. It is worth noting that the last sentence of Article 4(4) of the Birds Directive is still operative however.

During the drafting of the Habitats Directive, there was a view amongst some member states that the protection afforded to SPAs under the Birds

Box 3.2 European Court of Justice decisions under the EU Birds Directive

Three European Court of Justice (ECJ) cases – Leybucht Dykes (Case C-57/89 1991), Santona Marshes (Case C-355/90 1993) and Lappel Bank (Case C-44/95 1996) – are milestones in the interpretation of EU protected area legislation. They set important precedents for the designation and protection of SPAs, and have influenced subsequent policy.

The *Leybucht Dykes* case concerned the construction of flood defence works adjacent to an SPA in Germany, which the EC considered infringed Article 4(1) of the Birds Directive. The Commission argued that the works had led to deterioration in the habitats of birds for which the SPA had been designated. The German government argued that the damage to the SPA was minimal, that the works were necessary and in the public interest, and that they had exercised a member state's discretion in this respect. The UK government intervened in support of the German government's position. The Germans argued that the Commission had not provided evidence to support its contention that deterioration of the SPA had occurred as a result of the works, and that the works would actually improve conditions in the SPA, so having a compensatory effect.

The ECJ argued that whilst member states have 'a certain discretion with regard to the choice of territories which are most suitable for classification as Special Protection Areas', they do not have the 'same discretion ... in modifying or reducing the extent of areas'. By definition, these were the most suitable territories for the bird species in question. The ECJ stated that '... the power of the Member States to reduce the extent of a special protection area can be justified only on exceptional grounds'.

The judgement continued that 'those grounds must correspond to a general interest which is superior to the general interest represented by the ecological objective of the Directive'. The court stated that economic and recreational requirements as identified in Article 2 of the directive did not meet this test, but that construction of flood protection measures in this case did, as long as damage to the SPA was minimized. The court noted that other aspects of the works, while not meeting this test, would improve the quality of the SPA. So although the Commission actually lost this case, the point of principle was established that destruction of even part of an SPA could be sanctioned only if very strict conditions were met.

The *Santona Marshes* case turned on the need to designate 'the most suitable territories' as SPAs, and then ensuring their appropriate protection and management. The Commission argued that Spain had 'neglected the obligations of protection stemming from Articles 3 and 4 of the directive'. The Spanish government rejected the allegations. In common with the Leybucht case, it argued that the obligations of the directive 'should be subordinate to other interests', such as those of an economic or social nature, or 'at the very least balanced against those interests'. The Commission, of course, cited the Leybucht result as clear case law against this position. The Commission and the Spanish government did agree that the Marismas de Santona were indeed important wetland habitats, but the government argued that it had some discretion as to which areas it decided to designate.

The court ruled that the member state was obliged to designate the territory as an SPA, if it met the criteria set out in the directive – choosing not to designate was not an option. It also considered that the designation of the Marismas as a nature reserve under Spanish law did not meet the obligations of the directive, nor was the area so designated adequate to meet the requirements of the bird species involved. It followed that the management plan drawn up to protect the Marismas was also inadequate, and that Spain had not delivered its obligations under Articles 4(1) and 4(2) of the directive. The court also found that Spain had breached Article 4(4), as it had permitted the building of a new road and associated development, clam farms in the Marismas and pollution.

The Lappel Bank case concerned the exclusion of mudflats (Lappel Bank) from the Medway SPA in Kent on economic grounds, and the subsequent lack of any compensatory measures to restore the habitat damage. The case had been taken by the RSPB through the UK courts, and was eventually referred to the ECJ by the House of Lords. The House of Lords requested clarification as to whether member states could draw the boundaries of SPAs taking economic considerations into account. If not, was it possible to take a superior general interest into account (as per the Leybucht judgement), and whether any such economic considerations constituted 'imperative reasons of overriding public interest' as set out in the Habitats Directive.

The conservation case relied on both the Leybucht and Santona cases and on the Article 6 process (see above) contained in the Habitats Directive. The ECJ ruling was clear: (i) member states cannot take account of economic requirements when designating SPAs and defining their boundaries; (ii) economic requirements do not constitute a general interest superior to the ecological objective of that directive; and (iii), even if economic interests do constitute overriding public interest under the Habitats Directive, these matters could not enter into consideration at the designation stage, although they might be considered in any Article 6 process.

Directive was too absolute, and did not take account of social, cultural and, especially, economic factors. This concern seemed to reflect the call from Rio for sustainable development; indeed the preamble to the directive duly notes this responsibility (see below). Furthermore, the text of the Habitats Directive itself does allow for the possibility of otherwise damaging developments (provided that they are associated with mitigation or compensatory habitat action) under certain conditions of 'over-riding public interest'. A contrary view, of course, was that the level of protection afforded to SPAs had in fact been watered down by a decision-making process, which under certain conditions, would permit damaging development.

In the context of the debates which culminated in the Earth Summit, held in Rio in 1992, the Habitats Directive (adopted in the same year) took a wider approach than the Birds Directive in two important respects. First it looked beyond a strictly protected areas approach; and second it recognized the importance of sustainable development. This is apparent in the language used in the preamble: '... the main aim of this Directive being to promote the maintenance of biodiversity, taking account of economic, social, cultural and regional requirements, this Directive makes a contribution to the general objective of sustainable development; whereas the maintenance of such biodiversity may in certain cases require the maintenance or indeed the encouragement of human activities'.

The preamble goes on to set out the requirements for protected areas (in this case SACs), and notes that 'land-use planning and development policies should encourage the management of features of the landscape which are of major importance for wild flora and fauna'. But while the Habitats Directive is set in a wider context than was the Birds Directive, the earlier directive is brought into this new framework. Thus the protection and management of SPAs complement the SACs as part of the Natura 2000 network.

However, as with the Birds Directive, the main focus of the implementation of the Habitats Directive across the EU has been on the identification and eventual designation of SACs. This is a more complicated process than that for SPAs, involving initial selection of qualifying sites at the member state level, and then the moderation of these lists by biogeographic region in concert with the Commission. This process should have been completed by 2000, but is now severely delayed: a second round of moderation meetings has been required and is now in progress. They are several reasons for these delays. Site selection procedures are more complex, and interest groups (industry, landowners, sporting interests and nature conservation NGOs) have been much more actively involved than was the case for SPAs (in the UK at least) under the Birds Directive. The net effect is that delays at the national level have seriously impeded progress in implementing this EU-wide measure.

Article 10 of the directive aims to provide a wider framework within which the Natura 2000 series should sit. It is not, however, strongly worded: 'Member States shall endeavour, where they consider it necessary, in their land-use planning and development policies and in particular, with a view to improving the ecological coherence of the *Natura 2000* network, to encourage the management of features of the landscape which are of major importance for wild fauna and flora'. Having set this strategic overview, the text then continues: '... Such features are those which, by virtue of their linear and continuous structure (such as rivers with their banks or the traditional systems for marking field boundaries) or their function as stepping stones (such as ponds or small woods) are essential for the migration, dispersal and genetic exchange of wild species'.

One way to paraphrase these paragraphs is that they recognize that the land use planning system has a contribution to make in protecting and enhancing the wider countryside matrix within which Natura 2000 sites will sit. They also imply that targeted habitat management is needed to deliver conservation benefits.

DELIVERY MECHANISMS

In common with most member states, the UK has focused on the identification, designation and protection of *Natura 2000* sites. The first two components are still not complete for either SPAs or SACs (indeed at the time of writing, the European Commission was part way through a second series of so-called Biogeographic Moderation meetings which aim to finalize the SAC series across the Community). Setting up Natura 2000 involves a wide range of players, such as individual landowners and managers, major commercial concerns, NGOs, the statutory nature conservation agencies, civil servants and ministers. A national legal and policy framework is needed for such wide-ranging deliberations, designed to deliver the UK's obligations under the two directives.

The workings of the directives are transposed and given force in national law by a combination of regulations (some emanating from devolved administrations) and planning guidance. These are in turn cross-referenced to a still wider range of land use topics, concerning subjects as diverse as regional, county and district planning, transport and minerals planning, and an environmental impact assessment. There are also strong links with non-statutory processes and plans, such as the local to national Biodiversity Action Plans (BAPs) (H M Government, 1994; UK Biodiversity Group, 2001), and the Environment Agency's Local Environment Agency Plans (LEAPs) (Environment Agency, 1997) for river catchments. The introduction into UK law of the EU Water Framework Directive (CEC, 2000), which will be partially dependent on the implementation of the Birds and Habitats Directives, will add a further factor.

Even though the directives increase the level of obligation to meet EU requirements, UK governments have delivered the directives' obligations through existing legislation, including the introduction of regulations derived from this. No primary legislation has been enacted. Thus, with very few exceptions, the site designation provisions of the Birds and Habitats Directives have been delivered through Sites of Special Scientific Interest (SSSIs) (or Areas of Special Scientific Interest (ASSIs) in Northern Ireland), under the Wildlife and Countryside Act 1981. The Conservation (Natural Habitats &c.) Regulations 1994 (the Habitats Regulations), adopted in October 1994, gave effect to key elements of the Habitats Directive at the then UK level. The Wildlife and Countryside Act 1981 has now been amended by the Countryside and Rights of Way Act 2001 in England and Wales. As a result, the SPAs and SACs are essentially part, whole or composite suites of SSSIs. The use of SSSIs as the site designation delivery mechanism has important implications for the effectiveness of the Natura 2000 series in the UK, given that the SSSI selection criteria bear no direct relationship to the site selection criteria in the directives. As noted above, key Habitats Directive obligations, notably the concept of 'favourable conservation status' and the site safeguard provisions of Article 6, apply equally to SPAs. It is symptomatic of the patchy way in which both directives have been transposed that while site safeguard is dealt with at a UK level (through the Habitats Regulations), 'favourable conservation status' is not, even though it is critical to successful implementation.

So, whilst UK governments since 1979 have progressed, but not yet completed, action to implement the directives, the mechanisms through which this is being achieved do not necessarily fully reflect their intent. Whilst the concept of subsidiarity allows for a degree of national-level interpretation, it should not be taken so far as to undermine the necessarily uniform implementation which an EU-wide network implies. But it would be wrong to single out the UK government in this respect: as recent work by the World Wide Fund for Nature (WWF) makes clear, member states' performance on Directive implementation is highly variable, and the UK is in fact one of the better performers to date (World Wide Fund for Nature, 2001).

The approach adopted by many member states, the UK included, has been to take a national perspective, based on that member state's own interpretation of what is expected of them. It is only when country-based, directive-led decision-making is challenged by third parties, or perhaps by the Commission itself, that the Commission has become involved in enforcement action against the member states. As result, the EU overview tends to catch up with member states' interpretation, rather than lead it. This is true of the notable ECJ judgements (see Box 3.2) which have focused on the issues surrounding the designation of SPAs and SACs and the likely impacts of plans or projects that could affect them. It is also instructive that Commission guidance on Article 6 of the Habitats Directive emerged only in 2000, eight years after the directive had come into force; and that no guidance has yet been issued on site management and monitoring (also Article 6) and so-called wider countryside measures (Article 10).

So whilst it would seem reasonable to suggest that the directives do indeed 'Europeanise' conservation policy and decision-making, in practice this is a much more iterative and less complete process than might have been expected. But, in this respect, are the directives any different from much other legislation, the interpretation of which inevitably evolves over time?

IMPACT ON THE BRITISH PLANNING SYSTEM AND WIDER COUNTRYSIDE POLICY FRAMEWORKS

With the benefit of hindsight, it is clear that a range of related worldwide, European and national changes to policy and guidance affecting biodiversity was initiated in the early 1990s. The obligations of the Convention on Biological Diversity in 1992, the Habitats Directive itself, and new national planning legislation paved the way for an important change in the way in which the environment, and protected areas in particular, were dealt with through the planning system. Around the same time, the Town and Country Planning Act 1990 and the Planning and Compensation Act 1991 introduced a new emphasis on a plan-led system.

The weight to be accorded to nature conservation issues, especially those arising from international or European obligations, was formally underlined with the replacement of Department of the Environment Circular 27/87 on Nature Conservation (DoE, 1987) by Planning Policy Guidance Note 9 (PPG9) on Nature Conservation in October 1994 (DoE, 1994). This was accompanied by the so-called Habitats Regulations (see above). PPG9 and the regulations provide the framework for conservation within the planning system in the UK, although, as a result of devolution and new national legislation, both are now due for revision.

The magnitude of this change is well illustrated by the contrast between the full treatment given to biodiversity conservation in PPG9 and the cursory treatment in Circular 27/87. Thus, Circular 27/87 devoted a mere seven paragraphs to the treatment of SPAs in the planning system; and the key section is just two paragraphs re-iterating the text of Article 4(4) of the Birds Directive. By contrast, most of PPG9, which deals with the treatment of nature conservation issues in the planning system in general, is concerned with the implications of the Habitats Directive. This was inevitable; given that Articles 6(2) to 6(4) addressed the treatment of plans and projects which could impact on Natura 2000 sites.

The Habitats Directive Article 6 decision-making process, and its transposition into UK law through the Habitats Regulations and PPG9, has had a marked impact on strategic and site-specific planning policy and practice. This is evident both in the way that the requirement has been interpreted in general and in how it has been used to resolve site-specific planning issues. The cases cited in Box 3.2 have shaped evolving national policy and guidance in the UK. Furthermore, planning inquiries in the UK have produced decisions that have lent further interpretation to the application of the directive. These kinds of decisions, whether taken nationally or at the European level, can have significant long-term implications for the general thrust of a statutory development plan by affecting the likely locations for new housing development for example, or the proposed development of sensitive sites. None the less, ten years after the Habitats Directive came into force, we are now seeing the promotion of major infrastructure projects, such as new deep-water container port facilities in sensitive environments, which are seriously testing the concepts of site integrity, over-riding public interest and mitigation/compensation.

Thus a significant amount of time and energy has been spent on the site designation and protection issues raised by the directives, and on how these have been delivered through the planning system. But there are also questions about the management of Natura 2000 sites, and the wider countryside within which they are set.

Many *Natura 2000* sites are, or at least include, existing nature reserves that benefit from management plans which already take account of their international status. There is a specific obligation under Regulation 33 of the Habitats Regulations for all marine sites to have management plans drawn up, although a similar obligation does not apply to terrestrial sites. Similarly, agri-environment measures, such as Environmentally Sensitive Areas (ESAs) and the Countryside Stewardship Scheme (CSS) in England or Tir Gofal in Wales, do address particular habitats and habitat features, providing they operate appropriate prescriptions and are adequately funded. These measures fulfil, at least in part, the requirements of the second paragraph of Article 10, complementing the more traditional protected area approach in the UK. The importance of wider countryside measures has, however, come to the fore in recent years, mainly as a result of steep declines in farmland flora and fauna arising from agricultural intensification, encouraged and financed by the CAP. But as yet there is no overarching protection and management scheme that really works at a landscape scale – delivering the 'favourable conservation status' for habitats and species listed in the Habitats Directive for example.

THE CHANGING CONTEXT

The need for CAP reform, coupled with the recent Bovine Spongiform Encephalopathy (BSE) and Foot and Mouth outbreaks in the UK, have led efforts by government, statutory agencies, farming and landowning bodies, and nature conservation NGOs to promote more sustainable and integrated rural land use policies. The importance of a wider rural development framework chimes with the social, economic, cultural and sustainable development objectives set out at the beginning of the Habitats Directive.

This is the context in which a much more proactive and strategic nature conservation agenda is taking shape, involving large-scale habitat restoration through the UK Biodiversity Action Plan process and related biodiversity rebuilding initiatives. Action at the county and local levels reflects this; among many examples are Hampshire's Biodiversity Action Plan and Landscape Strategy (Hampshire Biodiversity Partnership, undated; Hampshire County Council, undated). While a landscape-level approach to nature conservation is not a new theme in the UK, it is only now coming to the fore. It would seem that the drivers for this are not, however, the Birds and Habitats Directives so much as the concerns and opportunities created by CAP reform and climate change, and the growing alarm at the erosion of biodiversity, landscape and local distinctiveness in the countryside as a whole. They also respond to the thinking behind other initiatives at the European level, which are less binding than the two directives, notably the European Landscape Convention (see Chapter 4), the Pan-European Biological and Landscape Diversity Strategy (PEBLDS) and the European Ecological Network (EECONET).

To quote directly from its website summary, PEBLDS 'presents an innovative and proactive approach to stop and reverse the degradation of biological and landscape diversity values in Europe' and emphasizes the need for integrated and coordinated action.[4] The strategy was developed under the auspices of the meetings of Europe's Environment Ministers and focuses on the whole of Europe. It grew out of the recognition that political, social and economic change across Europe, coupled with a growing public awareness and concern for biodiversity and landscape conservation, presented both a need and opportunity for better coordination. Whilst this is undoubtedly the case, the strategy has not received the publicity and political support it clearly needs to succeed. Not having been framed within the EU, PEBLDS has no legal teeth, but only aims to 'fill gaps where these initiatives are not implemented to their full potential or fail to achieve desired objectives'. Since even the Habitats Directive has received relatively little attention by many, even most, member states, it is not surprising that the PEBLDS should have had such a low profile.

Nevertheless, the strategy's ten key principles provide an excellent framework for what many would see as enlightened environmental and landscape decision-making. These include:

- careful decision-making;
- avoidance of damage;
- precautionary principle;
- translocation of species;
- ecological compensation;
- ecological integrity;
- restoration and (re)creation of habitats;
- best available technology and environmental practice;
- polluter pays;
- public participation and access to information.

The core objectives relate to, amongst other things, the maintenance and enhancement of key ecosystems, habitats and species to create EECONET, the sustainable management of the resources within the network, and sectoral integration and 'adequate financial means' to make it happen.

CONCLUSIONS

The Birds and Habitats Directives have had a major impact on the way in which nature conservation is operated in the UK. They have certainly affected the workings of the planning system and provided a rationale for many of the agri-environmental initiatives. Above all, the directives have helped to raise the profile of biodiversity conservation in the UK.

Yet the approach, certainly as it has been interpreted, has tended to be site focused. As has become clearer in recent years, the countryside agenda is changing rapidly and connections are being made between sectors that previously acted in relative isolation. Whilst site-based conservation still has a very important role to play in the protection of the countryside, there is a growing need for a more comprehensive approach. It is to be hoped that the implementation of the directives will be part of this strategic approach to shaping the countryside of the future, in which the welfare of people, the strength of the rural economy, and the health of biodiversity and natural systems are more strongly linked.

NOTES

1   Court of Justice of the European Communities (1991) *Case Number C-57/89: Commission v. Federal Republic of Germany.*
2   Court of Justice of the European Communities (1993) *Case Number C-355/90: Commission v. Spain.*
3   Court of Justice of the European Communities (1996) *Case Number C-44/95: Regina v Secretary of State for the Environment* ex parte *Royal Society for the Protection of Birds.*
4   See www.strategyguide.org/straabow.html

REFERENCES

Commission of the European Communities (CEC) (1979) *Conservation of Wild Birds*, Directive 79/409/EEC of 2 April 1979, Office for Official Publications of the European Communities, Luxembourg

Commission of the European Communities (CEC) (1992) *Conservation of Natural Habitats and of Wild Fauna and Flora*, Directive 92/43/EEC of 21 May 1992, Office for Official Publications of the European Communities, Luxembourg

Commission of the European Communities (CEC) (2000) *Framework for Community Action in the Field of Water Policy*, Directive 2000/60/EEC of 23 October 2000, Office for Official Publications of the European Communities, Luxembourg

Department of the Environment (DoE) (1987) *Circular 27/87: Nature Conservation*, Her Majesty's Stationery Office, London

Department of the Environment (DoE) (1994) *Planning Policy Guidance 9: Nature Conservation*, Her Majesty's Stationery Office, London

Environment Agency (1997) *Local Environment Agency Plans*, Environment Agency, Bristol

Hampshire Biodiversity Partnership (undated) *Biodiversity Action Plan for Hampshire, Volume 1: Strategic Framework and Main Course of Action*, Hampshire County Council, Winchester

Hampshire County Council (undated) *The Hampshire Landscape*, Hampshire County Council, Winchester

H M Government (1994) *Biodiversity: The UK Action Plan*, Cmd 2428, Her Majesty's Stationery Office, London

UK Biodiversity Steering Group (2001) *Sustaining the Variety of Life: 5 Years of the UK Biodiversity Action Plan*, Report of the UK Biodiversity Group to the UK Government, the Scottish Executive, the National Assembly for Wales and the Northern Ireland Executive, Department of the Environment, Transport and the Regions, London

World Wide Fund for Nature (2001) *A Race to Protect Europe's Natural Heritage*, WWF, Brussels

Chapter 4

Our Landscape from a Wider Perspective

Adrian Phillips and Roger Clarke

This chapter is about a new development: the harnessing of landscape as an international policy instrument, and the impact of this on conservation and land use policy and practice in the UK. It discusses two significant, parallel and related developments: how landscape has become a source of international attention, notably with the World Heritage Convention and the European Landscapes Convention (ELC), and how landscape has come to be seen both as a precious resource in its own right and as a means to achieve sustainable development. It concludes with a brief exploration of what these developments might imply for the UK.

LANDSCAPE – AN ELUSIVE CONCEPT FOR INTERNATIONAL POLICY

The topic of landscape has attracted many writers. Some have looked at it from a historical perspective, pointing out how tastes in landscapes have changed greatly over the years. Such students of landscape often recall how distant are 18th-century views from our own. William Cobbett wrote that he had 'no idea of picturesque beauty separate from fertility of soil', and William Gilpin said that there were 'few who do not prefer the busy scenes of cultivation to the greatest of nature's rough productions'. Even Wordsworth, that poet of the romantic landscape, could not deny that for many people the sight of 'a rich meadow, with fat cattle grazing on it, or the sight of what they would call a heavy crop of corn, is worth all … the Alps and Pyrenees in their utmost grandeur and beauty' (all quotations in Thomas, 1983).

Others have written about landscape more from a cultural and philosophical perspective. They would contrast the power of the ancient forest mythology on the peoples, and even the politics, of central Europe, with the poetic tradition of *la douce* France – 'sweet France' – as captured in the *Tres Riches Heures* of the duc de Berry (Scharma, 1995). Venerating the link between landscapes and culture appeals strongly to the English hunting classes, for whom a love of the pastoral landscape and a passion for the chase and field sports seem to be interwoven (Vandervell and Coles, 1980).

Others again have written of landscape from a more analytical standpoint, seeking to understand its physical elements, and how they relate to each other, to cultural and artistic associations and to the changing needs of society. A whole series of landscape studies of this kind have been undertaken in Britain in recent years, many of them pioneered by the former Countryside Commission, but now being pursued by its successors, other national agencies and local government. This work, which has supported a thriving industry of landscape consultancy, is drawn upon in several of the chapters that follow in Part 2. A common feature of these initiatives by public agencies is that they are multidisciplinary.

So landscape has many meanings, can be approached from numerous perspectives and draws on many disciplines. But as a basis for a policy-related discourse it has suffered from three distinguishing characteristics: landscape is a convergence ground for different disciplines; attitudes and responses towards it are culturally-related, change over time, and are considered to be subjective; and few of its qualities can sensibly be quantified.

The study of landscape involves ecologists, architects, archaeologists, historians, geographers, geologists, geomorphologists and others; it unites the natural and social sciences. This is the strength of the landscape approach to environmental management, as we will see. However, until quite recently, multidisciplinary approaches to the understanding of our environment were not fashionable, and landscape was therefore doomed to be everyone's interest, but no one's responsibility. As a result, there has been no strong disciplinary core to the topic, and indeed there are difficulties in defining what is meant by a 'landscape profession'. Its practitioners are involved in everything from the treatment of the curtilages of buildings to the management of broad tracts of countryside; and they come to the profession from many different primary disciplines.

The problem is compounded by the apparently subjective nature of people's responses to landscape. Landscape beauty is indeed in the eye of the beholder. To one person, the china clay pits on the south-west edge of Dartmoor are a gross violation of wild scenery. But others may see in them an industrial majesty, particularly if they are enthusiasts for the architectural notion of 'functionalism', which asserts that 'providing the *function* of the landscape ... finds visual expression through the *form* of the landscape itself, the result would be aesthetically pleasing' (Appleton, 1991, p73). There are indeed no universally agreed norms in this business, and prevailing attitudes change over time. The historical changes in landscape taste have already been touched on. Attitudes to the industrial revolution demonstrate this well: what were once seen as industrial intrusions – the Ribblehead viaduct in the Yorkshire Dales National Park, for example – have become essential parts of well-loved landscapes (but who would say that of lines of electricity pylons?). The National Parks and Access to the

Countryside Act 1949, which provided the framework for the current family of national parks and areas of outstanding natural beauty (AONBs), focused mainly on mountains, moors, upland and hilly country, omitting such places as the Somerset Levels. Today 'critics of the list of the range of landscapes covered by AONB designation cite the preoccupation with hills, seemingly at the expenses of flat landscapes, as a significant shortcoming' (Holdaway and Smart, 2001, p27).

Since landscape is a social construct, it is viewed very differently in different parts of the world. Each society has its own distinctive view of landscape and of its values; and each culture celebrates its landscape in different ways. Moreover, two cultures may look upon the same piece of landscape in quite different ways. For example, newly arrived Australians of European origin saw the outback of that continent quite differently from the aboriginal peoples who had lived there for millennia. To this day, the Maasai in east Africa see the wildlife spectacle of the Serengeti plains through different eyes to those of the safari tourist. In both cases, the indigenous peoples look upon their environment as a working landscape. They can locate in it those things that Europeans cannot: its food and water sources, and its dangers; but they are less impressed by the drama of the scenery. As a result, landscape was not initially a comfortable topic for international discourse. In particular, a 'euro-centric' view of landscape, with its heavy emphasis on a shared cultural heritage of painting, literature and music, had little appeal to those whose culture leads them to look on landscape very differently. It seems reasonable to assume that landscape could not become a topic for international debate until its advocates were ready to recognize and respect the diversity of views and attitudes towards the subject (Phillips, 2000).

In theory, it might be possible to overcome these problems by recourse to some objective means of measuring landscape and its qualities, and to reduce its infinite complexity and variety to a commonly agreed quantifiable base. But that is a chimera, since there can only be quantification when there is an agreed framework of values, and a good understanding of how those values and the measurable characteristics of the landscapes relate. Given the subjective nature of responses to landscape, it is unlikely that such a shared understanding exists within any one society, let alone between societies. Moreover not everything about landscape can be measured (its association with painters or writers, for example, or the spiritual values that many indigenous peoples and other communities attach to it). The assessment of landscape can be undertaken in a rigorous and comprehensive way (Countryside Commission, 1993), but it cannot be reduced to a set of computer-based calculations dealing only with numbers.

These characteristics of landscape make it an elusive concept, and a difficult topic to embed in policy. None the less, love of landscape has driven public policy for many years. The UK's legislation to designate and protect landscapes deserving special protection (national parks and areas of outstanding natural beauty in England and Wales) was enacted more than 50 years ago. It has also motivated millions of people to support powerful voluntary sector organizations like the National Trust and the Campaign to Protect Rural England (CPRE). But landscape has usually been seen as a second-class member of the environmental club. Lacking a coherent philosophy, thin on quantification and without a strong disciplinary core, it has often been viewed as a 'soft' topic, to be swept aside in the rush to develop and exploit the environment, a trend that is justified by that trite commentary: 'jobs before beauty'. In these respects, landscape protection, management and planning contrast strongly with conservation of nature, and with the protection of clean air and water.

The contrast is particularly evident at the international level. Until just a few years ago, there were no international measures at all that specifically addressed the topic of landscape: the reasons for this reluctance have already been identified. In contrast, by 1980, there were already two global biodiversity-related agreements, the Convention on Wetlands of International Importance (Ramsar), and the World Heritage Convention (see below). There were also a number of regional nature conservation conventions, for example, in South-East Asia, Europe, Africa, the western hemisphere and in a number of marine regions. In 1992, the Convention on Biological Diversity was signed by many countries at the Earth Summit (see Chapter 2), but in the last few years landscape has at last become a topic of international discourse as well; it is interesting to consider why this came about.

Landscape Comes in from the Cold

Landscape has emerged on the international agenda in several places in recent years. 'Cultural landscapes' have been included as a specific category under the World Heritage Convention; and increasing interest is being taken in 'protected landscapes' as a World Conservation Union (IUCN) category of protected area; a Pan-European Biological and Landscape Diversity Strategy has been agreed; and a European Landscape Convention (ELC) has been adopted. In light of such developments (which will be discussed below), it is possible to make a bold claim for landscape: that it provides a 'medium' through which to address the challenge of sustainable development. There are four reasons for this.

First, landscape can be seen as a 'bridge' between two perceptions of the world: one that focuses both on people and their cultures, *and* on nature and its systems. Thus landscape is a unifying notion: 'it is used as a theoretical concept and social construct around which an array of disciplines, including geography, art, literature and science coalesce to explore ... nature–human relationships' (Benson and Roe, 2000, p3). The idea of landscape already embraces both the human and natural dimensions that must be addressed in the pursuit of sustainable development. In this, landscape contrasts with biodiversity, which is but one – albeit very important – element in the sustainability agenda.

Second, landscape introduces a sense of time into our understanding of the environment. 'The English landscape itself, to those who know how to read it aright, is the richest historical record we possess' (Hoskins, 1955, p14). An understanding of the time-depth in the landscape of today is important to taking the right management decisions for the future. This is due to the fact that the archaeological dimension in the environment is significant in itself, but also because it 'allows management decisions for tomorrow to be made in light of the fullest knowledge of the effects of past practices' (Macinnes and Wickham-Jones, 1992, p2).

Next, landscape provides an appropriate scale for many sustainable development policies. Many writers believe that governance for sustainability needs to be based on bioregional landscape units (eg Miller, 1996), arguing that 'there is an increasing appreciation of the need to manage defined landscape units, such as coastal zones or river basins' (Maltby et al, 1999, p28). While it is true that the word 'landscape' may be used here to mean a bio-physical unit, in practice such units – a river basin, say, or a mountain range – almost invariably have social and cultural significance too. While it may be desirable to divide the landscape into quite small units for on-the-ground delivery of policy (eg Warwickshire County Council, 1991), it seems that the basic units for shaping a policy response need to be relatively large. Examples are the UK's national parks and its AONBs, or the comparable protected landscapes in many other European countries.

Finally, landscape is a popular notion. The very word is far more accessible than a term such as 'biodiversity'. Landscape can inspire intense affection; its protection can engender great dedication. People care about the landscape of the places that they live in or visit. Landscape sums up experience of place, and people can often engage more easily in sustainable development and environmental issues through the medium of landscape.

So an understanding of landscape brings four critical perspectives to our appreciation of the environment and human interaction with it: it is a unifying theme, requiring an inter-disciplinary approach; it reveals a time-depth understanding; it can only be addressed meaningfully on a relatively large scale; and it involves engaging in a cause close to many people's hearts. Similarly, policies for landscape protection, management and planning – the core activities encouraged by the ELC – can be a way of pursuing much of the sustainable development agenda. Traditionally, care for the landscape was often linked to access to beautiful countryside and opportunities for healthy outdoor recreation. But in a sustainable development context, landscape offers much more than that. It 'is inescapably connected to policy initiatives which seek to improve the quality of life, including the natural systems which support life itself' (Selman, 2000, p98). 'It is a principal means of enhancing the "identity" of places, associated with a sense of stability, continuity and attachment. It is a setting and a resource for the attraction and indigenous growth of industry. It supports biodiversity and the functioning of environmental life-support systems' (op cit). It is a means of encouraging the participation of people in shaping their own environment, and blends local knowledge with expert analyses. Hence today's concept of landscape is vastly more than attractive scenery for tourists to view. It is no longer located at the outer margins of political interest, but nearer the heart of the agenda for sustainable development and thus a 'key element within a nationally and internationally significant policy agenda' (op cit).

Another way to look at the topic is chronologically: landscape is at the beginning and the end of the sustainable development process. At the outset, how a place looks and feels is a good way to begin to address issues: whether a place is beautiful or derelict, improving or deteriorating can be diagnostic evidence of environmental health. In shaping a sustainable development strategy for an area, policies for the various sectors, such as transport, housing, water or agriculture, need to be integrated: as we have seen, landscape provides a tool for such an integrated approach. National park management plans already offer an example of how a landscape-based tool can be used to pull all the various elements – economic, social and environmental – together. Finally, the landscape can provide a means to measure the success of the strategy when it is implemented: does this place look and feel a better one to live and work in?

To conclude this part of the argument: landscape is both an environmental resource in its own right with a strong appeal to society, but which has been relatively neglected by policy-makers in the past; and a *medium* by which sustainable development programmes can be pursued in the future. These ideas are captured in the Oxford Landscape Declaration, adopted in May 2000 (see below).

CULTURAL LANDSCAPES AND THE WORLD HERITAGE CONVENTION

This treaty, the full title of which is the Convention Concerning the Protection of the World Cultural and Natural Heritage, is one of the oldest environmental agreements; it was adopted in 1972, the year of the Stockholm Conference, and came into force three years later. As of December 2002, 172 states were party to it. The convention aims to promote cooperation among nations to protect and conserve natural and cultural heritage of 'outstanding universal value'. It does this mainly by inscribing sites on the World Heritage List. These must be endowed with exceptional natural and/or cultural values. The list currently (at the end of 2001) includes 730 sites: 563 are cultural sites (such as the Pyramids of Egypt, or Westminster Abbey); 144 are natural sites (such as the Grand Canyon in the USA, or St Kilda in Scotland); and 23 are mixed (such as Machu Picchu in Peru) (UNESCO, 2002). Designation as a World Heritage site, which is undertaken by the World Heritage Committee, carries with it the expectation of strict protection.

Although the convention brings together cultural and natural sites within one international framework, there was no way, until recently, of recognizing sites which were important precisely because of the interplay between cultural and natural values – ie outstanding cultural landscapes. This became a source of concern during the 1980s for several reasons. It was felt that the split between culture and nature in the implementation of the convention excluded some important areas from consideration. A domestic example was the Lake District, which was nominated by the UK government in 1985; consideration by the World Heritage Committee was deferred because there were no appropriate criteria against which the area's landscape qualities could be assessed (Jacques, 1995). Also, the convention seemed to be failing if it could not offer protection to landscapes at the very time when preparations for the Rio Earth Summit in 1992 stressed the need to safeguard all forms of environmental capital. Moreover, sharp distinctions between nature and culture had become discredited in light of evidence that people had in fact modified nearly all so-called natural environments in the world, often over millennia. Finally, a reassessment was also called for because many societies were claiming the cultural significance of landscapes: in some places, such as Australia, indigenous groups see protection of such landscapes as a political issue tied to the fate of their own identity (Lowenthal, 1978).

As a result of such arguments, in 1992 criteria were adopted to allow cultural landscapes to be recognized as a special kind of World Heritage cultural site (but often with important natural values too). Several sub-categories were identified:

- designed landscapes,
- organically evolved landscapes (sub-divided in turn into living and 'fossil' landscapes of this type),
- associative landscapes (Plachter and Rössler, 1995).

Since 1992, about 30 cultural landscapes have been added to the World Heritage List. These include:

- designed landscapes: eg Sintra (Portugal), and Lednice-Valtice (Czech Republic);
- organically evolving landscapes: eg the astonishing rice terraces of the Philippines Cordillera, in Luzon, and the terraced vineyards of the Cinque Terre (Italy); and
- associative landscapes: eg Tongariro National Park (New Zealand) and Uluru-Kata Tjuta (Ayer's Rock) National Park (Australia), landscapes of great significance to the Maori and Aboriginal peoples respectively.

The inclusion of cultural landscapes in the World Heritage Convention

> *enables landscapes of outstanding universal value to take their place on the list alongside the world's great cultural monuments and natural sites, recognising them as part of the world's environmental capital. [It] sends a signal to all concerned with the better understanding and protection of the environment that landscapes merit attention at the international and – by extension – the national level too. (And) through its threefold division of landscapes types, the convention is encouraging debate around the idea that landscapes may be designed, may evolve organically, or may be found in the mind* (Phillips, 2000, p81).

UNESCO is due to publish guidelines on the management of Cultural Landscapes, as an impetus to encourage more states to designate such places. Already, the World Heritage Convention is acting as an international driver in this field; as we shall see, the UK is among the countries that are responding.

PROTECTED LANDSCAPES

In parallel with the growing interest in cultural landscapes of 'outstanding universal value' under the World Heritage Convention, a similar enthusiasm is

---

BOX 4.1 IUCN PROTECTED AREA MANAGEMENT CATEGORIES

I   Protected area managed mainly for (Ia) science or (Ib) wilderness protection (Strict Nature Reserve/Wilderness Area)

II   Protected area managed mainly for ecosystem protection and recreation (National Park)

III   Protected area managed mainly for conservation of specific natural features (Natural Monument)

IV   Protected area managed mainly for conservation through management intervention (Habitat/Species Management Area)

V   Protected area managed mainly for landscape/seascape conservation and recreation (Protected landscape/Seascape)

VI   Protected area managed mainly for the sustainable use of natural ecosystems (Managed Resource Protected Area).

Source: IUCN, 1994

---

being shown in new ideas about protected areas. These involve using protected areas to help conserve lived-in environments, which thus complements their traditional role of safeguarding more natural areas. The focus of this new approach is as much on landscapes as it is on biodiversity. Such ideas crystallize within the international categorization system for protected areas.

This system is based on the IUCN definition of a protected area as 'an area of land or sea especially dedicated to the protection and maintenance of biological diversity, and of natural and associated cultural resources, and managed through legal or other effective means' (IUCN, 1994, p7). More than 30,000 sites meet that definition (IUCN, 1998). In order to rationalize the many different kinds of protected area set up for a range of different purposes, IUCN has developed six management categories for protected areas (see Box 4.1). The system was prepared by IUCN's World Commission on Protected Areas (WCPA), which is a world-wide body of experts on protected areas.

Categories I to III focus on areas which are in a broadly natural state – though in practice there is little if any truly natural environment remaining anywhere. Categories IV and VI are subject to rather greater manipulation, whether for conservation purposes (Category IV sites, which include UK National Nature Reserves and Marine Nature Reserves) or so that local communities can exploit natural resources sustainably (Category VI sites).

Category V, or 'Protected Landscapes', involves the greatest degree of modification: they exist to protect valuable humanized and managed landscapes. They are lived-in, working landscapes, which have special natural and cultural values deserving recognition and protection. This category is therefore specifically intended to recognize a class of protected area established for the purpose of landscape protection. The UK's national parks, AONBs and National Scenic Areas (in Scotland) are all regarded as Category V protected areas (IUCN, 1998).

In recent years there has been a growing interest in Category V, in particular at the international level. The reasons are easy to understand. The world's environmental crisis calls for more and better-managed protected areas of all kinds, but there are problems with strictly protected areas such as the traditional North American model of a national park – wild areas dedicated to nature and to visitors. In poor countries especially, they may be seen as anti-people, excluding them from access to resources that they may have used in the past. So there is often resistance to the creation of new parks of this kind because they are thought to impose unreasonable burdens on local people. Such areas cannot protect places where people live and work, but which are still important for conservation, such as some farming areas. Also the scope for bringing natural or near-natural areas into strictly protected parks and reserves is fast diminishing as the world becomes ever more densely populated.

So new models of protected areas are needed to complement Categories I–IV, and to protect places where people live and work. Hence the interest in the Category V or protected landscapes approach. As with the new category of cultural landscapes under the World Heritage Convention, the concept is based on the links between nature and culture which are the essence of what is meant by the term 'landscape', ie people plus nature. Local communities are central to the management of protected landscapes. The economic, social, cultural and environmental aims for the landscape embody the community's traditions and values. Protected landscapes are thus managed to maintain the integrity of the relationship between people and their environment.

The UK has itself played an important part in promoting awareness of the Category V approach. In 1987, the then Countryside Commission organized the Lake District Symposium, an international event to focus on protected landscapes (Countryside Commission, 1988). In 1988 the IUCN General Assembly in Costa Rica (1988) called for the wider use of Category V. A guide to protected landscapes was published (Lucas, 1992) and the International Centre for Protected Landscapes (ICPL) was established in Aberystwyth around the same time, both with the help of the Commission and both carrying the message more widely. Renewed impetus was given to this work with a workshop in Vermont, US in 1999, which helped to launch a global programme on Category V areas (Brown et al, 2000). This programme will develop published guidance on Category V areas; will set up a network of managers or other practitioners; and will consolidate the global experience in this field as a contribution to the Fifth World Parks Congress, to be held in Durban, South Africa in September 2003.

These developments have two main implications for the UK. First, as pioneers of the approach, it is likely that the UK's expertise in this field will be drawn upon in giving advice on Category V areas in many countries. Already UK experts of this kind are active in a number of UK-funded programmes, such as the Know-How Fund for Eastern Europe. In addition, international exchange programmes, such as those run by the EUROPARC Federation and the US Glynwood Center, have made considerable use of UK knowledge in landscape protection and management (LaBelle, 2000). The other implication is more subtle: this trend amounts to an international recognition and validation for the conservation and sustainable development work undertaken in the UK's national parks and AONBs. While the UK nature conservation sector has long been used to working with international partners, and gaining some esteem from this, such appreciation has come only recently to those engaged in landscape protection in this country.

EUROPEAN LANDSCAPE CONVENTION

In October 2000, amid the splendours of Florence's Palazzo Vecchio, 18 European states signed the European Landscape Convention (ELC), the first international agreement specifically addressing landscape issues. This treaty, which was developed under the auspices of the Council of Europe, illustrates the way in which landscape has come to be seen as a legitimate topic for international action. Even though the UK was not among the countries signing in Florence, the door is still open to signature at a later date. In view of the potential importance of the ELC to the UK, it is necessary to understand the thinking behind the convention and its implications.

Europe has a particularly rich and varied heritage of landscapes. It is, therefore, no surprise that an interest in them and a concern for their protection go back several hundred years. The painting of landscape has been a strong tradition in many countries, notably France, the Low Countries and Britain, along with its celebration in poetry, song and literature. Nineteenth-century French and German geographers pioneered the systematic study of landscape. The English landscape movement took root with the founding of the National Trust in 1895 (Waterson, 1994). In 1949, England and Wales comprised one of the first countries to legislate for comprehensive landscape protection, with powers to set up its system of National Parks and AONBs based on landscape quality. Many other European countries now have similar legislation, and have developed systems of landscape protection through the designation of special areas, known nationally under many titles, such as regional nature parks, nature parks and landscape parks. As result, land in Category V protected areas in Europe, as a proportion of land in all protected areas, is about 66 per cent. This contrasts with only 8 per cent globally (IUCN, 1998).

Despite this continent-wide interest in landscape protection at the national level, the topic was strictly off the international agenda until around 1990. In this it contrasted with other aspects of Europe's shared heritage. Thus the Council of Europe (COE), with its pan-European responsibilities, adopted the Berne Convention on wildlife and natural habitats in 1979. The EC Birds Directive, applying to the member states of the European Union, came into force in the same year. The COE also developed two other conventions: those on the Architectural Heritage (Granada, 1985) and on the Archaeological Heritage (Valetta, adopted in 1969, revised in 1992). The EC's Habitats Directive was adopted in 1992.

The rationale for adopting an international approach to landscape protection is very similar to that successfully argued in the past for the protection of wildlife and of the architectural and archaeological heritage. Thus, many landscapes are of importance to the people of Europe as a whole and may therefore be regarded to some extent as a common heritage and a shared responsibility. Often landscapes face threats that arise at the international level, and these must be addressed through international cooperation. There is also a particular need to support less wealthy countries. Only in one respect does the conservation of wildlife have an added claim to international cooperation: because some species migrate from one country to another, countries must work together to protect them.

Such arguments were advanced during the early 1990s in support of a Europe-wide instrument for landscape, for example: in the proceedings of the Anglo-French Landscape Conference in Blois, France in October 1992 (Phillips, 1992); the IUCN Parks for Life Programme for Protected Areas in Europe (IUCN, 1994); and in *The Dobris Assessment* of Europe's Environment (Stanners and Bourdeau, 1995). This last report, prepared at the request of Europe's Environment Ministers, meeting in Dobris Castle in 1991(at that time in Czechoslovakia), devoted a whole chapter to the topic of landscapes. It commented sympathetically on ideas for the development of a landscape convention under the auspices of the COE. 'Its broad aim would be to strengthen the conservation of rural landscapes of Europe' (Stanners and Bourdeau, 1995, p187). It speculated that its objectives might be to 'encourage states to record their landscapes and put into place measures to protect or enhance them; to develop a network of landscapes of European significance; and to support this with training, information exchange and perhaps a centre of European landscape expertise' (op cit).

Another important development was the inclusion of landscapes both in the title and the content of the Pan-European Biological and Landscape Diversity Strategy (PEBLDS), the cumbersomely titled programme adopted by the European Environment Ministers at their meeting in Sofia in October 1995. The Dutch government sponsors of the PEBLDS initiative were not at first sympathetic to the inclusion of a landscape theme but, with lobbying from the Central and Eastern Europe countries in particular, the concept was eventually established. As a result, and for the first time, landscape diversity was placed alongside biological diversity as an aim for international action; and this was supported by a special action theme in the PEBLDS.

However, the critical factor in moving the landscape convention idea forward to reality was the interest shown by the Congress of Local and Regional Authorities (CLRAE) of Europe, a constituent part of the COE. In 1994, inspired by the Mediterranean Landscape Charter, its Standing Conference adopted a resolution to draw up 'a framework convention on the management and protection of the natural and cultural landscape of Europe as a whole' (COE, 2000, p2).

The complex consultative process by which the CLRAE developed the text for adoption in Florence over seven years later is instructive in several respects. As drafts were drawn up and debated by experts and others (a process in which, incidentally, UK experts made a central contribution), the original ideas, with their emphasis on protection and rurality, were significantly widened. Certainly, it was recognized that the convention was needed to fill a gap in existing international measures to protect the natural and cultural heritage; and also that landscapes were of value to all Europeans, and therefore that all countries had an interest in their care. The final version of the convention was more ambitious than originally envisaged. Thus it:

- applies to the whole of the national territory of a signatory (natural, rural, peri-urban and urban landscapes);
- is concerned with the creation (planning) and management of landscapes, as well as their protection;
- seeks to make landscape protection, management and planning key processes in sustainable development;
- sees landscape as a democratic issue, and a concern of all, especially at the local and regional levels, rather than as an elitist or specialist interest.

While these aspects of the ELC are indeed radical, other features show the restraining influence of governments, fearing that the ELC would be too intrusive or too heavy a burden. Thus the convention does not include the idea of landscapes of European significance which had been promoted by IUCN and UNESCO (the latter hoping thereby to complement World Heritage cultural landscapes in Europe with other important landscapes recognized at the European level). Scarred perhaps by experience with the Habitats Directive, several governments saw this as yet another layer of international bureaucratic interference, and reported 'designation fatigue' among their rural electorates. More serious shortcomings are the lack of a free-standing convention secretariat and the absence of earmarked funds. The treaty will be serviced by two committees of the COE, one on biological and landscape diversity and one on cultural heritage. This arrangement is given a positive twist in the COE report to member states: 'the Council of Europe provides the ideal framework since it has the competent committees on which all States parties to the convention can be represented' (ibid, p22), which overlooks the problems that usually face conventions without their own secretariats. However, over the years, the COE has not found it easy to bridge the divide between the staff divisions responsible for nature and for culture. Therefore, shared responsibility for the convention could become a major constraint on its effectiveness. So the landscape convention is a curious paradox: very ambitious in scope, but its ability to make an impact is compromised by the absence of teeth and resources. More so than is the case with most environmental conventions, the ELC will be only as good as its members allow it to be. The ELC's main provisions are summarized in Box 4.2.

The states that signed up to the ELC in Florence were: Belgium, Bulgaria, Croatia, Denmark, Finland, France, Italy, Lithuania, Luxembourg, Malta, Moldova, Norway, Portugal, Romania, San Marino, Spain, Switzerland and Turkey. By December 2002, Cyprus, the Czech Republic, Greece, Ireland, Poland, Macedonia, Slovenia, Switzerland and Sweden had joined them. However, the UK has so far been reluctant to sign on the grounds that the convention might be invoked as a constraint on development and economic investment. But it is to be hoped that it is only a matter of time before the UK does join. We consider at the end of the chapter what that might mean.

BOX 4.2 MAIN PROVISIONS OF THE EUROPEAN LANDSCAPE CONVENTION

National measures

States parties will:
- recognize landscapes in law as essential for human well-being (Article 5a)
- establish policies for their protection, management and planning (5b)
- encourage the participation of the public etc. in implementing planning policies (5c)
- integrate landscape into all planning and all other relevant policies (5d)
- raise public awareness of landscape issues (6A)
- provide education and training in landscape issues (6B)
- identify and analyse their landscapes, the trends affecting them etc. (6C)
- set landscape policy objectives for landscape (6D)
- put instruments in place to protect, manage and plan landscapes (6E)

European cooperation

States parties will cooperate with each other to:
- reinforce the landscape dimensions of international policies and programmes (7)
- provide mutual assistance and exchange information on landscape issues (8)
- cooperate over trans-frontier landscapes (9)
- monitor the implementation of the convention (10)
- make a Landscape Award to recognize and encourage high standards in landscape protection, management and planning (11)

RECENT DEVELOPMENTS IN THE EUROPEAN UNION

Meanwhile an interesting development has occurred within the European Union. Hitherto, landscape has not been a topic on the EU's agenda. No doubt it was, in the past, regarded as a matter within member states' competence, rather than that of the European Commission (EC). The word's appearance in the 1992 Habitats Directive is only in the context of 'landscape features which are of major importance for wild fauna and flora' (Articles 3 and 10). But the Dobris assessment (Stanners and Bourdeau, 1995) and the ELC appear to have helped the EC to recognize that the topic is of EU-wide relevance. Thus the Sixth European Environmental Action Programme, drawn up during 2000, acknowledges landscape as a proper subject for EC attention. It sees improved land use planning as one of five approaches that need to be at the centre of the new strategy, and identifies landscape protection and management as critical elements in such an approach. It refers supportively to the ELC, with its wider geographic scope, and declares that, 'at the Community Level, regional and agricultural policies need to ensure that landscape protection, preservation and improvement is [*sic*] properly integrated into the objectives, measures and funding programmes' of the EC (CEC, 2001, p34). Landscape is being recognized as a particularly important means of making the application of the Common Agricultural Policy (CAP), and spatial planning, more geographically sensitive. While the full significance of this in terms of EC or member state activity is not yet clear, reference to the topic in an EC programme marks an important advance in establishing landscape as a matter for debate and action at the international level. In sharp contrast to the position only ten years ago, landscape now appears in a global treaty, in IUCN programmes, in a Europe-wide convention and is on the agenda of the EC. It has become a respectable subject of international discourse.

THE IMPLICATIONS FOR THE UK

The central argument of this chapter is that landscape is now an international driver, albeit a new one, in shaping UK environmental and rural policy; forces outside the UK are helping to push the subject up the agenda. Of course the case must not be overstated: the instruments which have been described are all relatively soft in their impact. Landscape is not the subject of binding EC requirements, comparable with those in the Birds and Habitats Directives, and the UK has not yet (2002) signed the ELC. But the various instruments of international agreement that have been described above can be used by those concerned with the protection, management and planning of the landscape of the UK. In particular the ELC offers great opportunities to raise the profile of landscape work in the UK and to establish it as a core element in programmes for sustainable development.

So what specifically are the implications of these international developments for the way in which we address landscape and related issues in future?

In respect of the World Heritage Convention, the UK has set out its plans in a consultation paper (DCMS, 1998) on the tentative list of sites for possible future World Heritage nomination (an administrative requirement before any new sites can be nominated). This commits the government to nominating two potential Cultural Landscape sites, the New Forest and the Lake District, hoping thereby to give these areas global recognition. It emphasizes the natural qualities of the former and the associative qualities of the latter: the Lake District was not only the home of the Lakeland poets and painters but also the birthplace of the National Trust and the UK's National Parks movement. Moreover, the UK government has said that it intended to carry out further studies to identify other cultural landscapes (ibid), a potentially important initiative which is now being pursued by UK Committee for the International Council on Monuments and Sites (ICOMOS).

World Heritage nomination is a very rigorous process, and it is by no means certain that all the UK's list of candidate sites will in fact be inscribed. None the less, the nomination of the Lake District and the New Forest will raise intense local interest in World Heritage issues, and generally help focus public and media attention on the significance of the World Heritage Convention. Already the successful nomination of the Dorset and East Devon coast (inscribed as a natural World Heritage site on geological, palaeontological and geomorphological grounds in December 2001) has given rise to much more media and local interest than surrounded the first round of nominations in the 1980s.

By comparison, the categorization of protected areas by the United Nations Environment Programme's World Conservation Monitoring Centre

(UNEP/WCMC) and WCPA for inclusion in the UN list is a far less exacting exercise and has not hitherto generated much interest outside a small circle of experts. But the IUCN system of protected area management categories is becoming more widely known, used and referenced. As result, the international recognition of a site as a protected area, and its allocation to an individual protected area category, is emerging as a topic of concern to some in the UK. Questions arise, for example, over Sites of Special Scientific Interest (SSSIs), which have so far been excluded from the list because it was felt that, apart from National and Marine Nature Reserves, the protection afforded to such areas was insufficient to merit inclusion. Thus in 1997, the great majority of SSSIs were not recognized by the IUCN as protected areas at all (IUCN, 1998). The strengthened protection given to such sites under the new Countryside and Rights of Way Act 2000 may be considered sufficient to 'lift' the whole suite of SSSIs into the list. Also where should the new National Parks go? The New Forest is probably best kept under Category IV, to which it is presently assigned, since protection of habitat will remain the central aim of management. Loch Lomond and the Trossachs and the South Downs would appear to be suitable candidates for Category V. Some will think that the proposed Cairngorms National Park has the potential to be a Category II site. Others may argue that Scotland's National Scenic Areas are of such limited impact that they should be removed from the list altogether. At first sight such debate might seem arcane, but this is to miss the point: the discussion over categorization (which provokes passions in some continental countries) is a debate about whether and how the UK's protected areas match up to international standards, a dimension hardly addressed at all in the past. It seems certain that there will be more interest in this question as UNEP/WCMC begins to compile the revised list in time for the next World Parks Congress in 2003.

The impact of the ELC will of course depend on whether, and if so when, the UK ratifies the agreement. A call for it to do so was made in May 2000 at the Oxford Landscape Conference (see Box 4.3). If the UK does sign, then one modest but immediate practical implication is that it may consider entering sites for the European Landscape Award. However, a more far-reaching impact is to be hoped for: a recognition that landscape issues should be more strongly included in the development, implementation and evaluation of public policy. This might take many forms, for example:

- so far, biodiversity concerns have probably been the strongest environmental considerations in driving the UK demand for reform of the CAP. But if landscape becomes the topic of an international treaty signed by the UK, it will become more influential in the debate over the future of the CAP;
- NGOs and others are likely to find that they can use the convention to begin to influence the nature of the debate in other areas, such as transport policy and planning. In conjunction with the new Human Rights Act 2000, they may feel they are sufficiently empowered to *require* the UK government, country administrations in Scotland, Wales and Northern Ireland, English regional government, and local government throughout, to give landscape its proper due;

Box 4.3 The Oxford Landscape Declaration

We, 100 participants from the United Kingdom and abroad, gathered in Oxford from 3–5 May 2000 for the ICOMOS UK Conference on Europe: a Common Heritage – the Cultural Landscape, have adopted the following declaration.

We believe that landscape is of fundamental importance. It brings enormous cultural, social, spiritual, ecological, environmental and economic benefits, and is a vital element in the quality of life of all people and in their sense of local identity.

We recognise that European landscapes combine both natural and cultural components, reflecting the long-standing interaction between people and the land, and that they thus embrace a vital part of both the cultural and the natural heritage of Europe.

We declare:

• our recognition that landscapes inevitably change and evolve over time, in response to natural processes and to the changing needs and activities of people, and that such change is bound to continue;
• our concern, however, that many present-day changes are progressively reducing the quality and diversity of landscapes;
• our belief that it is necessary and possible to guide the processes of change in ways which meet essential human needs but which also ensure that the character, diversity and quality of landscapes are maintained or enhanced rather than diminished;
• our conviction that the peoples of Europe must be involved, notably at local level, in making this happen;
• our affirmation that future generations should be entitled to inherit and enjoy landscapes at least as rich as those which now exist; and
• our conviction that this implies the need both for a comprehensive and integrated approach to the understanding, protection, management and planning of the landscape as a whole, and for specific measures related to landscapes of particular significance, as a key part of sustainable development.

We therefore welcome:

• the increasing recognition, among peoples and governments throughout Europe, of the importance of landscape and the need to care for it;
• the growth, in many European countries, of action at all levels to record and assess the landscape heritage, to protect, manage and plan landscapes in general, and to protect key landscape areas;
• the initiatives at European level, including the proposed European Landscape Convention, the Pan-European Biological and Landscape Diversity Strategy, and the inclusion of landscape as a central element in the Council of Europe's 1999/2000 campaign on 'Europe: A Common Heritage'; and
• the addition of cultural landscapes to the categories of sites on the World Heritage List, and the willingness of the governments of the United Kingdom and other European countries to bring forward landscapes of outstanding universal value as candidates for inclusion on that List.

We strongly support the adoption of the European Landscape Convention, and urge its early opening for signature.

We call on the Government of the United Kingdom, and (as appropriate) on the administrations in Scotland, Wales and Northern Ireland, to promote the cause of landscapes by:

- giving active support to the adoption of the European Landscape Convention, and then using it (when it is signed and ratified) as a positive framework for management of landscapes in the United Kingdom;
- promoting public awareness of landscape as an asset to local communities, from which they can benefit through knowledge, use and enjoyment;
- encouraging involvement of owners and managers of property, and of the general public, in measures to identify, evaluate, protect, manage and plan landscapes;
- recognising the importance of protecting, managing and planning landscape in all relevant legislation and government policies and programmes, notably those which relate to:
  - the operations of the town and country planning system, noting the need for planning and other policy guidance on the subject of landscape;
  - alterations and additions to infrastructure, including roads;
  - agriculture, noting the need for further expansion of agri-environment programmes, forestry, and other economic activities, noting particularly the importance of tourism;
  - programmes for creation of new landscapes where these are needed, as in the community forests;
  - education, training and provision of information, at all levels; and
  - the allocation of lottery and other funds;
- requesting national agencies in the fields of protection of the historic environment, of countryside protection and enjoyment, and of nature conservation, to work together, and with regional bodies and local authorities, in the assessment of both rural and urban landscapes, and to encourage local authorities, owners and managers of property, professional advisers and all relevant others to protect, manage and enhance landscapes;
- resourcing the national, regional and local bodies concerned in the above work;
- working vigorously within the European Union to ensure that agricultural, regional, structural and other relevant policies and funds take the landscape, and its human and other benefits, fully into account; and undertaking a comprehensive assessment of sites within the United Kingdom suitable to be nominated for recognition as cultural landscapes under the World Heritage Convention of UNESCO.

- Local Agenda 21 and community planning processes (see Chapter 5) can be expected to give more attention to landscape issues, especially where creativey-thinking local authorities can see the relevance of the requirements of the ELC to the interests of local communities;
- landscape training and teaching institutions, landscape consultancy, the Countryside Agency and others directly involved in landscape work may be expected to benefit from a greater interest in landscape issues as they pertain to public policy. There should be expanded opportunities for practitioners and academics to share expertise with other countries, notably but not exclusively with those in Europe;
- Landscape-based programmes, such as *LANDMAP* in Wales and Countryside Character in England (see Chapters 7 and 12) should receive a boost, since they already address some of the new obligations that the UK government will take on if they sign the CEL.

Britain has been among the leaders in the field of landscape for many years. It still has a rich heritage of landscape. Some of its public agencies, like the

Countryside Agency, have been pioneers in landscape study and policy work. Among NGOs working in this area, the National Trust especially has outstanding achievements to its credit. It is a topic certain to stir interest in the public mind. Particularly if the UK joins the ELC, we can expect that the status of landscape in public policy will be enhanced. This would give the UK a unique opportunity to play to one of its strengths, both at home and abroad.

REFERENCES

Appleton, J (1991) *The Funny Thing about Landscape*, The Book Guild, Lewes

Benson, J and Roe, M (eds) (2000) *Landscape and Sustainability*, Spon Press, London

Brown, J, Mitchell, N and Sarmiento, F (2000) 'Introduction', *The George Wright Forum*, vol 17(1), pp12–14

Commission of the European Communities (CEC) (2001) *Sixth Environment Action Programme*, Commission of the European Communities, Brussels

Council of Europe (COE) (2000) *European Landscape Convention*, Council of Europe, Strasbourg

Countryside Commission (1988) 'Protected Landscapes: Summary Proceedings of an International Symposium', Lake District, UK, 5–10 October, Countryside Commission, Cheltenham

Countryside Commission (1993) *Landscape Assessment Guidance*, Countryside Commission, Cheltenham

Department of Culture, Media and Sport (DCMS) (1998) *UNESCO World Heritage Sites – A Consultation Paper on a New United Kingdom Tentative List of Future Nominations*, DCMS, London

Holdaway, E and Smart, G (2001) *Landscapes at Risk? – The Future for Areas of Outstanding Natural Beauty*, Spon Press, London

Hoskins, W G (1955) *The Making of the English Landscape*, Hodder and Stoughton, London

IUCN (1994) *Guidelines for Protected Area Management Categories*, IUCN, Cambridge

IUCN (1998) *The United Nations List of Protected Areas 1997*, IUCN, Cambridge

Jacques, D (1995) 'The Rise of Cultural Landscapes', *International Journal of Heritage Studies*, vol 1(2), pp91–101

LaBelle, J (2000) International Exchange of Ideas, *PARKS*, vol 10(3), pp15–26

Lowenthal, D (1978) 'Finding Valued Landscapes', *Progress in Human Geography*, vol 21(3), pp373–418

Lucas, P (1992) *Protected Landscapes*, Chapman and Hall, London

Macinnes, L and Wickham-Jones, C (eds) (1992) *All Natural Things – Archaeology and the Green Debate*, Oxbow Books, Oxford

Maltby, E, Holdgate, M, Acreman, M and Weir, A (eds) (1999) *Ecosystem Management – Questions for Science and Society*, Royal Holloway College, London

Miller, K (1996) *Balancing the Scales*, World Resources Institute, Washington

Phillips, A (1992) 'The Conservation of the Rural Landscapes of Europe – Proposal for a Convention', *Paysage and Amenagement*, no 21, pp74–77

Phillips, A (2000) 'International Policies and Landscape Protection', in Benson, J and Roe, M (eds) *Landscape and Sustainability*, Spon Press, London, pp78–96

Plachter, M and Rössler, M (1995) 'Cultural Landscapes: Reconnecting Culture and Nature' in von Dioste, B, Plachter, M and Rössler, M (eds) *Cultural Landscapes of Universal Value – Components of a Global Strategy*, G Fischer, New York

Scharma, S (1995) *Landscape and Memory*, Harper Collins, London

Selman, P (2000) 'Landscape Sustainability at the National and Regional Scales', in Benson, J and Roe, M (eds) *Landscape and Sustainability*, Spon Press, London, pp97–110

Stanners, D and Bourdeau, P (eds.) (1995) *Europe's Environment – the Dobris Assessment*, European Environment Agency, Copenhagen

Thomas, K (1983) *Man and the Natural World*, Allen Lane, London

United Nations Educational, Scientific and Cultural Organization (2002) *The World Heritage Convention*, UNESCO, Paris

Vandervell, A and Coles, C (1980) *Game and the English Landscape*, Debrett's Peerage Ltd, London

Warwickshire County Council and Countryside Commission (1991) *Arden Landscape Guidelines*, Warwickshire County Council, Warwick

Waterson, M (1994) *The National Trust: The First Hundred Years*, National Trust and BBC Books, London

Chapter 5

Policy Context for Community Involvement in Countryside Planning

Diane Warburton

Community involvement has been on the mainstream land use planning agenda since the 1960s, but there has been a massive shift in emphasis towards public and community participation since the mid-1990s. Some profound political, social and economic forces have brought about this change.

The ownership and management of the land in Britain have been contested for centuries. Raymond Williams dates this to the 14th century, following the Black Death, in which more than a million people died, many settlements were abandoned, woodlands were cleared for timber and pasture, land was enclosed and many arable villages were destroyed. This fundamentally altered relations between feudal landlords, tenants and labourers (Williams, 1993). Since then, there have been organized struggles over ownership and control of changes to the countryside. The Great Society of peasants in the 14th century, the 17th-century Diggers and Levellers, the 19th-century Land Chartists, and the early 20th-century Land Settlement Association could be seen as the antecedents of modern protest movements, from NIMBYs (who are caricatured as rejecting any development near them: Not In My Back Yard) to Dongas (the 'tribe' responsible for some of the best known anti-road building protests in rural England in the 1990s).

These groups, and many others, have essentially focused on oppositional protests against the ability of wealthy and powerful public and private landowners, to enclose, control, use and develop land with little or no consideration for the impacts this had on the people affected. Alongside these protest movements (and perhaps partly because of them), decision-makers have gradually come to accept that the 'public' or 'communities' have a right to participate in decisions which affect them – and public involvement in planning is now a mainstream element in public policy.

A conventional public policy approach to the history of community involvement in countryside planning would be most likely to take the report of the Skeffington Committee on Public Participation in Planning (Skeffington, 1969) as the seminal event. But, in fact, Skeffington drew on a number of themes emerging in the 1960s, particularly the growing community development movement.

Community development has always been about improving living conditions through community participation and action (Craig and Mayo, 1995). It has involved both protest and partnership, with some community and interest groups using both strategies at the same time to increase their influence and effectiveness (Craig et al, 2001). Its development in the 1960s needs to be understood in the wider political context of that time, during which protest and the adoption of alternative lifestyles were increasingly common (a period now recognized in social science literature as a burst of activity in new social movements). Community development was also stimulated in the 1960s for several more specific reasons: because of the perceived failure of both the welfare state and increasing levels of affluence to do away with poverty; because the government response to urban unrest, racial tension and rising crime was considered inadequate; because of dissatisfaction with the quality of public services; and because of the emergence of movements for civil rights and feminism (Taylor, 1992). In 1969, the same year as the Skeffington report was published, community development moved into the mainstream of social policy in the UK with the launch of the government-sponsored national Community Development Projects (CDP) programme.

The land use planning system, of course, developed from different roots. Thus, the 1947 Town and Country Planning Act, on which the UK planning system is still largely based, was the product of a powerful vision and drive for change at a time of enormous social upheaval which also created the National Health Service, extended the state education system and implemented the Beveridge report to provide welfare benefits: measures made possible by the post-war consensus which affirmed principles of social democracy and increased equality (TCPA, 1999).

At a time when nationalization was readily accepted, the Town and Country Planning Act 1947 nevertheless stopped short of nationalizing land, and instead nationalized the right to develop and use land. Although agriculture and forestry were exempted from the Act (and largely remain so), the provisions applied equally to urban areas and to the countryside (as the title of the Act makes explicit).

The links between the planning profession, which was growing in confidence and ambition, and the radical community development movement (which included the CDPs but also the strengthening tenant movement, squatting campaigns, campaigns for child care, etc) were clearly expressed in the Skeffington report. The report specifically recommended that 'community development officers should be appointed to secure the involvement of those people who do not join organisations. This job would be to work with people, to stimulate discussion, to inform people and give people's views to the authority' (Skeffington, 1969, p47). Skeffington formalized the link between community development and participation in planning, although many community development activists saw their role as extending far beyond this limited intermediary role and much more in terms of organizing at community level for radical social change (Taylor, 1992; Batson and Smith, 1996; Hallet, 1987), and as aiming for community involvement as transformative (eg about social and personal change) rather than merely instrumental in planning processes (eg about improving practical outcomes).

Through the 1980s and 1990s, there was increasing participatory activity coordinated by planning departments in local authorities, both around the formal development of plans (Bishop et al, 1994; Royal Town Planning Institute (RTPI), 1996) and associated with environmental strategies and policies (Local Government Management Board (LGMB), 1993). There was also a strong and continued growth in the planning aid movement, offering planning advice to community groups and individuals who would otherwise be unable to afford these services. There has been particular interest in community involvement in planning in rural areas at the local scale through village appraisals and parish maps, the Rural Action programme, discussions of citizenship and citizens' rights, and the devolution of development control powers to some parishes (Owen, 1998). The influential government report *Quality in Town and Country* (DoE, 1994) emphasized that local people should feel able to participate in the planning process to make sure that development enhances their surroundings, perhaps a tacit recognition that, in the past, development had often not enhanced rural areas.

There has also been intensive community involvement in various other local planning processes and other local authority activities such as provision of schooling and community care, concern about development pressures and environmental issues including community-based environmental action (Moseley et al, 1996). Local city farms, community gardens, Groundwork trusts and development trusts were all expanding the opportunities for local communities to get involved in or actually take control of development and management of their living environments, both in cities and the countryside. The activities of development trusts in rural areas has been growing particularly fast: there are now more than 70 such trusts working across rural areas, one-third of all the Development Trusts Association's members (Development Trusts Association, 2001).

Throughout this period, there was also enormous expansion in community and public participation in regeneration programmes – primarily in urban areas where much of the regeneration investment was targeted, but also (and increasingly) in rural development programmes as well (eg Aston Business School 1991; Rural Development Commission 1997; Vittery, 1989; Warburton and Wilcox, 1988). Community involvement has grown through a range of government-led or supported initiatives over the past 20 years: the Urban Programme in the 1980s, City Challenge, Rural Challenge, Single Regeneration Budget, Rural Development Areas and Rural Development Programmes, Local Rural Regeneration Programmes in Scotland, EU LEADER programmes, Local Agenda 21 and local biodiversity action plans. Many of these programmes required public and community consultation as a condition for securing funding from central government.

But despite all this action, until relatively recently real partnership and participation in local regeneration projects remained the exception rather than the norm (Clarke, 1995). However, the most recent national government regeneration programmes, such as the New Deal for Communities (launched in 1999) and the National Strategy for Neighbourhood Renewal (published in 2001), have included much more community involvement in the initial design stages, and there is expected to be much more powerful community involvement in their implementation. As always, though, practice will have to be reviewed before any final judgements can be made. In these newer programmes, the role of participation is changing from merely being a means (either to get the funding from central government, or to improve the quality of the project) to also being an end (community ownership and commitment being among the indicators of success of these programmes).

Thus, there has been a wealth of both bottom-up and top-down initiatives which have aimed to involve local communities in urban and rural planning, as well as in land management in the wider sense. However, the links between these initiatives remain rather tenuous, and the contributions of the various professional disciplines of planning, community development and participatory working are as yet poorly articulated (Cannan, 2000).

GLOBAL AND EUROPEAN DRIVERS TOWARDS SUSTAINABLE DEVELOPMENT, HUMAN RIGHTS AND ENVIRONMENTAL POLICY

Important policy developments in the fields of sustainable development, human rights and environmental policy have taken place at global and European levels, especially in the past ten years, which have given an impetus to community involvement in the UK.

Sustainable development remains a contested concept, but there are a number of areas where there is clarity. As readers of this book will know, the concept emerged from a debate in the early 1970s about the *Limits to Growth* within a finite global system, and concerns about environmental problems (Meadows et al, 1983). These culminated in the 1972 UN Conference on the Human Environment (UNCHE), in Stockholm, which was followed by a series of United Nations and other initiatives, including the World Conservation Strategy (1980), the Brandt Commission on international development and north/south inequalities (1983), and the Brundtland Commission on Environment and Development (1987). The report of the Brundtland Commission recognized the importance of wide public involvement in policy and practice if development were to be sustainable, stating:

> *The law alone cannot enforce the common interest. It principally needs community knowledge and support, which entails greater public participation in the decisions which affect the environment. This is best secured by decentralising the management of resources upon which local communities depend, and giving these communities an effective say over the use of the resources. It will also require promoting citizens' initiatives, empowering people's organisations, and strengthening local democracy* (World Commission on Environment and Development, 1987, p63).

The United Nations Conference on Environment and Development (UNCED) in Rio in 1992, known as the Earth Summit and at which Agenda 21 (the agenda for sustainable development in the 21st century) was signed, made public and community participation a key feature in all the programmes on sustainable development which followed (Warburton, 1998).

Longstanding international statements of environmental principles and declarations of human rights underpin the Rio Declaration and Agenda 21. These provide a range of moral or legal rights (and responsibilities) to enable citizen participation in planning and decision-making.

Thus the 1972 Declaration from the UNCHE formalized concepts of environmental rights and duties as covering both the physical and social conditions of human life. The first principle of that declaration states:

> *Man has the fundamental right to freedom, equality and adequate conditions of life, in an environment of a quality that permits a life of dignity and well-being, and he bears a solemn responsibility to protect and improve the environment for present and future generations.*

The UN Declaration of Human Rights in 1948 was the basis for the UK Human Rights Act 1998, which was formally brought into UK law in October 2000 to give further effect to rights and freedoms guaranteed under the European Convention on Human Rights. The impact of the Human Rights Act on the planning system has still to become clear, but comments range from it having impacted on the planning system with the force of a high-speed tilting train (Lock, 2001a), to the rather more restrained conclusion that it was still pretty much 'business as usual', although with third party rights of appeal and difficulties between public interests and private rights as 'unfinished business' (Crow, 2001).

At the European level, the signing of the UN Economic Commission for Europe's Convention on Access to Information, Public Participation in Decision-Making and Access to Justice in Environmental Matters, (the Aarhus Convention) will affect EU instruments. It will upgrade public participation in relation to EU directives in relation to environmental impact assessment, waste, water pollution, air quality, landfill etc.

The EC has played an important part in promoting community involvement in many fields of public policy. In commenting on the Aarhus Convention, EC Commissioner Margot Wallstrom said 'Real environmental progress can only be achieved with the participation of the citizens concerned'. The legislation is not only based on the belief that it is right for the public to be involved in decisions which affect them but also on the objective of making environmental legislation be more effective and work better in practice (CEC, 2001a). The theme is taken up in the EU's 6th Environmental Action Programme, entitled *Environment 2010: Our Future. Our Choice*. In setting out environmental priorities for the coming ten years, it acknowledges that this is not just an issue for politicians and industry but that it concerns all of us, and recognizes that people want to be consulted more when decisions are made which affect the environment, and that means access to clear and trustworthy information (CEC, 2001b). Finally, the Europeanization of rural development policy through the structural funds has brought new ways of working and a wider range of actors into rural partnerships (Ward, 2001). It has also brought greater participation, at least notionally, in development programmes.

THE UK RESPONSE

Such thinking runs through the UK strategies for sustainable development: the latest version states that 'Public involvement is essential for a truly sustainable community' (DETR, 1999, para 7.87), and 'Opportunities for access to information, participation in decision-making, and access to justice should be available to all' (ibid, para 4.1). However, there is also a growing focus on the local environment. Prime Minister Tony Blair's second speech on the environment in as many months (just prior to the 2001 General Election) was entitled 'Improving Your Local Environment'. In this speech he made the point that 'We ... need stronger local communities and an improved quality of life ... where the environment in which we live fosters rather than alienates a sense of local community and mutual responsibility' (Blair, 2001).

These sentiments underpin the government's far-reaching Modernising Government programme, through the various new legislation which begins to implement this agenda (eg Local Government Acts 1999 and 2000, and the Greater London Area Act 1999). As Beverley Hughes, then Minister for Local Government, said of the Local Government Act 2000, 'At the heart of our modernisation agenda was the promise to give local people a better deal, a bigger say in how their communities are run' (Hughes, 2001). The community strategies, local strategic partnerships, Best Value (which has its own requirements for consultation) and opportunities for local government to restructure their decision-making processes (with directly elected Mayors, cabinets, etc) – all these are designed to promote greater community involvement in planning and delivering services. Community strategies in particular take planning into new territory, as they move away from simply planning those services that are delivered by the local authority, aiming to creating a new 'community leadership' role for local government in which they coordinate all the services which are being provided within their area.

Local Agenda 21

There have been concerns that the introduction of community strategies will mean simply starting all over again, and ignore previous community participation exercises, particularly around Local Agenda 21 (LA21) strategies. Certainly sustainable development and LA21 staff often remain marginalized in many local authorities. However, the government has made clear that they 'expect community strategies to build on the best of the work done to prepare Local Agenda 21 strategies, both of which have the aim of sustainable local communities at their heart' (Hughes, 2001; Chanan et al, 1999, 2000).

LA21 makes knowledge of (if not understanding about) sustainable development available more widely. A survey by the government's Sustainable

Development Unit (SDU) in December 2000 found that 93 per cent of local authorities had completed LA21 strategies (SDU, 2001). Of course, producing a strategy is not any guarantee that broader policies and programmes will change as a result, and it has been suggested that LA21 might not have achieved everything it could have and did not connect with the heart of authorities (Bennett and Pilling, 2001).

However, whether LA21 strategies have made the UK more sustainable generally, a key achievement of the process has been the involvement of local communities: 'whilst many of the claims about LA21 are intractable to test, there is some evidence of genuine attainment... This relates mainly to processes of strategy production, stimulation of environmental citizenship, inclusion of various sectors, challenging traditional assumptions and actions, and assisting local democracy' (Selman, 1998, pp287–302).

Indeed, research from 1996 onwards (Young, 1996, 1997) showed that 50–60 councils had aimed to produce bottom-up LA21 strategies (although this may be more of an aspiration than a reality). The research also showed that LA21 has promoted many innovative solutions to community involvement, such as visioning, community profiling and village appraisals, focus groups, Planning for Real exercises, forums, round tables and advisory committees. LA21 processes have also encouraged partnerships between communities and local agencies, with projects for recycling, housing cooperatives, LETS, credit unions and environmental improvement. These partnerships had three main features in common: they were not-for-profit, they were local community level (both locality communities and communities of need, eg black and minority ethnic groups, across wider areas), and they emphasized local democracy and involvement. More recent research (LGMB, 1999) showed that, of the 72 per cent of local authorities in England, Scotland, Wales and Northern Ireland which had completed LA21s, 70 per cent had provided support for community and voluntary groups as part of their awareness raising approaches, 42 per cent had multi-stakeholder forums coordinating their strategies, and 30 per cent had involved the community. These are self-reported findings, and the practice on the ground may not always have lived up to these results (Bennett and Pilling, 2001).

In practice LA21 has encountered real problems with community involvement. Thus, some potentially contentious environmental problems (eg roads) were placed outside the process; it was difficult to maintain the momentum of involvement, especially from business; there were conflicts over the roles of local councillors; and it was often difficult to integrate the participatory experiments with mainstream strategic planning, at different spatial levels (eg regional policies on waste, or transport) (Young, 1997). However, sustainability is concerned as much with process as with product, and it can be argued that the journey is as important as the destination (Selman, 1995). Taking that view, LA21 has been a pioneer of many of the approaches that will need to be followed in community strategies, initiatives that seem to be much closer to the heart of local government.

The Rural White Paper 'Our countryside: the future'

The Rural White Paper published in 2000 continues the rhetoric of community involvement. Richard Wakeford, Chief Executive of the Countryside Agency, has described the White Paper as follows: 'together these [proposals] have the potential to ensure that the rural voice is heard at all levels and that local communities are better placed to shape their own futures' (Wakeford, 2001, p17). The White Paper promises to 'empower local communities so that decisions are taken with their participation and ownership' (DETR and MAFF, 2000, p11), mainly through strengthening (and rewarding) 'quality' parish councils, and encouraging the production of town and village action plans that will feed into community strategies.

The Rural White Paper is intended to build on past programmes, and previous partnership schemes such as rural development programmes. These partnerships were evaluated under the major Partnerships in Rural Integrated Development programme in six EU countries. The evaluation concluded that there needs to be a more user-friendly approach, more flexible, devolved, long-term and reliable funding, wider involvement of individuals and groups, and better ways to involve local communities (Cherrett, 2001). Similar evaluations of other rural partnership programmes have reached similar conclusions; but it is widely recognized to be particularly difficult to secure effective community participation in programmes which are competitive and sometimes result in no funding at all (eg Little et al, 1998 on Rural Challenge; Scottish Executive, 1998, on the Local Rural Partnership Scheme).

Underlying Trends in a Changing Context

The trend towards greater community involvement and the nature of that involvement are affected by two kinds of changes taking place at the turn of the century. Some are essentially organizational:

- greater devolution (to Scotland, Wales and Northern Ireland, as well as increasingly to the English regions), which is creating some fundamental challenges to traditional public involvement in land management and ownership (especially in Scotland);
- the emergence of an audit culture (Royal Geographical Society, 2000), which is part of the Modernising Government agenda (eg Best Value inspections), but is also being adopted by government agencies. It has been suggested that, as a result of the proposals in the Rural White Paper 'The [Countryside] Agency is thus thrust from being the rural champion ... to become a rural watchdog' (Lowe, 2001, p19);
- the continuation of a trend that began in the 1980s, in which government is envisaged as being less about 'doing' and more about 'enabling'. Partnerships with NGOs, public/private partnerships and so forth are features of this, and both political and economic rationales are advanced for moving in this direction.

Other trends are more profound:

- Governments are perceived to have lost power in a globalized economy, and people have less trust in the ability and willingness of governments to act on behalf of citizens (Macnaghten et al, 1995). Peter Hain, then in the Foreign Office, said 'as governments face diminishing control over events, those they govern want more control over their lives ... people want more say in the decisions that affect them. And they want to have this say more directly' (Hain, 2001). However, the rhetoric about a reduced role for national governments can be seen as a tactical discourse in the globalization debate, or simply as wishful thinking on the part of other international interests (Christie and Warburton, 2001). Meanwhile NGOs may now be more trusted by the public than governments or official bodies, as well as having public support expressed, not least, through their membership – 'In Britain, almost five times as many people belong to environmental groups as to all the political parties put together' (Hain, 2001). However, NGOs face similar issues to government in relation to having to balance leadership and participation, accountability and effectiveness (Craig et al, 2001).
- Authority of all kinds is increasingly challenged. 'Experts' are less trusted, as are scientists. Governments face a continuing challenge to convince a sceptical electorate that they do have the answers to the complexities that face society in the 21st century (Beck, 1992; Macnaghten et al, 1995).
- There is declining involvement in the formal processes of democracy. The turnout at the General Election in 1997 was 71 per cent, the lowest figure since 1951; a figure which dropped again at the 2001 General Election, where it was the lowest since universal franchise. In local government elections, the turnout in England and Wales was only 28 per cent in the 1999/2000 elections, and in the elections for the European Parliament in July 1999 it was only 24 per cent. The Select Committee on Public Administration suggests that 'politicians are increasingly mistrusted and representative government is adversely affected' (Select Committee on Public Administration, 2001, p2), yet the government has argued that participation in elections is crucial to, and a barometer of, the health of democrarcy (DETR, 1998).

Declining participation in elections allow the legitimacy of government to be questioned, which further undermines government claims to represent 'the people' and therefore confront other powerful forces. For the Select Committee on Public Administration, voting figures have powerful implications for government accountability to the public: if so few people consider elections to be important, there is a growing need to find alternative methods. The Committee proposes innovations, such as deliberative democratic methods (eg citizen's juries), experimenting with e-governance, and the creation of a People's Panel. They see that 'the health of representative and participative democracy are intertwined' (Select Committee on Public Administration, 2001, p3).

While such conclusions may not yet be shared by most elected politicians and others in government, they are provoking a debate about the role of community and citizen involvement more generally. It is against that background that the current emphasis in public policy on 'community' deserves particular attention.

Community as Panacea?

One recent analysis suggests that the lack of trust and the sense of a lack of power in local and national governments has led to the growing focus on 'values-led' government, where government gains its legitimacy not from establishing public programmes which serve the people, but from 'moral leadership' based on espousing values which reflect people's concerns (Allen, 2001). This analysis is used to explain the emphasis in the US on 'community' as the basis of 'the communitarian philosophy, which aims to bolster the foundations of civil society – including families, schools and neighbourhoods – and foster a commitment to the community' (ibid). British Prime Minister Tony Blair has made similar comments including that 'Britain is ready to rebuild a sense of community, common purpose and shared promise. To give new energy to old traditions of self-help and mutual aid' (Blair, 1999). He also declared that:

> *The central belief that brought me into politics, and drives everything that I do, is that individuals realise their potential best through a strong community based on rights and responsibilities. I have always believed that the bonds that individuals made with each other and their communities are every bit as important as the things provided for them by the state* (Blair, 1999).

In his first speech on the environment in October 2000, Blair used similar terminology: 'The root of my political beliefs is the idea of community; of solidarity' (Blair, 2000).

There have now been a whole raft of policy initiatives focused on community especially around regeneration but also community planning/strategies and the promotion of community action, active citizenship and volunteering through the Active Communities Unit, based at the Home Office, and strategies for community care, community health, etc.

Modern politics and policy in the UK invokes 'community' in a number of ways:

- As an aim. Community is used to explain why various programmes are undertaken, what is to be achieved and how people want to live. Community becomes the ideal society made up of people who know and care about each other. More specifically, in some programmes (eg regeneration) the aim is to 'build' or 'rebuild' community or communities, or to create sustainable communities.
- As the participants. Community is used to describe who is (or should be) involved in policy. This is usually taken to mean local residents, and sometimes local businesses as well, as in the 'local communities' which are being involved in developing and implementing plans, policies and programmes.

- To describe the process. Community action or involvement is used to mean how things should happen – through participation and involvement, grassroots, local action and self-help.
- As the location for policy. Community is used to describe where policy is enacted: the local place – neighbourhood, small town or village.

Community is obviously a contested concept, but it does provide a useful focus for government policy. It lies somewhere between *individualism* and traditional *collectivism*, between *family* and the more distant '*society*', with a predominantly *local* and *geographical* focus (although there are many other types of communities). And it offers a symbolic counter to alienation and apathy, individualism and materialism – summarized by Tony Blair as rejecting selfishness and embracing community (Blair, 1999).

Current UK government policy seems to draw at least as much on ideas of community developed in the US, particularly Amitai Etzioni's communitarianism (Etzioni, 1995), as on concepts of community developed in the UK. In the US, community is used to symbolize traditional social institutions, such as the family, church, civic societies and schools, and focuses on the role of these institutions as the 'glue' which creates the social, moral and political foundations of society.

There are always dangers in assuming that a model from another country can be transposed wholesale into a cultural context which is very different. While the basic aim of communitarianism – that is, to find an alternative to the increasingly individualistic and materialistic lifestyles in the modern world – remains valid in many places, the cultural assumptions on which US communitarianism are based may to a large extent be inappropriate in the UK.

In the UK, community has some of the traditional connotations of the US, but has an equally strong history and tradition based on ideas of mutuality and cooperation, on radical liberal politics and on a whole variety of idealistic (and occasionally utopian) initiatives and values. What have been labelled 'community initiatives' in the UK have included small community projects and campaigns by tenants and residents, community bookshops, community schools and 'alternative' communities including those set up alongside road protests or land occupations. There have also been attempts to create much larger utopian communities since the 17th century, from the beginning of the Industrial Revolution (eg Robert Owen's new communities) right up to the development of the New Towns, created between the 1940s and the 1990s to provide better living places than city slums. All these types of 'community' initiatives have an element of idealism, of creating a better world, where people can live together well. But the word has also been used more cynically, to attach a warm glow to unpopular policies, eg the Community Charge (better known as the poll tax).

The ways in which recent government policies on poverty and social exclusion have focused around 'community' provides a useful focus to analyse the concept. Indeed, the concept of community has become central to contemporary politics as politicians vie to find viable forms of community to promote national renewal (Brickell, 2001).

The work of the government's Social Exclusion Unit (SEU) has been widely welcomed and admired – for consulting widely, for sophisticated analysis and sensitive solutions. It has been a great advance to recognise that, while the areas targeted suffer from multiple and complex problems, they also contain great resources in terms of the people who live there. In his introduction to the first SEU report, Tony Blair said: 'Too much has been imposed from above, when experience shows that success depends on communities themselves having the power and taking the responsibility to make things better' (Social Exclusion Unit, 1998). Proposals for the National Neighbourhood Renewal Strategy, for the New Deal for Communities, and for the later rounds of Single Regeneration Budgets, have encouraged community involvement, and have moved local management and community self-help to the centre of the national policy on local regeneration.

Dangers in Assumptions about Community

All these developments have been welcomed by campaigners and by local communities. But there are dangers in not clarifying the assumptions behind the word 'community'. These assumptions include:

• That everyone shares a view about what 'community' means, and that it relates in some way to idealized communities (often rural) of the past. In practice, there is no shared view of what an ideal community is or would be, and few specific examples of previous communities (other than in literature) which epitomize those ideal communities.
• That poverty and social exclusion are essentially *local* problems for poor people to solve themselves by gaining skills (through capacity building and training). This avoids any hint that poverty and social exclusion may be structural problems created by the nature of the current economic and political system.
• That community is a solution for poor people, but not for everybody. The focus in community development, community regeneration, etc, is on the poorest and most disadvantaged neighbourhoods, and not (at least not until the development of community strategies) on wider neighbourhoods, towns or whole parts of major cities, irrespective of the different levels of wealth they contain.
• That people need to have their 'capacity' built before they can participate in community action or in decisions which affect their lives and those of their neighbours: few would suggest that a stockbroker or bank manager needs to have her or his capacity built before they can engage in political/democratic activity or community action, although they are no more likely to be able to create responsible, caring, supportive, including community relationships, than their neighbours in poorer neighbourhoods.
• That social exclusion is about economic status and skills, and not about politics or power. Much less attention has therefore been paid to political exclusion (or increasingly environmental exclusion, environmental rights and environmental justice) than it has to social and economic exclusion.

The use of community to help set policy creates special difficulties. For example, it is not obvious what types of community should be aimed for. The traditional community (often imagined as a rural village) has not always been ideal: too often it has been oppressive, divisive, hierarchical, rigid, sexist, racist. And contemporary communities have some additional negative images: as ghettos, or exclusive, gated communities.

When pressed, government and others (including agencies responsible for rural areas) are able to provide a vision of a 'good' community which has none of these traditions, but which:

- is diverse – with mixed ages, skills and professions, ethnic backgrounds, religions, wealth, etc;
- welcomes difference;
- is active, with many opportunities for involvement; and
- has extensive relationships and formal and informal networks.

However, this type of community rarely exists, and is unlikely to have often existed in the past. It is not something that can be 'rebuilt' or 'returned to' as if there were a golden age of community. In practice, 'community' may best be seen as an aspiration rather than a return, and as a choice rather than an inheritance.

Williams points out that 'In many villages, community only became a reality when economic and political rights were fought for and partially gained, in the recognition of the unions, in the extension of the franchise, and in the possibility of entry into new representative and democratic institutions' (Williams, 1993, p104). Community, political participation, power and representative democracy continue to be fundamentally intertwined.

The concept of the 'sustainable community' is a recent addition to the debate. The Local Government Management Board guidance for local authorities on LA21 was the first coherent summary of the characteristics of a sustainable community (LGMB, 1998). And SCAN (the Sustainable Communities Action Network) – which includes organizations such as Community Development Foundation and Going for Green – have developed criteria for a sustainable community. At local levels, others are attempting to create their own visions and manifestations of sustainable communities: the Millennium Village in Greenwich (and others planned); a growing network of Zero Emission Developments (including in BedZed in Surrey and Sherwood Energy Village in Nottinghamshire) and smaller initiatives such as Hockerton Houses; research into local economic self-sufficiency, and developing the building blocks for healthy local economies (Countryside Agency and the New Economics Foundation); and the Whole Settlements Strategy, an approach initiated in Hertfordshire which builds on Local Agenda 21 and foreshadowed community strategies. These disparate initiatives have fed the major proposals for development launched by the UK government as the programme for sustainable communities in 2003. Although this programme is essentially focused on meeting housing need, environmental factors and social facilities are essential to the guiding principles.

Community is often used as a simple way of describing local residents, but it is not only local residents who will have views, rights and responsibilities to the countryside. There is a whole range of other stakeholders, such as established voluntary and community groups and organizations, land users, visitors, professionals and politicians. Beyond them are those who attach an existence value to the countryside, as well as excluded groups who do not feel they can actively use it, or live in it, such as black and minority ethnic groups and many young people (Warburton, 1997). Any involvement with the community in the countryside must take all these other interests into account.

Social Capital and Trust in Communities

Social capital and trust have become code words for some of the basic principles that policy-makers would like to see operating in strong communities. American academic Robert Putnam popularized the term 'social capital' in his study of civic life in Italy. Putnam describes social capital as '... features of social life – networks, norms and trust – that enable participants to act together more effectively to pursue shared objectives' (Putnam, 1993, p15). He argues that the strong civic community is 'marked by an active, public spirited citizenry, by egalitarian political relations, by a social fabric of trust and co-operation' (ibid), expressed in the existence of strong local social institutions and networks in civic society (from labour unions to choral societies).

Putnam provides evidence that a strong civic culture 'turned out to be the best (in fact the only strongly significant) predictor of economic success for a locality over the long term ... The key differential factor is the presence of community, specified as those norms of reciprocity and networks of civic engagement which Putnam calls social capital ... social capital is thought of as a moral resource and public good which activates the latest human capital of individuals and populations' (Sullivan, 1995, p28–89).

The current promotion of social capital as a way of analysing successful communities raises some concerns:

- Many analyses do not properly recognize the importance of local groups, associations, etc to Putnam's analysis. These organizations provide the infrastructure for the otherwise rather nebulous relationships.
- The analysis of social capital is usually static rather than dynamic, explaining what it is and how it is manifested, rather than how it may be created where it does not exist.
- The concept can be used to avoid addressing issues of power, structural inequality and conflict. For many commentators, social capital exists somewhat apart from such complex hierarchies of power and dispute.

The Rural Perspective?

So far it has been assumed that the public policy framework on community involvement should apply to rural areas just as it does to urban ones. But is that right? Or is the countryside so different that the same principles do not apply there? Much of the literature suggests that the difference may be less than is often assumed.

Williams argues that ideas about the countryside as a 'separate' and different place grew up as a contrast to the town, and particularly as seen by a relatively small but wealthy group who had the means to travel between town and country. He argues that the development of ideas about the special qualities of the countryside 'evidently involves response to a whole way of life largely determined elsewhere' (Williams, 1993, p290). More recent analysis sees the relationship of countryside to landscape as a key to understanding its significance. Thus, landscape is likened to a text and its interpretation to reading (Daniels and Cosgrove, 1988). Taking this view, analysis has to look beyond the apparently obvious differences of town and country, and consider how concepts of the 'countryside' have been produced, and maintained. There are likely to be conflicts between many conservationists' ideas of an ideal landscape (ie remote and with no people), and those thrown up by public participation.

There are clearly distinct challenges in devising effective community involvement in rural areas: poverty may be present, but not as obvious; communities may be very dispersed, or just very small; the voluntary and community infrastructure is different; and social relations may be more entrenched. However, differences seem to be lessening all the time. The Countryside Agency found that rural and urban populations held very similar views about land use and development in the countryside (Countryside Agency, 2001). Research for the CPRE and WWF UK came to similar conclusions: the shared priorities of the participants, drawn from Birmingham and rural Worcestershire and Herefordshire, are much more important than the things which divide them (Office for Public Management, 2000). The OPM research also concluded that groups highlighted the need to bridge the gap in policy-making and political leadership which deals with town and country separately and gives more power to local communities over decisions which affect their quality of life (CPRE, 2000).

It has also been argued that 'much of what is called 'countryside' is just a new type of town: housing commuters who work in towns, or in non-rural professions but happen to live in villages or new developments in rural areas' (Lock, 2001b, p47). Another recent examination about the future of rural land use concluded that 'differences in the needs and aspirations of urban and rural populations have long since eroded and are now almost indistinguishable, as too is the economy ... These changes demand joined-up policies that will regenerate the countryside in sustainable ways whilst benefiting the whole nation' (Royal Geographical Society, 2000). The convergence of town and country is not unique to Britain. A recent ten-nation scoping study on rural development concluded 'In several of the national reports, it has been stated strongly that rural development policy cannot be sustainable on its own as rural areas are strongly interlinked with urban regions in economic, social and environmental terms ... Understanding the many and various interconnections and interdependencies between rural and urban areas, whether neighbouring or spaced apart, is one of the keys for interpreting sustainability in a coherent and holistic way' (Baldock et al, 2001, p37).

It seems as though the similarities between urban and rural communities, in the UK in the 21st century, are much more important than the differences. Which suggests that there is a need to share learning between rural and urban areas about community involvement in planning, as on other issues, much more often and more effectively.

CONCLUSIONS

The growing importance of participation in planning, and particularly community involvement, is clear. It is now very rare for any policy initiatives related to planning (including rural regeneration or any related topic) to be launched without parallel proposals for community involvement. More broadly, community, although a contested concept, is deeply entrenched as a guiding principle in current political debate and public policy. Although there is no very clear, and certainly no shared, idea of what 'community' actually looks like, there are attempts to create ideas of a sustainable community, which is diverse, open and welcoming of difference. The UK as a community of communities and citizens (Runnymede Trust, 2001) remains a powerful vision for many, although it is to be hoped that the orientation remains firmly on the present and future and the potential for harking back to a mythical idea of the ideal community (especially when based on a fantasy of the rural village) is limited to works of fiction.

The reasons for these trends are less obvious, but include the distrust of science and scientists, and public institutions; the perceived loss of political legitimacy for governments in the light of falling electoral turnouts and globalization; growing protests against unwanted development; demands that the public voice be heard alongside the wealthy and powerful lobbies with established access to government; and a growing realization that a healthy democracy requires more than a vote once every few years. At the same time, there is growing evidence that participatory schemes are more effective and sustainable than conventionally managed projects and programmes. These are powerful arguments of principle and practice which seem to be reflected in the many public policy developments outlined in this chapter.

However, in spite of the rhetoric and the policy changes, there remains a lack of understanding about community involvement in countryside planning at all levels of government, and in the other public, private and voluntary organizations that bring about change in the countryside. There is also an ambivalence in government (and its agencies) at all levels between centralized control and direction, and listening to the needs, desires and knowledge of local people and others. Often government may be confronted by a range of views (often conflicting) which emerge from any community. Often too, government finds that other institutional stakeholders are focused on internally derived priorities, targets and goals rather than on meeting the broader needs and priorities being articulated from the grassroots.

All these issues can only be resolved by greater experience of working with communities. Practice, in this case, makes better – if not perfect – as long as it feeds back into policy development. There has been much written in recent years about the need for policy to be based on evidence and experience, but the resources to gather the evidence and learn from experience of community involvement in countryside planning remain meagre (the Countryside Agency is among a few honourable exceptions).

The failure to make community involvement mainstream to countryside planning in practice, as well as in principle, is a reflection of a wider failure of policy-making in the UK. Community involvement can only make sense as part of a completely new policy-making process which moves away from reliance on bright new ideas and media-friendly wheezes towards solid experience, evidence, knowledge and wisdom. At present, it still seems that headline-grabbing sound bites or concepts have more impact on action, even though community involvement leads to better quality countryside planning processes and outcomes. For all the good ideas in recent rural white papers, there are few indications that implementation will be examined thoroughly in discussion with those likely to directly experience the impacts. Even when those with real experience of practice are encouraged to be involved in policy design (such as in the Social Exclusion Unit's Priority Action Teams), the tendency has been to focus on identifying ideas for action rather than establishing long-term – indeed permanent – processes for involvement.

This book shows the vital importance of countryside planning to those who live in the countryside, and to those who live elsewhere. It is too important to be left to a policy-making and delivery process that all too often focuses on the short term. A sustainable countryside, which meets human needs and enhances environmental quality, requires the involvement of the people who live in, use, visit and care about the countryside in shaping policy. Of course, elected politicians will still be required to make major decisions on behalf of the community as a whole (at different spatial levels), but these decisions need to reflect the priorities and concerns of the people affected as well as being the product of brave and clear-sighted leadership. Community involvement can then play a central role in new policy-making and delivery processes for sustainable countryside planning.

Community involvement, then, is not simply a box in a flow chart in a countryside planning process but a profound challenge to policy-makers. But it can be a positive challenge which should enable future countryside planning decisions to be more legitimate, accountable and appropriate, and implementation to be more successful in contributing to sustainable development.

REFERENCES

Allen, M (2001) 'Bush Plans Values-Based Initiative to Rev Up Agenda', *The Washington Post*, 29 July 2001

Aston Business School (1991) *Managing Social and Community Development Programmes in Rural Areas: An Evaluation of the Rural Development Commission's Social Programme*, Aston Business School, Birmingham

Baldock, D, Dwyer, J, Lowe, P, Petersen, J and Ward, N (2001) *The Nature of Rural Development. Towards a Sustainable Integrated Rural Policy in Europe. A Ten Nation Scoping*

Study, WWF UK, Countryside Agency, Countryside Council for Wales, Scottish Natural Heritage, English Nature, Centre for Rural Economy (University of Newcastle upon Tyne) and Institute for European Environmental Policy, Godalming

Batson, B and Smith, J (1996) *Organisational Development in the Community*, ISPRU Publications, Leeds Metropolitan University, Leeds

Beck, U (1992) *Risk Society: Towards a New Modernity*, Sage Publications, London

Bennett, J and Pilling, A (2001) 'Putting Theory into Practice: How to have a mainstreaming sustainable development authority', *EG Magazine*, vol 7(7), pp3–6

Bishop, J, Davison, D, Hickling, D, Kean, J, Rose, J and Silson, R (1994) *Community Involvement in Planning and Development Processes*, Her Majesty's Stationery Office, London

Blair, T (1999) Speech to National Council for Voluntary Organisations, 8 February 1999

Blair, T (2000) 'Richer and Greener', Speech to the CBI/Green Alliance Conference on the Environment, 24 October 2000

Blair, T (2001) 'Improving Your Local Environment', Croydon, 24 April 2001

Brickell, P (2001) *People before Structures: Engaging Communities Effectively in Regeneration*, Demon, London

Cannan, C (2000) 'Green social theory, the environmental crisis and community development', *Community Development Journal*, vol 35(4), pp365–376

Chanan, G, West, A, Garratt, C and Humm, J (1999) *Regeneration and Sustainable Communities*, Community Development Foundation, London

Chanan, G, Garratt, C and West, A (2000) *The New Community Strategies: How to Involve Local People*, Community Development Foundation, London

Cherrett, T (2001) 'Rural Partnerships – Do they add value?', *EG Magazine*, vol 7(3), pp13–16

Christie, I and Warburton, D (2001) *From Here to Sustainability: Politics in the Real World*, Earthscan, London

Clarke, G (1995) *A Missed Opportunity: An Initial Assessment of the 1995 Single Regeneration Budget Approvals and their Impact on Voluntary and Community Organisations in England*, Urban Forum, London

Commission of the European Communities (CEC) (2001a) *Commission Takes a Further Step towards Ratification of the Aarhus Convention*, Press Release, 26 January 2001, Brussels

Commission European Communities (2001b) *Environment 2010: Our Future, Our Choices*, Sixth European Action Programme, CEC, Luxembourg

Countryside Agency (2001) *State of the Countryside 2001*, Countryside Agency, Cheltenham

Council for the Protection of Rural England (2000) *Town and Country. More United than Divided*, CPRE Press Release, 29 February 2000, London

Craig, G and Mayo, M (eds) (1995) *Community Empowerment*, Zed Books, London

Craig, G, Monro, S, Taylor, M, Warburton, D and Wilkinson, M (2001) *Willing Partners? Voluntary and Community Organisations in the Democratic Process*, Interim findings of research project, part of ESRC Democracy and Participation programme, University of Brighton and University of Hull, Brighton.

Crow, S (2001) 'Back to the all-powerful centralised state? Or a blow for democracy?', *Town and Country Planning*, vol 70(6), pp168–169

Daniels, S and Cosgrove, D (1988) 'Introduction: iconography and landscape', Cosgrove, D and Daniels, S (eds) *The Iconography of Landscape. Essays on the Symbolic Representation, Design and Use of Past Environments*, University Press, Cambridge, pp1–10

Department of the Environment (DoE) (1994) *Quality in Town and Country*, DoE, London

Department of the Environment Transport and the Regions (1998) *Modernising Local Government: Local Democracy and Community Leadership*, The Stationery Office, London

Department of the Environment Transport and the Regions (1999) *A Better Quality of Life. UK Strategy for Sustainable Development*, The Stationery Office, London

Department of the Environment Transport and the Regions and Ministry of Agriculture, Fisheries and Food (2000) *Our Countryside: The Future. A Fair Deal for Rural England*, Cmd 4909, The Stationery Office, London

Development Trusts Association (2001) *Rural Agenda for Community-Led Enterprise*, Development Trusts Association, London

Etzioni, A (1995) *The Spirit of Community. Rights, Responsibilities and the Communitarian Agenda*, Fontana Press, London

Hain, P (2001) *The End of Foreign Policy? Britain's Interests, Global Linkages and Natural Limits*, Fabian Society, Green Alliance and Royal Institute of International Affairs, London

Hallet, C (1987) *Critical Issues in Participation*, Association of Community Workers, Newcastle

Hughes, B (2001) 'Putting Councils in Touch with Local People: The role of community strategies and the well-being power', *EG Magazine*, vol 7(1), pp2–3

InterAct (2001) *Evaluating Participatory, Deliberative and Co-operative Ways of Working*, InterAct Working Paper, London

LGMB (1999) *Progress with Local Agenda 21 in England and Wales*, LGMB, London

LGMB/DETR/LGA (1998) *Sustainable Local Communities for the 21st Century: Why and How to Prepare and Effective Local Agenda 21 Strategy*, DETR, London

Little, J, Clements, J and Jones, O (1998) 'Rural Challenge and the Changing Culture of Rural Regeneration Policy', in Oatley, N (ed) *Cities, Economic Competition and Urban Policy*, Paul Chapman, London, pp127–145

Local Government Management Board (LGMB) (1993) *Customer and Citizen Involvement*, LGMB, London

Lock, D (2001a) 'Gold, Frankincense and Mud', *Town and Country Planning*, vol 7(1), p13

Lock, D (2001b) 'Rural is Not Another Country', *Town and Country Planning*, vol 7(2), p47

Lowe, P (2001) 'Sifting Through the Bran Tub', *Town and Country Planning*, vol 7(1), pp18–19

Macnaghten, P, Grove-White, R, Jacobs, M and Wynne, B (1995) *Public Perceptions and Sustainability in Lancashire. Indicators, Institutions and Participation*, Lancaster University, Lancaster

Meadows, D, Meadows, D, Randes, J, Behrens, I and William, W (1983) *The Limits to Growth: A Report for the Club of Rome's Project on the Predicament of Mankind*, Pan Books, London

Moseley, M, Derounian, J and Allies, P (1996) 'Parish Appraisals – a spur to local action?', *Town Planning Review*, vol 67(3), pp309–329

Office for Public Management (2000) *Urban and Rural Futures*, Council for the Protection of Rural England and World Wide Fund for Nature, London

Owen, S (1998) 'The Role of Village Design Statements in Fostering a Locally Responsive Approach to Village Planning and Design in the UK', *Journal of Urban Design*, vol 3(3), pp359–380

Putnam, R (1993) *Making Democracy Work: Civic Traditions in Modern Italy*, Princeton University Press, Princeton

Royal Geographical Society (2000) *Rural Land Use in the 21st Century*, Royal Geographical Society London

Royal Town Planning Institute (RTPI) (1996) *The Local Delivery of Planning Services*, RTPI, London

The Runnymede Trust (2001) *A Community of Communities and Citizens: Cohesion and Justice in the Future of Britain, Report of the Commission on the Future of Multi-Ethnic Britain*, Runnymede Trust, London

Rural Development Commission (1997) *Rural Challenge: The Story so Far*, Rural Development Commission, London

Scottish Executive (1998) *Evaluation of the Local Rural Partnership Scheme*, Scottish Executive, Edinburgh.

Select Committee on Public Administration (2001) *Innovations in Citizen Participation in Government*, Sixth Report, HC 373-I, The Stationery Office, London

Selman, P (1995) 'Local Sustainability', *Town Planning Review*, vol 66(3), pp287–302

Selman, P (1998) 'Local Agenda 21: Substance or spin?', *Journal of Environmental Planning and Management*, vol 45(5), pp533–553

Skeffington (1969) *People and Planning. Report of the Committee on Public Participation in Planning*, Her Majesty's Stationery Office, London

Social Exclusion Unit (1998) *Bringing Britain Together: A National Strategy for Neighbourhood Renewal*, Cmd 4045, The Stationery Office, London

Sullivan, W M (1995) 'Reinventing Community: prospects for politics', in Crouch, C and Marquand, D (eds) *Reinventing Collective Action. From the Global to the Local*, Blackwells, Oxford, pp20–32

Sustainable Development Unit (2001) 'Survey of Progress on Local Agenda 21', Information from the Government's Sustainable Development Unit, *EG Magazine*, vol 7(5), p18

Taylor, M (1992) *Signposts to Community Development*, Community Development Foundation, London

Town and Country Planning Association (TCPA) (1999) *Your Place and Mine: Reinventing Planning*, TCPA, London

Vittery, A (ed) (1989) *Partnership Review*, English Nature, Peterborough

Wakeford, R (2001) 'The Parish Discovery Trail', *Town and Country Planning*, vol 70(1), p17, January 2001

Warburton, D (1997) *Participatory Action in the Countryside: A Literature Review*, Countryside Commission, Cheltenham

Warburton, D (1998) 'A Passionate Dialogue: community and sustainable development', in Warburton, D (ed) *Community and Sustainable Development: Participation in the Future*, Earthscan, London, pp1–39

Warburton, D and Wilcox, D (1988) *Creating Development Trusts*, Her Majesty's Stationery Office, London

Ward, N (2001) *Actors, Institutions and Attitudes to Rural Development. The UK National Report*, WWF UK, Countryside Agency, Countryside Council for Wales, Scottish Natural Heritage, English Nature, Central for Rural Economy and Institute for European Environmental Policy, Godalming

Williams, R (1993) *The Country and the City*, Hogarth Press, London (first published in 1973)

World Bank (1994) *The World Bank and Participation: Report of the World Bank Learning Group on Participatory Development*, World Bank, Washington, DC

World Commission on Environment and Development (1987) *Our Common Future*, Oxford University Press, Oxford

Young, S C (1996) *Promoting Participation and Community-based Partnerships in the Context of Local Agenda 21*, Department of Government, University of Manchester, Manchester

Young, S C (1997) 'The Significance of Local Agenda 21 Participation Programmes in the Broader Context of Regenerating Local Democracy', in Jacobs, M (ed) *Greening the Millennium? The New Politics of the Environment*, Blackwell, Oxford, pp138–147

Part 2

New Concepts and Tools

Chapter 6

The Natural Area Experience

Keith Porter

Against a backdrop of declining biodiversity, English Nature has developed a biogeographic framework – Natural Areas – to help deliver a sustainable future for habitats and their species. This chapter provides an analysis of why Natural Areas were developed, how this was done and how the framework has been used by English Nature and others. The Natural Areas concept is not static, it continues to evolve and is helping to shape thinking on the integration of land use within the countryside. The story of Natural Areas should therefore be seen as part of a continuing saga whose final chapter has still to be written, but will hopefully tell of a more sustainable countryside in the future where people live in better balance with the natural environment.

NEW SOLUTIONS TO OLD PROBLEMS

In 1991, the Nature Conservancy Council (NCC), the government's statutory adviser on nature conservation, was split into separate country agencies. This was viewed by many as a major setback for nature conservation in the UK (Scott, 1992; Marren, 1993; Evans, 1997) yet it also created an opportunity for fresh thinking. The new agency for England – English Nature – set about a fundamental review of its purpose, structure and function. A basic principle that had underpinned the NCC was that nature conservation would be delivered through the designation/notification of protected areas, and the collective effort of the previous 40 years had been to secure a network of Sites of Special Scientific Interest (SSSIs) which held a representative sample of the full range of wildlife and natural features. The establishment of English Nature provided an opportunity to challenge the belief that site-based conservation alone would deliver the new agency's goals. As ecologists, the majority of staff understood the need for a wider context for sites. In particular they recognized that a site-based approach in a fragmented landscape would inevitably lead to local extinction of species and continual loss of overall diversity. The outcome of this root and branch review was a much stronger focus on people as the beneficiaries of nature conservation, an emphasis on 'wildlife gain' and a commitment to explore the potential of developing a new strategic framework that would guide the work of English Nature. Thus, from the ashes of the NCC arose the concept of a new geographical framework that would reflect the variety of England's wildlife and natural features and help the public to relate to nature conservation through a 'sense of place'. The pain of organizational change was used as a tool to advance thinking and make a single large leap in corporate culture that might not have otherwise been possible.

Why did English Nature need Natural Areas?

The development of 'Natural Areas', as the new biogeographic framework became known, was driven by the specific needs of English Nature. The Agency believed that a strategic biogeographic framework would provide a series of related internal and external benefits. Internally, it was hoped the development of a strategic framework would facilitate better targeting of the Agency's resources and the removal of artificial barriers between different departments. Working across England meant that communication between different teams could be problematic. Most decisions on site selection or management were driven from a local perspective at best, and from an individual site viewpoint at worst. One of the early benefits of Natural Areas was that is was seen as a way of linking sites with similar characteristics, and thereby created a wider awareness of issues and solutions. A good example of this was found in Oxfordshire, where the Midvale Ridge Natural Area (see Figure 6.1) is bounded by a series of fens along a spring line. A few sites were known to include open fen habitat and had been recognized as similar to one another. A further set of sites were wooded with no explicit fen interest identified. When these wooded sites were looked at from the perspective of the spring line fens, they were discovered to contain springs and small fens which supported many rare, key, fen species characteristic of that Natural Area. Defining the boundary of the Midvale Ridge had the immediate effect of extending knowledge of the distribution and abundance of species of conservation concern. The new framework, released from the artificial administrative divisions, had liberated thinking about ecological associations.

The NCC had always struggled with the concept of a network of SSSIs. No formal reason had ever been given as to what the series represented or when it would be complete. Natural Areas provided a rationale for revising the coverage and priority for SSSIs in England. Linked to this was the ability of Natural Areas to invite a wider consideration of the similarities and differences between SSSIs. For example, the Chilterns had been recognized as a distinct geographic unit for many decades, but until the mid-1990s all the SSSIs and National Nature Reserves in the Chilterns were treated in isolation (see Figure 6.2). Today a more integrated view is being taken, as a direct result of the Natural Areas framework, and the whole suite of sites is considered when deciding priorities for conservation management.

A key factor in the development of Natural Areas was the recognition that delivering a sustainable outcome for nature conservation was beyond the

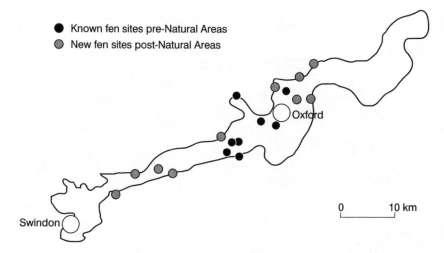

Figure 6.1 *Oxfordshire Midvale Ridge Natural Area showing known fen locations and those 'discovered' through application of predictive search*

resources of English Nature alone. It was hoped that a strategic biogeographic framework would provide a means to target the resources of other organizations and land managers; and that it would become a practical framework for partnership, helping English Nature to communicate its own priorities to a range of partners in the public and private sectors.

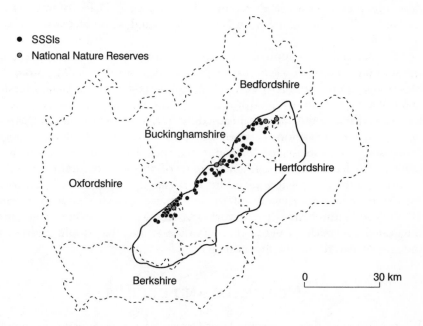

Figure 6.2 *Chilterns Natural Area showing National Nature Reserves and Sites of Special Scientific Interest*

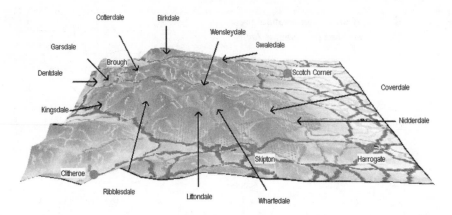

Source: English Nature

Figure 6.3 *The Yorkshire Dales Natural Area*

It was hoped that the framework would help relate nature conservation/ biodiversity issues to the wider public through the identification of features and values that created a 'sense of place'. The experience has been rather different. The large size of Natural Areas means that this aim has yet to be achieved in many parts of England. A finer treatment is needed to reflect the scale to which the local community relates, rather than the ecological scale needed for nature conservation. As can be seen from Figure 6.3, the Yorkshire Dales Natural Area does not pick up on the differences between each Dale community and landscape. Thus, the link between Natural Areas and 'sense of place' remains a priority for future work.

The Natural Areas approach was also prompted by external thinking about the need for conservation action at a regional or landscape scale. The promotion of ecological corridors (Bennett, 1999; Council of Europe, 1996; Marshall, 2000; Wascher, 2000) as a tool for nature conservation was led by concerns about the disruption to dispersal caused by fragmentation of habitats, and the need to ensure connections between protected sites so as to facilitate ecological processes. The problems of 'disconnected sites' has particular resonance in lowland England where the fragmentation of the semi-natural resource has occurred to the point where each 'site' is effectively isolated and vulnerable to the irreversible local extinction of the rare species that they contain (Bennett, 1999). The Natural Areas framework was seen as a way of ensuring a more integrated approach to nature conservation – one that would address the mobility of nature and the functioning of ecosystems.

NEW NEEDS AND DRIVERS

While initial work on the Natural Areas framework was essentially prompted by internal thinking and priorities within English Nature, as the framework developed it has had to respond to a series of external needs and drivers.

Thus the UK Biodiversity Action Plan (UKBAP) (H M Government, 1994) and the Birds and Habitats Directives (CEC, 1979, 1992) have established a clear set of priorities for nature conservation. The UKBAP sets out clear targets for habitat and species conservation (see Chapter 2). The Birds and Habitats Directives place a statutory obligation on the UK government to identify sites for priority species and habitats, and to secure 'favourable conservation status' for these features (refer to Chapter 3 for a fuller explanation). This implies a two-strand approach combining site-based action with positive conservation measures in the wider countryside (Articles 3 and 10 of the Habitats Directive). Even though the directives pre-dated the start of Natural Areas, their influence on the work of the statutory conservation agencies took several years to emerge. It was not until the late 1990s that the implementation of the directives became a high priority. Likewise, biodiversity action planning emerged as a key work area towards the end of the 1990s when the Natural Areas were defined. Unlike the European directives, the biodiversity action plan (BAP) process has no statutory basis but, since the passage of the Countryside and Rights of Way Act 2000, the government is required to have regard to the purpose of the conservation of biological diversity in the exercise of their functions. This is meant to underpin the BAP process in England and Wales. There are now more than 400 species and habitat action plans (UK Biodiversity Group, 2001). Implementation of such a large number of plans on an individual basis is clearly not practical and could even lead to potentially conflicting management activities being promoted on the same patch of ground. To further complicate matters, both the Birds and Habitats Directives and the BAPs introduce a new way of describing habitats, the former based upon European classification of vegetation types and the latter through a holistic view of habitat on a landscape scale. Resolving these issues for England is being dealt with through the Natural Areas framework with a strong emphasis on integrating species with habitats, establishing simple, multipurpose objectives and delivering actions through a single management package for each site. The challenges presented by the directives and UKBAP have led to one of the most valuable uses of Natural Areas: they provide a rational geographic framework to help translate international and national targets into plans for local delivery.

Greater public accountability and freedom of access to environmental information have led to the need for better information on the state of designated sites and the justification for establishing new sites. For example, the UK government is required under the provisions of the Birds and Habitats Directives to report on progress with the establishment of Natura 2000 and the conservation status of designated sites. The UKBAP requires the operation of a number of reporting cycles to provide feedback on progress towards the published targets in action plans (UK Biodiversity Group, 2001). Natural Areas have been used to provide a framework to establish clear targets against which to measure progress, in a manner that facilitates local, regional and national interpretations.

In the past, an understanding of the state of nature through the measurement of outcomes, or the use of indicators, has been tackled through the periodic use of repeat survey or special campaigns to produce distribution atlases (Porter, 2001). Given the pace of change and the demand for more up to date information, the traditional solution of periodic survey activity no longer meets current needs. A new, dynamic process is needed where information is continually collected and made available on the status of wildlife in order to assess the success of policies and actions. The National Biodiversity Network (NBN) (www.nbn.org.uk) is capitalizing on improvements in technology to establish such a process and enable greater sharing and integration of information on biodiversity. This initiative involves developing the means to give access to data and setting new standards for the collection, management and provision of data. The allocation of targets to Natural Areas requires access to all available information on status and distribution. At present, collating any information on biodiversity is a resource intensive activity as the data on species and habitats are widely dispersed among volunteer recorders, national societies, record centres and conservation agencies. The purpose of the NBN is to improve access to existing data and ensure that data collected in the future is easily accessed through a network of data centres. Providing access to existing data will help enormously, however, there are gaps in knowledge that need filling in order that we can satisfy reporting requirements. A key need is for information on the extent and quality of habitats. This is being approached through the establishment of a catalogue or inventory of habitat parcels, and the Natural Areas framework provides a filter to help stratify sampling of habitats and species monitoring and to ensure that samples reflect differences in the distribution of these features across England.

DEVELOPING THE FRAMEWORK

Drawing on the Past

The initial challenge facing English Nature was to explore if a framework could be found to meet the needs above and reflect the variety of nature conservation features in a meaningful way. The earliest attempt in 1992 involved asking each national habitat and species specialist to devise a geographical framework that would best describe the national heterogeneity of his or her particular specialism. This exercise produced a series of maps which suited the needs of each specialism (Brown and Grice, 1993), but provided no common basis for a single map of England. The map created by overlaying all the maps of specialists was not a practical starting point due to differences in scale and area definitions.

The next step was to undertake an open exploration of potential approaches which involved looking at the experience of other countries, a literature review of geographic frameworks and discussion with a wide range of bodies. The aim was to find a framework which was ecologically sound, practical to use and would be recognized by a wide range of users. Most of the initial possibilities were too strongly biased towards one particular sector (see Box 6.1). The most hopeful approach was that taken by geographers and exemplified by Dudley Stamp in his work on land utilization maps (Stamp, 1950). A literature review revealed a range of 'landscape divisions' for every county in England, often supported by associated publications on agriculture (Grigg, 1967) or county

---

BOX 6.1 EXAMPLES OF APPROACHES EXPLORED IN DEVISING THE NATURAL AREAS FRAMEWORK

Approach	Notes
Administrative boundaries	Politico-administrative boundaries did not reflect ecological character and had been explored at great length for 40 years
Habitats and taxon groups	Works for each specialism, but no coherent overall pattern emerges for England
River catchments	Large scale, covers a very wide range of different ecological patterns
Land cover or land use datasets	Fine scale of data provides useful input to characterization, but too fine a scale for identifying contiguous, coherent areas

---

flora (Sinker and Oswald, 1985). Each source provides a simple starting point for the division of a county into areas which are recognized locally as distinctive. Each map had a common basis in geology, soils and topography which were expressed in the land utilization maps as 'capability' for agriculture. The conclusion is that these physical factors are the fundamental drivers for vegetation cover. This approach, using geology, soils and topography, has been adopted in modern county floras to explain the different vegetation character across a county (Jermyn, 1974) and the challenge was to ascertain whether the same approach could be replicated at an all-England level.

Starting with the landscape accounts for each county, the maps were collated into an all-England map. This showed that virtually all the county sub-divisions were linked across county boundaries to produce a coherent pattern of geographic areas which cut across administrative areas. The majority of landscape accounts emphasize in-county distinctivenss, with less recognition given to the larger areas which cross county boundaries. The obvious exceptions were the Cotswolds and Chilterns, but even there, each county segment was treated in isolation by administrative and conservation organizations. By joining up the individual county level areas the first draft of what was named the Natural Areas map came into being.

Securing an Organizational Mandate

Following the literature review and development of the first map, the next challenge was to see if this framework matched up to the perceived corporate need. This new way of looking at nature conservation demanded changes to the culture of English Nature and the adoption of new approaches to working practice. Any such change takes time and can often been viewed as unwelcome. The adoption of the Natural Areas approach within English Nature took several years and required change at three levels: senior management, national specialists, and local officer levels. Given the potential initial resource investment, and the impact on strategy, it was critical to secure the commitment of senior management. This was the organizational level that had initially commissioned an exploration of biogeographic frameworks and thus was presumably receptive to new ideas. In addition, they were best placed to see emerging issues at the international, national and political levels that would require organizational change.

Therefore the first step in establishing Natural Areas within English Nature was for the project team to discuss with senior managers how the framework would meet the agency's requirements. This process lasted almost six months and involved the use of real examples to demonstrate the potential of the approach. The concept gained support, but it was evident that it needed to be tested through public consultation, so as to gauge the reaction of conservation partners and other interested parties. Before undertaking a consultation exercise it was necessary to check that the 'Natural Areas map' would be widely supported within English Nature. The first map was used as the basis of extensive internal consultation to test and confirm its value for English Nature. Following seminars and consultation across English Nature, the map was revised to improve the definition of each area. The basis of this revision was a more detailed consideration of existing information on soils, vegetation and local knowledge. The process involved a wide range of bodies in the conservation field and local authorities and was undertaken by each of the 21 English Nature local teams. The subsequent version of the map was subject to a national consultation exercise (English Nature, 1993, 1994) to engage a wide range of bodies.

On the basis of an encouraging response, the next phase of securing English Nature support was to hold a series of workshops with English Nature local teams and national staff. This provided an opportunity to raise awareness using examples and case studies and air concerns that needed further exploration. These workshops challenged some of the assumptions about nature conservation, particularly the notion that site-based conservation alone will secure a sustainable future for wildlife. While sites still remained as the single most powerful part of the nature conservation 'tool kit' they had to be supported by a wider countryside in which ecological processes could continue to operate. English Nature staff recognized the problems of habitat fragmentation and supported the need for a mechanism to help deal with this issue. The local teams readily adopted the concept and played an active role in defining lines on maps. They rapidly developed a strong sense of ownership over 'their' Natural Areas and acted as champions for the concept when consulting external bodies. National science teams took on the role of producing national overviews after recognizing the value of a single common framework rather than different frameworks for different topics. Following the consultation and internal workshops, information was fed back to the local teams and this was used to create draft three of the Natural Areas map which was published in 1994. This version included an increase in the number of areas and further refinement of the boundaries, and broadly established the number and shape of areas that are in use today (see Figure 6.4 in Plate section).

In summary, English Nature developed the Natural Areas concept because it saw it as a means of helping to advance other areas of work to which it was committed. In particular, Natural Areas provided a way to 'get a handle' on the complex diversity of nature conservation features across England, in a way that would help to deliver more effective wildlife conservation with limited resources. Thus Natural Areas evolved as a framework driven by need. But they also represented a significant departure for an agency, which had historically based its initiatives on strong science and traditional 'expert' approaches. Being intuitively-based, Natural Areas attracted some criticism for being 'soft science' and lacking in rigour. Some of this rigorous underpinning had yet to come, but English Nature was convinced that the Natural Areas would help to take forward the national nature conservation agenda.

The Countryside Character Map

Unbeknown to those working on Natural Areas within English Nature, the Countryside Commission had been piloting a New Map of England in the south-west (Countryside Commission, 1994 – see also Chapter 7). This work explored the use of 1 kilometre square resolution data to produce a consistent methodology for defining regional character areas. Once it was realized that the two parallel initiatives existed, both organizations agreed to work together to explore the development of a common 'map'. Comparison of the two approaches rapidly showed that, at the broadest scale, the Natural Areas and the character areas in the south-west of England were compatible: the Countryside Commission's 38 character areas were the same as, or nested within, Natural Areas. The agencies were joined in their collaborative work by English Heritage, and were supported by the then Department of the Environment. The outcome was the Countryside Character Map (Countryside Commission, English Heritage and English Nature, 1996). This provided some of the scientific rigour needed to underpin the Natural Area framework and so addressed the concerns of critics.

The collaborative work between the Countryside Commission, English Heritage and English Nature in preparing a single map for England took about 18 months. The methodology involved the collation of a series of datasets at 1 kilometre square resolution for all major attributes that underpin countryside character (see Box 6.2) and a correspondence analysis using TWINSPAN[1] to create geographic areas (Countryside Commission, 1997). This technical view of an England-wide framework was then used to inform a series of regionally-based consultations with a wide range of partner organizations. The regional consultation exercise emphasized the need to refine the technical output with local knowledge and experience. The datasets which underpin the computer-generated framework are rarely precise, as many of the data points are extrapolated from sample-based data collection. The outcome of this work was a map, virtually identical to the Natural Areas map, with the definition of distinct character areas lying hierarchically within some large Natural Areas and coincident with others. This collaborative work allowed the agencies involved to explore the commonality of visual, cultural and ecological aspects of countryside character. The published map was supported by integrated statements for each Character Area, which summarized the key elements for landscape, wildlife and natural features.

BOX 6.2 VARIABLES USED TO ESTABLISH THE COUNTRYSIDE CHARACTER MAP

Variable (all data defined at 1 km² units)	Number of attributes
Field pattern and density	16
Visible archaeology	12
Settlement patterns	12
Industrial history	16
Designed parkland	3
Farm type/patterns	15
Surface geology	27
Altitude	10
Landform/relative relief	10
Ecological character	13
Land capability patterns	8
Woodland cover patterns	8

NATURAL AREAS IN PRACTICE

Targets and Priorities

The main value of Natural Areas for English Nature has been to help identify the most important nature conservation features in each area and understand what has to be done to achieve their effective conservation. The key features are prioritized in terms of international, national and local significance; top priority goes to the features listed in the annexes of the European directives, and thus of international significance. In practical terms, Natural Areas provide the framework through which national scale targets can be broken down into manageable blocks which reflect areas of England where features, or associated groups of features, can be maintained, restored or re-created in a sustainable way.

The Natural Areas are supported by a range of products that help English Nature staff and others to improve the targeting of nature conservation activities. A set of national overviews provides a breakdown of the significance of habitats, species groups and earth science features across Natural Areas. The national overviews have helped to ensure an appropriate balance between national priorities and those of local area staff. In addition, a profile document has been prepared for each Natural Area which describes the character of the area, the key nature conservation features, their objectives and the main factors affecting these features. These profile documents provide a standardized view of the most important nature conservation features in each Natural Area and the issues that need to be considered by decision-makers and land-managers when considering plans for new development or changes to land use within a Natural Area. The aim is that the national targets be broken down in a way that reflects the existing semi-natural resource and the need and practicality of restoring habitats or species.

Boundary Issues

Any product has to reflect the needs of its users, and those who are interested in biodiversity and earth science features work at a range of scales. Very few, if any, operate at the Natural Area scale. The mismatch between the ecological coherence of Natural Areas and administrative boundaries was a barrier to many potential users, especially local authorities. Local agency staff played a critical part in overcoming this barrier, and were helped by improvements in data access and technology. Each Natural Area has a definable character; an almost unique mix of habitats and species which reflects the physical characteristics and land use history of each area. Even when a Natural Area crosses a county border, the ecological 'signature' remains intact. English Nature local staff had for long advised on the priorities for nature conservation at the county scale, and were thus able to repackage the Natural Area key features into other area-based plans, while drawing out their national, regional and local significance. With emerging computer technology, many local authorities were able to re-cast the site-based information from Natural Areas into any scale or shape of area they wanted.

Summarizing at scales larger than an individual Natural Area has been done to support the work of Government Regional Offices (English Nature, 1999) and certain regional biodiversity plans (Selman et al, 1999). Such summaries are derived from an analysis of the component Natural Area profile documents and are aimed at informing regional level decision-making. Given the important role that Government Regional Offices now play in respect of all sectors, it is important that appropriately packaged summaries of nature conservation priorities should be available at this scale.

Targeting in Practice

The UK BAP (see Chapter 2) provides national-scale quantified targets for species and habitats: for habitats, the targets are for areas that need to be restored, created or re-introduced. However, there is no indication of how this target should be broken down to local areas. This is where the Natural Areas can act as the framework through which the national target is divided into area-based targets. Similarly, for each Natural Area a list of targets can be produced with associated information to enable the link to be made with the national action plans. Each Natural Area target is translated into action through relevant local delivery mechanisms, such as a local biodiversity action plan. While this may appear to help to meet the targets, there are doubts about whether a sustainable scale and pattern of habitat is being created, and whether restoration (or creation) is being done in the best place to ensure linkage with other habitats and maximum interchange of species.

The government's agri-environment schemes are a key mechanism for delivering biodiversity. Both the Environmentally Sensitive Area and the Countryside Stewardship Schemes have benefited from target setting through Natural Areas. Knowledge of which key species and habitats exist in each Natural Area enables the scheme project officers of the Department of the Environment, Food and Rural Affairs (DEFRA) to respond to applications in a way that supports the delivery of national targets. The partnership between

English Nature and DEFRA is critical in targeting funds so as to maximize biodiversity and environmental benefits. Natural Areas have helped to improve the effectiveness of this partnership.

Countryside and Landscape

Using the example of lowland heathland, the Natural Area framework provides a mechanism to understand better heathland character, with all its local variants. Lowland heathland is a focus both for the Habitats Directive (with Britain seen as containing a high proportion of the European resource) and the UK BAP (which contains a clear set of targets for the maintenance, restoration and creation of this habitat). However, clarity over habitat definitions is essential to target setting and measuring progress over plans, especially as many definitions exist for lowland heathland (Webb, 1986). The recognition of local character and the link with definitions of lowland heathland have been explored in two related studies: one by English Nature and the other by the Vegetation Unit of Lancaster University. The English Nature work arose from the development of an information system to support the monitoring of SSSIs. In this work each site is divided into broad habitat features, such as heathland. Each broad feature is further defined by the component vegetation communities, described by the National Vegetation Community (NVC) (Rodwell, 1991). By grouping SSSIs into Natural Areas, then looking at the NVC communities linked to heathlands on these sites, it was clear that a pattern exists for each Natural Area. In parallel with this work, the Lancaster University team had been developing a concept called 'contact communities'. This recognized that in different parts of the country the same broad habitat contained a different mix of vegetation communities (Rodwell and Cooch, 1997). Based upon this work, maps were produced to explain the differences between – say – the Lizard heaths and the Thames Basin heaths in a systematic way. This characterization of heathland Natural Areas is a useful tool to aid target setting and definition of character in heathland restoration and creation schemes (English Nature, 1998b). This type of analysis appears obvious in hindsight, but would have been difficult to do for the whole country without the benefit of the Natural Areas framework.

Knowledge about the character of each Natural Area is a useful tool when defining priorities for nature conservation as it informs decisions about the pattern and detail of landscape. This has been explored in four discrete areas of England under the Habitat Restoration Project (Thomas, 2000). This identified four different types of landscape, each covering approximately 100 km². Two of these areas contained heathland as a key habitat. In each of the four pilot areas the key habitats species and character of the landscape were defined and data collected on the current land cover pattern. This information was then used to develop a 'vision' map for each area, which identified the potential for expansion of existing habitat and the restoration of ecological connectivity. Each area was considered typical of the Natural Area in which it lay, and provided an opportunity to explore the issues helping or preventing the restoration of a biodiversity-friendly landscape.

For example, the River Alde provided a focus for one of the project areas in the Suffolk Coast and Heaths Natural Area (Figure 6.5 in Plate section). It contains a typical mixture of all the key habitats which characterize the whole Natural Area. Taking the lead from a national target for lowland heathland, the proportion allocated to the Suffolk Coast and Heaths Natural Areas can be further broken down into this particular study area. The vision map process enables this target area to be compared with existing habitat, and areas with potential for restoration, and provides options for particular parcels of land (see Figure 6.5 in Plate section). In essence, the landscape map is the final stage in the targeting process and allows the breakdown of national targets to be validated and modified better to reflect reality. However, the focus of the Habitat Restoration Project was solely upon biodiversity, with no consideration given to other 'heritage' land uses. The establishment of the vision maps did include extensive consultation with farmers, foresters and other land managers, but the project was focused on biodiversity. Since biodiversity is only one of many potential uses of the wider countryside, one lesson learnt from this project work was the need to reflect a wider range of other uses.

WHERE NEXT?

Character is wider than biodiversity and must include those cultural, historic and socio-economic aspects that have shaped the landscape if a sustainable outcome is to be achieved (Antrop, 2000). Because of this, and because about 20 per cent of UKBAP priority species depend upon the landscape outside designated sites, (Simonson and Thomas, 1999; English Nature, 2000) English Nature is now looking at new ways of delivering biodiversity as part of a multi-user landscape.

'Lifescapes': Integration through Landscape

The framework of Natural Areas and Countryside Character provides a way forward. Nature conservation needs a mechanism to help us move from Natural Area scale targets to individual land parcels; this is where biodiversity is delivered through land management. In delivering biodiversity outside SSSIs, conservationists are effectively competing with a wide range of other countryside users. A process is needed to bring together the information necessary to support more balanced decisions on land-use and reflect the social and economic issues in the countryside. From a nature conservation point of view, this includes an indication of the pattern of habitat needed to achieve biodiversity targets in each Natural Area. These ideas are behind the development of an approach called Lifescapes (English Nature, 2000). The aim is to bring together the parallel work of the Countryside Agency, English Heritage and English Nature so as to create a more integrated view of landscape. Similar approaches are being explored by some local authorities (such as Kent County Council) as an aid to strategic development planning.

From the perspective of biodiversity, Lifescapes are a development of Natural Areas and will help to target effort and increase the chance of habitat creation or restoration being carried out in the right place, in terms of biodiversity, landscape and heritage. Each Natural Area has a set of national priority targets for habitats, species and earth science features. The Lifescapes approach will help decisions on where best to seek opportunities for delivering these targets by giving them a spatial identity. Lifescapes will build upon experience gained from four Habitat Restoration Project pilots (see above), which shows that a map-based approach, which links information to parcels of land, is the best way to communicate with land managers. Discussing options with a farmer is much easier if they can see the links with their neighbours, and indeed with other parts of a county and the overall aims of a proposal, rather than considering how a particular field might be managed in isolation. Many landowners welcomed the overview provided by a map as it allowed them to take more informed decisions when considering opportunities for entering agri-environment schemes.

Lifescapes are aimed at providing direct benefits for biodiversity through a focus on special sites and the countryside matrix in which they sit. The disruption of dispersal is a major factor in the decline of species which rely upon semi-natural habitat. The most obvious benefit of a landscape approach is to reduce the isolation of fragmented sites, or 'join up the dots' through habitat links or corridors. Knowing where, and how, to restore species flows is a critical issue for restoring sustainability to the existing resource on designated sites. Using knowledge of the pattern of land cover and the needs of key species, Lifescapes will identify gaps and areas of land with potential for recreating habitat and linkage.

A key aspect of Lifescapes is the recognition of the central role of socio-economic factors in achieving change in the countryside. Promoting an agenda centred upon biodiversity, or even 'heritage', is impossible unless the social and economic factors are included. The intimate linkage between farming, land use and tourism has been graphically brought to the fore by the Foot and Mouth epidemic of 2001. To secure a sustainable outcome for biodiversity, any actions must include the wider needs of society, including employment, health and leisure; a community threatened with the loss of their livelihood is unlikely to be worried about maintaining a nice flower-rich meadow. The key functions of Lifescapes are indicated in Box 6.3.

The development of the Lifescapes concept is an explicit recognition that biodiversity targets in the countryside cannot be achieved through a narrow focus on species, habitats and natural features. Delivery needs to recognize and respect other users of landscape, and ensure that social and economic benefits are achieved through restoration of a more sustainable landscape. The concept of heritage is central to thinking about Lifescapes. This includes the visual, cultural and historic elements, as well as biodiversity, which collectively encompass what the public see as landscape. The potential synergy between biodiversity targets and those for historic or cultural landscapes needs to be explored. While the establishment of the Countryside Character Map in 1996 was a milestone towards achieving an integrated view of heritage interests in England, the Lifescapes concept should further facilitate an integrated approach to countryside planning by providing the detail necessary to deliver at the local

---

BOX 6.3 KEY FUNCTIONS OF LIFESCAPES

The key functions of Lifescapes are to:

Biological:
- facilitate species movement between sites through wildlife corridors or stepping stones;
- mitigate the affects of pollutants or water-level changes on sites through buffer zones;
- establish a 'wildlife friendly' landscape which helps species cope with climate change;
- establish habitat pattern which supports the 20 per cent of Biodiversity Plan target species reliant upon wider countryside.

Social:
- integrate biodiversity targets with cultural and historical objectives;
- promote the recognition of the value of local heritage to local communities;
- facilitate local decision-making through the provision of information for community planning;
- encourage new partnerships to influence positive change in the countryside.

Economic:
- improve the cost–benefits of public money through the targeting of agri-environment scheme resources;
- increase the quality of decisions on sustainable land use throughout England through influence on planning decisions; and
- facilitate economic growth, rather than constrain it, through integrated land use planning.

---

scale. Through the use of geographic information systems, key data on existing and potential heritage resource can be linked to equivalent data on agricultural potential, preferred development areas, land use and a wide range of socio-economic information. Ready access to such data for individual land parcels will improve the quality of decisions on land use and encourage more flexible, responsive strategic planning

CONCLUSIONS

Natural Areas have proved to be an extremely useful tool for nature conservation, both as an aid to English Nature core work and as a framework for other national bodies. The creation of the Character Map in 1996, and subsequent work by the Countryside Agency and English Heritage, presents an opportunity for the future. The recognition of nested boundaries within a national framework will enable each agency to work at a range of scales, to identify common objectives and recognize where differences exist. This spatial approach is increasingly supported by computer technology as information is accessed and analysed by geographical areas, with the data linked to patches of land. Data integration becomes possible through a series of layers, each

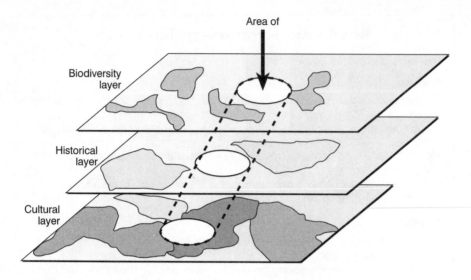

Figure 6.6 *A 'layered' approach to data integration*

representing a particular sectoral interest and value-system (see Figure 6.6). Thus we do not need to force different scales or type of data together and thereby create over-simplistic interpretations that are supported by none of the contributors. Much of the work on Natural Areas has been predicated on the belief that good decisions on land use in the countryside are made possible through better access to appropriate information. This has yet to be tested, but the early signs are encouraging.

In the future, technological developments (such as web-based mapping software) will assist 'joined-up' conservation. The NBN model of local and national data nodes, connected through the Internet, has the potential to work for all environmental data and could thus provide a template for the promotion of integrated decision-making. Data, linked to land parcels, can be overlain and used to derive new information of instant practical value. It is now a good time to bring together the diverse users of the countryside, using map-based views of data. This approach will allow different scales of need to be catered for, and will provide the vertical linkage between national targets and local action.

NOTE

1   TWINSPAN is a statistical package which helps group similar sets of data.

REFERENCES

Antrop, M (2000) 'Background concepts for integrated landscape analysis', *Agriculture, Ecosystems and Environment*, vol 77(1), pp7–28

Bennett, A F (1999) *Linkages in the Landscape: The Role of Corridors and Connectivity in Wildlife Conservation*, IUCN, Cambridge

Brown, A F and Grice, P V (1993) *Birds in England: Context and Priorities*, English Nature Research Report No 62, English Nature, Peterborough

Commission of the European Communities (CEC) (1979) *Conservation of Wild Birds*, Directive 79/409/EEC of 2 April 1979, Office for Official Publications of the European Communities, Luxembourg

Commission of the European Communities (CEC) (1992) *Conservation of Natural Habitats and of Wild Fauna and Flora*, Directive 92/43/EEC of 21 May 1992, Office for Official Publications of the European Communities, Luxembourg

Council of Europe (1996) *The Pan-European Biological and Landscape Diversity Strategy: A Vision for Europe's Natural Heritage*, Council of Europe, UNEP and European Centre for Nature Conservation, Strasbourg

Countryside Commission (1994) *The New Map of England: A Directory of Regional Landscapes*, Countryside Commission, Cheltenham

Countryside Commission (1997) 'Countryside Character Initiative: National Mapping Project', unpublished technical report of the computer phase, Countryside Commission, Cheltenham

Countryside Commission, English Heritage and English Nature (1996) *The Character of England: Landscape, Wildlife and Natural Features*, English Nature, Peterborough

Dawson, D (1994) *Are Habitat Corridors Conduits for Animals and Plants in a Fragmented Landscape? A Review of the Scientific Evidence*, English Nature Research Reports No 94, English Nature, Peterborough

Department of the Environment, Transport and the Regions (1999) *Quality of Life Counts: Indicators for a Strategy for Sustainable Development for the United Kingdom*, Department of the Environment, Transport and the Regions, London

English Nature (1993) *Natural Areas: Setting Nature Conservation Objectives: A Consultation Paper*, English Nature, Peterborough

English Nature (1994) *Natural Areas: Responses to English Nature's Consultation Paper*, English Nature, Peterborough

English Nature (1998a) *Natural Areas: Nature Conservation in Context*, CD-ROM, English Nature, Peterborough

English Nature (1998b) *Tomorrow's Heathland Heritage: A Heritage Lottery Fund Supported Lowland Heathland Restoration Programme*, Information Note 1, English Nature, Peterborough

English Nature (1999) *Natural Areas in the Yorkshire and the Humber Region*, English Nature, Peterborough

English Nature (2000) *Annual Report: 1 April 1999–31 March 2000*, English Nature, Peterborough

Evans, D E (1997) *A History of Nature Conservation in Britain*, Routledge, London

Grigg, D B (1967) 'The Changing Agricultural Geography of England: A commentary on the sources available for the reconstruction of the agricultural geography of England 1770–1850', *Transactions of the Institute of British Geographers*, vol 41, pp73–96

H M Government (1994) *Biodiversity: The UK Action Plan*, Cmd 2428, Her Majesty's Stationery Office, London

Jermyn, S T (1974) *Flora of Essex*, Essex Naturalist Trust, Fingeringhoe, Colchester

Marren, P (1993) 'The Siege of the NCC: Nature conservation in the Eighties', in Goldsmith, F B and Warren, A (eds) *Conservation in Progress*, John Wiley, Chichester, pp283–300

Marshall, I (2000) *LIFE ECOnet: A European Project to Demonstrate Sustainability Using Ecological Networks (Inception Report)*, Cheshire County Council, Chester

Nature Conservancy Council (1984) *Nature Conservation in Great Britain*, Nature Conservancy Council, Peterborough

Nature Conservancy Council (1989) *Guidelines for the Selection of Biological SSSIs*, Peterborough, Nature Conservancy Council

Porter, K (2001) 'Tracking Future Trends: The Biodiversity Information Network', in Hawksworth, D L (ed) *The Changing Wildlife of Great Britain and Ireland,* Taylor & Francis, London, pp422–434

Rodwell, J S (ed) (1991) *British Plant Communities: Volume 2 Mires and Heaths*, Cambridge University Press, Cambridge

Rodwell, J S and Cooch, S (1997) 'Red Data Book of British Plant Communities', unpublished report for World Wide Fund for Nature, Godalming

Scott, M (1992) 'NCC and After: The changing face of British nature conservation', *British Wildlife*, vol 3(4), pp214–221

Selman, R, Dodd, F, and Bayes, K (1999) *A Biodiversity Audit of Yorkshire and Humberside*, Royal Society for the Protection of Birds, Sandy

Simonson, W and Thomas, R (1999) *Biodiversity: Making the Links*, English Nature, Peterborough

Sinker, C A and Oswald, P H (1985) *Ecological Flora of the Shropshire Region*, Shropshire Trusts for Nature Conservation, Shrewsbury

Stamp, D L (1950) *The Land of Britain: Its Use and Misuse*, Longmans, London

Stamp, D L and Beaver, S H (1971) *The British Isles: A Geographic and Economic Survey*, 6th edition, Longmans, London

Thomas, R (2000) *English Nature Habitat Restoration Project: Final Report*, English Nature Research Reports No 377, English Nature, Peterborough

UK Biodiversity Action Plan Steering Group (1995) *Biodiversity: The UK Steering Group Report Volume 1: Meeting the Rio Challenge*, Her Majesty's Stationery Office, London

UK Biodiversity Steering Group (2001) *Sustaining the Variety of Life: 5 Years of the UK Biodiversity Action Plan*, Report of the UK Biodiversity Group to the UK Government, the Scottish Executive, the National Assembly for Wales and the Northern Ireland Executive, Department of the Environment, Transport and the Regions, , London

Wascher, D M (ed) (2000) *The Face of Europe: Policy Perspectives for European, Landscapes*, European Centre for Nature Conservation, Tilburg

Webb, N (1986) *Heathlands*, New Naturalist, Collins, London

Chapter 7

The Assessment of Countryside and Landscape Character in England: An Overview

Carys Swanwick

In the last five years the concept of 'countryside character' has become central to a wide range of activity in landscape and environmental planning and management in England. It is largely, but not completely, synonymous with the term 'landscape character'. Both focus on the use of character as a framework for decision-making on environmental issues. The main differences between the two are: first, that countryside character is a broader integrating concept that draws together landscape, wildlife and archaeological and historical aspects of the countryside; and second that it focuses largely on the rural environment, while landscape character is concerned with all types of landscape in both town and country.

This chapter provides an overview of approaches to the assessment of countryside and landscape character in England. It explores the evolution of current thinking about countryside and landscape character from its origins in earlier work on landscape evaluation and landscape assessment, and examines the way that methods for assessing character have developed and been applied in a wide range of practical situations. It also considers the links that exist between this approach and other emerging tools that have been developed to assist with planning for sustainable development. There are now a number of decision-making tools that can contribute to achieving sustainability. Some, such as the use of Village Design Statements to explore the character of village environments, have been in existence for some time and are relatively well tried and tested. Others, notably the approach known as Quality of Life Capital, are new additions and are still emerging and developing. An understanding of countryside and landscape character often makes an important contribution to these tools although it is usually only one of several parallel topics that need to be addressed.

THE EVOLUTION OF COUNTRYSIDE AND LANDSCAPE CHARACTER ASSESSMENT

Landscape is now widely recognized as an important integrating concept (see, for example, Benson and Roe, 2000). Although there is always likely to be debate about exactly how such an elusive and contested term should be defined, most people seem to accept its importance as an expression of the relationship between people and place. The range of different interpretations of this relationship has been reviewed by many people in the academic literature, (summarized recently in Muir, 1999 and by Phillips in Benson and Roe, 2000) but writers like Richard Mabey have perhaps best captured the importance of landscape to society writing, for example, that:

> *Landscapes are a physical record of our history and labour, our inventiveness and sense of community. They are also records of the continuing struggle between private ambition and social need. In this sense they are a kind of common concrete language... 'A link between what we were and what we are'... Landscapes are not static. They are owned, worked, changed, sometimes by the vitality of the natural world – that supposedly enduring cornerstone-itself* (Mabey, 1985).

Given the importance of landscape to society, it is not surprising that the need to incorporate landscape considerations into environmental decision-making has been recognized for some time. It has, however, grown in importance as the emphasis on sustainability has increased. For many years, and especially in the 1970s at the time of local government reorganization in England, the main emphasis was on the idea of landscape evaluation, that is on what makes one area of landscape 'better' than another. The search for a consensus about such approaches to landscape at this time did not succeed. Emphasis on supposedly objective, scientific, often quantitative approaches to determining landscape value, which was very much the fashion at the time (exemplified by the *Manchester Landscape Evaluation Study* (Robinson et al, 1976)) led to a considerable disillusionment with this type of work. This was largely because many believed it inappropriate to reduce landscape, which is complex, often perceived in emotional terms and intertwined in our culture, to a series of numerical values and statistical formulae. As a result, something of a vacuum emerged. Those involved in landscape planning were sometimes reluctant to tackle the visual and perceptual aspects of landscape, as opposed to the specific and often more tractable aspects of land use and management, such as agriculture, forestry, recreation and nature conservation.

Some of the impetus for change grew from the involvement of the former Countryside Commission in the public inquiry into the proposed designation of the North Pennines as an Area of Outstanding Natural Beauty (AONB). This was the first ever inquiry into proposals for such an official designation, and during it, it became clear that there was no widely accepted systematic approach to assessing the character or quality of different landscapes (Countryside Commission, 1985). As a result, the approach that became known as landscape assessment emerged in the mid-1980s as a different kind of tool. Most importantly it set out clearly to separate the classification and description of landscape character, that is what makes one area different or distinct from another, from the then more usual approach of landscape evaluation, with its obsession with relative value. A study in the Mid Wales Uplands (Land Use Consultants, 1986) initially explored the approach and it was later developed further in work in the lowlands of England in the Warwickshire Landscapes Project (Countryside Commission, 1991). Further inputs to the emerging method came from a review of the literature relating to both practice and research in landscape assessment (Landscape Research Group, 1988).

Landscape assessment developed from these initiatives during the late 1980s and early 1990s as practitioners and policy-makers gained practical experience of its use. Guidance on the approach and methods first appeared in the Countryside Commission's internal document on the subject (Countryside Commission, 1987) and was followed by a more detailed examination of the principles and practice in a Scottish context (Countryside Commission for Scotland, 1991). These documents played a major role in drawing the attention of practitioners to the potential of this new tool. Publication of the Countryside Commission's first major guidance document was directed at practitioners in the public and private sectors (Countryside Commission, 1993a). It helped to reinforce this message and played a major part in applying landscape assessment in a wide range of different situations. Local authorities have been increasingly active, with a 1997 study (Diacono, 1997) suggesting that 83 per cent of English counties had by then carried out assessments and that half of these had been completed since 1993 when the guidance was issued. More recent unpublished research by the Countryside Agency suggests that the proportion is now even higher, although the quality of the assessments is variable.

The Emergence of Landscape Character Assessment

Since 1993, more and more emphasis has been placed on landscape character as a concept central to landscape assessment. As a result, the tool has now come to be widely described as Landscape Character Assessment (LCA) in order to reflect this. Although the idea of character underpinned much of the previous work on landscape assessment, this was often implicit rather than explicit. Its role in assessment work was first set out explicitly in the Countryside Commission project to characterize the lowland landscapes of Warwickshire (Countryside Commission, 1991).

Landscape character can be considered as the distinct and recognizable pattern of elements that occur consistently in a certain type of landscape. It is created by particular combinations of: geology, landform, soils, vegetation, land use, field patterns and human settlement. Character is what makes landscapes distinctive and creates a particular sense of place in a locality. Everywhere has character and all landscapes are distinctive.

Identifying and describing landscape character requires recognition not only of the individual elements that make up the landscape, but also of the way that they work together to create distinctive patterns. This requires that character be examined in a structured and systematic way. Current approaches to LCA are designed to achieve this by providing a common framework and a toolkit of methods and techniques that can be used in different combinations according to the particular circumstances.

How we identify the character of landscapes, and how we value them are now recognized as two separate questions. So the emphasis is now placed on dividing the relatively value-free process of characterization, which means identifying areas of distinctive character, classifying and mapping them, and describing their character, from the second stage of making judgements, based on the characterization, in order to inform decisions that may be required in relation to specific applications of the assessment. Characterization normally results in the identification of one or both of the following:

- *Landscape character types*: these are distinct types of landscape that are relatively homogeneous in character. They are generic in that they may occur in different parts of the country, but wherever they occur they share broadly similar combinations of geology, topography, drainage patterns, vegetation and historical land use and settlement pattern.
- *Landscape character areas*: by comparison, these are discrete geographical areas of a particular landscape type, and are in themselves unique. Each has its own individual character and local identity, even though it may share the same generic characteristics with other areas of the same landscape type.

Potential for application at different scales

LCA in its current form can be applied at a number of different scales, from the national, or indeed European level, down to the local parish level. Assessments carried out at different scales can fit together as a nested series, or a hierarchy of landscape character types and areas so that assessment at each level adds more detail than is present in the one above. The three main levels at which LCA may be carried out are:

- *National/regional scale*: work at this level is large-scale (typically 1:250,000) and may cover the whole of a country or a large region. It seeks to identify broad patterns of variation in landscape character resulting from the underlying geology and landform, which is overlaid with the influence of broad ecological associations and key aspects of settlement and enclosure history.
- *County/district scale*: within these broad overarching patterns it is possible to identify a finer grain of variation in landscape character, which can be mapped and described through LCA applied at the country or district (or unitary authority level), typically at a scale of 1:50,000 or 1:25,000.
- *Local scale*: sometimes it may be necessary to carry out an assessment of a smaller area such as an individual parish, an estate or farm in single ownership, or the area of a proposed development site. Such work is usually carried out at 1:10,000 or less and will add detail to larger-scale assessments.

It is common to refer to the first two categories as assessment at the 'landscape scale', to use the landscape ecological planning term, while the third category can generally be thought of as site assessment.

Links to Historic Landscape Character Assessment

As LCA has emerged in the 1990s, it has been accompanied by a growing emphasis on historic landscape (or land use) characterization as a parallel freestanding tool for exploring the historic or 'time-depth' dimension of the landscape. In England, the method of Historic Landscape Characterization has been developed by English Heritage (Fairclough, 1999) and in Scotland the method of Historic Land Use Assessment has been adopted by Historic Scotland (see Chapter 10). Such work can be carried out either before or alongside an LCA, but increasingly the benefits of integrating the two approaches are being realized. There is no doubt that where resources and time constraints allow, work which combines the two approaches is likely to produce the most satisfactory results.

Involving the stakeholders

In the early stages of its development, landscape assessment was seen primarily as a professional process, the work being carried out by professionals and for professionals. Over the years, however, there has been growing recognition of the need to involve a much wider constituency of people who have a particular concern for, involvement with or stake in the landscape, now captured in the term 'stakeholders'. This approach is particularly important given the new emphasis in government on community planning, cultural strategies and best value performance plans and indicators. Practitioners are still learning about the best ways of engaging stakeholders in the process of LCA but it is widely recognized that investment in this area is likely to produce both better informed assessments and greater ownership of the results when they are applied in practice.

Box 7.1 summarizes the key differences that have emerged as approaches to the assessment of landscape have evolved over the last three decades.

National approaches to countryside and landscape character

In the early 1990s, the then Countryside Commission felt the need to look beyond the system of protected landscapes, reflecting a general move from concentration on the special landscapes to a more general concern for the wider countryside. This new emphasis brought into focus the lack of a comprehensive and consistent analysis of the character of the English landscape (Countryside Commission, 1996a). This led the Commission to begin its innovative work on the Countryside Character programme. The programme flowed directly from the work on landscape assessment, briefly outlined above, and had the twin objectives of: identifying, describing and analysing the character of the English landscape; and identifying specific opportunities to conserve or enhance this character. The precise reasons for the change in terminology from 'landscape character' to 'countryside character' are not entirely clear. They undoubtedly include the view that countryside is a more fully integrated concept than landscape, which was particularly significant at a time when the remits of both the Countryside Commission and English Nature were both under review (see below). It may also, however, reflect a reluctance to rely too overtly on the term 'landscape' because of the ongoing debate about its cultural meanings and a perception that in some

---

BOX 7.1 THE EVOLUTION OF LANDSCAPE CHARACTER ASSESSMENT

Early 1970 Landscape evaluation	Mid-1980s Landscape assessment	Mid-1990s Landscape Character Assessment
• Focused on landscape value • Claimed to be an objective process • Compared value of one landscape with another • Relied on quantitative measurement of landscape elements	• Recognized role for both subjectivity and objectivity • Stressed differences between inventory, classification and evaluation of landscape • Provided scope for incorporating other people's perceptions of the landscape	• Focused on landscape character • Divided process of characterization from making judgements • Stressed potential for use at different scales • Linked to Historic Landscape Characterization • Emphasized need for stakeholders to be involved

---

people's minds it is too heavily orientated towards aesthetic rather than functional considerations. Whatever the reasons, the Countryside Character Initiative has now become the umbrella term for all character-based work in England, subsuming LCA within it.

A pilot study, under the title of the *New Map of England*, was originally carried out in the south-west region of England in 1993/94 (Brooke, 1994). This developed a robust methodology for large-scale character assessment, combining map analysis of the different variables that give the landscape its character at this large-scale, with Geographical Information Systems (GIS) data handling and computer classification methods and with more traditional techniques of landscape description (New Map Consortium, 1993). While the Countryside Commission was piloting this large-scale character assessment approach, English Nature independently launched its own Natural Areas programme to provide a similar national framework for setting nature conservation objectives (see Chapter 6). The 1994 government organizational review of both the Countryside Commission and English Nature encouraged the organizations to work together to produce a single national map which would underpin both landscape and nature conservation measures in future.

The Countryside Character programme adopted this broad approach through one of its components, the National Mapping Project, although in the final analysis the computer-based classification played a less significant role in the final definition of character areas than was originally anticipated. Regional assessments, developed by the Commission's consultants in collaboration with regional staff and other regional stakeholders, eventually played the dominant part in the process of producing published national and regional maps and descriptions of Countryside Character, with the GIS maps of landscape variables informing rather than leading the process.

The concept of Countryside Character finally found expression in the Character of England map, produced by the Countryside Agency and English Nature with support from English Heritage (Countryside Commission and English Nature, 1996); it is also sometimes referred to as the 'Joint Map'. This combined English Nature's Natural Areas and the Countryside Commission's Countryside Character areas from the National Mapping Project, into a map of joint character areas for the whole of England. The map is accompanied by descriptions of the character of each of the 159 character areas, the influences determining that character and the pressures for change. All this information is described in eight regional volumes (Countryside Commission, 1998a, 1998b, 1998c; Countryside Agency, 1999a, 1999b, 1999c, 1999d, 1999e).

The national map and the descriptions together provide the top tier of the hierarchy of LCA in England. They deal only with character areas at this scale and do not define landscape character types. This framework has, however, been further strengthened by the development of a national landscape typology prepared by the Countryside Agency in collaboration with English Nature and English Heritage, with support from the then Department of the Environment, Transport and the Regions (see Swanwick and Land Use Consultants, 2002). This takes forward and develops the original approach to the National Mapping Project using a GIS database as its foundation and with greater emphasis on professional judgement rather than use of computer classification in developing the typology.

The Countryside Character areas provide the necessary broad framework for more detailed assessment at lower levels in the LCA hierarchy. Many English counties, and some unitary authorities and district councils, have prepared assessments describing more detailed variations in the character of their areas at 1:50,000 or 1:25,000 scale, and the Countryside Agency has published assessments of all the AONBs in England. There is some variation in the approach in these assessments, because they have been prepared at different stages in the evolution of landscape assessment methods, often by different consultants working to different briefs. They vary particularly in whether they identify landscape character types, landscape character areas, or both of these. A number of these assessments preceded publication of the character of England map and so do not make use of this national framework. A growing number do, however, use the national set of Countryside Character areas as a basis for more detailed assessment.

It is worth noting that in Scotland the broad approach has been different. Scottish Natural Heritage (SNH) has, over the last five years, completed a comprehensive national programme of LCA. A total of 29 separate regional studies have been carried out, in partnership with local authorities and other organizations. Together, the published assessments document the rich variety of Scotland's landscape. They cover all of the council areas in Scotland, together with some more detailed assessments, including the countryside around certain towns, and in special areas such as Loch Lomond. The individual assessments classify, map and describe the landscape, usually at a scale of 1:50,000, but with some areas at 1:25,000. Subsequently these fine-grained landscape character types have been grouped together on the basis of similarities in their key characteristics, into a hierarchy which defines landscape types at three different levels by aggregation. This hierarchy allows the character of the landscape to be examined at a number of different scales, from the broad national level, to the regional level, and sometimes down to the local level.

Scotland does not have an exact equivalent of the Countryside Character map in England. At the national level, government departments, agencies and other organizations can, however, use the highest level of aggregated information from the national programme of assessments, together with the framework of Natural Heritage Futures (as described at greater length in Chapter 11) to deal with strategic land use and development issues.

The two countries have adopted a broadly similar approach to LCA and in both cases there is now a much improved database of information about landscape character, and about the factors which shape it, at both the national and local authority levels. This has an invaluable role to play in ensuring that land use, management and planning decisions are well founded. Both countries have also relied heavily on private sector consultants to carry out much of the LCA work, although in some cases individual local authorities have completed the task. This is quite different from the work carried out in, for example, Norway, where one national institution has carried out mapping of landscape character for the whole of the country.

Because of the similarities in their approach, the two country agencies have worked together to prepare new guidance on LCA to help the many people who are now seeking to apply the approach in practice (Swanwick and Land Use Consultants, 2002). The guidance provides a wide-ranging update of the principles and practice of LCA and reflects the wide range of accumulated experience among practitioners. It stresses the new emphasis on character as the key to the approach, clarifies the roles of both characterization and of making judgements in the decision-making process, and explains the hierarchical approach. The key practical steps in the process (see summary in Box 7.2) are a core part of the guidance but it also seeks to reflect the changing context and the evolving agenda surrounding the use of LCA.

MAKING JUDGEMENTS BASED ON COUNTRYSIDE AND LANDSCAPE CHARACTER

The main value of having an LCA is to help in the process of managing change in our surroundings. All sorts of change will shape the landscapes of the future and applying this tool in an appropriate way, along with other environmental tools, can help to ensure that such changes make a positive contribution rather than causing unacceptable loss and damage, or degradation of the landscape.

For this reason, most assessments will usually move beyond the characterization stage to that of making judgements to inform particular decisions. Making judgements as part of an assessment does not concentrate only on the maintenance of existing character, although this will be one of the considerations. The real focus, however, is on ensuring that land use change or development proposals are planned, designed and executed to achieve a good

Box 7.2 Main steps in Landscape Character Assessment

Stage 1: Characterization

Step 1: Defining the scope. All Landscape Character Assessments need to have a clearly defined purpose as this will critically influence the scale and level of detail of the assessment, the resources required, those who should be involved in its preparation, and the types of judgement that are needed to inform decisions. As part of defining the scope, it is normally essential that a familiarization visit be undertaken to allow those involved in commissioning or carrying out the assessment to become familiar with the nature of the landscape.

Step 2: Desk study. This involves review of relevant background reports, other data and mapped information, and the use of this information to develop a series of map overlays to assist in the identification of areas of common character (usually draft landscape character types and/or areas).

Step 3: Field survey. Field data are collected in a rigorous way with these purposes: to test, refine and if necessary modify the draft landscape character types/areas; to inform written descriptions of their character; to identify aesthetic and perceptual qualities which are unlikely to be evident from desk information; and to identify the current condition of landscape elements.

Step 4: Classification and description. The output of the characterization process is refined and finalized by classifying the landscape into landscape character types and/or areas and mapping their extent, based on all the information collected, followed by preparation of clear descriptions of their character.

Stage 2: Making judgements

Step 5: Deciding approach to judgements. Further work is usually needed to decide on the approach that will be taken to making the judgements needed to meet the objectives of the assessment. This requires thought to be given to the overall approach, the criteria to be used and the information that will be needed to support the judgements to be made. Decisions will be needed on the role to be played by interested parties (the stakeholders in the landscape). Especially if judgements are needed about landscape value, it may sometimes be necessary to look for evidence about how others, such as artists and writers, for example, have perceived the area. Additional fieldwork may be required, especially when additional applications of the assessment emerge only after the characterization has been completed. Information from the field survey will need to be reviewed on topics such as the condition of landscape elements and features and the sensitivity of the landscape to change.

Step 6: Making judgements. The nature of the judgements and the outputs that may result from the process will vary according to the purpose of the assessment. The main approaches to making judgements within the landscape assessment process are:

* landscape strategies;
* landscape guidelines;
* attaching special status to the landscape;
* landscape capacity.

'fit' with their surroundings, and wherever possible to contribute to enhancement of the landscape, in some cases by creating a completely new character.

Making judgements based on landscape character must also take account of several other factors. Most importantly, it is vital to decide who is going to be involved in making the judgements. For practical reasons some assessments may still rely mainly on judgements made by professionals. It is, nevertheless, particularly important to find ways of involving stakeholders in this part of the process if the judgements intended are to command wide support. Many different stakeholder groups, including those who manage the land, members of local communities and other users of the land, all need to have their say about the future of the landscape.

A historical perspective can also be very important, helping to understand the way in which a landscape has evolved, over time, to arrive at its present character, and how both natural forces and human intervention have contributed to its evolution. With such understanding, decisions about future change can be placed in a historical context and ideas about, for example, restoration of some earlier historic character can be well-informed and based on a sound historical rationale.

Approaches to making judgements about landscape are generally based on consideration of character linked to understanding of the quality and value of the landscape and its sensitivity to change. These terms need to be understood if there is to be some consistency in the approaches taken:

- *Landscape character* creates the particular sense of place of different areas. Assessments are usually used to establish those characteristics of the landscape which are key to its character (key characteristics). Landscape guidelines can be drawn up to indicate the actions required to ensure that these distinctive characteristics are maintained or, if appropriate, enhanced.
- *Landscape quality* is related to the character of the landscape within a type and so does not involve comparisons of different types. It reflects the state of repair or condition of the individual landscape elements which make up a landscape, and also the integrity and intactness of the landscape and the extent to which its distinctive character is apparent in a particular area. Considerations of quality usually lead to the production of a strategy for the landscape, to guide thinking on the desirability of one of these alternative strategies: maintaining existing character; enhancing character; restoring some former landscape character; creating a new character altogether; or some combination of these.
- *Landscape value* refers to the relative value that is attached to different landscapes, often through official policy-making, and is usually the basis for recognizing, by designation or other means, certain highly valued landscapes.
- *Landscape capacity* refers to the degree to which a particular landscape character type or area is able to accommodate change without unacceptable adverse effects on its character. This is not an absolute matter and capacity is likely to vary according to the type of change that is being considered.

In practice these considerations of character, quality, value and capacity, and the different strategies, guidelines or designation/recognition developed from them, are often combined in various ways depending on the particular application for which an assessment is to be used.

Links to other Sustainability Tools

LCA is only one of a growing number of tools that can be used in planning for sustainability. Moreover, making judgements about landscape often contributes to wider environmental decision-making tools where landscape is only one of several topics to be addressed. Two examples are discussed below.

Quality of Life Capital

This is a new decision-making tool, developed by the four conservation agencies in England: the Countryside Agency, English Nature, English Heritage and the Environment Agency (CAG Consultants and Land Use Consultants, 2001). The approach offers an integrated and systematic way of recording which aspects of quality of life matter to people, and why. At the heart of the approach is concern for the environmental service or benefits that areas or features of the environment provide, rather than with the features themselves. Such services or benefits are normally grouped under the following headings:

- *health/survival*: such as absorbing greenhouse gases, reducing pollution or controlling soil erosion;
- *biodiversity*: by providing habitats for, or supporting populations of rare species;
- *appreciation of the environment*: including, for example, birdsong or habitat for urban wildlife;
- *sense of place*: aspects which give an area its particular character including perceptual qualities such as isolation, remoteness or wildness;
- *historical character*: including archaeology, built heritage and associations with well-known people or events;
- *education*: use for both formal teaching and informal study;
- *recreation*: use for sports and for informal leisure;
- *value to the local economy*: including revenue from tourism and direct or indirect employment from use or management of resources.

This approach provides an understanding of why people value the environment, allowing stakeholder values to be set alongside professional concerns. Like LCA, the approach can be applied at any scale, from strategic national or regional planning to dealing with local site-specific issues.

Quality of Life Capital applies a consistent evaluation framework to all aspects of the environment (ie to all identified benefits or services) by asking a series of questions: at what scale is the service important? How important is it at that scale (judged against integrated criteria)? Could the service be substituted or re-created if lost? Do we have enough of that service? This last question is important in that it seeks to focus attention on those aspects of the environment that are declining in quality and/or quantity.

The answers to these questions then generate the relevant management or policy aims. So, for example, for a service that is important, non-substitutable and scarce (ie there is not enough of it) policy is likely to have a strong emphasis on conservation. On the other hand, if the service is important, substitutable and scarce, the policy might emphasize enhancement and the need for any further loss to be compensated for.

In the context of LCA this complementary tool can be particularly valuable in reaching decisions where it is important to set judgements based on landscape character alongside other broader environmental concerns. This may particularly be the case where:

- it is important to understand how different aspects (eg biodiversity, cultural heritage and sense of place) of the environment interact, for example, in the development of integrated management objectives;
- it is important to give equal attention to the different aspects of the environment; where stakeholder concerns need to be taken account of alongside those of professionals;
- in conflict resolution, where conservation and enhancement of landscape character need to be seen alongside other interests such as recreation provision. This is particularly relevant to management planning.

LCA can contribute to an assessment of Quality of Life Capital. This may be by providing an important input to an integrated characterization, combining considerations of landscape, ecological and historical character (which can often provide a useful starting point for a Quality of Life Capital evaluation), or in considering the range of services and benefits encompassed by the heading 'sense of place"

Identifying indicators and monitoring change

There is now great interest in the development of environmental indicators to monitor trends and assess progress towards the achievement of sustainable development. There is potential to develop local indicators to reflect the nature of change in landscape character at the local level. Ideally, LCAs undertaken at this level should indicate one or more key indicators relevant to each landscape character type or area identified. At the national level, countryside character and quality are particularly difficult to summarize in national indicators, as there is so much variation in the nature of the landscape throughout England. Not surprisingly, therefore, practical indicators have proved somewhat elusive at this level. The Agency is, however, seeking to use information on landscape character, and the various factors which influence it, to help to identify headline indicators of countryside quality and of countryside character.

PRACTICAL APPLICATIONS OF LANDSCAPE CHARACTER ASSESSMENT

In practical terms, LCA can already be seen in action in a wide range of applications throughout the UK and its role is likely to increase in the future. It is emphatically not a tool designed to resist all types of change that may influence the landscape in the future. Rather it is an aid to decision-making – a tool designed to ensure that we understand as much as possible about what the landscape is like today, about how it came to be like this, and about how it may change in the future. Its role is to help ensure that change does not undermine whatever it is that may be characteristic or valued about a landscape. It is a powerful tool to aid the planning, design and management of our future landscapes. The main applications of LCA are briefly summarized below to illustrate the range. (Further details are provided in Julie Martin's contribution to this volume, Chapter 13).

Planning

Landscape Character Assessment is making a valuable contribution to: the formulation of planning policies at strategic (regional and structure plan) and local level; development control activities; the allocation of land for development; strategies for particular forms of development such as wind energy; and providing an input to Environmental Impact Assessment (EIA), both at the strategic level relating to plans and policies, and at the level of individual development projects.

An understanding of landscape character can be particularly helpful in informing the design and location of new elements in the landscape, and especially the design of new built development. Design guidance is increasingly used to ensure that such essential change is sympathetic to the character of the landscape and where possible enhances it. In England the Countryside Agency has developed complementary techniques, alongside LCA, for assessing the character of the built environment and its relationship to the landscape through its Design in the Countryside Programme.

These techniques include: Countryside Design Summaries (CDS), which are intended to provide a broad overview of the pattern of built development in an area and its relationship to the surrounding landscape; and Village Design Statements (VDS), which focus on managing change and demonstrating how new and locally distinctive design can add to the visual quality of rural settlements (see Countryside Commission, 1993b, 1996b; Atkins, 1998). It is becoming quite common for an LCA and a CDS to be prepared in parallel or in close association with each other, with the CDS concentrating particularly on the inter-relationship between buildings, settlements and the landscape.

Landscape Conservation, Management and Enhancement

LCA has in recent years been widely applied to landscape conservation and management. Traditionally the focus has been on the designation of special areas of valued landscape, including the identification of areas, mapping of boundaries, preparation of justifications for special treatment, and input to management plans and other management initiatives. More recently, though, there has been a growing emphasis on devising strategies and guidelines to help to conserve and enhance the diversity of character in the wider landscape.

LCA has been drawn on in shaping such strategies, so as to influence decisions about land use change. Examples are to: guide the planned increase in the extent of woodland in the landscape; inform the targeting of agri-environment schemes such as Countryside Stewardship; inform strategies for regeneration, including Community Forests and their equivalents, and land reclamation and restoration strategies; and contribute to wider environmental initiatives, such as Local Agenda 21, Biodiversity Action Plans and State of the Countryside Reports.

An emphasis on assessing the current character of the landscape is not a barrier to the creation of new landscapes. Where an LCA indicates that a strategy of enhancement is appropriate for a particular landscape type or area, this signals scope for significant change to the landscape, often by creation of a new landscape to suit a new function. In many respects, landscapes with degraded features and elements offer the greatest scope for positive change to improve the local environment and people's quality of life. Initiatives such as the National Forest and the Community Forests in England, and schemes to recreate new wetland and fenland areas, provide good examples of the type of large-scale landscape creation which can be informed by LCA.

CURRENT AND FUTURE ISSUES

The assessment of countryside and landscape character is now firmly established as an important practical tool for planning and managing countryside and other environmental resources at all scales. Interest in its use and development is growing – for example, the Countryside Agency's Countryside Character Network – established to forge links between the many different parties with an interest in this subject – has grown rapidly and at the time of writing has a membership approaching 500.

Several emerging issues will need to be tackled in the future. Expansion in the scope of this form of assessment, including the addition of techniques for involving stakeholders and the need to embrace work on the historic dimension of landscape character, adds to the complexity and cost of such work, potentially making it more difficult to persuade local authorities to give it priority. At the same time there is as yet no conclusive evidence about the benefits of using this technique. Although it is in wide use no one has so far researched the value it has added in terms of the quality of decisions made about the landscape, the nature of landscape change or the character of new development. The value of character assessment in informing decisions in highly contested areas such as the fringes of towns and cities is particularly worthy of further examination, as this is where the most difficult problems arise in finding land suitable for development and in maintaining environmental quality. There is therefore a need to assess the value of LCA in the decision-making arena, leading – it is hoped – to a strong body of well-informed support for its application. Above all, it requires the raising of awareness and understanding among policy-makers and senior managers, in both the public and private sectors, to complement the enthusiasm of practitioners.

REFERENCES

Atkins, W S (1998) Design in the Countryside: Monitoring Countryside Design Summaries and Village Design Statements, unpublished report to the Countryside Commission, Cheltenham

Benson, J F and Roe, M H (eds) (2000) *Landscape and Sustainability*, Spon Books, London

Brooke, D (1994) 'A Countryside Character Programme', *Landscape Research*, vol 19(3), pp128–132

CAG Consultants and Land Use Consultants (2001) *Quality of Life Capital: Managing Environmental, Social and Economic Benefits – Overview Report*, Countryside Agency, English Heritage, English Nature, Environment Agency, Cheltenham

Countryside Agency (1999a) *Countryside Character Volume 4: East Midlands*, Countryside Agency, Cheltenham

Countryside Agency (1999b) *Countryside Character Volume 5: West Midlands*, Countryside Agency, Cheltenham

Countryside Agency (1999c) *Countryside Character Volume 6: East of England*, Countryside Agency, Cheltenham

Countryside Agency (1999d) *Countryside Character Volume 7: South East and London*, Countryside Agency, Cheltenham

Countryside Agency (1999e) *Countryside Character Volume 8: South West*, Countryside Agency, Cheltenham

Countryside Agency (2001) 'Development of a National Landscape Typology for England', in *Countryside Character Newsletter*, No 6

Countryside Commission (1985) Public Inquiry on the proposed North Pennines Area of Outstanding Natural Beauty, unpublished Proof of Evidence, Cheltenham

Countryside Commission (1987) *Landscape Assessment – a Countryside Commission Approach*, Countryside Commission, Cheltenham

Countryside Commission (1991) *Assessment and Conservation of Landscape Character. The Warwickshire Landscapes Project Approach*, Countryside Commission, Cheltenham

Countryside Commission (1993a) *Landscape Assessment Guidance*, Countryside Commission, Cheltenham

Countryside Commission (1993b) *Design in the Countryside*, Countryside Commission, Cheltenham

Countryside Commission (1996a) *The Countryside Character Programme: Briefing Pack*, Countryside Commission, Cheltenham

Countryside Commission (1996b) *Village Design: Making Local Character Count in New Development (Parts 1 and 2)*, Countryside Commission, Cheltenham

Countryside Commission (1998a) *Countryside Character Volume 1: North East*, Countryside Commission, Cheltenham

Countryside Commission (1998b) *Countryside Character Volume 2: North West*, Countryside Commission, Cheltenham

Countryside Commission (1998c) *Countryside Character Volume 3: Yorkshire and the Humber*, Countryside Commission, Cheltenham

Countryside Commission and English Nature (1996) *The Character of England – Landscape, Wildlife and Natural Features*, Countryside Commission, Cheltenham

Countryside Commission for Scotland (1991) *Landscape Assessment: Principles and Practice*, Countryside Commission for Scotland, Battleby

Diacono, M (1997) Landscape Character Assessment – Present Practice and the Future, unpublished Masters' thesis, Oxford Brookes University, Oxford

Fairclough, G (1999) *Historic Landscape Characterisation – "The State of the Art"*, English Heritage, London

Land Use Consultants (1986) Mid Wales Uplands: Landscape Assessment, unpublished report to the Countryside Commission, Cheltenham

Landscape Research Group (1988) *A Review of Recent Practice and Research in Landscape Assessment*, CCD 25 Countryside Commission, Cheltenham

Mabey, R (1985) *In a Green Shade*, Unwin Paperbacks, London

Muir, R (1999) *Approaches to Landscape*, Macmillan Press Ltd, London

New Map Consortium (1993) *New Map of England Pilot Project Technical Report 1: Regional Landscape Classification*, Land Use Consultants, London

Robinson, D G, Laurie, I C, Wager, J F and Traill, A L (1976), *Landscape Evaluation*, University of Manchester, Manchester

Swanwick, C and Land Use Consultants (2002) *Landscape Character Assessment Guidance*, Countryside Agency, Cheltenham, and Scottish Natural Heritage, Edinburgh

Chapter 8

Policies and Priorities for Ireland's Landscapes

Michael Starrett

The Irish landscape has been the focus of attention for generations. Whether through publications, such as *Irish Geographical Studies* (Stephens and Glasscock, 1970) or the *Atlas of the Irish Rural Landscape* (Aalen et al, 1997), or through the myth and legend of storytellers, our landscape holds a significant place in the culture of Ireland. The sense of place in Ireland is part of that culture, epitomized in the retention of townland and place names, many of which, in the native Irish language, reflect the relationships between people and their environment. The influence of humankind on Ireland's wild and savage natural beauty is pervasive. Ireland enjoys no wilderness, and even its highest peaks and its deepest bogs can yield marvellous examples of the influence which people have had upon the shaping of that landscape. Its development and future now face unprecedented change as Ireland's rapid economic growth places stresses and strains on the systems which are there to protect its landscape. Protecting the landscape in this time of change demands partnership and coordination between all those agencies and activities which have a potential to impact on it. Furthermore, people must be involved in the decisions which affect their landscape. This is the approach which the Irish Heritage Council has promoted since its establishment in 1995.

THE HERITAGE COUNCIL

The Irish Heritage Council is a semi-state body, which was established by the Irish government under the Heritage Act 1995, to propose policies and priorities for the national heritage. What is very unusual about this organization, when compared with similar advisory bodies in the UK and the Republic of Ireland – indeed throughout Europe – derives from the definition of 'national heritage' which is used in the Heritage Act 1995, Section 6(i). This embraces most aspects of Ireland's natural and cultural heritage, including its landscape. There is no separation of responsibility for the built and natural heritage, as there is, for example, between the duties of Scottish Natural Heritage (SNH) and of Historic Scotland (although Chapter 11 shows how SNH is working to overcome this separation), or between those of English Heritage and English Nature. Only the Heritage Lottery Fund in the UK has a comparably broad remit.

Shortly after its establishment in 1995, the Heritage Council grasped the opportunity presented by this inclusive definition to develop integrated policies for the future management and development of the national heritage. The Council sought to break down the compartments into which the heritage had previously tended to be viewed. In all its work, it has emphasized the value and significance of the whole heritage to the everyday life of the Irish people.

While the Heritage Council is essentially an advisory rather than an executive body, it can promote policies, priorities, strategies and structures that will benefit the national heritage. The Council cannot compel others, nor forbid them, to undertake a specific course of action. While it is enjoined by the Heritage Act, Section 6(3)C, to 'promote the coordination of all activities relating to the functions of Council', it has to do this by cooperating with, and seeking to influence its many partners, including government departments and agencies, and local planning authorities.

The Council recognized from very early on the special place of landscape in its work. Landscape is both a physical embodiment of many heritage values and a context within which these values can be conserved in years to come (Phillips, 1999). Given the general lack of awareness of landscape issues in Ireland (see below), and the low priority accorded to it in legislation (Landscape Alliance Ireland, 1998), the size of the task facing the Council cannot be overstated. In its own evaluation of environmental designations, the Council had already highlighted the scale of the problem facing Ireland (Hickie, 1997). However, there have been encouraging developments elsewhere in Europe which offered the potential to raise the profile of landscape issues in Ireland itself. Indeed landscape is increasingly being seen as an important issue at a European level, and not only through the designation of protected landscapes (IUCN, 1994). The emerging European Landscape Convention, signed in Florence in October 2000 (see also Chapter 4), together with the Council's membership of the EUROPARC Federation, encouraged the Council to develop landscape policies for Ireland as well. At the same time, the Irish government was moving away from a centralized approach to planning and related matters, towards a system that allowed more responsibility and autonomy at regional and local levels. This process was reflected in the Planning and Development Act 2000, which gave new responsibilities to local authorities, and responded to the requirements associated with funding under programmes of the European Union. As a result, the Council identified local authorities as key partners in its work on the Irish landscape.

THE FIRST STEPS

Since its establishment, and the publication of its first strategic plan in 1997, the Heritage Council has exercised its functions under the Heritage Act 1995 so as to raise awareness of the value of the heritage in all aspects of everyday life. Because it recognized that the information needed to take decisions about the national heritage was often lacking, the Council's strategic plan for 1997–2000 set as an objective 'to provide information which will improve the quality and effectiveness of heritage input into Government policy at the national level' (Heritage Council, 1997).

The Council has had some success in the pursuit of this objective. For example, it has had an influence on national policy initiatives, such as Ireland's *Sustainable Development Strategy* (Department of Environment, 1997), the *National Biodiversity Plan* (Department of Arts, Heritage, Gaeltacht and the Islands (DAHGI), 2002b), and the *National Heritage Plan* (DAHGI, 2002a), as well as helping to bring about some changes in legislation. Certainly the Council can claim to have influenced changes in the Planning and Development Act 2000, which now provides the legislative basis upon which it can promote its own policy advice on landscape. For example, sections 10 (2e) and 204 of the Act make mention of landscape character and landscape conservation, and draft regulations require local authorities to take landscape into account in their planning.

The Emergence of Heritage and Landscape Policy in Ireland

Ireland's *National Development Plan 2000–2006* (Government of Ireland, 1999) was framed after an extensive consultation process to reflect the broad consensus on future national development needs. The plan lays the foundation for Ireland's continued economic and social development, and sets out a coherent development strategy supported by a quantified commitment to invest £40.588 billion over the plan period. The funding will come from public, EU and private sources. It will be mainly directed towards infrastructure development, education and training, the productive sector and the promotion of social inclusion, but will also support a framework for a more balanced regional development.

While the Council was not itself involved in the preparation of the *National Development Plan*, it commented upon it. It recognized the need for substantial infrastructure improvements throughout Ireland, but argued that much of the information which decision-makers required in order to plan for these was not available (Heritage Council, 2000a). This could lead to lengthy delays in the planning process, and thus the targets set in the plan might not be realized. The Council believed that an integrated and effective landscape policy could help achieve the objectives of the *National Development Plan* by providing a context within which to plan infrastructure schemes. Moreover, the incorporation of heritage concerns, especially landscape, into development planning would encourage awareness of the value of the national heritage and so help improve the quality of life for all. The Council therefore advocated its emerging landscape approach and argued that planning policies should be made heritage-proof through heritage appraisal of development plans.

Heritage appraisal is a methodology developed by the Heritage Council to raise awareness of the significance of the national heritage within the development planning process. County Development Plans are the foundation for planning and development responsibilities as exercised by Ireland's local authorities, and the policies they contain provide the strategic framework within which development decisions are taken. Heritage appraisal is targeted at assessing the policies contained within local authority development plans, and at the evaluation of specific developments. The methodology, which was developed in partnership with local authorities and compliments the more specific work on landscape expanded on in this chapter, was presented to the Minister for Arts, Heritage, Gaeltacht and the Islands (AHGI) in July 2000. It has also helped to open a dialogue between the Heritage Council and the National Roads Authority, which is important in view of the growing opposition from local communities around Ireland to proposals for new motorways.

The Heritage Council has taken a holistic and integrated approach to landscape. It believes that landscape policy should embrace all landscape elements, and recognize their significance. This calls for a multidisciplinary approach to the way in which Ireland manages and develops landscapes. Recent work in the forestry sector undertaken through the Forestry Inventory Planning System (FIPS), initiated by the Department of Marine and Natural Resources, is one positive illustration of such an approach. Similarly, the recent consultative draft guidelines on landscape characterization, published by the Department of the Environment and Local Government (DOE&LG), aimed specifically at local authorities, will assist in the ongoing debate and the raising of awareness (see also Chapter 9).

The Vision for Landscape

In order to inform the development of its landscape policy, and consolidate international experience, the Heritage Council organized an international conference on landscape at Tullamore in 1999. This meeting heard a challenge from Professor Michael Ryan:

> *I wonder is it possible to write a simple short statement, a vision of what we want for the Irish landscape? If we can write that and accommodate within it all the social, economic, developmental, protective and other needs everything else will flow from that vision* (Heritage Council, 1999).

Agreement on such a vision could be the starting point. It should then be possible to develop a framework for actions that would help achieve the vision, including the negotiations which are required with different interests. Thus the vision becomes the goal to which everyone's efforts are directed. Lessons drawn from best practice from abroad, the planning of new initiatives and the adjustment of on-going practical work in a variety of sectors can all be harnessed to the achievement of that vision.

The challenge to formulate a vision for Ireland's landscape was accepted by the Heritage Council, which referred this task to a working group on policy development for Ireland's landscape. The establishment of such a group was a critically important step. While, in general, working groups tend to be small and very task oriented, on this occasion the size of the group was less important than ensuring that all those who wished to participate had the opportunity to do so.[1]

On being asked for their *vision* for the Irish landscape, the members of the group identified the relationship between society and environment as a central theme. The link between cultural and natural elements of the landscape heritage was self-evident. The underlying implication was that people recognized that they had an influence over the 'shape' of the landscape and wished to maintain their power to exercise that influence in future. Landscape was seen as dynamic and changing over time. The group believed that people wished to retain a dynamic landscape and that there was no call for its fossilization.

Validation of the Vision

Any work on landscape in Ireland has to recognize that there is at present a low level of public awareness. For example, research undertaken for the Council showed that less than 3 per cent of the population considered landscape as part of their national heritage (Landsdowne Market Research, 2000). It was, none the less, felt necessary to validate the group's views about landscape through further market research. (Landsdowne Market Research, 2000). As a result, the group felt that its initial views had been confirmed. It then put forward this vision for the Irish landscape: 'The Irish landscape will be a dynamic landscape, one that accommodates the physical and spiritual needs of society with the needs of nature in a harmonious manner, and as a result brings benefits to both in kind'.

The research confirmed the view that people accept a dynamic landscape, which is both changing and developing. There was also broad agreement amongst respondents on which changes were viewed as beneficial and which were not. The results demonstrated the need for an integrated approach to rural and urban landscapes. They showed that perceptions of landscape in rural areas focused on mountains and rivers, whilst those of city dwellers focused more on parks and green space. A landscape policy needs to address the aspirations of both constituencies, and should allow them to influence the quality of landscape change. For example, design, location and species composition are critical to the impact of new woodland in the Irish landscape; design, location and building materials are equally critical in determining the impact of new housing.

THE PILOT LANDSCAPE CHARACTERIZATION – COUNTY CLARE

A pilot project was initially proposed at the Tullamore conference. It was designed to test and resolve a number of the issues surrounding the development of policy for Ireland's landscapes, including the availability, accessibility and quality of baseline information. The pilot was seen as a way to inform the Heritage Council on the development of an approach towards landscape policy across sectoral divides. County Clare was selected for two main reasons:

- the national and international recognition afforded to its cultural and natural landscapes. This is apparent in the range of protective designations in the area (both the European designations of SACs (Special Areas for

Conservation) and SPAs (Special Protection Areas), and the national designation of National Park and its archaeological landscapes) and in the wide range of academic work which has been carried out in Clare over many years;

- much information is available for the area, since work had already been carried out by forestry interests on the FIPS, by Duchas the Heritage Service (the executive arm of the Department of AHGI) and by the Department of Agriculture.

In developing the pilot exercise on landscape character, the Council drew on the work on landscape characterization undertaken since the early 1980s elsewhere in Europe, and in particular in the UK. This work has been fraught with problems in its initial conceptual stages and many lessons have been learnt by the agencies involved in promoting what is now clearly emerging as a most useful tool (see Chapters 7 and 14). The Council looked particularly to experience in Scotland and the emphasis there on involving stakeholders in the process (see Chapter 11).

From the Heritage Council's perspective, the process of characterization was attractive because it is essentially value-free and judgement-free. It also provided the opportunity to involve all stakeholders in the process, since the approach recognizes that all agencies and individuals can identify with the physical attributes of landscape. What is more difficult is to impart the importance and significance which landscape has to our overall quality of life. Because characterization work requires access to a wide range of information and the cooperation of the various bodies that control this, the process has the potential to bring together many different agencies and organizations. Some of these would not normally consider that they had a role in landscape policy development, or could provide information that contributed to the process of landscape characterization. Thus, becoming involved in a landscape characterization project can be a learning experience for them. This applies to several of the following government departments that were involved in the pilot project in County Clare:

- Department of AHGI (which provided information on habitats and monuments);
- Department of Agriculture, Food and Rural Development (which provided information needed for monitoring agri-environment packages);
- Department of Marine and Natural Resources (which provided information from the FIPS);
- Ordnance Survey of Ireland;
- Geological Survey of Ireland;
- Teagasc (which provided information on soils).

For some of the above involvement in the process was effectively the first time that they were consciously involved in landscape work. The Department of AHGI, for example, had previously confined its involvement to protected landscapes, such as national parks, and the Department of Agriculture was concerned primarily with the impact of agriculture and the agri-environment packages on a farm by farm basis. However, the moves towards sustainable forest management and the anticipated 30 per cent increase in forestry cover envisaged over a 20-year period in the national forestry plan (Department of Agriculture, Food and Forestry, 1996) had encouraged the forestry sector to look at landscape on a much broader front, work which proved very beneficial in the Clare pilot.

Any agency that has sought to coordinate the activities of various government departments will be familiar with the difficulties faced by the Council in getting the departmental representatives to focus on issues which they considered to be outside their remit. The challenge faced by the Council was compounded by the initial absence of the DOE&LG and the need to establish special arrangements to accommodate that department's involvement in the process. Some departments initially took the view that they had no responsibility for landscape and so were unable to participate. However, following a series of meetings with individuals in each area of activity, the group came together and worked well, sharing an understanding of how the activities of each impacted on the landscape. Once the agreed vision had been arrived at, it became easier to obtain inter-departmental involvement.

Technical Challenges faced in the Pilot Project

The final report on the pilot project demonstrates how a number of technical challenges might be overcome, it also afforded Ireland the opportunity to develop the landscape characterization process beyond what has been achieved elsewhere (ERM and ERA-Maptec, 2000). The opportunity arises primarily from the development of the application of Geographical Information Systems (GIS), its potential to achieve initial landscape characterization profiles, and the links being forged between the evaluation and understanding of cultural and natural landscapes.

When provided with high quality and consistent data layers, GIS can replicate more traditional but time-consuming and expert-dependent methodologies. The landscape characterization produced by the use of GIS was considerably strengthened through the integration of data which would traditionally have been thought of as part of the cultural heritage (eg data on archaeological landscapes) with data sets relating to the natural heritage, such as landform, geology and habitats. The implications of these findings, and the benefits that can be derived from them for local authorities, which now have added responsibility in this area, are considerable. They are explored further below.

A number of problems have been reported in the development of landscape characterization in England and in Scotland (see Chapters 7 and 11). For example:

- the use of characterization by sectoral interests (especially if this occurs early on in the process) tends to obscure the integrated nature of the landscape and hence the impact of one use on another;

- local planning authorities have tried to use landscape characterization as a planning tool without recognizing the need for a standardized approach to ensure quality control and consistent decision-making;
- too general a national framework for characterization will fail to pick up subtle but significant differences, introducing difficulties at the local level;
- there has been a tendency to rely too heavily on physical and natural landforms without fully incorporating the significant contribution of cultural heritage.

Since such difficulties have undermined the credibility of characterization in the eyes of potential user groups, and reduced its utility in the decision-making process, the approach adopted in the pilot study sought to overcome these.

Methodology

The pilot represented a significant advance in the use of GIS in the initial characterization work. The success of the work depended on the availability of certain key data, such as: topography, surface geology and soils, land cover, habitat types, historic landscape character types, townlands, settlements, communications and field patterns. Much of the data had to be converted to digital format, and this required close liaison between the landscape architect and the information technologist. The pilot demonstrated that Ireland had information of an appropriate quality to allow initial characterization to be made through an agreed and standardized methodology, although, of course, agreement is needed on the sharing of information and a willingness to make it available to all those who will benefit from it.

Landscape characterization studies typically begin with a desk review of key data, documents and maps. This is supplemented by a familiarization visit to the study area which helps to give a 'feel' for the scale of the landscape and an understanding of the broad patterns of landform, land cover and settlement. Mapped data are usually reviewed by a process of overlay mapping; the resultant preliminary landscape character types provide the basis for detailed analysis and field verification.

An aim of the pilot study was to compare the usual manual overlay technique with a computer-based approach. The overlay process can then be tested by rigorous analysis, laying the foundations for a robust, reputable landscape characterization as a basis for landscape policy.

The GIS experts worked closely with landscape architects to develop a computer model which mimics the thought processes involved in overlay mapping and the development of preliminary landscape character types. This section describes the manual overlay process and then the GIS analysis. These parallel processes resulted in the production of two separate maps showing preliminary landscape character types in County Clare. The two maps were then compared and the overall method reviewed.

Manual analysis
Each of the data sets was printed in colour onto film at a scale of 1:50,000 (the chosen scale of analysis). They were then overlaid on the Ordnance Survey base

and the dominant landscape patterns marked up on a separate layer of tracing paper. The data sets were compared and overlaid repeatedly until an overall pattern of landscape character types gradually emerged.

The data sets have differing levels of complexity. For instance, the geology map for Clare is relatively simple, but the historic landscape character types form a more complex pattern. It proved easier to start with the simpler data sets and those describing physical aspects of the landscape (geology, elevation, slope, etc) and then continue to the cultural aspects (historic landscape character types, road/settlement patterns, etc). As the analysis progressed, the data sets could be overlaid in various combinations to test and amend the emerging pattern.

With the exception of the aspect data (which was found to be too complex to assist in the analysis), all the data sets contributed to the characterization:

- *geology* – this provides an overall understanding of the underlying rock structure, and is the key influence on rocks, soils and patterns of land use. It would have been useful to have had data for drift as well as solid geology, as the soils data set was not very helpful in understanding landscape character;
- *elevation* – this is useful in defining upland and lowland areas, since contours on OS maps are not very legible;
- *slope* – an excellent indication of landform, which defines alignment and form, including ridges, escarpments and lowland landforms, such as drumlins;
- *land cover* – the Europe-wide habitats recording system, CORINE, defines a relatively complex mosaic of land uses; the combinations and proportions of land cover types vary in different parts of the county;
- *soils* – this provides broader patterns than the land cover map and can assist in its interpretation, particularly in defining areas of gleyed soils and peat (lowland and upland);
- *historic landscape character types* – this provides a detailed analysis of the historic evolution of land cover patterns. The analysis of field boundaries (of enclosed land) is especially useful and helped to define some of the landscape character types;
- *the OS base* contributed particularly to analysis of patterns of roads and settlements; the townland boundaries data set had been used in compiling the historic landscape character types and was not overlaid separately;
- *the Land Parcel Information System (LPIS) data*, showing present-day field patterns, were not available when the manual analysis was undertaken. However, this additional data might provide a comprehensive analysis of field boundary patterns and a substitute for the historic landscape character types data set which is relatively costly to prepare. Further analysis is required to test the potential application of this data set within the landscape characterization process.

The principal constraint in the manual analysis was the difficulty in handling the large maps and in achieving consistent and accurate justification of the different layers. It would therefore be preferable to undertake the preliminary overlay analysis on the computer, using a standard GIS programe. Background research, particularly into local geology, soils and the evolution of landscape patterns, is an essential prerequisite for this type of analysis.

The preliminary landscape character types map which emerges from the manual analysis is presented as Figure 8.1 (see Plate section).

GIS analysis

The aim of the GIS analysis was to ascertain the degree to which GIS can automate the landscape characterization process. Two main approaches were adopted during this study. The first was a purely statistical approach, that analysed mathematical relationships between the various data sets. The second approach involved the use of the expert knowledge gained during the preceding phase of manual landscape characterization. A technical explanation of the statistical approach adopted is given in Box 8.1.

BOX 8.1 TECHNICAL EXPLANATION OF THE
STATISTICAL APPROACH

The GIS analysis and classification were performed using the ESRI ArcView and ERDAS IMAGINE 8.4 products. ArcView was used mainly for data storage, preparation of univariate products and map printing. Multivariate analysis and classification were performed with IMAGINE. Results were printed at 1:50,000 scale (on four A0 sheets) and at 1:100,000 on a single A0 sheet.

Univariate analysis was mainly used to derive products to assist in the manual landscape characterization, or as input to the multivariate/expert classifications. ArcView was used to derive the following univariate data sets:

* Elevation
* Slope
* Aspect
* Land cover
* Soils
* Solid geology
* Record of Monuments and Places Register – density

All these data sets were converted to raster grids for the multivariate and expert classifications.

There are many techniques that can be used for *multivariate analysis*. Hierarchical methods, such as Twinspan, have been used previously in some GIS landscape classifications. Twinspan was designed to analyse data sets which have a natural hierarchical classification, such as botanical data, where one species is a sub-set of a genera. Some landscape classes may be hierarchical, but are more likely to be distinct units with little or no hierarchical relationship. In these cases, Twinspan may not be the most appropriate tool.

Another method of multivariate analysis is cluster analysis, which attempts to define mathematical relationships between the different variables. In applying cluster methods to the data sets, both at a 500m pixel level and at a townland level, expectations for these methods were low, mainly because clustering does not account for the spatial relationships within the data.

Expert classification

Traditional methods of classification, such as those outlined in the section above, cannot easily deal with data of different kinds. They also have difficulty in dealing with spatial contexts (for example, a certain landscape class may be defined as being close to rivers). Expert systems attempt to overcome the shortcomings of traditional statistical classifiers. A technical explanation of the approach adopted is given in Box 8.2.

The modelling process using the expert classifier was undertaken in three stages:

- The first level classification was based on physical aspects of the landscape, using such data sets as geology, elevation and land cover. The framework of the model was constructed according to the preliminary landscape character types as described above.
- The second stage classification made use of extra data sets, including road density, enclosure patterns (from the historic landscape character types data set) and settlements. This enabled some of the classes to be more accurately defined.
- The third stage classification was based on a statistical analysis of the landscape character types, against each of the data sets.

Thus the pilot project sought to develop a computer model which would mimic the conventional approach of an experts' assessment in overlay mapping and the preparing of preliminary landscape types. These parallel processes resulted in the production of two separate maps showing preliminary landscape types in County Clare. The main conclusion that can be drawn is that combining manual and GIS analysis techniques results in a successful preliminary landscape characterization which is significantly more robust than traditional techniques would allow, and that the methodology does indeed provide an opportunity to develop a new approach to landscape characterization. However, the GIS expert classification does not represent a fully automated process since the system relies on a preliminary traditional overlay analysis to provide the initial descriptions of landscape character types from which the expert classification is derived. Some of the other lessons learnt are these:

- The results of a manual analysis can be cross-checked against those of a GIS model.
- Each system relies on the other and both have an important role to play. Analysis of both physical (geology, landform, soils, land cover) and cultural (field patterns, roads, settlement) data sets is required to develop a meaningful preliminary landscape characterization.
- There is insufficient differentiation between landscape character types if only physical data are used.
- The agricultural LPIS data may provide a valuable addition to the system within Ireland, and may be a complement to the historic landscape character types data set.

Box 8.2 Technical explanation of the expert analysis

The new version of ERDAS IMAGINE has a tool for building (and executing) geographic expert systems for image classification, post classification refinement, and advanced GIS modelling. ERDAS IMAGINE is one of the first commercial packages for creating expert systems using geographic data to solve geographic problems.

The IMAGINE Expert Classifier interface captures the intellectual process that an expert in a particular field of expertise would normally use to sift through geographic data, process and analyse it, and compare and combine results, in order to infer some form of information about a geographic location. The captured process can then be repeated by someone else. Because the IMAGINE Expert Classifier has recorded the expert's process of inference, and can repeat it with new data, reliable and repeatable analysis results are always produced. The software consists of two parts – the Knowledge Engineer and the Knowledge Classifier.

The Knowledge Engineer provides a graphical user interface for the 'expert' to build a knowledge base. The knowledge base is represented as a tree diagram consisting of final and intermediate class definitions (hypotheses), rules (conditional statements concerning variables), and variables (raster, vector or scalar). Hypotheses are evaluated by the use of rules: if one or more rules are true, then that hypothesis may be true at that particular location. A rule is evaluated based on input variables to determine if it is true. For instance, a rule could be that slopes must be gentle (less than five degrees). To evaluate this, a variable is required determining the slope at every location. This could be in the form of an existing image specifying slope angles, it could come from a spatial model calculating slope on the fly from an input DTM, or it could even be an external programme. Variables can also be defined from vectors and scalars. If the variables' value indicates that the rule is correct, this (combined with other correct rules) indicates that the hypothesis (class allocation) is true.

The Knowledge Classifier may then be applied by a less experienced user to the previously created expert knowledge base in order to perform a classification. This programme is designed with a simple, user-friendly wizard interface.

This knowledge-based approach can be applied to new data or locations without re-training, with reliable, repeatable justifiable results. The 'pathway cursor' in the Knowledge Engineer allows the user to point to any pixel in the classified image and see the exact path that was taken in the decision tree to arrive at the classification. The end user does not need to be an expert in either the application field, or the operation of individual software tools. All he or she needs to do is to provide their own data as inputs to the Knowledge Classifier.

Further work is required to refine the GIS expert classifier approach. In particular there is a need to include modelling of landform and of the frequency of land cover types. None the less, the pilot study supports the establishment of a basic, consistent, agreed landscape characterization for Ireland as a whole. Such a National Landscape Characterization would assemble the same data sources and GIS layers as those used for County Clare. Although significant further analysis is required to ensure a consistent comprehensive approach across the country, there is now the potential to develop a national landscape database as a the foundation for a national typology of Irish landscapes.

THE NEXT STEPS

There are several elements of follow-up to the Clare pilot. For example, the current pilot will be extended within the pilot area. This work would aim to produce a full County-based LCA (CLCA) in association with partner agencies, such as the County Council, Shannon Development, the forestry sector of the Department of Marine and Natural Resources, the DOE&LG, the Department of Agriculture and the DAHGI.

Following the Clare pilot, the Heritage Council has started to work closely with local authorities elsewhere in Ireland on the application of characterization to help assess major development proposals which would affect historic designed landscapes (such as Lough Rynn in County Leitrim and Durrow Abbey in County Offaly). The characterization process is also being used in examining the impact of infra-structural improvements, such as the New Ross by-pass. A further opportunity to apply the work done on landscape characterization arises with the requirement, under the Planning and Development Act 2000, that local authorities should produce CLCAs as advised in the final version of the DOE&LG guidelines referred to above.

It is desirable that this follow-up work should include a strong element of stakeholder participation. In the pilot, the Heritage Council work took into account the views expressed at a stakeholders' meeting, which helped to shape the policy document on the Heritage Awareness in Ireland that was presented to the Minister in October 2000 (Heritage Council). What was most striking about this exercise was the pleasant surprise expressed by many local people that they should be involved by a national agency in such a process at the outset. This reaction reflects the past tendency in Ireland to run public agencies in a very centralized manner. While the Council was not able to maintain direct contact with all those involved in the partnership group at a local level in County Clare, it has done so through the local authority and its Heritage Officer in the County. In fact, the Heritage Council currently funds Heritage Officers in 18 local authorities and sees these post holders as essential in communicating the effectiveness of its policy work at the local level back up to the national level.

Developing the Heritage Council Policy

As the major output of its work on landscape in recent years, in late 2000 the Heritage Council submitted its pre-publication proposals for integrated policies for Ireland's landscape to the Minister for Arts, Heritage, Gaeltacht and the Islands. This document articulated the rationale behind the Council's thinking on landscape and contained recommendations which support the production of a standardized and consistent national landscape policy, which in turn will support the development of County landscape characterization. In preparing its recommendations, the Council wished to allay fears of a top-down approach, and to avoid encumbering local authorities and others with burdensome work; at the same time it was determined to raise the profile of landscape issues in shaping development policy in Ireland.

BOX 8.3 SUMMARY OF RECOMMENDATIONS ON LANDSCAPE POLICY BY THE HERITAGE COUNCIL

That government should recognize the central and positive role integrated landscape policies can play in achieving national and international objectives by:

1. Acknowledging the value of a consistent and agreed methodology for landscape characterization, identifying an adequately resourced central agency to complete a programme of national landscape characterization, and providing funding for this work.
2. That the potential benefits of sharing and making accessible information are realized through the further development of the computerized system applied in the Clare pilot project, through its continued application in County Clare, and its application to the production of national landscape characterization.
3. That government recognizes the importance of linking the cultural and natural aspects of landscape by applying the lessons from the Clare Pilot Project at a national scale, by making accessible data held by government departments and by funding the completion of a National Landscape Charaterization.
4. That all key partners cooperate in the completion of the Clare Pilot Project by implementing a complete County landscape characterization and by local initiatives.
5. That emphasis is placed on the significance of our landscape at all levels of the decision-making process by ensuring: enforcement of the new planning Act; endorsement of the concept of heritage quality appraisal as part of the development plan process; and publication of national landscape guidelines.
6. That a review of legislation as it relates to the designation of national parks and other protected landscapes is completed as a matter of urgency.
7. That the significance of Heritage Council policy papers on land uses, such as agriculture and forestry are fully recognized through: their application in EU-funded packages, such as the rural development programme; and the application of the broad principles they contain at a national scale.
8. That government uses these recommendations to help achieve the objectives in the national development plan and uses the recommendations to strengthen links between urban and rural landscapes in the National Spatial Strategy.
9. That the potential to complement the work of landscape characterization in the North of Ireland is realized.

The nine recommendations in the report are summarized in Box 8.3. The landscape policy now proposed by the Heritage Council, and the recommendations which flow from that policy, are designed to allow those with responsibility for the management and development of landscape (and whose use of land impacts on it) to assess the policies they are implementing against specific indicators. They also allow a fully integrated approach to the landscape to be adopted by the government. If acted upon, these recommendations will help to ensure that the quality of life becomes an integral part of the implementation of the National Development Plan. The Heritage Council now awaits a full response from government on the detail of the proposals contained in its policy document.

CONCLUSIONS

In the absence of the consistent and standardized approach to landscape that is sought by the Council, there is a danger that planning authorities and development agencies will act in an ad hoc and ill-informed way. In the current climate of rapid economic development, this would represent a real threat to the well-being of the Irish landscape. The work of the Heritage Council therefore seeks to place the national heritage (including landscape) much higher on all agendas. The Council has sought to raise awareness of the significance of that heritage to the quality of life of all those who live in, work in and visit the Irish landscape. It believes that, through the integrated approach to landscape characterization developed for Clare and now advocated for the whole of Ireland, all those with an interest in the future of Ireland's landscape heritage can have a say in how it will evolve.

Indeed the greatest danger to the future well-being of the Irish landscape is that the focus and vision are too narrow. The landscape is where people live and represents many of the aspects of Ireland that people take a pride in sharing with others. While it allows the Irish people to enjoy a quality of life which is the envy of many, its future cannot be taken for granted. The well-being of the landscape is entrusted to the Irish people and it is they who must value it if its qualities are to survive. To rely on one group or another to look after it will inevitably fail. The responsibility is that of society as a whole.

NOTES

1   The members of the Landscape Policy Working Group (April 1999–2000) were Freda Rountree, Former Chairperson The Heritage Council; Niall Sweeney, Offaly County Council; Vincent Hussey, Offaly County Council; Terry O'Regan, Landscape Alliance Ireland; Fred Aalen, Trinity College; Ross Millar, DOE NI; Gabriel Cooney, University College Dublin; Alan Craig, National Parks and Wildlife Service; Diarmuid McAree, Forest Service; Finnain MacNaeidhe, Teagasc; Joe Hamill, Department of Arts, Heritage, Gaeltacht and the Islands; Brendan McGrath, Clare County Council; Representatives from the Department of Agriculture, Food and Rural Development.

REFERENCES

Aalen, F H A, Whelan, K and Stout, M (eds) (1997) *Atlas of the Irish Rural Landscape*, Cork University Press, Cork

David Tyldesley & Associates (in association with Donegal County Council) (2000) *Heritage Appraisal of Development Plans: A Methodology for Planning Authorities*, David Tyldesley & Associates, Nottingham

Department of Agriculture, Food and Forestry (1996) *Growing for the Future a Strategic Plan for the Development of the Forestry Sector in Ireland*, Department of Agriculture, Food and Forestry, Dublin

Department of Arts, Heritage, Gaeltacht and the Islands (2002a) *The National Heritage Plan*, Department of Arts, Heritage, Gaeltacht and the Islands, Dublin

Department of Arts, Heritage, Gaeltacth and the Islands (2002b) *The National Biodiversity Plan*, Department of Arts, Heritage, Gaeltacth and the Islands, Dublin

Department of Environment and Local Government (1997) *Sustainable Development a Strategy for Ireland*, Department of Environment and Local Government, Dublin

Environmental Resource Management (ERM) and ERA-Maptec Ltd (2000) *Pilot Study on Landscape Characterisation in County Clare*, unpublished report to the Heritage Council, Kilkenny

Government of Ireland (1999) *National Development Plan 2000–2006*, Stationery Office, Dublin

Heritage Council (1997) *Strategic Document The Plan 1997–2000*, The Heritage Council, Kilkenny

Heritage Council (1999) *Policies and Priorities for Ireland's Landscape: Conference Papers, Tullamore, Co. Offaly. Ireland, April 1999*, The Heritage Council, Kilkenny

Heritage Council (2000a) *Submission on the National Development Plan 2000–2006*, The Heritage Council, Kilkenny

Heritage Council (2000b) *Policy Paper on Heritage Awareness in Ireland*, The Heritage Council, Kilkenny

Hickie, D (1997) *Evaluation of Environmental Designations in Ireland*, The Heritage Council, Kilkenny

IUCN (1994) *Parks for Life: Action for Protected Areas in Europe*, IUCN – The World Conservation Union, Cambridge

Landscape Alliance Ireland (1998) *Survey on Legislative Framework for Landscape Policy*, Waterfall, Cork

Landsdowne Market Research Ltd (2000) Report on the Future of the Irish Landscape – Unpublished Report, The Heritage Council, Kilkenny

Phillips, A (1999) pp5–14 in Heritage Council 1999: *Policies and Priorities for Ireland's Landscape: Conference Papers, Tullamore, Co. Offaly. Ireland, April 1999*, The Heritage Council, Kilkenny

Stephens, N and Glasscock, R E (1970) in Honour of E. Estyn Evans, *Irish Geographical Studies*, Department of Geography Queen's University of Belfast

Chapter 9

Development and Application of Landscape Assessment Guidelines in Ireland: Case Studies using Forestry and Wind Farm Developments

Art McCormack and Tomás O'Leary

Until recently, the only document providing guidance on landscapes at a national level in the Republic of Ireland were the publications entitled *Outstanding Landscapes* (An Foras Forbartha, 1976) and National Coastline Study (Anon, 1973). These tended to associate landscape with scenic quality which often resulted in planning considerations being focused on landscapes of high scenic value rather than on rural areas generally. More recent approaches to landscape (such as that advocated by the European Landscape Convention (see Chapter 4)), are based on an entirely different understanding, the most significant feature of which being that all landscapes are important to someone and thus warrant assessment as well as appropriate management.

The need for a clear understanding of what landscape is, and the impact and acceptability of change brought about by different kinds of land use and development, prompted the Forest Service and the Department of the Environment and Local Government (DoE&LG) to fund research to develop a landscape assessment methodology. This was intended to assist these organizations, and their partners, to take a more proactive view of the role of development and land use change in landscape management. This chapter outlines the approach adopted in the development of the Landscape and Landscape Assessment Guidelines (which was written by the authors of this paper for the DoE&LG, (2000)) and evaluates their application through case studies concerned with forestry and wind farm developments.

IRISH LANDSCAPE ASSESSMENT GUIDELINES

The approach adopted for landscape assessment in Ireland involves the description and evaluation of landscape as a basis for considering possible development and land use change. This should be distinguished from an evaluation of development in a landscape, as is more typical of the development-led approach where an environmental impact statement (EIS) is carried out for a specific project. Nevertheless as will become clear later, the part of the approach concerning assessment of landscape sensitivity does advocate an understanding of specific kinds of land use and development.

The approach that has been developed is intended to provide the basis for strategic planning and, thus, attempts to provide the following:

- Structured way of understanding landscape from different perspectives as a means to determine landscape character areas. This calls for a holistic approach to landscape character assessment (LCA), going beyond quantifying physical aspects of the landscape, and including also the qualitative perceptions of spatial structure and landscape image.
- Link between LCA, through the identification of values, to the consideration of landscape sensitivity. This will ensure the relevance of landscape character to decision-making.
- Structure for involving stakeholders as well as for the determination and evaluation of their values as a means of establishing landscape sensitivity.
- Back-up planning and design criteria. These will help evaluate how different kinds of land use will impact on different landscape character types.
- Input into, for instance, regional and county planning policies, studies of development potential, development strategies, capacity studies, the national spatial strategy and agri-environmental strategies.

The process of landscape assessment that has been developed involves landscape character as well as landscape sensitivity. Landscape character can be established for an area where there is visual distinctiveness and identity through a continuity of similar characteristic. Landscape sensitivity is established by considering the various values associated with a given landscape and provides the basis for production of landscape sensitivity classification regarding different kinds of change.

Landscape Character Assessment

The methodology developed for character assessment reflects three ways of understanding landscape, namely the objective and physically tangible composition of landscape, the visio-spatial structure as perceived and the landscape of the mind comprising its image. Each of these involves a stage in the assessment process which may result in the identification of units of landscape peculiar to the stage, and these are named physical units, visual units and image units (Figure 9.1).

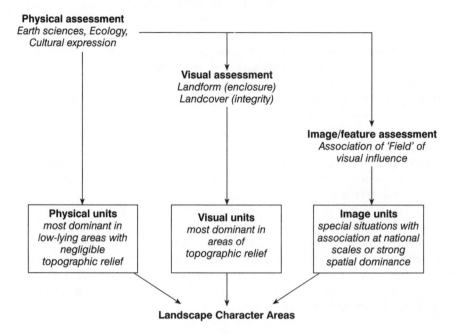

Figure 9.1 *Model for the identification of landscape character areas*

Physical units are, as the term suggests, defined by physical elements and components that result primarily from a combination of landform and land cover. They are established using, for example, geology, soils and land cover, as well as historical land use and settlement patterns. This stage of the assessment is carried out as a desk study mapping exercise and is greatly facilitated by the use of a Geographical Information Systems (GIS) where the relevant data sets are used to establish landform and land cover and also provide much of the information necessary for the physical aspects of landscape character description.

Visual units are areas defined primarily by spatial enclosure, as determined by landform and to a lesser degree by land cover. They are based on cohesion and similarity of, for instance, form, pattern, proportion, complexity and visual dynamic within a viewshed. Thus, unlike the plan-based assessment relevant to the identification of physical units, this stage involves the three-dimensional perception of landscape. It is of greatest relevance in areas of appreciable topographic relief, where views are typically limited to adjacent ridges and peaks, so defining a viewshed or a discrete context for a given land use change. The establishment of visual units in the process of landscape character identification is regarded as important for it is within such enclosed areas that the compatibility of land use change will often be judged. This stage involves on-site landscape assessment but can be initiated as a desk-study involving manual drawing on contour maps so as to identify catchment areas, or by using digital river catchment maps on a GIS.

Image units relate to the apprehension of unity in an area due to (a) cultural associations with land use, mythology, history and/or religion or (b) a feature of such dominance that it acts as a major focal point establishing spatial cohesion of its physical surrounds. The resulting visual and/or mental association creates an image or sense of place which is distinct from that derived simply from either the physical components or visio-spatial structure. Many landscapes lack such dominant features and so image units are often absent. Nevertheless, where such an association exists at a national scale, it will likely be a significant influence on landscape character identity and thus worthy of assessment. In Ireland the prime example is Croagh Patrick: it has a striking physical presence on the shores of Clew Bay on the west coast, an association with St Patrick (the nominal founder of Christianity in Ireland) and remains to this day a place of pilgrimage for many thousands of people.

The identification of landscape character areas and their mapping using polygons is usually based on a combination of the above three stages. Any one of them, however, may be more dominant than the others. Physical units, for example, are more likely to predominate in determining landscape character areas in flatter terrain where viewsheds are not so easily defined. Visual units are likely to be more important in determining landscape character in hilly and mountainous areas where viewsheds delimit viewing and thus define clearly identifiable character areas. A visual unit may include a number of physical units, especially in a broad valley or lake basin comprising, for example, mountain, moorland, marginal scrub, fertile farmland and bogs. A number of viewsheds, however, can be within the same character area if they present similar physical characteristics. An image unit is more difficult to define with a polygon, but will usually act as qualifier of the character identified under the other two stages.

Landscape Sensitivity

Landscape sensitivity is the extent to which an area can accommodate change without unacceptable loss of existing landscape character or unacceptable degradation of its associated values. Depending on the character of a given area, including its visual complexity, sensitivity will vary for different kinds of land use. For example, while few, if any, landscapes can successfully accommodate overhead power lines and towers, forestry and housing, where properly planned and designed, can potentially enhance many areas. Thus, there should not be a presumption that change per se will be detrimental to character. Rather, each kind of change or land use needs to be considered for its likely impact on the landscape.

While a proactive approach to land use change is in many cases important to help meet socio-economic objectives and for environmental enhancement, it is also necessary that peoples' values regarding their environment, and hence the sensitivity of landscape, be taken into account. This is the part of landscape assessment that particularly entails direct public involvement.

The overall sensitivity of a landscape to development, and therefore to change, will vary according to the significance of that landscape as well as to the nature of the development, and the benefits or dis-benefits that could result. The Quality of Life (QoL) Capital approach provides a practical tool in the assessment of the acceptability of new development and in its design within a specific landscape (CAG Consultants and Land Use Consultants, 2001). The approach is useful in the evaluation of the different values or benefits derived from the resources of an area, whether environmental, social or economic. As it is based on the characterization of landscape, it is particularly useful in the identification of landscape values, such as recreation, aesthetic, ecological, health and sense of identity. The assessment is concerned with anything of tangible and intangible importance to communities, whether local, regional, national or international. It follows that the identification of the values of a given area requires wide-ranging consultation.

The landscape assessment methodology developed in Ireland adopts some aspects of the QoL approach. Thus the assessment of landscape sensitivity is based on an evaluation of values according to three related criteria: importance, sufficiency and substitutability. The importance variable relates to the level of importance (high, medium or low), the scale of importance (ranging from international to local) and the identification of to whom it is important. Sufficiency is concerned with whether there is enough of these values, if they are under threat and whether they can be improved. Substitutability requires an assessment of whether the resource that provides a given value can be substituted for by another resource providing the same value.

The results of applying these criteria are brought together to help evaluate and classify landscape sensitivity. Five classes of sensitivity for different kinds of land use and development are proposed:

- *Class 1* – low sensitivity;
- *Class 2* – moderate sensitivity;
- *Class 3* – high sensitivity;
- *Class 4* – special; and
- *Class 5* – unique.

This part of the assessment can be used to consider the acceptability of different kinds of development in a given landscape and, for where it is acceptable, to what extent and how it might best fit in respect of planning and design. Use of the QoL Capital approach is also optimized by considering how the values ascribed to an area would be affected differently by specific kinds of development. It is, therefore, important to produce sensitivity maps that are development specific. Accordingly, the benefits of the development, such as possible enhancement of values, as well as consequential dis-benefits, can be integrated into the assessment. Potential substitutability can also be more accurately identified when there is a specific development in mind, rather than considering it in the abstract. Without such a grounding in specific development and land use change, the assessment might remain too general to be of practical application.

CASE STUDY 1: LANDSCAPE ASSESSMENT IN THE PLANNING AND DESIGN OF FORESTRY

The afforestation programme in Ireland over the next 30 years is intended to increase forest cover from approximately 9 per cent of the land surface to 17 per cent (Department of Agriculture, Food and Forestry, 1996). Given the perceived adverse impacts of a considerable proportion of commercial forestry upon the landscape, it is important to establish planning and design guidelines and strategies so as to ensure overall positive results and avoid damage to the landscape. To facilitate this, the Irish Forest Service has developed a GIS system, known as the Forest Inventory and Planning System (FIPS), to ensure proper forestry planning and to make information available to all interested parties. A pilot study was carried out by the authors for the Irish Forest Service regarding the landscape component of FIPS, which involves the landscape assessment methodology outlined above.

Use of Character and Sensitivity

Figure 9.2 is a holistic model proposed for strategic forest landscape planning and design and illustrates the approach followed in the forest landscape assessment process. This model proposes, in outline, a relationship between three key determinants of forest landscape planning and design: landscape physiography, landscape character and sensitivity. Landscape physiography is used to establish forestry capability, that is what species will grow in which location. Landscape character is used to determine the potential for enhancement (of each character area) through afforestation. Landscape sensitivity is used to determine constraints to afforestation by reference to the landscape character types used in the national *Forestry and the Landscape Guidelines* (McCormack and O'Leary, 2000). The first two determinants provide for a framework for the introduction of forests to the landscape, while the evaluation of landscape sensitivity acts as a filter to ensure that only appropriate afforestation that enhances landscape character and responds to different values receive grant aid.

The approach developed was piloted in parts of counties Cork, Leitrim, Mayo and Wicklow. These counties were of particular interest for landscape research given the variation in landscape character, silvicultural potential, socio-economics and public opinion regarding forestry. The pilot focused on those parts of the counties that, when considered as a whole, seemed representative of the different forestry development scenarios in Ireland.

Landscape character
The process of identifying landscape character in these study areas used the approach described above. In most cases, the identification of landscape character was based mainly on physical and visual units. The physical units were found to determine the character areas on lower and flatter ground, while in upland and mountainous areas visual units were more appropriate.

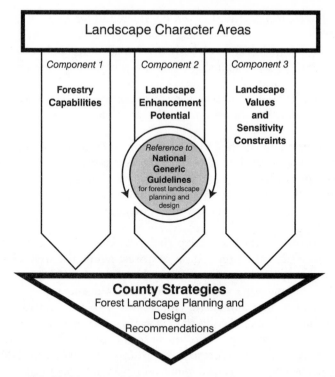

Figure 9.2 *Model proposed for strategic forest landscape planning and design*

In order to develop planning and design recommendations for forestry, the concept of 'forest landscape planning' first needed to be established. Forest landscape planning, as distinct from forest design, is concerned with spatial organization and the effects of forests and forestry practices on landscape at a broad scale, especially in regard to area-wide character and quality. Forest landscape design is concerned with the appearance of the forest in relation to its immediate context, and includes silvicultural and management implications. Forest landscape planning and design criteria and associated factors were established (see Table 9.1).

As FIPS is primarily a planning tool, the forest landscape planning factors were applied to each of the identified landscape character areas as a means of describing how each one could be enhanced by forestry, while design recommendations were treated more synthetically in prose:

Table 9.1 *Forest landscape planning and design criteria and factors*

	Forest landscape planning		Forest landscape design	
Criteria	Extent	Disposition	Configuration	Composition
Factors	Scale	Arrangement	Shape	Margin
	Size	Location	Pattern	Texture
			Proportion	Colour
			Edge	

- *scale*: Overall area of forest cover, considered in terms of 'low', 'moderate' or 'high';
- *size*: Area of individual forests, whether 'small', 'medium' or 'large';
- *arrangement*: Spatial relationship of forests whether 'clustered' or 'scattered'; and
- *location*: Position of a forest or forests in a landscape, considered in terms of 'upper ground', 'middle ground' or 'lower ground'.

The GIS component of the FIPS landscape study incorporated a computer automated 'point and click' facility. This allows a user to click on a given area of interest and be simultaneously provided with a character map, representative photograph, character description, the relevant character type for cross reference to the forest landscape guidelines and succinct planning recommendations.

Referring back to the model depicted in Figure 9.2 above, the third major determinant used in the preparation of forest landscape strategies is that of landscape sensitivity. This was investigated by first identifying different values contained in the landscape, so as to facilitate an assessment of the impact upon them of forestry. The immediate aim was to produce landscape sensitivity classes which could be applied to the relevant landscape character areas as part of forestry decision-making. In the longer term, however, the assessment could be used to guide and control forestry, taking account of its acceptability, primary function (recreation/amenity or commercial), planning, design and management recommendations and administrative requirements. Guidance and control are least restrictive and demanding in Landscape Sensitivity Class 1 and most restrictive in Class 5. The classes proposed were as follows:

- *Class I: Low Sensitivity* – new forests in this class would be subject to relatively few aesthetic constraints, as the need for visual integration would not be regarded as of critical importance.
- *Class II: Moderate Sensitivity* – in this class, new forests would be expected to fit visually into the landscape: only modest aesthetic and environmental impacts would be acceptable.
- *Class III: High Sensitivity* – new forests in these landscapes should provide visual quality and should be appear naturalistic, depending on whether the context comprises, for example, open mountain moorland or an enclosed patchwork of fields.
- *Class IV: Special Landscape* – only those forests designed for passive or active recreation, and/or for ecological purposes, would be permitted in this class. The stress here (though not necessarily exclusively) would be on conservation rather than commercial exploitation.
- *Class V: Unique Landscape* – this class includes landscapes, whether with or without forests, in which avoidable change through afforestation is not acceptable.

The five Landscape Sensitivity Classes as proposed reflect the aesthetic impact brought about by forestry, and involve an indication of the planning and design requirements in respect of each of the criteria established in the forest landscape guidelines already mentioned. Forestry management practices can also be determined by involving the three components of the model, with the aim of greater visual integration of forest and more sensitive design. The classes proposed would have implications for the main functions of the forests: whether, for example, they are to be predominantly managed for timber production, recreation or nature conservation. They would also have a bearing on management requirements, as well as for the type and detail of documents to be submitted to the Irish Forest Service when seeking grant aid or planning permission.

Determination of sensitivity in the study involved not only a literature review of county development plans and of tourism and artistic literature, but also public consultation through focus group meetings. These meetings included professional evaluation using a checklist of assessment criteria. They were held in each of the four counties, involving people who were intimately familiar with the county, most of whom worked and/or resided there. They included local farmers and rural development groups as well as decision-makers such as local authority officials, representatives of local and corporate land users, inspectors from statutory and research authorities, experts, NGO representatives, outdoor pursuit representatives and academics from a range of relevant fields.

The meetings involved a field trip in the morning, which was intended to stimulate discussion, focus the mind on forests in the landscape and prepare the participants for the afternoon session. The latter was concerned with the exchange of ideas, opinions and preferences regarding alternative forest landscape scenarios produced specifically for the groups. These sessions involved four components:

- Participants identifying areas of value to them (reflecting their respective interests) on a map of the county, the results of which were later incorporated into a GIS-based sensitivity map.
- Participants completed a questionnaire that aimed to determine values and landscape sensitivity.
- Participants were then asked to evaluate posters depicting seven different landscape types and five different forms of forestry development (in terms of scale, size, format, etc).
- In the final component, the focus group participants took part in an open debate about forestry development in the county, focusing on forestry planning and design issues. The record of these discussions was analysed to identify the main concerns and aspirations regarding forest planning and design.

The authors of this chapter took account of the findings of the focus group meetings in designating landscape sensitivity, and also examined each landscape character area using a checklist of aesthetic sensitivity assessment criteria which included:

- number of viewers;
- likely mental disposition of viewers (eg commuters hurriedly driving on

busy national route versus golfers enjoying panoramic views in a leisure mode);
- recreational facility;
- provision of elevated panoramic views;
- degree of perceived naturalness and sense of remoteness;
- presence of water (river, lake, sea);
- mountains present;
- ruggedness of landform/exposure of rock outcrops;
- presence of striking or noteworthy features;
- integrity of character;
- historical, cultural and/or spiritual significance evident or sensed;
- sense of awe; and
- rarity or uniqueness.

Following this assessment, each character area was assigned a sensitivity classification ranging from Class 1 (lowest sensitivity) to Class 5 (highest classification). This latter exercise was performed by professionals integrating the findings and producing county sensitivity maps.

The findings of the above sensitivity assessment were incorporated into a GIS-based map. This map indicated areas identified as sensitive, grouped under such headings as ecology, planning, commercial forestry, scenic and artistic value and fisheries. Here again a 'point and click' device was employed to identify the landscape sensitivity classification and corresponding forest landscape planning, design and management recommendations for any given location. The aim was to produce a product that is easy to use and of practical value to those concerned with planning and designing forestry schemes. Only time will tell whether this objective has been realized, although it appears that further investigation and refinement of the approach will be needed in order to improve the integration and weighting of the different kinds of sensitivity.

CASE STUDY 2: LANDSCAPE ASSESSMENT IN THE PLANNING AND DESIGN OF WIND FARMS

The landscape assessment methodology outlined above was also piloted in a study examining the potential for wind energy development initiated by Cork County Council (2001). The aim of this project was to test whether the methodology could help formulate planning policies to guide wind farm developments.

In total, 71 distinct draft landscape character areas were identified throughout the county. A full range of physiographic data sets were not available to facilitate a thorough study. Given the hilly and mountainous landscape of much of County Cork, these character areas primarily comprised visual units. No feature or location was deemed so commanding, whether spatially or in respect of national image, that it warranted consideration as an image unit. As with the study carried out for forestry, in order to facilitate the development and application of planning and design guidelines the landscape character *areas* were

Plates

Figure 6.4   The Natural Areas framework, 2002
Figure 6.5   Vision map of the Alde project area
Figure 8.1   Preliminary landscape character types in County Clare
Figure 9.3   Suggested landscape character types in County Cork for wind
               farm planning and design
Figure 9.4   Suggested landscape sensitivity classification of County Cork
               for wind farm planning and design
Figure 11.2   Natural Heritage Units of Scotland
Figure 15.1   Development at the Hedgerows, Leigh on Mendip
Figure 15.2   Development at Townsend Farm, Leigh on Mendip

Key
— County boundary
Character Area boundary (Natural Areas consist of one or more Character Areas)

Source: English Nature

Figure 6.4 *The Natural Areas framework, 2002*

1	North Northumberland Coastal Plain	60	Black Mountains and Golden Valley
2	Border Uplands	61	Dean Plateau and Wye Valley
3	Solway Basin	62	Bristol, Avon Valleys and Ridges
4	North Pennines	63	Thames and Avon Vales
5	Northumbria Coal Measures	64	Midvale Ridge
6	Durham Magnesian Limestone Plateau	65	Chilterns
7	Tees Lowlands	66	London Basiin
8	Yorkshire Dales	67	Greater Thames Estuary
9	Eden Valley	68	North Kent Plain
10	Cumbria Fells and Dales	69	North Downs
11	West Cumbria Coastal Plain	70	Wealden Greensand
12	Forest of Bowland	71	Romney Marshes
13	Lancashire Plain and Valleys	72	High Weald
14	Southern Pennines	73	Low Weald and Pevensey
15	Pennine Dales Fringe	74	South Downs
16	Vale of York and Mowbray	75	South Coast Plain and Hampshire
17	North York Moors and Hills		Lowlands
18	Vale of Pickering	76	Isle of Wight
19	Yorkshire Wolds	77	New Forest
20	Holderness	78	Hampshire Downs
21	Humber Estuary	79	Berkshire and Marlborough Downs
22	Humberhead Levels	80	South Wessex Downs
23	Southern Magnesian Limestone	81	Dorset Heaths
24	Coal Measures	82	Isles of Portland and Purbeck
25	Dark Peak	83	Wessex Vales
26	Urban Mersey Basin	84	Mendip Hills
27	Meres and Mosses	85	Somerset Levels and Moors
28	Potteries and Churnet Valley	86	Mid Somerset Hills
29	South West Peak	87	Exmoor and the Quantocks
30	White Peak	88	Vale of Taunton and Quantock Fringes
31	Derbyshire Peak Fringe and Lower	89	Blackdowns
	Derwent	90	Devon Redlands
32	Sherwood	91	South Devon
33	Trent Valley and Rises	92	Dartmoor
34	North Lincolnshire Coversands and	93	The Culm
	Clay Vales	94	Bodmin Moor
35	Lincolnshire Wolds	95	Cornish Killas and Granites
36	Lincolnshire Coast and Marshes	96	West Penwith
37	The Fens	97	The Lizard
38	Lincolnshire and Rutland Limestone	98	Northumberland Coast
39	Charnwood	99	Tyne to Tees Coast
40	Needwood and South Derbyshire	100	Saltburn to Bridlington
	Claylands	101	Bridlington to Skegness
41	Oswestry Uplands	102	The Wash
42	Shropshire Hills	103	Old Hunstanton to Sheringham
43	Midlands Plateau	104	Sheringham to Lowestoft
44	Midland Clay Pastures	105	Suffolk Coast
45	Rockingham Forest	106	North Kent Coast
46	Breckland	107	East Kent Coast
47	North Norfolk	108	Folkestone to Selsey Bill
48	The Broads	109	Solent and Poole Bay
49	Suffolk Coast and Heaths	110	South Dorset Coast
50	East Anglian Plain	111	Lyme Bay
51	East Anglian Chalk	112	Start Point to Land's End
52	West Anglian Plain	113	Isles of Scilly
53	Bedfordshire Greensand Ridge	114	Land's End to Minehead
54	Yardley–Whittlewood Ridge	115	Bridgwater Bay
55	Cotswolds	116	Severn Estuary
56	Severn and Avon Vales	117	Liverpool Bay
57	Malvern Hills and Teme Valley	118	Morecambe Bay
58	Clun and North West Herefordshire Hills	119	Cumbrian Coast
59	Central Herefordshire	120	Solway Firth

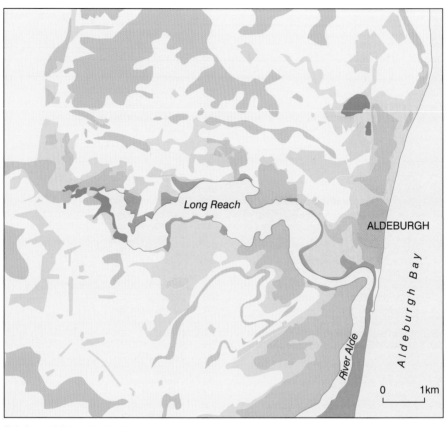

Long Reach

ALDEBURGH

Aldeburgh Bay

River Alde

0   1km

Existing habitats suitable for restoration management

Heathland and acid grassland
Coastal floodplain grazing marsh
Reedbed
Saltmarsh

Zones where habitat creation should be technically feasible

Heathland and acid grassland
Wetland habitats (coastal grazing marsh, reedbeds and saltmarsh)
Farmland habitats

Source: English Nature

Figure 6.5 *Vision map of the Alde project area*

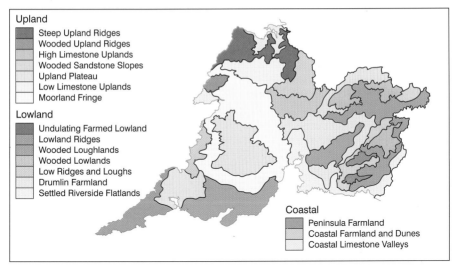

Upland
- ▨ Steep Upland Ridges
- ▨ Wooded Upland Ridges
- ▨ High Limestone Uplands
- ▨ Wooded Sandstone Slopes
- ▨ Upland Plateau
- ▨ Low Limestone Uplands
- ▨ Moorland Fringe

Lowland
- ▨ Undulating Farmed Lowland
- ▨ Lowland Ridges
- ▨ Wooded Loughlands
- ▨ Wooded Lowlands
- ▨ Low Ridges and Loughs
- ▨ Drumlin Farmland
- ▨ Settled Riverside Flatlands

Coastal
- ▨ Peninsula Farmland
- ▨ Coastal Farmland and Dunes
- ▨ Coastal Limestone Valleys

In West Clare, the Peninsula Farmland dominates the distinctive, exposed lowlands and cliffs of the Kilkeel Peninsula and recurs to the north, on the smaller peninsula near the Cliffs of Moher. Linking these two areas, the Coastal Farmland and Dunes landscape includes the sequence of promontories and sweeping sandy bays of the West Clare coast, which extend from Doonbeg to Milltown Malby. Inland, the Moorland Plateau is a broad elevated plateau with a mosaic of upland moor, peatlands and conifer plantations. It is surrounded by a Moorland Fringe landscape of gleyed pastures, conifer plantations, loughs, wetlands and farmsteads. This area has a relatively dense network of roads and tracks. Together the Upland Plateau and Moorland Fringe landscapes dominate central West Clare. To the south, the Lowland Ridges landscape has a more regular pattern of gleyed fields, small woodlands and some drained farmland. The straight roads often follow the ridges and there is a sequence of rocky coves along the Shannon estuary.

To the north there is a gradual transition to the distinctive limestone scenery of the Burren. The exposed dramatic cliffs, limestone pavements, caves and archaeological sites on the high tops of the Burren are described as High Limestone Uplands. To the south, the Low Limestone Uplands is a transitional open landscape, with extensive semi-natural grasslands, some settlements and occasional woodlands. On the north coast, the dramatic Coastal Limestone Valleys are enclosed by the distinctive curved rock terraces of the Burren. There are numerous archaeological sites on the fringes of the uplands and the valley field patterns are of ancient origin.

The landscapes of East Clare are dominated by Silurian uplands. The Steep Upland Ridges landscape of Slieve Bearnagh is the highest upland in Clare. It has a series of sharp ridges and summits with a large-scale mosaic of peat, moorland and conifer plantations. To the southwest and north of Slieve Bearnagh, the Wooded Upland Ridges include the lower, more rounded uplands of Scalp, Maghera, Knockaunnamoughilly and Woodcock Hill. The landform of these summits is partially masked by extensive conifer plantations which are interspersed with moorland and peat bogs. These Silurian uplands are fringed by Wooded Sandstone Slopes to the north, and the Undulating Farmed Lowlands to the south and east. The former is a remote landscape of extensive conifer plantations and bog. It is relatively inaccessible and there are few farmsteads or roads. By contrast, the Undulating Farmed Lowlands have numerous dispersed farmsteads in a landscape of small, mostly marginal pastures.

The East Clare uplands are separated by a broad lowland belt. The underlying limestones of this Drumlin Farmland are plastered with dense boulder clays. The area has scattered, relatively shallow drumlins, with some loughs and inter-drumlin wetlands. There are also many small woodlands. In the centre of the lowland, the Wooded Loughlands are found on an outcrop of Silurian rock. The landform in this part of the lowland is more rugged, with rocky knolls, woodlands, heaths and pastures. There are also numerous designed parklands and wooded estates within a relatively small area.

To the north of Ennis the Wooded Lowlands is an area of less distinct, but discernible drumlins with quite a high proportion of woodland and relatively marginal farmland. This area, together with the Low Ridges and Loughs to the north is a transitional landscape linking the drumlin lowlands of East Clare and the Burren to the north. The Low Ridges and Loughs are a low-lying limestone landscape with long loughs and marshy wetlands. The area has the thin soils and sparse vegetation typical of limestone landscapes.

The Settled Riverside Flatlands alongside the River Shannon have a very distinctive landscape of drained pastures, wetlands and tidal flats. This area has a concentration of settlement and infrastructure and is dominated by Shannon airport.

Source: Heritage Council

Figure 8.1 *Preliminary landscape character types in County Clare*

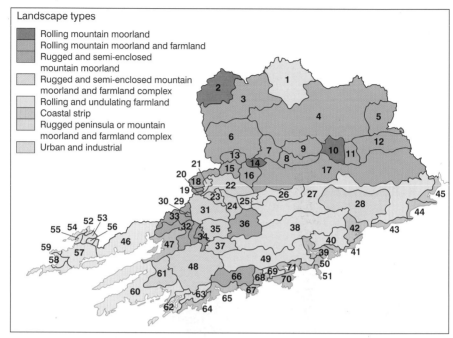

Figure 9.3 *Suggested landscape character types in County Cork for wind farm planning and design*

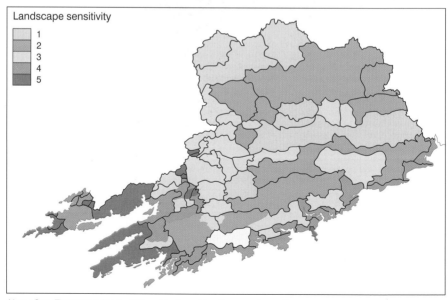

Figure 9.4 *Suggested landscape sensitivity classification of County Cork for wind farm planning and design*

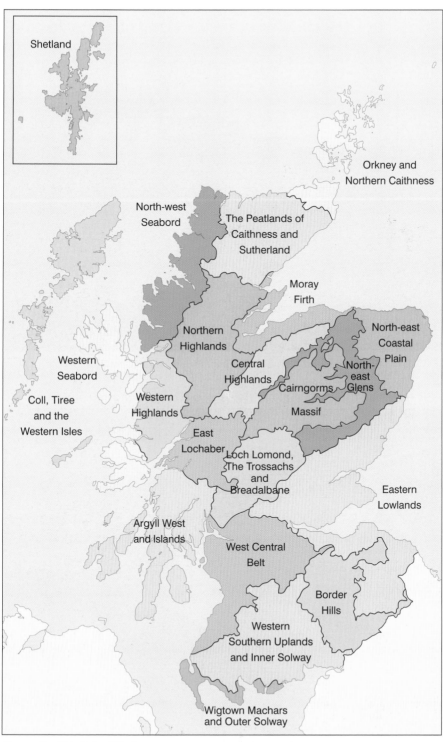

Shetland

Orkney and
Northern Caithness

North-west
Seabord

The Peatlands of
Caithness and
Sutherland

Moray
Firth

North-east
Coastal
Plain

Northern
Highlands

Central
Highlands

North-
east
Glens

Cairngorms
Massif

Western
Seabord

Western
Highlands

Coll, Tiree
and the
Western Isles

East
Lochaber

Loch Lomond,
The Trossachs
and
Breadalbane

Eastern
Lowlands

Argyll West
and Islands

West Central
Belt

Border
Hills

Western
Southern Uplands
and Inner Solway

Wigtown Machars
and Outer Solway

Source: Scottish Natural Heritage

Figure 11.2 *Natural Heritage Units of Scotland*

Figure 15.1 *Development at the Hedgerows, Leigh on Mendip*

Figure 15.2 *Development at Townsend Farm, Leigh on Mendip*

grouped into eight *types* (see Figure 9.3 in Plate section) on the basis of overall similarity regarding elevation, scale, degree of enclosure, degree of ruggedness, sense of the naturalistic, predominant land cover and proximity to the coast. Distinct landscape planning and design recommendations were specified for each character type taking into account the following factors:

- wind farm size – *planning*, whether small, medium or large;
- wind farm plan complexity – *design*, whether deep plan (multiple lines of turbines) or linear plan (single line); and
- turbine spacing – *design*, whether random or equal.

The next phase of the study was to apply a landscape sensitivity analysis so as to indicate areas where, from a landscape perspective, wind farms would either be acceptable or not acceptable. Public consultation regarding landscape sensitivity was not possible in this study due to time and budgetary constraints. Professional assessment was thus carried out using a checklist similar to that applied in the above forestry project. The entire county was classified into five sensitivity classes (see Figure 9.4 in Plate section), the suggested implications of which are specified in Table 9.2.

The final stage in the research was to combine the landscape sensitivity assessment with a map indicating commercially viable locations for wind farm development. This combination highlighted those areas where development, at least from a landscape perspective, was likely to be acceptable and commercially viable. This map could help planners, landowners and developers alike by identifying preferred locations for wind farm development. Cork County Council is now considering progressing the assessment in greater detail, using all data sets in a GIS for use as a basis for development plan policies on wind farms.

CONCLUSIONS

Landscape assessment has begun to receive much needed attention in Ireland over the past three years. Landscape and the accommodation of change are finally moving up the political agenda. This has resulted in the preparation of guidelines for all local authorities by the DoE&LG. The production of such guidelines, however, represents just the first small step along the road towards developing a consistent approach to the planning and design of different types of development in the landscape.

The experience gained in the two case studies outlined in this chapter as well as in some current work being undertaken by others would suggest that the new guidelines are reasonably robust. They provide a systematic methodology as a basis for achieving greater consistency and compatibility. These studies also indicate that landscape character and sensitivity can provide the framework for dealing with development in the landscape in a manner that balances the need to protect existing resources with encouragement of change. The character areas identified can be used in the consideration of how new development or

Table 9.2 *Proposed implications of the five sensitivity classes for wind farm development in County Cork*

Landscape planning and design criteria	1 (Lowest)	2	Sensitivity class 3	4	5 (Highest)
Size	Large	Medium/large	Small	Small (in secluded location only)	None
Cumulative effects	100% of total capacity	50% of total capacity	30% of total capacity	30% of total capacity	None
Locational pattern	Clustered/ dispersed	Dispersed	Dispersed	None	N/a
Layout	Any	In response to character	In response to character	In response to character	N/a
Phasing multiple wind farm developments	Not required	Recommended	Mandatory	N/a	N/a
Hub height	High	High	Medium	Low	N/a
Mast form	Solid tapered	Solid tapered	Solid tapered	Solid tapered	N/a
Mast colour	Matt light grey	Matt white or light grey	Consider alternatives to white or light grey	As appropriate to backdrop	N/a
Rotor speed	Any	Any	Any	Slower preferred	N/a
Visibility of transformer station	Exposed	Partially screened	Complete screening	Complete screening or buried	N/a
Visibility of national grid connection	Above ground	Above ground	Burying preferred	Buried	N/a
Treatment of service roads	Any	Minimal contrast with surrounds	Low contrast mandatory	Low contrast mandatory	N/a
Flicker	Acceptable	Acceptable	Acceptable	Not acceptable from key viewpoints	N/a
Consultation through public displays	Preferred	Preferred	Mandatory	Mandatory	N/a
Production of visualizations	Mandatory	Mandatory	Mandatory	Mandatory	N/a

land use will change that character – without comment as to *whether* it should – whereas landscape sensitivity provides the basis for decision regarding, first, *whether* change is acceptable and, second, if so, *how*.

However, real progress can only be made through the application of the guidelines in different geographic locations and under different socio-economic conditions, thus allowing for further testing and refinement. In order to achieve this, and to ensure optimum methodological benefit, the entire process will require careful monitoring of results by a central body, probably headed by the DoE&LG.

This process of advancing landscape assessment in the Republic of Ireland should include the following:

- Further development of the tripartite approach to landscape character identification, ie the use of the three levels or ways of understanding landscape and how they are combined to produce maps that are useful for strategic planning.
- Computer automation, using GIS, of part of the landscape assessment process. The success of this depends on the availability of the required data sets in digital form and on close cooperation between landscape and computer experts.
- Identification of the most effective scale for use of landscape character in regard to different kinds of land use and development. While it may be interesting academically to identify many landscape character areas and have them as a reference in a county development plan, it is quite possible that only a few more broadly scaled types are sufficient for the practical needs of planners to help guide and control change in the landscape.
- Establishment of the optimum way(s) of involving the general public, professionals and land use agencies, especially in relation to landscape sensitivity. This should involve investigation and testing of evaluation methods in the identification of the values attached to landscape by different groups.
- Production of development-specific planning and design guidelines as well as sensitivity maps at a county level.
- Determination of the process by which assessment results can be translated into county development plan policy, while ensuring compatibility throughout Ireland.

At this point in the history of land use and development in Ireland there is an opportunity to develop policies, structures and measures to guide the process of landscape change. Change need not necessarily be a problem, but rather can provide an opportunity to enhance landscape. The need is to ensure that consideration of change in the landscape is based on a balanced, comprehensive and transparent process. While not referring to Ireland, the quotation below captures something of the complexity of this challenge:

> *We need at this moment, as much as any country ever needed, the development which makes clear the influence of nature upon intellectual and spiritual life; an integration that involves science, the arts, and human interest in order to give clear expression to what is most significant in our relation to nature* (Smith, 1936, in regard to the US).

REFERENCES

Anon (1973) *National Coastline Study: County Reports, Notes on Development Strategy*, An Foras Forbartha and Bord Fáilte, Dublin

An Foras Forbartha (1976) *Outstanding Landscapes*, An Foras Forbartha, Dublin

Bulfin, M (2000) 'Physical Planning for Forestry in Ireland' in Weber, N (ed) *NEWFOR – New Forests for Europe: Afforestation at the Turn of the Century*, Proceedings of the Scientific Symposium, Freiburg/Germany, 16–17 February, EFI Proceedings No 35, pp89–100

CAG Consultants and Land Use Consultants (2001) *Quality of Life Capital*, English Heritage, Environment Agency, Countryside Agency and English Nature, Cheltenham

Cork County Council (2001) *Wind Energy and Landscape ALTNER Project AL/98/542*, Cork County Council, Cork

Department of Agriculture, Food and Forestry (1996) *Growing for the Future*, Department of Agriculture, Food and Forestry, Dublin

Government of Ireland (1999) *National Development Plan 2000–2006*, Stationery Office, Dublin

McCormack, A and O'Leary, T (2000) *Forestry and the Landscape Guidelines*, The Forest Service, Department of the Marine and Natural Resources, Dublin

McCormack, A, O'Leary, T and Dubháin, A (2000) *Landscape Component of the Forest Inventory and Planning System*, The Forest Service, Department of the Marine and Natural Resources, Dublin

Smith, H A (1936) 'Editorial', *Journal of Forestry*, vol 34(4), p1

Starrett, M (2002) 'Policies and Priorities for Ireland's Landscapes', in Bishop K and Phillips, A (eds) *Countryside Planning: Global drivers, joined-up planning, local action*, Earthscan, London, pp125–140

Chapter 10

Historic Landscape Characterization

Lesley Macinnes

The whole landscape bears the imprint of its long human history. This imprint is most apparent in the plethora of archaeological and historical remains, but increasingly the historic complexity of settlement and field patterns, and the extent of human influence on vegetation cover and landscape character, are gaining wider appreciation. This chapter offers an overview of recent initiatives to identify and map these influences, a process known as historic landscape characterization (HLC).

BACKGROUND

Our understanding of the human impact on the landscape derives from a wide range of academic disciplines, including landscape archaeology, historical geography, history and palaeobotany (see Aalen, 1996 and Muir, 1999 for recent summaries). Conservation policy and practice have, however, tended to focus on specific features and to treat the natural and cultural aspects of landscape separately.

Existing legislation relating to the cultural heritage affords protection primarily to specific features and areas. Ancient monuments and archaeological sites are scheduled under the Ancient Monuments and Archaeological Areas Act 1979, while historic buildings are listed and conservation areas designated under Town and Country Planning legislation (Breeze, 1993; Suddards, 1993; Baker, 1993). The planning system gives some protection to larger areas of historic interest, such as historic parks and gardens, as do some land management schemes and policies for designated landscapes, for example, national parks (Macinnes, 1993). However, there is no specific protection for the historic landscape as such, and little acknowledgement in policy of the historic dimension of the environment as a whole (though there has been a recent governmental statement on the historic environment in England, entitled *The Historic Environment: A Force for Our Future* (DCMS and DTLGR, 2001).

Within the natural heritage, in contrast, there has been a drive in recent years towards landscape characterization (for example, Usher 1999; Swanwick and Land Use Conultants, 2002). However, the standard approach to landscape character assessment (LCA) has generally under-represented the complex ways in which humans have impacted on the appearance of the landscape and the length of time over which this influence has occurred. With a focus on the more recent past and highly visible historic features, the more subtle connections between vegetation cover, land use and human history have tended to be under-played in the LCA process.

The site-specific nature of most archaeological records, and the site-focused approach of much archaeological work, have contributed to this situation and made it difficult for the wide range of archaeological evidence to be incorporated into the more landscape-based approach of LCA. Consequently, though individual LCAs may have tried to embrace the chronological range of human history evident in the landscape, initial results have normally taken the form of an accompanying historical narrative rather than played a meaningful part in the process of characterization itself. At the same time, archaeological and historic landscape projects have tended to concentrate on understanding the past, rather than on considering how past use has influenced the present landscape (Fairclough, 1999a, pp4–5).

Nevertheless, the attempt to represent historical influences within landscape characterization programmes has led gradually to the development of techniques for characterizing the dominant historical processes which have affected the landscape and which are still evident within it. Such techniques of HLC are beginning to provide a powerful insight into how people have influenced the landscape over time, reflecting its time-depth and highlighting the degree of continuity and change within it. These complement the LCA approach and offer an enhanced understanding of some landscape character types (Herring, 1998; David Tyldesley and Associates, 2001). The ultimate aim of this work is to demonstrate that our environment has far greater time-depth than is usually appreciated, and to show how this has influenced its current character. Indeed, it can be said with some justification that 'we live in an historic environment' (Wills, 1999, p39).

HISTORIC LANDSCAPE CHARACTERIZATION

HLC was first developed in England between 1992 and 1994, through a research project funded by English Heritage. The aims of this project were to 'investigate methods of defining historic landscape, in order to allow proper attention to its conservation' (McNab, 1999, p18). The project comprised a review of historic landscape surveys at parish, estate and farm level; a review of historic landscape assessment within Environmental Statements; and two geographical pilots, in Oxfordshire and in County Durham. As a result of this work, the terms *historic landscape assessment* and *historic landscape characterization* were introduced as a process of describing, analysing and identifying patterns within the historic landscape (McNab and Lambrick, 1999, p55). The process defined is broadly comparable to LCA and moves through the setting of clear objectives for the study to data collection, analysis and characterization, and finally to policy recommendations. Evaluation can be built into the process but is not an essential component of it (McNab and Lambrick, 1999). The methodology was first applied more widely in 1994, when the Cornwall Archaeological Unit undertook a character assessment of the historic landscape of its county, partly to assist with the preparation of the character map for the area and partly in response to the English Heritage initiative (Herring, 1998). Other HLC projects have since been developed across Britain, generally building on the original methodology and adapting it to local needs and circumstances. All of these are seeking to enhance our understanding of the historic depth in the landscape and depict this in mapped form. In the following discussion, Cornwall is used as an exemplar for the methodology, in view of its scale and scope, its links to LCA and its pioneering influence on subsequent projects. The chapter contains an overview of comparable work that has been carried out elsewhere in Britain and elsewhere in Europe. It concludes with a preliminary review of the use and application of the technique.

Cornwall and the Basic Methodology

In many ways, Cornwall saw the first practical application of HLC. It was developed there to assist in the preparation of the Character Map of England in 1994, in an attempt to represent the historic dimension more fully than individual sites and monuments allowed (Herring, 1998). As the HLC sprang directly from the LCA process in Cornwall, it was closely related to it and offers a good example of the inter-play between the two techniques. The Cornwall HLC tried to identify which elements of the landscape had greatest antiquity and to clarify the dominant historic influences that have helped shape the Cornish countryside and contribute to its present character. Thus, farmland was dated to the medieval or post-medieval periods, or to the 20th century; woodland was classified as ancient or modern; the early cores of settlements were distinguished from their modern extents (Herring, 1998). This approach provided an understanding of the historic depth behind the characteristic appearance of the modern landscape of Cornwall: it indicated, for example, that some of its field patterns were likely to be medieval in origin, or even prehistoric; and that some parts of the county are still dominated by evidence of the industrial activity that transformed the landscape in the 19th century.

The HLC brought to light 17 historic landscape types across the county (Herring, 1998); each of these identify the dominant historic land use, based on professional assessment and local knowledge. Information was derived from data sets that were available for the whole county (such as Cornwall Wildlife Trust's 1:10,000 habitat maps, early Ordnance Survey maps and local place-name data). The work was desk-based and mapping was carried out manually at a scale of 1:50,000, using reduced 1:25,000 maps which is the smallest scale that depicts field boundaries.

The historic landscape types were subsequently generalized into 18 zones to aid understanding and for ease of comparison with the smaller-scale and broader-brush LCA (Herring, 1998). The zones amalgamated some character types and sub-divided others to present a simplified view of historic character and depict broad patterns more clearly (op cit). This simplified view offered a strong visual image of the predominant historic types within the landscape, but lost much of the detailed definition provided by the full range of types. The zone maps, therefore, provided an overview of the predominant historical process within the county, while the type maps added greater local context. Each zone map was accompanied by a textual description which explained the nature of the historical process within the zone, including its typical archaeological and historic features, assessed the zone's condition and sensitivity to change, and considered its potential for research, amenity and education.

However, as each type and zone represented only the dominant historical influence evident in a given area, it was realized that the resultant maps could not easily depict the full range and time-depth of historic evidence that actually survived within the landscape. In reality the landscape is a complex palimpsest of influence from different periods. In order to show this, time-depth matrices were prepared to accompany the zonal maps, while significant areas of relict land use were depicted on the maps by hatching (Herring, 1998).

The Cornwall project succeeded in showing that historic information can do more than provide interesting background information to landscape analysis. It can be an integral part of understanding the character of the modern landscape, showing how people have influenced their environment in ways that have lasted through time, in some cases over several millennia. This achievement has since been developed further in other projects across Britain.

England: Strength in Diversity

In England, several HLC projects have been undertaken, or started, since the Cornwall project, covering in all about one-third of the country. Areas covered include (former) Avon, Peak District National Park, Cotswolds AONB, Nottinghamshire, Hampshire, Herefordshire, Surrey, Lancashire, Somerset, and Eastern England (a single project encompassing Suffolk, Hertfordshire, Essex, Cambridgeshire, Norfolk and Bedfordshire) (Fairclough, 1999b).

The characterization process is generally based on the same type of data as that used in Cornwall, identifying historic landscape types, simplified into categories or areas for an easier overview (for example, Barnatt, 1999; Lambrick, 1999; Miller 1999). Subsequent projects have generally been GIS-based from the outset, making the product more flexible. Most of these are financially supported by English Heritage in partnership with the relevant local planning or national park authorities, which are usually the lead bodies. To an extent, therefore, they are bottom-up projects, which give greater weight to local circumstances than to an over-arching national design.

Individually the projects vary quite considerably in scope: for example, the Hampshire work was very detailed, identifying 85 historic landscape types (Lambrick, 1999, p52), while in the Peak District National Park, work concentrated on identifying changes over time (Barnatt, 1999). Most projects relate directly to planning policy (Sydes, 1999) and countryside management (Miller, 1999). Some are associated with landscape character work, as in the case of Hampshire (Tartaglia-Kershaw, 1999), while in the Peak District National Park the HLC has been undertaken in advance of an LCA for the area (Barnatt, 1999).

English Heritage aim to continue to promote this work throughout the country with their partners (Fairclough, 1999b). The focus is very much on mapping local distinctiveness for local uses. Although developed from a common methodology, there is no standardized typology in the characterization projects across England and no definite plan to link these to form a national historical character map. Nevertheless, there is the potential to produce national or regional overviews as most HLCs are GIS-based and the data are capable of generalization or simplification (Fairclough, 1999b). This emphasis on the local is a particular strength in relation to planning policy and sustainability issues, which mostly have a local focus and aim to depict local character (for example, Lambrick, 1999; Miller, 1999).

Scotland: A National Overview

In Scotland, Historic Landuse Assessment (HLA) is being undertaken as a partnership between Historic Scotland (HS) and the Royal Commission on the Ancient and Historical Monuments of Scotland (RCAHMS). Inspired by the Cornwall model, though differing significantly from it, HLA is similarly seeking to map the historic influences still evident in the modern countryside (Dyson Bruce et al, 1999; Dixon et al, 1999). It is based on the OS 1:25,000 map, and uses topographical and land cover maps and datasets, vertical aerial photographs and archaeological and historical data to identify historic land use patterns and relict landscapes over one hectare in extent. The resultant HLA, which is contained in a GIS database, depicts the dominant historical land use processes that have affected the present day landscape.

HLA defines historic land use types, based on the period of origin, the form and/or the function of current land use patterns. HLA also identifies relict types: these are either historic land use types no longer used for their original purpose, but still identifiable in the landscape, or archaeological areas. There can be up to three relict types in the same area, reflecting real time-depth in the landscape. This addition of information on relict types makes HLA slightly different from other approaches, though cross-referencing with relict data can be achieved fairly readily in other cases. Both historic and relict land use types can be grouped into categories to provide a clearer, but simplified, overview of historic and relict patterns, which aids regional comparison.

At the time of writing, some 25 per cent of Scotland has been covered, taking in a reasonable spread of landscape types and including the first two National Parks in Scotland, Loch Lomond and the Trossachs (RCAHMS and Historic Scotland, 2000), and the Cairngorms (RCAHMS and Historic Scotland, 2001). The eventual aim is to have full national coverage.

Unlike the approach in England, the HLA is essentially a top-down process carried out centrally. Some areas have been analysed at the request of, and with financial assistance from, other bodies, including Scottish Natural Heritage (SNH), the Forestry Commission and the Ayrshire Joint Structure Plan Committee. To date, however, there has been very little partnership with local authorities. The HLA, therefore, focuses more on the national overview than on local variety. There are advantages to this: national coverage will be to a consistent style and standard; a national overview is helpful for strategic purposes, such as setting agri-environment priorities; and the national picture can be used to identify regional patterns. At the same time, however, there is a loss of local knowledge and detail, and, as a result, HLA may be considered of less use to the local planning system. Nevertheless, it has value for strategic planning, it can be harmonized with local sites and monuments records (SMRs), and other local information can be built in at any stage.

Unlike Wales's unifying *LANDMAP* (see below and Chapter 12) or some of the projects in England, the HLA is not linked directly to SNH's LCA of Scotland. However, a recent preliminary review of the relationship between HLA and LCA in the World Heritage area in Orkney suggests that they complement each other fairly well (David Tyldesley and Associates, 2001). A comparable study is currently underway for the area of the new National Park in Loch Lomond and the Trossachs.

Wales: Registration and Characterization

In Wales, the approach has been slightly different. Cadw, the Countryside Council for Wales (CCW) and ICOMOS UK, in association with the Welsh Archaeological Trusts, the Royal Commission on the Ancient and Historical Monuments of Wales (RCAHMW) and the Welsh unitary authorities, have produced the non-statutory *Register of Landscapes of Outstanding Historic Interest in Wales* (Cadw et al, 1998) and *Register of Landscapes of Special Historic Interest* (Cadw et al, 2001).

The first register identified 36 landscape areas across Wales which were deemed to have outstanding historic value; the second listed 22 generally smaller landscapes of special historic interest. Both registers were identified through extensive consultation with specialists in archaeology, history and historical geography rather than through the application of any formal analytical technique (Cadw et al, 1998, ppxxiii–xxiv). The registers contain descriptions of the main historic processes and features within each historic landscape identified, together with a summary of their significance. Although the Welsh Registers concentrate on specific landscapes rather than the whole countryside, this does not mean that areas not on the register are considered to have less historic value. Rather, the purpose of the registers is to educate and raise awareness, particularly among planners and land managers, of the historic quality of the Welsh landscape and thereby improve the management of this across the landscape as a whole (Cadw et al, 1998).

Indeed, the overview provided through the registers is being complemented by the more detailed process of HLC (Cadw et al, 1998, pxxvii). This is being carried out by the four Welsh Archaeological Trusts, with support from Cadw and CCW, and is gradually being undertaken both for register landscapes and elsewhere as part of the *LANDMAP* programme (Cadw et al, 2001, pxvii; and Chapter 12). Using the methodology established in a study of the Gwent Levels (Rippon, 1996a) and subsequently developed by Gwynedd Archaeological Trust in the Llyn Environmentally Sensitive Area (Thompson, 1998), this HLC exercise is mapping historic character areas, based on dominant patterns, historical processes and coherent character within the landscape. As elsewhere, this draws on land use type and physical features relating to land use and settlement (David Thompson, personal communication). For the register landscapes, this process will both refine their key characteristics and test the appropriateness of their boundaries. More generally, HLC is beginning to reveal that historical processes have influenced present landscape character considerably (for example, *Gwynedd Landscape Strategy* (Gwynedd County Council, 1999, p13)).

While the process of identifying historic landscapes for the two Welsh Registers was essentially top-down, historic landscape characterization is a more bottom-up approach. Within Wales, therefore, HLC can be applied in both national and local contexts: guidelines have already been drawn up to help assess the impact of development on register landscapes, while HLC is being used to advise on applications for Tir Gofal, the Welsh agri-environment scheme (Cadw et al, 2001). As part of *LANDMAP*, CCW, in partnership with others, has developed the HLC approach further to identify the cultural associations and influences of landscape (CCW, 2001).

Beyond Britain

The recent production of an atlas of the rural landscape has provided an excellent base for understanding the historical development of the landscape in Ireland. This combines general description with details of regional variation and discussion of sensitivity to change (Aalen et al, 1997).

In Northern Ireland, a landscape characterization programme has recently been completed through the Environment Service, for use by planners within all district council areas. Although information and advice has been supplied by the Archaeological Service, this does not include a specific HLC at this stage (Claire Foley personal communication).

HLC has, however, recently been piloted for Counties Clare and Limerick, complementing a survey of archaeological landscapes which is being carried out at the same time.[1] As described in Chapter 8, HLC was applied in County Clare as part of a wider landscape characterization project, based on the Cornwall methodology and funded by the Irish Heritage Council. Around the same time, a new methodology for HLC, adapted from the Cornish and Scottish models, was tested in County Limerick and in County Clare as part of the Archaeological Landscapes Project, also funded by the Heritage Council. A key element of this new methodology was to use the Irish townland boundaries as the primary mapping unit, as townlands are considered to be a central contributor to historic character and important in the public perception of the Irish landscape. Like the Scottish methodology, the Irish HLC includes a Relict Landuse Component to reflect the chronological depth of the historic character. The mapping sources are early six-inch and recent 1;50,000 OS maps, from which information on, for example, topography, townland boundaries, settlements, woodland and nature reserves was extracted. Data on relict land use are derived from the Record of Monuments and Places.

The new Irish HLC identifies types, zones and areas. HLC types consist of a historic land use component which is based on the dominant historic land use in a townland, and a relict landuse component, which reflects historic land use traces no longer in use. They therefore show both the dominant historic process visible in the landscape and the most significant underlying relict elements. HLC zones are derived from the types through simplification and generalization, to show the broader patterns of the historical processes within the landscape. HLC areas represent an aggregation of zones to produce a simplified map of historical processes at county or regional level. At each level, accompanying text describes the main historic land use and relict land use components and considers issues such as significance, sensitivity and potential.

Mapping and analytical work on the historical development of the landscape are being carried out elsewhere in Europe. Examples are the preparation of general historical atlases, as in Sweden (Selinge, 1994); detailed case studies, such as the collaborative project between the Netherlands, Germany and Denmark in the Wadden Sea (Lancewad, 2001); the development of policy for the cultural heritage in spatial planning, as in Denmark and the Netherlands (Danish Forest and Nature Agency, 2001); and the EU-funded programme, *European Pathways to the Cultural Landscape*. As in Britain, the purpose of such work in continental Europe is to aid understanding, identify important historical or cultural landscapes and inform landscape management.

Summary

Although terminology varies and there are differences in the data that are available for specific areas, the various methodologies are derived from similar sources. Conceptually they share a common core, and the information conveyed is broadly comparable. Data on relict components are only included as part of the HLC process in Scotland and in the Republic of Ireland, but elsewhere relict data can be cross-referenced to available sources such as SMRs (for example, Sydes, 1999; Johnson, 1999a) or published atlases (for instance, Roberts and Wrathmell, 2000). HLC methodologies are predominantly desk-based, with selective field checking, while outputs are generally GIS-based and are normally accompanied by reports which describe the historical characteristics of the landscape and offer some guidance on issues of sensitivity and management.

Historic character is generally indicated by historic (or relict) land use (for example, 18th- and 19th-century improvements, industrial or military activity), the nature of field patterns and field boundaries (including size, date and regularity), the pattern of settlement (such as nucleated, scattered or planned) and the vernacular style of buildings. Generally, the results reveal that, while much of the present land use pattern was established in the 18th or 19th centuries, there is significant time-depth in many areas. Indeed, in some places, field boundaries can be traced back to the medieval period, if not earlier. The strength of HLC is that it shows how much present day local landscape character has been influenced by historical processes (Swanwick and Land Use Consultants, 2002).

Thus HLC enhances our understanding of the modern landscape. It is beginning to offer an insight into the historic complexities behind it and to depict regional variation and local character related to this. This information is not available from another single source. Like LCA, the focus of HLC is on the wider environment, not on special places; and its purpose is to inform and manage the process of landscape change. At the same time, it provides a context for individual archaeological and historic features and is potentially a powerful analytical tool for research.

Needless to say, there are problems to be addressed. Current HLC projects have the capability of enabling broad comparison in historic landscape development within, and between, the component parts of Britain. Yet this will ultimately need full national coverage, an aspiration which offers challenges of funding and timing. Although a broad-brush approach, HLC is more detailed than LCA and will take considerably longer to complete at a national level. There is an attendant problem of up-dating: as HLC reflects field boundaries and current land use patterns, some detail could become out of date more quickly than for LCA, though this is not likely to affect the broad historic patterns.

Finally, while HLC makes historical data more widely accessible and understandable, it none the less needs interpretation for the non-specialist. It is important that accompanying reports are accessible to a wide audience of users and that, where relevant, they include guidance on trends, pressures/sensitivities and on managing change. Some material has already been produced for the general public, in the form of published reports and leaflets, such as those produced by the Welsh Archaeological Trusts. Nevertheless, further work needs to be done in this area if the full significance of the historical dimension of the landscape is to be more widely understood.

THE APPLICATION OF HLC

Since HLC is a relatively recent development, it has not yet been sufficiently used to allow a comprehensive critical review. However, it is already apparent that the product is highly valued for its role in aiding an understanding of the development and character of the modern landscape, and influencing decisions about its future development. Its major potential application lies in the following areas: planning, land management, landscape policy, local distinctiveness and community-based initiatives, research, and education and communication.

HLC has so far been used most often by local archaeological services to advise on planning issues, relating to both policy and development control (for example, Sydes, 1999; Johnson, 1999a, 1999b; Rippon, 1996b). It is considered an aid to the understanding of the landscape by planners because it focuses on land use, with which they are familiar, in contrast to the more specialized archaeological and historical data held in most SMRs. At the same time, it gives a landscape context for those individual features. HLCs are beginning to be used in strategic planning policy where they can contribute to national or regional objectives and the planning of major developments like wind farms. Just as LCA has now been accepted as an established element in the planning process – widely referred to in planning guidance (Swanwick and Land Use Consultants, 2002; Cadw et al, 2001) – it is likely that HLC will gradually come to be used in the same way, helping to define the characteristics of an area irrespective of any formal designation.

HLC has also been used to advise on land management issues, particularly in respect of agri-environment schemes and Woodland Grant Schemes (Miller, 1999; Cadw et al, 2001). Although at present this is done most often in response to specific applications, it is also being used more strategically. For example, in Cornwall HLC has been used to help direct and prioritize heathland regeneration schemes by identifying areas of former heathland (Nick Johnson, personal communication). HLC can also assist in the development of Indicative Forestry Strategies and specific tree-planting schemes by indicating areas where trees have traditionally formed part of the land use, where they have played an important part in the character of settlement or where particular sensitivity is called for in relation to planting. In the Peak District National Park, for instance, a coincidence has been noted between surviving woodland and the presence of cruck-framed buildings (Ken Smith, personal communication). At Mar Lodge in the Cairngorms, HLA has been used to assess the likely impact of natural regeneration on areas of relict landscape (Dyson Bruce et al, 1999). More generally, HLC can assist in the process of monitoring landscape change by providing baseline information against which change can be measured. Alongside LCA, it can also facilitate an integrated approach to countryside management, improving communication and minimizing conflict (Bishop, 1999).

HLC can play a role in helping to develop strategic policy for cultural landscapes and rural land management. It can both provide national overviews and help to define regional and local characteristics as a basis for prioritizing actions from the national to the local level. National overviews can help develop strategic policy in relation to international provisions such as those of the World Heritage Convention and the European Landscape Convention (see Chapter 4). In these contexts, HLC can provide an overview of cultural sites and landscapes, and combine with LCA to define key landscape characteristics for protection, management and interpretation. In Orkney, for example, HLA and LCA are being used together to develop the Management Plan for the World Heritage site, *The Heart of Neolithic Orkney* (David Tyldesley and Associates, 2001). HLC can similarly play a strategic role in defining national policy for, for example, monument and landscape protection, rural development or agri-environment schemes.

HLC can be a useful tool in helping local communities gain an insight into the historical roots of their area, enhancing their sense of place. It helps highlight local distinctiveness and diversity, by clarifying how areas have developed differently (for example, Lambrick, 1999; Miller, 1999). It is being used actively to inform community-based local projects such as the Common Ground Parish Map of Cornwall (Nick Johnson, personal communication). In the Peak District National Park, it is seen as a useful tool for informing and stimulating discussion about what local communities view as the key characteristics of their local landscape (Barnatt, 1999). In this respect, it has clear potential for use in Local Heritage Initiatives, a set of three country programmes funded by the Heritage Lottery Fund in partnership with the

Countryside Agency, SNH and the CCW. It may also be relevant to determining issues relating to access in the countryside and in Local Agenda 21 sustainability initiatives. It can help inform environmental decision-making where a balance is needed between continuity and change, and between conservation and development. This lies at the very heart of policy for sustainable development.

The potential value of HLC in research is considerable. As a broad brush landscape assessment, it can be used to clarify rapidly what is known about a landscape, and to help identify gaps in knowledge and target priority areas for survey or further research. It helps predict what kind of historic information is likely to survive in different areas, based on the use of an area in the past and the impact of that use on the survival and visibility of physical evidence. The HLC helps show patterns and connections within the landscape, including the variety of sites and their relationship with other landscape features; and relationships between topography, the natural environment and historic land use and settlement. It aids investigation into how the landscape and land use have changed through time, particularly in relation to human influence. HLC is thus a potentially powerful tool for predictive modelling for planning and management objectives, and for research.

The HLC can both raise issues for further research and offer a broader context for detailed research. Its broad brush approach can be made more sensitive by the addition of further layers of information or analysis at larger scales. For example, it can help in exploring settlement patterns and associated land use through time (Wills, 1999). The Peak District National Park has produced a series of period characterization maps, relating to 50-year intervals from 1650 to the present. These show how different landscape types have changed through time and thus help establish relevant conservation and management strategies for the landscape of the park (Barnatt, 1999).

HLC is a flexible tool which can assist greatly with the communication of specialist data. It can be adapted to suit national, regional and local levels of need; and it can be integrated with, or reviewed against, a variety of datasets. In this respect, its greatest value is obtained through inter-active GIS rather than the static maps. HLC can help make specialist data meaningful to a wider audience by focusing on landscapes rather than sites, and on land use, with which non-specialist users are generally more familiar. This makes it easier for archaeological specialists to talk to a variety of audiences, including planners, land managers and local communities, and it makes it easier for those audiences to understand the relevance of the history in the landscape to modern strategies for landscape management (see Herring, 1998). This gives it immense potential in the fields of training, education and interpretation.

Relationships with other data sets

No work has yet been carried out to relate the various types of HLC to each other. HLCs can already be linked directly with SMRs, giving a wider landscape and land use context for specific site information. In fact, the Cornwall County Archaeologist has expressed the view that the HLC has become fundamental to the County SMR (Nick Johnson personal communication), since the HLC identifies the historic influences across the landscape of Cornwall, while a conventional SMR shows only the individual features that have survived. As result, site specific data becomes, in effect, a sub-set of the broader record (Johnson, 1999a, 1999b; Sydes, 1999). The HLC clarifies the historical processes that created individual features on the one hand, and facilitated their survival on the other.

Because HLCs are mostly GIS-based, they can also be linked relatively easily to other archaeological data sets, such as those for wetlands or urban areas. Furthermore, they are capable of analysis in a variety of ways and against different sets of information, such as settlement types (Roberts and Wrathmell, 2000) or vernacular buildings. They can also be linked to environmental records so as to analyse, for instance, the correlation between historical processes and biodiversity.

In some instances HLC is formally linked to the LCA for the same area, as in the original Cornwall study, in the Peak District National Park and in Hampshire (Barnatt, 1999; Lambrick, 1999). In many cases, however, this relationship has not yet been explored in detail. Correlation can be difficult because different scales and methods of production are used for HLC and LCA, and they are generally distinct products. Nevertheless, HLC forms an important layer of information in the preparation of the broader brush LCA, and GIS makes it entirely possible to relate the two techniques closely to each other, as the Welsh *LANDMAP* in particular demonstrates. HLC and LCA clearly convey complementary information about the landscape, and, used in combination, the two approaches considerably enhance our understanding of the modern landscape and the human influence on it (David Tyldesley and Associates, 2001; Tartaglia-Kershaw, 1999).

CONCLUSIONS

Landscape is a palimpsest, a combination of natural forces and cultural influence. It is also the product of historical processes. In many parts of Britain, historical influence is paramount; elsewhere it is less obvious, but it is present everywhere. HLCs are enhancing our appreciation of the time-depth within the landscape and our understanding of how its character has been influenced by its human history. Alongside LCA, HLC offers us a powerful new tool to aid understanding of the modern environment and to inform decisions about management and change in a more integrated and creative way than ever before.

POSTSCRIPT

Since this chapter was written, a new publication has appeared, *Europe's Cultural Landscape*, which presents further detail of several of the projects mentioned (Fairclough and Rippon, 2002).

ACKNOWLEDGEMENTS

I would like to thank the many colleagues and friends who kindly assisted with the preparation of this chapter, offering information, discussion or textual comment, principally: David Breeze, Gabriel Cooney, Aled Davies, Piers Dixon, Graham Fairclough, Claire Foley, Sarah Govan, Peter Herring, Nick Johnson, Lee Jones, Richard Kelly, Adrian Phillips, Ken Smith, Jack Stevenson, David Thompson, Peter Herring and the Cornwall Archaeological Unit. Any errors or inaccuracies are, of course, entirely my own.

NOTE

1 The following information is derived from an unpublished report by Gabriel Cooney and colleagues (Cooney *et al.* 2001).

REFERENCES

Aalen, F H A (1996) *Landscape Study and Management,* Office of Public Works, Dublin

Aalen, F H A, Whelan, K and Stout, M (eds) (1997) *Atlas of the Irish Rural Landscape,* Cork University Press, Cork

Baker, D with Shepherd, I (1993) 'Local Authority Opportunities', in Hunter, J and Ralston, I (eds) *Archaeological Resource Management in the UK: An Introduction,* Sutton Publishing Ltd, Stroud, pp100–114

Barnatt, J (1999) 'Peak National Park: A changing landscape', in Fairclough, G (ed) *Historic Landscape Characterisation: Papers Presented at an English Heritage Seminar,* English Heritage, London, pp41–50

Belvedere Memorandum (undated) *The Belvedere Memorandum: A Policy Document Examining the Relationship between Cultural History and Spatial Planning,* available from Distributiecentrum VROM, PO Box 2727, 3430 GC Nieuwegein

Bishop, M W (1999) 'Relating Research to Practice with Historic Landscape Character in Nottinghamshire', in Fairclough, G (ed) *Historic Landscape Characterisation: Papers Presented at an English Heritage Seminar 11 December 1998,* English Heritage, London, pp83–89

Breeze, D J (1993) 'Ancient Monuments Legislation', in Hunter, J and Ralston, I (eds) *Archaeological Resource Management in the UK: An Introduction,* Sutton Publishing Ltd, Stroud, pp44–55

Cadw, Countryside Council for Wales and ICOMOS UK (1998) *Register of Landscapes of Outstanding Historic Interest in Wales,* Cadw, Cardiff

Cadw, Countryside Council for Wales and ICOMOS UK (2001) *Register of Landscapes of Special Historic Interest in Wales,* Cadw, Cardiff

Cooney, G, Condit, T and Byrnes, E (2001) *The Archaeological Landscapes Project: Final Report (Draft for Comment),* The Heritage Council, Kilkenny

Countryside Council for Wales (2001) *LANDMAP Manual,* CCW, Bangor

Danish Forest and Nature Agency (2001) *Cultural Heritage in Planning: Identifying Valuable Cultural Environments through Planning,* Danish Forest and Nature Agency, Copenhagen

David Tyldesley and Associates (2001) *Landscape Studies of the Heart of Neolithic Orkney World Heritage Site,* Report to Scottish Natural Heritage and Historic Scotland, Edinburgh

Department for Culture, Media and Sport (DCMS) and the Department for Transport, Local Government and Regions (DTLR) (2001) *The Historic Environment: A Force for Our Future*, Report by the DCMS and DTLR, London

Dixon, P, Dyson-Bruce, L, Hingley, R and Stevenson, J (1999) 'Historic Land Use Assessment Project', in Usher, M B (ed) (1999) *Landscape Character: Perspectives on Management and Change*, The Stationery Office, Edinburgh, pp162–129

Dyson Bruce, L, Dixon, P, Hingley, R and Stevenson, J (1999) *Historic Landuse Assessment (HLA): Development and Potential of a Technique for Assessing Historic Landuse Patterns*, Historic Scotland Research Report, Edinburgh

Fairclough, G (1999a) 'Historic Landscape Characterisation: Theory, objectives and connections', in Fairclough, G (ed) *Historic Landscape Characterisation: Papers Presented at an English Heritage Seminar 11 December 1998*, English Heritage, London, pp3–14

Fairclough, G (1999b) 'Historic Landscape and the Future', in Fairclough, G (ed) *Historic Landscape Characterisation: Papers Presented at an English Heritage Seminar 11 December 1998*, English Heritage, London, pp60–67

Fairclough, G, Lambrick, G and McNab, A (1999) *Yesterday's World, Tomorrow's Landscape: the English Heritage Historic Landscape Project 1992–4*, English Heritage, London

Fairclough, G and Rippon, S (with Bull, D) (2002) *Europe's Cultural Landscape: Archaeologists and the Management of Change*, European Archaeologiae Consilium, Brussels

Gwynedd County Council (1999) *Gwynedd Landscape Strategy Volume 1: Strategy Framework*, Gwynedd County Council, Caernarfon

Herring, P (1998) *Cornwall's Historic Landscape: Presenting a Method of Historic Landscape Character Assessment*, Cornwall Archaeological Unit, Truro

Hunter, J and Ralston, I (eds) (1993) *Archaeological Resource Management in the UK: An Introduction*, Sutton Publishing Ltd, Stroud

Johnson, N (1999a) 'Context, Meaning and Consequences: Using the map in Cornwall', in Fairclough (ed) *Historic Landscape Characterisation: Papers Presented at an English Heritage Seminar 11 December 1998*, English Heritage, London, pp117–122

Johnson, N (1999b) 'Preface to Historic Landscape Characterisation: The Cornwall study', in Macinnes, L (ed) *Assessing Cultural Landscapes: Progress and Potential*, ICOMOS UK, pp15–26

Lambrick, G (1999) 'Hampshire: historic landscape character and the community', in Fairclough (ed) *Historic Landscape Characterisation: Papers Presented at an English Heritage Seminar 11 December 1998*, English Heritage, London, pp51–63

Lancewad (2001) *Lancewad: Landscape and Cultural Heritage in the Wadden Sea Region*, Project Report, Wadden Sea Ecosystem No 12, Common Wadden Sea Secretariat, Wilhelmshaven

Macinnes, L (1993) 'Archaeology as Land Use', in Hunter, J and Ralston, I (eds) *Archaeological Resource Management in the UK: An Introduction*, Sutton Publishing Ltd, Stroud, pp243–255

McNab, A (1999) 'Introduction to the Project', in Fairclough, G (ed) *Historic Landscape Characterisation: Papers Presented at an English Heritage Seminar 11 December 1998*, English Heritage, London, pp18–23

McNab, A and Lambrick, G (1999) 'Conclusions and Recommendations', in Fairclough, G (ed) *Historic Landscape Characterisation: Papers Presented at an English Heritage Seminar 11 December 1998*, English Heritage, London, pp54–59

Miller, K (1999) 'Using Historic Landscape Characterisation for Land Management in the Isle of Axholme', in Fairlcough (ed) *Historic Landscape Characterisation: Papers Presented at an English Heritage Seminar 11 December 1998*, English Heritage, London, pp91–112

Muir, R (1999) *Approaches to Landscape*, Macmillan Press Ltd, Basingstoke

Rippon, S (1996a) *The Evolution of a Wetland Landscape*, Council for British Archaeology Research Report 105, York

Rippon, S (1996b) *The Gwent Levels Historic Landscape Study: Characterisation and Assessment of the Landscape*, Cadw and CCW, Cardiff

Roberts, B and Wrathmell, S (2000) *An Atlas of Rural Settlement in England*, English Heritage, London

Royal Commission on the Ancient and Historical Monuments of Scotland and Historic Scotland (2000) *The Historic Landscape of Loch Lomond and the Trossachs*, RCAHMS and Historic Scotland, Edinburgh

Royal Commission on the Ancient and Historical Monuments of Scotland and Historic Scotland (2001) *The Historic Landscape of the Cairngorms*, RCAHMS and Historic Scotland, Edinburgh

Selinge, K G (ed) (1994) *Cultural Heritage and Preservation: National Atlas of Sweden*, Royal Swedish Academy of Sciences, Stockholm

Suddards, R W (1993) 'Listed Buildings', in Hunter, J and Ralston, I (eds) *Archaeological Resource Management in the UK: An Introduction*, Sutton Publishing Ltd, Stroud, pp77–88

Swanwick, C and Land Use Consultants (2002) *Landscape Character Assessment Guidance*, Countryside Agency and Scottish Natural Heritage, Cheltenham

Sydes, B (1999) 'Building on the Map: Avon', in Fairclough, G (ed) *Historic Landscape Characterisation: Papers Presented at an English Heritage Seminar 11 December 1998*, English Heritage, London, pp67–82

Tartaglia-Kershaw, L (1999) 'Integrating Historic Landscape Characterisation to Landscape Assessment in Hampshire', in Fairclough, G (ed) *Historic Landscape Characterisation: Papers Presented at an English Heritage Seminar 11 December 1998*, English Heritage, London, pp113–115

Thompson, D (1998) *Historic Landscape Characterisation on Llyn: A Methodological Statement*, Gwynedd Archaeological Trust unpublished report No 287, Caernarfon

Usher, M B (ed) (1999) *Landscape Character: Perspectives on Management and Change*, The Stationery Office, Edinburgh

Wills, J (1999) 'Cotswolds AONB: characterisation, classification and GIS', in Fairclough, G (ed) *Historic Landscape Characterisation: Papers Presented at an English Heritage Seminar 11 December 1998*, English Heritage, London, pp33–40

Chapter 11

Connecting the Pieces: Scotland's Integrated Approach to the Natural Heritage

Roger Crofts

Scotland's natural heritage is immensely diverse, despite the small size of the country. This arises from Scotland's complex earth history, its location between continental and maritime influences, and its altitudinal range. Not only is the proper stewardship of this heritage important in its own right, but it provides opportunities for increasing economic wealth and improving social well-being. Historically, however, as in other parts of the UK, the approach to the protection and management of Scotland's natural heritage has been fragmented: species and habitats have been dealt with by a nature conservation agency, whilst landscape, amenity and recreation have been the responsibility of a separate countryside agency. Other parts of the public sector have been poorly connected with natural heritage management and often their activities have resulted in its progressive deterioration.

A number of changes occurred in the early 1990s which presented opportunities for a more integrated approach and achieving a wider range of benefits. The institutional structure was remodelled: Scottish Natural Heritage (SNH) was established in 1992 with an integrated remit for the conservation and enhancement of the natural heritage as a whole and with a responsibility to promote its sustainable use. The agenda from the UNCED Earth Summit in Rio in 1992 encouraged more integrated approaches by placing the pursuit of economic and social needs and aspirations alongside the stewardship of natural resources. There was growing interest in experience in many other parts of the world where the delivery of policy and action within biogeographic regions or zones, rather than administrative units, had proved valuable (Miller, 1996). And, finally, there was a growing commitment to including the various local and national communities of interest in visioning, planning and action for the conservation, enhancement and sustainable use of the natural heritage.

It was because of these developments that SNH decided, in the mid-1990s, to initiate its Natural Heritage Futures Programme (the Futures Programme).[1] This chapter sets out the thinking behind the approach, explains the methodology used to define the natural sub-divisions of Scotland, and describes the main elements of the Futures Programme. The main part of the text focuses on an assessment of the actual and expected benefits of the Futures Programme.

THE OVERALL PHILOSOPHY

For far too long there have been fragmented and sectoral approaches to dealing with rural countryside and environmental issues in Britain. When philosophies and cultures of segmentation and separation are deeply entrenched, they become barriers to coherence and integration. This was reflected in, and was in turn reinforced by, the way in which natural heritage business was organized in the UK. Since the development of statutory environmental organizations in Britain in the late 1940s, there have been over 50 years of fragmented approaches to dealing with the natural environment. It has been dealt with from either a nature conservation perspective, focusing particularly on species and habitats, or a countryside perspective, embracing landscape, amenity and recreation (Smout, 2001).

There are profound philosophical and practical reasons for integrating the two strands of the natural heritage business – countryside and nature conservation – into one organization, as practised in Scotland through Scottish Natural Heritage (SNH) and in Wales through the Countryside Council for Wales (CCW) (Crofts, 1994, 2000, 2001). First, there is the argument that biological and landscape diversity are so intimately inter-related that it makes no sense to separate them. Landscape character depends in part on its physical (ie geological and geomorphological) elements, and in part on its vegetation cover: landscape diversity is therefore partly a function of biological diversity. Second, the natural heritage of plants and animals, geological and geomorphological features, natural beauty and amenity (as it is defined in the Natural Heritage (Scotland) Act 1991) is highly dynamic. Changes in one element, eg land use, can have profound effects on other elements, eg wildlife and amenity; changes made now will have an impact over many years into the future, eg forestry. Third, much of nature conservation, and to a lesser extent landscape protection, is based on a strategy of protected areas. Yet there is much evidence within Scotland, and elsewhere, to show that achieving protection of critical features through protected areas alone, whilst ignoring what is occurring outside their boundaries, makes no sense. Pollution effects and migration of species can make protected area boundaries meaningless; moreover, many existing protected areas are too small to serve the purpose for which they were established (see, for example, Runte, 1997). Next, the conservation of diversity in Britain is primarily undertaken on private land. To be successful, therefore, the legitimate interests and roles of owners and managers of land need to be recognized. However, the finer points of difference between a nature conservation policy and a landscape protection policy will often be lost on the landowners and occupiers: indeed many would regard having to deal with different institutions, policies, designations, etc as irritating. And finally – and of central relevance to the topic explored in this chapter – administrative boundaries rarely recognize the diversity of landscape or biological features; moreover, such boundaries are subject to adjustment for political reasons. In Britain, for example, some administrative counties that ceased to exist as long ago as 1974 are still used as the basic units for identifying Sites of Special Scientific Interest (SSSIs), the foundation of site-based nature protection in Britain. With advances in the collection and analysis of spatial data, we are better placed to define natural units that make sense in terms of both biological and landscape diversity.

As a new organization forged out of these two previously separate streams, SNH was determined to bring together its nature conservation and countryside functions in a coherent and integrated manner. It developed a means of addressing these challenges in the mid-1990s by defining the Natural Heritage Zones of Scotland. On the basis of the above analysis, the Futures Programme had the following initial principles:

- a new approach, founded on the interaction between activities within and outside protected areas and sites;
- an integrated approach to wildlife, landform and landscape protection and management;
- a rigorous but practical sub-division of the country to recognize its diversity;
- active engagement of the communities of interest in the management of protected areas and the wider countryside; and
- integration of environmental, economic and land use policies and schemes of assistance.

At the outset of its work on the Futures Programme, SNH did not have entirely clear objectives. Attention was focused on replacing administrative units as Areas of Search for SSSIs. Work elsewhere of a similar nature was not appraised until later, and a major exercise of Landscape Character Assessment (LCA) for the whole of Scotland was still at an early stage. However, by the time of writing this chapter, SNH has taken this work far beyond its original limited intentions. It has linked it to the emerging requirements of the organization and the changing needs of the natural heritage and it changed the name from the Natural Heritage Zonal Programme, which had connotations of another system of designations, to Natural Heritage Futures to recognize the forward looking and strategic nature of the programme. It has learnt the lessons from similar activities undertaken elsewhere in the UK and overseas (see, for example, Chapters 6, 7, 8 and 12 and Crofts et al, 2000), and it has tried to reflect its experience in engaging with partner organizations in the post-Rio era, bringing together social, economic and environmental concerns (see Crofts, 2001) (Box 11.1).

BOX 11.1 TIMETABLE FOR THE FUTURES PROGRAMME

1994/95	Development of basic concepts
1995/96	Review of approaches elsewhere
Late 1996	Approval of the Natural Heritage Zone (NHZ) programme by SNH Board
1996/97	Implementation of first phase of NHZ programme combined with SNH Organizational Development Programme
April 1997	Establishment of corporate NHZ team and re-structuring of organization
1997/99	Development of six national assessments
1997/98	Development of pilot local prospectus for Shetland
1998/2000	Development of other 20 local prospectuses
1999/2000	Development of six national prospectuses
Late 2000	Approval by SNH Area Boards of local prospectuses for external consultation
December 2000	Approval by SNH Board of six national prospectuses and overview for external consultation
Early 2001	External consultation
Early 2001	National assessments on to SNH web site
Late 2001	Revisions following consultation: new name of 'Natural Heritage Futures' adopted for what was the NHZ programme; 'Prospectuses' replaced by 'Perspectives'
Early 2002	Publication of all perspectives

BASIC STRUCTURE OF APPROACH

SNH believes that conservation, resource use and development must be integrated if natural functions, local character, and species and habitat patterns are to be maintained. It defines the Futures Programme as a visionary, practical and partnership approach for meeting, in an integrated way, the needs of all of Scotland's diverse terrestrial natural heritage. Thus it embraces the delivery of SNH's statutory responsibilities, as well as its role in meeting international obligations, (eg those under the Convention on Biological Diversity and the EU Natura 2000 programme (see Chapters 2 and 3)), in achieving national targets, including those set by biodiversity action plans (BAPs), and supporting other policy frameworks, such as Agenda 21.

The approach to the Futures Programme involves taking:

• a longer-term vision, focusing on what can be achieved in 25 years' time;
• an analytical stance in describing, nationally and locally, the diversity of the resource and the drivers of change; and
• an action-orientated approach by identifying objectives and specific actions for SNH and its partners.

As a result, Scotland has been classified into a series of geographic units within each of which there is a commonality of natural heritage characteristics and which, taken together, reflect the diversity of Scotland's natural heritage.

> ## Box 11.2 Stages in the definition of Natural Heritage Futures Units
>
> 1. Taxonomic classification: 6 species
> 2. Climatic data: 16 variables
> 3. First stage zonal map
> 4. Literature review of spatial sub-divisions of Scotland
> 5. Soil and geographic data
> 6. Land use data
> 7. Landscape character data
> 8. Final map of 21 Natural Heritage Futures areas

The Futures Programme is primarily related to the terrestrial natural heritage. An attempt was made to apply a zonal approach to the marine environment (Kiemer et al, 1998) but there was insufficient material to allow geographic units to be identified in any meaningful way. There was also no coherence between the boundaries of terrestrial and marine zones. Coastal and marine issues are, however, dealt with in all relevant local documents and in the national document on the coast and sea (see below).

A brief account of the methodology is needed to explain how the various elements of the natural heritage were brought together (see Box 11.2). The starting point was to find indicators which were sensitive to the diversity of the natural biogeographic regions of Scotland. Work commissioned from the Institute of Terrestrial Ecology revealed that a particular series of plants and animals were most effective in providing a logical sub-division of Scotland (Carey et al, 1994, 1995). Data for six taxonomic groups formed the basis of the first level of classification: breeding birds, diurnal insects, non-marine molluscs, liverworts, mosses and vascular plants. In addition, 16 climatic variables were added. The outcome of this first stage analysis was a ten-zone map of Scotland. A schematic version (Figure 11.1) shows that the diversity of Scotland's natural heritage is determined by altitudinal and oceanic/continental gradients. This was then cross-checked in two ways. An extensive literature review was commissioned on the classification of Scotland into biogeographic regions (Mather and Gunson, 1995); this showed that there was a great deal of consistency between the more historic qualitative work and the later quantitative work. In a separate exercise, other relevant biogeographic data were added (ie on soils and topography).

The next stage was to ensure that non-biogeographical elements of the natural heritage, ie landscape character and land use, were incorporated in the classification. This was vital if the spatial units were to reflect the whole of SNH's remit, which covers landscape diversity as well as biodiversity. The detailed Landscape Character Assessment of Scotland was still at an early stage, although the methodology had been established jointly with the then Countryside Commission for England (Swanwick and Land Use Consultants, 2002). The expertise of SNH's own landscape advisers was used to distil the patterns into landscape character types and then to superimpose these onto the biogeographic data (Thin, 1999).

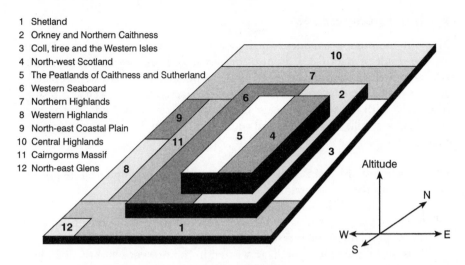

1 Shetland
2 Orkney and Northern Caithness
3 Coll, tiree and the Western Isles
4 North-west Scotland
5 The Peatlands of Caithness and Sutherland
6 Western Seaboard
7 Northern Highlands
8 Western Highlands
9 North-east Coastal Plain
10 Central Highlands
11 Cairngorms Massif
12 North-east Glens

Figure 11.1 *Systematic diagram of Natural Heritage Units*

A composite picture of the natural heritage character of Scotland was built up in a series of layers, including: plant and animal distributions; climate, soils and topographical factors; landscape character and land use. The spatially-referenced data were aggregated at different levels in order to identify the level at which clear patterns emerged. It was never the intention to allow the data alone to determine the number of natural heritage sub-divisions of Scotland, but to confirm the choice which was to be made by informed judgement. If there were too many sub-divisions, the result would be fragmented, and major units which have wide public recognition would be lost; if there were too few units, identity, diversity and sense of place would not be revealed.

Examination of the composite data sets led to the judgement that 10–12 units would be too few to reflect adequately the diversity of Scotland's natural heritage but that more than two dozen would result in too great a fragmentation. After detailed discussions with colleagues and others knowledgeable about Scotland's natural heritage, 21 units were determined (see Figure 11.2 in Plate section).

The next step was to develop documentation for the Futures Programme. It was decided to focus attention on three sets of documents: national assessments, national and local documents.

National assessments

These are the foundation documents. They comprise the best available information and interpretation about key aspects of the natural heritage and its use: recreation and access, landscape, physical characteristics, earth heritage, species, habitats and fresh waters. The data are presented in tabular and map form and made available through the SNH website (www.snh.org.uk) and on a CD Rom (SNH, 2002a). The information gathered is the most comprehensive and up-to-date available and represents a baseline from which to measure future change.

National perspectives

Many of the human activities, which drive change within each of the 21 units, are the result of national, European or global policies. Also, many units share common themes. Hence a series of national perspectives has been prepared to address nationally relevant issues. The topics covered were chosen as a result of discussion with key constituencies: farmland, forests, woodlands, fresh waters, coast and sea, hills and moors, and settlements. Each document comprises six parts:

- summary of the main environmental, social and economic features and the key issues for the natural heritage;
- a description of the natural heritage;
- an assessment of the key influences on the natural heritage both in the recent past and in the foreseeable future;
- a vision of the natural heritage written in the present tense of 2025 based on better stewardship of natural resources;
- objectives, priorities and actions required to work towards the vision; and
- identification of national stakeholders to help in pursuing the actions identified against each objective.

These documents have been published and are also available on the SNH website.

Local perspectives

For each of the 21 units, a local perspective has been drawn up. As with the national perspectives, each local perspective contains six parts:

- summary of the main environmental, social and economic features and key issues for the natural heritage;
- description of the natural heritage at present;
- an assessment of the key influences on the natural heritage both in the recent past and the foreseeable future;
- a vision for the natural heritage written in the present tense for 2025 based on better stewardship of natural resources;
- objectives, priorities and actions required to work towards the vision; and
- identification of key local and national stakeholders to help in pursuing actions identified against each objective.

These local prospectuses have also been published and are available on the SNH website.

Overview

In addition to these three types of document (national assessments, and national and local perspectives), An *Overview* has been prepared (SNH, 2002b). This explains Scotland's natural heritage and why it is important; the link between the natural heritage and sustainable development; what changes are taking place; and mechanisms for influencing change (policy measures, consensus, partnership working and community involvement).

WHAT ARE THE BENEFITS – ACTUAL AND EXPECTED?

The Futures Programme documents were subject to two stages of consultation with key partners, were revised and then formally published in March 2002. Clear action plans will be prepared and implemented. Since the programme is still at a formative phase, one must be cautious about drawing conclusions. None the less, it is possible to assess the impact of the Futures Programme under eight headings. These are: benefits for the natural heritage, improving collaboration with key stakeholders, stimulating policy integration, delivering an integrated remit, providing a new basis for strategies, providing a new basis for resourcing actions, defining targeted action and achieving improved corporate culture.

Achieving Tangible Benefits for the Natural Heritage

It is, of course, far too early to identify what the benefits of the Futures Programme to the natural heritage itself have been. However, by defining visions of the natural heritage in 2025 in 21 local variants and six national variants, SNH has set out its own aspirations. Box 11.3, which contains quotations from one local perspective and one national perspective, indicates the kind of long-term targets which have been drawn up.

From these vision statements, which were amended following the stakeholder consultation exercises, SNH has drawn up more specific action plans and identified milestones in the progress towards achieving a shared vision. Monitoring and evaluation of the programme, and the modification of objectives and actions, will be an integral part of the process of implementation.

Improving Collaboration with Key Stakeholders

SNH operates largely by influence and persuasion. It is not a regulatory agency and has no statutory powers to stop activities. SNH cannot fulfil its statutory responsibilities – 'to secure the conservation and enhancement of and foster the understanding and facilitate the enjoyment of the natural heritage of Scotland and have regard to the desirability of securing that anything done, whether by SNH or any other person, in relation to the natural heritage of Scotland is undertaken in a manner which is sustainable' – in any other way than through partnership.

So working with others sets the tone and culture for SNH's work. Indeed, it is one of its Operating Principles: 'we work in partnership by co-operation, negotiation and consensus, where possible, with all relevant interests in Scotland: public, private and voluntary organisations and individuals' (SNH, 2000a). Moreover, a specific objective of SNH's Management Strategy is 'improving collaboration with key stakeholders'. The articulation of this

Box 11.3 Defining visions for the natural heritage

Vision for the Peatlands of Caithness and Sunderland

> *There is a sense of optimism in Caithness and Sunderland because the economic decline has been halted. The local economy has been restructured to ensure co-ordinated, sustainable development that serves the needs of the people and the environment. Partnership projects continue to show positive results ... and still greatly influence integrated development and nature conservation policies...*

Diverse low-intensity farming and sensitive management are supported by agricultural and conservation incentive schemes ... the continuation of traditional land management, such as grazing and muirburn, helps to maintain diverse and distinctive managed landscapes, reinforcing the local character and identity of the area ...

Some forest plantations on deep peat, which have reached the end of their first rotation, are being clear-felled to initiate the restoration of peatland habitats ... through reductions in grazing and improved native woodland management, large areas of intact blanket mire are developing natural edges. These merge into regenerating woodland and scrub on steeper slopes and dryer soils ...

The characteristic wild landscapes of the area are protected through development control. Where possible these are restored by supporting activities that enhance those qualities, for example, the removal of obtrusive structures and the promotion of vernacular buildings of local stone ...

Affordable non-fossil fuel alternatives are now utilised in the area minimising the release of greenhouse gases... The economic value of the local environment has increased as tourism and other leisure activities have diversified and increased.

The rich natural heritage of crofting land and coastal fringes is maintained through diverse, low-intensity management supported by UK and European agriculture and environment incentive schemes...

The peatlands are designated as a World Heritage Site, helping to stimulate a co-ordinated approach to sustainable development and ensuring that all natural and cultural features are maintained and enhanced...

Through increased education, interpretation and an awareness of the economic value of the local environment, many habitats and species of local, national and international value are seen in a positive light by all in the area. The conservation of these features is consequently a priority for everyone.

Source: SNH (2002c)

Vision for Hills and Moors

> *there is a common agreement that the best way forward is a sustainable approach, based on sound understanding of the physical limitations and potential of our hills. This approach has secured greater care ... there has been substantial action to raise the quality and diversity of natural vegetation ... the recovery of natural woodland and scrub is being encouraged ... improvements to hill vegetation across extensive areas are now visible ... including the early development of natural treelines ... bird and mammal populations are heading towards a more natural balance ... however, climate change has led to some loss of biodiversity ... pressures for development have continued ... proposals to exploit natural resources of wind, water and minerals, and increased timber*

> production, have been sensitively handled through a more strategic and
> planned approach ... field sports continue as a major land use ... grouse
> populations are now more stable and red deer populations are in better
> balance with their habitat ... there is a stronger management for access
> ... for all these changes have had wider community benefits.
>
> *Source:* SNH (2002d)

objective was informed by a formal analysis of stakeholders as part of its management strategy work assisted by Colin Eden and Fran Ackerman of Strathclyde University (Eden and Ackerman, 1998). Each stakeholder was identified in terms of its relative power and interest in SNH's activities and the natural heritage. Mapping these on a grid provided a perception of the likely stance of the stakeholders (on a continuum from negative to positive) and the relative priority, in general terms, which should be given to working with each of them. Those stakeholders whose power and interest were greatest were identified as the most critical.

As part of the stakeholder interaction process, there has been a programme of introductory presentations to key national stakeholders. This was essential preparation for a more focused discussion on the contributions which key stakeholders could make. Reactions have perhaps been predictable. On the positive side, there has been support for SNH clarifying its own position, for using spatial units which make sense, for wishing to be both strategic and action-orientated in its endeavours with stakeholders and for having the courage to set out a clear and coherent vision for the future. On the negative side, concern has been expressed that SNH was spreading beyond its remit and that the spatial units made no sense in the real world and that its proposals and the resource requirements were far too ambitious. The negotiating process on the drafts has resulted in the removal or the diminution of the more negative messages and building on the positive support.

SNH has enjoyed national-level engagement with key stakeholders for many years, through formal liaison arrangements, and in some cases written Concordats or Memoranda of Understanding. The establishment of the Scottish Parliament with its legislative powers for the natural heritage and other relevant issues has stimulated more debate and policy development. The Scottish Executive has initiated dialogue on policy development, legislation and action, and aims to reallocate resources in areas affecting the natural heritage. The National Perspectives therefore provide SNH with an informed basis for formal engagement not only with representative bodies in environmental and other sectors of public policy, but also with the Scottish Parliament and the Scottish Executive.

At the local level, engagement with stakeholders has, perhaps inevitably, been variable. Success depends on the priorities of other bodies and their culture of cooperation and partnership, as well as on SNH's own priorities and cultures. In the last two or three years, major strategic roles have been given to local councils. Thus local councils lead on the Local Agenda 21 process, and in preparing and implementing sustainable development plans, Local Biodiversity Action Plans (LBAP) and Community Plans. All these involve input from local communities and other interests, and affect the delivery of the local council's functions. SNH has sought to influence the content of these plans, and the councils' developing thinking has, in turn, shaped SNH's local perspectives. This is not a seamless approach but an iterative process.

Officials within partner organizations, particularly key advisory staff, have welcomed the information provided by SNH on the natural heritage and its use. The information available to partner organizations is objective, consolidated, easily manipulated and therefore suitable for their use. It has enabled them to develop their own policies with confidence.

The engagement with stakeholders nationally and locally is still at an early stage. However, clear synergies are emerging. Partner organizations are showing themselves ready to take both a more strategic and a more analytical view of their role and work in respect of the natural heritage, and to take this forward in partnership with SNH.

Stimulating integrated policies for the Natural Heritage

The past ten years have been a period of strategic policy development locally, nationally, regionally and globally, stimulated largely by outputs from the UNCED Earth Summit of 1992, particularly the various approaches to sustainable development and biological diversity. SNH was established, and its statutory terms of reference and government policy statement determined, just before Rio. However, as noted above, SNH's founding legislation recognized its role in promoting sustainability, whilst the development of UK and local strategies and action plans in response to the decisions arrived at in Rio provided a further stimulus to SNH activity in this area. It thus became essential that SNH should set out its own approach to sustainable development (SNH, 1993) and develop the implications of this for key sectors such as agriculture and forestry, across Scotland and in different parts of the country. The timing of development work on sustainability was critical: moving too early would have been criticized externally: moving too late would have missed a unique opportunity.

SNH's Corporate Strategy (see below) took as its framework the three elements of sustainable development: environmental, economic and social. This was to demonstrate, internally and externally, that SNH, and the natural heritage, had important contributions to make to economic prosperity and social well-being. Whilst some organizations are concerned with the social or economic aspects only (eg housing or enterprise agencies), the integration of policy and action required to achieve sustainable development cannot be achieved unless there is recognition of the linkages. An obvious example is that access to the countryside near to where people live has social inclusion and health benefits, and can bring economic benefits to the locality. Similarly, the footprint of economic activity on natural resources, landscape and wildlife, cannot be ignored. Therefore, all national and local perspectives formulate views and aspirations for social and economic benefits in relation to each of six national settings and to the 21 units.

Ensuring integrated delivery of the remit
SNH was given a duty by government and Parliament (Scottish Development Department, 1990) to integrate the various functions for wildlife and landscape protection, and for environmental education and enjoyment of the natural heritage. SNH's responsibilities included access, landscape character, and the delivery of obligations under the European Union Directives on Birds and Habitats, as well as its sustainable development duties. The Futures Programme was an ideal vehicle through which to pursue the challenge of integrating this wide remit. It enabled SNH to achieve a more coherent and coordinated approach to scientific activity, policy development and advocacy – indeed, to integrate the delivery of all its functions.

Three examples illustrate how the Futures Programme can be used to overcome the tendency to address issues in a compartmentalized fashion:

•   It would be relatively easy, for example, for SNH to pursue its remit to improve access to the countryside without regard for other considerations. However, a comprehensive approach to access, such as is provided though the Futures Programme, must take into account the potential impact on sensitive habitats, species and landforms, and the need to influence the behaviour of visitors to the countryside. Hence, a conservation sensitivity test on the organization's access policy and action was an important element in integrating the remit.

•   In Scotland, as in many other parts of the world, soft coasts are undergoing net retreat. This creates problems for coastal settlements, affects economic activities, such as golf, and directly impacts on coastal habitats. The traditional response has been that of hard engineering. Such an approach is often a short-term palliative which ignores the reality of coastal dynamics. Hence it may create long-term problems along the coast, sometimes many miles away. Moreover, the removal of coastal vegetation, and continuation of intensive grazing, can accelerate the natural instability within the coastal system. The national perspective on the coasts and seas analyses these issues and proposes solutions. The objectives are to manage the coastline in sympathy with natural processes through, for example, the use of soft engineering solutions, removal or abandonment of hard sea defences, and changing agriculture management practice at the coast.

•   Protected areas work tends to concentrate on those wildlife features which merit special measures for their protection, eg safeguarding spawning beds for Atlantic salmon or maintaining hydrological systems for mires. However, it has been clear for many years that activities beyond the site boundaries affect the status of habitats and/or of the individual species within the protected areas. For the Futures Programme to be effective, therefore, it is essential that policies and action for land and water management outside protected areas, which influence the status of wildlife within them, are included in the relevant national and local perspectives.

Providing a new basis for strategic documents
The Futures Programme also provides a new basis for SNH's corporate strategic planning. The Scottish Executive requires SNH to adopt a three-year corporate

plan and a one-year operational plan. These documents are, however, relatively short-term and resource constrained, and SNH wishes to look ahead over a longer time horizon. Many factors could affect its work over a longer timescale, others in the sector operate on longer timescales, and the timescales for achieving significant benefits for the natural heritage tend to be measurable in decades rather than years. Moreover, a policy statement in the 'Partnership for Government' document from the new coalition government, elected in Scotland in 1999, emphasized the *strategic* importance of social sustainability and environmental sustainability (Scottish Executive, 1999). To take advantage of this opportunity, and to address the need for a longer-term strategy, SNH has prepared *A Natural Perspective – Corporate Strategy for Scottish Natural Heritage for the next 10 years* (SNH, 2000b). This new SNH Corporate Strategy, was developed in late 1999 and completed in mid-2000, and is based on the three elements of sustainability: environmental, social and economic. The three themes and accompanying goals are:

- *Caring for the natural world*: for the whole of Scotland's natural heritage to be cared for more effectively;
- *Enriching peoples lives*: for the link between the natural heritage and personal well-being to be widely recognized and acted upon; and
- *Promoting sustainable use*: for renewable resources to be harvested within their carrying capacity, for management operations to provide multiple benefits, and for natural resources to be used efficiently.

The section in the Corporate Strategy on 'Delivering the Strategy' identifies the Futures Programme, along with the Management Strategy, as the two main strategic delivery programmes of SNH. The national and local perspectives have all been checked to ensure that these are consistent with the overall goals and priorities of the Corporate Strategy. There is scope for evolving the Corporate Strategy, given that its time horizon is only ten years, and therefore considerably shorter than the vision elements of the perspectives (around 25 years).

Targeting Resources for Actions Nationally and Locally

Like many organizations within the public sector, SNH finds it difficult to accommodate radical shifts in expenditure programmes without substantial additional resources. For instance, the balance of expenditure between the inherited components of its pre-merger remit of wildlife conservation on the one hand and landscape conservation, recreation and access on the other, remained largely unchanged for some time, as did the balance of expenditure across the country. Major external pulses, such as the quickening pace of implementation of European Union Directives and the implementation of SNH's Access Action Programme, helped to bring about changes in the distribution of resources between programmes and around Scotland. However, it was not a systematic approach. The Futures Programme allows a more objective assessment of the needs of the natural heritage and therefore the application of resources by SNH and others. Having set a baseline of information and visions for the future, the National Assessments, and the national and local perspectives, will provide the means to assess progress and to identify remedial actions and expenditure needs, including financial input from partner organizations.

The Futures Programme, therefore, needs to be developed to help identify resource requirements and to shape the allocation of resources. Potentially, it could help SNH develop a more objective basis for assessing such needs, provide better information for decisions on relative needs and improve the objectivity of resource allocation to: individual programmes; different parts of the country; and, different operational units. In developing their annual budget proposals, SNH's area teams are encouraged to use the local perspectives to help them to assess the relative expenditure needs of different programmes.

Defining Targeted Actions

The national and local perspectives focus on action. This helps to reshape current work towards the attainment of the integrated, long-term goals and visions that have been set for SNH and for the natural heritage.

Defining actions in this way enables SNH to move from a largely reactive approach to a more proactive one. Of course, SNH alone does not determine what actions are undertaken affecting the natural heritage and the timescales for them. The pace of policy development and delivery has increased since the establishment of the Scottish Parliament, and more attention is being given to the implementation of the UK government's obligations under the European Union's Birds and Habitats Directives. It has been found helpful to include the required response to these policy developments as actions within the draft perspectives, which thus help to focus discussion, negotiation and ultimately agreement with key partners. In drafting the required action, a balance has to be struck between being overly prescriptive and too generalized. The way that actions in the Futures Programme are described will depend on the circumstances and on the stakeholders involved.

A good example is the series of actions which are set out in most of the local perspectives on renewable energy, now a major thrust of public policy. SNH must define the locations and sites which it considers suitable and those which it does not. It must seek to persuade the planning authorities to take strategic approaches and adhere to their policies in making decisions on individual proposals. It needs to persuade the government in Scotland of the need for strategic locational guidance, and the UK government for a balanced approach to the pricing of different technologies, bearing in mind their environmental impacts. And it must work with developers to identify locations that are both operationally credible and environmentally acceptable. The local perspectives can assist in this challenging work.

Improving Internal Collaboration

When the Futures Programme was being developed, SNH embarked on a fundamental review of its operational effectiveness and corporate culture. An Organizational Development Programme was established with the explicit aim of 'ensuring that SNH is a credible, effective and efficient organization, delivering its natural heritage remit and living within our means'. Seven specific objectives were identified: integrating the remit, effective working with key stakeholders, improved internal collaboration, developing efficient and effective management, providing effective leadership, developing staff, and reducing excessive workloads.

It should by now be apparent that the Futures Programme has had a fundamental part to play in integrating the remit and working with stakeholders. But it also helped to achieve a more positive and collaborative corporate culture within SNH. A radical re-shaping of the organizational structure was carried through: there was increased delegation locally to 11 area teams, a corporate advisory services of natural heritage specialists was set up, and a new policy facilitating group established, called Natural Strategy.

The Futures Programme gave leading roles to each of the main elements of SNH's staff structure (Areas, National Strategy and Advisory Services): Areas in the drawing up of local perspectives, National Strategy in drawing up national perspectives, and Advisory Services in drawing up national assessments. The allocation of responsibilities in this way was not undertaken as three separate exercises but as a collaborative programme. For the first time, local staff had an opportunity to specify their needs for policy development and for information, and to have a formal input into the policy development process. Thus area staff were able to develop policy objectives and needs for the uplands. For example, they identified the importance of land valuation for sporting purposes, and the objectives pursued by sporting estate owners; these are matters that had not previously been considered adequately in the reform of the Common Agricultural Policy. The outcome was a re-balancing of priorities, which took better account of local needs and circumstances.

Lead staff have been nominated as 'Perspective Coordinators' for each national assessment, national perspective and local perspective, and a member of the corporate futures team has been named as their link. Each coordinator was required to exchange information, provide guidance to colleagues working on particular aspects of the programme, and generally to undertake a promotional role. As a result, a wider body of knowledge and expertise has been focused on the programme, its context and relevance.

Within a Non-Departmental Public Body such as SNH, Board members have ultimate authority for the strategy and resource disposition of the organization. The Board of SNH approved the overall programme and the national perspectives to ensure consistency in the overall policy approach, and comprehensive and credible coverage of the issues. Each of the 21 local perspectives has been approved by one of SNH's three Area Boards. The Area Boards comprise members with substantial local knowledge and expertise and it was essential to gain their commitment to the process of engagement with local stakeholders and to the content of the prospectuses.

Each part of the organization which has become involved in taking forward an element of the Futures Programme has recognized the overall benefits of the strategic integrated approach. The level of 'ownership' has increased as it has become more tangible through direct engagement by staff and board members. The lesson is that, however well a concept may be promoted, it is only when it becomes fully embedded in all relevant parts of the organization that it will enjoy complete support and its relevance be recognized.

CONCLUSIONS

SNH embarked on the Natural Heritage Futures Programme to achieve greater integration and a more holistic approach to the natural heritage, both in respect of its activities and in the work of others. Some important lessons were learnt as result.

In taking forward such a programme, account must be taken of changing circumstances, and of the need to utilize new approaches which could not have been foreseen at the outset. Attitudes to this type of long-term programme will vary within the organization and between external stakeholders. Responses will also change over time as individuals and groups engage with the programme and become associated with its successes (and setbacks). Management within the lead organization must ensure that both positive and negative elements are recognized, and that action is taken to build on success and address problems.

Integrated approaches to the natural heritage must have as their primary focus the benefits to the natural heritage itself and to those who depend upon it, and use it both directly and indirectly. At the same time, it must be pursued in ways that are linked with economic and social agendas. Although the development of a long-term vision does not necessarily find favour with all interests, it is essential, not least because the decisions which others take will help to shape the natural heritage, and affect other interests too. Visions must, however, be both realistic and imaginative. Mapping out the programme of action and defining the role for stakeholders are also critical. All stakeholders must be willing to re-order priorities and resources in order to attain the longer-term vision. As a result, the benefits of utilizing integrated approaches to the natural heritage should accrue to the lead organization itself and to its partners.

SNH's experience with the Futures Programme shows that it can be used to advance the culture of an organization, particularly in its management and motivation. This can be done if the programme is linked to a management strategy. Similarly, a precise articulation of the vision, objectives and actions will help to develop further the relationship with working partners.

This chapter has described the genesis of a new approach to integrating the various aspects of the natural heritage and its use in Scotland, and the stages of its development and implementation. Only time will tell whether real benefits for the natural heritage are realized. However, without such an approach, work would continue in an isolated and fragmented manner. It would lack the essential sense of vision for the natural heritage, with the resultant incremental impoverishment of the natural heritage and its non-sustainable use. The Scottish experience suggests that a more coordinated and integrated approach is possible.

NOTE

1   The Natural Heritage Futures Programme was initially called the Natural Heritage Zonal Programme.

REFERENCES

Carey, P D, Dring, J C M, Hill, M O, Preston, C D and Wright, S M (1994) *Biographical Zones in Scotland*, SNH Survey and Monitoring Report no 26, Scottish Natural Heritage, Perth

Carey, P D, Preston, C D, Hill, M O, Usher, M B and Wright, S M (1995) 'An environmentally defined biogeographical zonation of Scotland designed to reflect species distribution', *Journal of Ecology*, vol 83, pp833–845

Countryside Commission and Scottish Natural Heritage, Land Use Consultants and Sheffield University (1999) *Interim Landscape Character Assessment Guidance*, Countryside Commission and Scottish Natural Heritage, Cheltenham

Crofts, R (1994) 'An Integrated Natural Heritage Organisation in Scotland', in Bishop, K D (ed) *Merits of Merger*, University of Cardiff, pp28–36

Crofts, R (1995) 'Natural Heritage Zones: A new approach in Scotland', in Fladmark, J M (ed) *Sharing the Earth*, Donhead, London, pp227–244

Crofts, R (2000) *Sustainable Development and Environment: Delivering benefits globally, nationally and locally*, SNH Occasional Paper 8, Scottish Natural Heritage, Perth

Crofts, R (2001) 'Delivering benefits globally, nationally and locally', in Smout, T C (ed), *Nature Landscape and People Since the Second World War: A Celebration of the 1949 Act*, Tuckwell Press, East Lothian, pp195–218

Crofts, R, Maltby, E, Smith, R and Maclean, L (eds) (2000) *Integrated Planning: International Perspectives*, Scottish Natural Heritage, Perth

Eden, C and Ackermann, F (1998) 'Scottish Natural Heritage – a conservation organisation formed from merging two organisations', in Eden, C and Ackermann, F (eds) *Making Strategy: The Journey of Strategic Management*, Sage, London, pp194–208

Kiemer, M C B, Casey, P D, Palmer, S C F and Roy, D B (1998) *The Bio-geographical Zones and Biodiversity of the Coastal Waters of Scotland*, SNH Research Survey and Monitoring Report no 103, Scottish Natural Heritage, Perth

Maltby, E and Crofts, R (2000) 'From Concept to Action: Challenges for the Implementation of Integrated Management', in Crofts, R, Maltby, E, Smith, R and Maclean, L (eds) *Integrated Planning: International Perspectives*, Scottish Natural Heritage, Perth, pp83–88

Mather, A and Gunson, R (1995) *Biogeographic Zones in Scotland: A review*, SNH Review no 40, Scottish Natural Heritage, Perth

Mitchell, C and Balharry, D (2000) 'Natural Heritage Zones: Working with Scotland's Natural Diversity and Planning for its wise use', in Crofts, R, Maltby, E, Smith, R and Maclean, L (eds) *Integrated Planning: International Perspectives*, Scottish Natural Heritage, Perth, pp41–44

Miller, K (1996) *Balancing the Scales: Guidelines for Increasing Biodiversity's Chances Through Bioregional Management*, World Resources Institute, Washington

Runte, A (1997) *National Parks: The American Experience*, University of Nebraska Press, Lincoln (US)

Scottish Development Department (1990) *Scotland's Natural Heritage: The Way Ahead*, SDD, Edinburgh

Scottish Executive (1999) *Partnership for Government*, Scottish Executive, Edinburgh

Scottish Natural Heritage (SNH) (1993) *Sustainable Development and the Natural Heritage: The SNH Approach*, Scottish Natural Heritage, Perth

Scottish Natural Heritage (SNH) (2000a) *Scottish Natural Heritage: An Introduction*, Scottish Natural Heritage, Perth

Scottish Natural Heritage (SNH) (2000b) *A Natural Perspective: A Corporate Strategy for SNH for the next 10 years*, Scottish Natural Heritage, Perth

Scottish Natural Heritage (SNH) (2002a) *National Assessments*, Scottish Natural Heritage, Perth

Scottish Natural Heritage (SNH0 (2002b) *Natural Heritage Futures: An Overview*, Scottish Natural Heritage, Perth

Scottish Natural Heritage (SNH) (2002c) *Natural Heritage Futures: The Peatlands of Caithness and Sutherland*, Scottish Natural Heritage, Perth

Scottish Natural Heritage (SNH) (2002d) *Natural Heritage Futures: Hills and Moors*, Scottish Natural Heritage, Perth

Smout, T C (ed) (2001) *Nature, Landscape and People Since the Second World War: A Celebration of the 1949 Act*, Tuckwell Press, East Lothian

Swanwick, C and Land Use Consultants (2002) *Landscape Character Assessment Guidance*, Countryside Agency and Scottish Natural Heritage, Cheltenham

Thin, F (1999) 'Landscape Assessment in the Natural Heritage Zones Programme', in Usher, M B (ed) *Landscape Character: Perspectives on Management and Change*, The Stationery Office, Edinburgh, pp23–33

Usher, M B and Balharry, D (1996) *Biogeographic Zonation of Scotland*, Scottish Natural Heritage, Perth

Chapter 12

LANDMAP: A Tool to Aid Sustainable Development

Rob Owen and David Eagar

This chapter explores the development of *LANDMAP*. It sets out the reasons why the Countryside Council for Wales (CCW) and others developed *LANDMAP* and how the methodology evolved. It looks at how *LANDMAP* is being used and concludes by analysing how the methodology may develop in the future.

ORGANIZATIONAL CHANGE

CCW was established in 1991, by bringing together the Nature Conservancy Council and the Countryside Commission in Wales. The new organization was responsible for a wide range of functions, including statutory duties to protect biodiversity and advisory roles on landscape, countryside recreation and enjoyment, as well as enhancing the public's understanding and appreciation of the Welsh environment. Soon after its formation there was pressure on CCW to develop a method for assessing the qualities and character of the Welsh landscape. In England, the Countryside Commission and English Nature had joined forces to produce two separate but related tools: Countryside Character (see Chapter 7) and Natural Areas (see Chapter 6). Initially, there was a move to undertake a similar approach in Wales. However, because of CCW's integrated remit and its general emphasis on trying to develop a more holistic approach to the countryside (see, for example, CCW, 1993), it was decided that a single method should be developed that combined both landscape and biodiversity and was thus applicable at the 'landscape scale' and a more detailed level for nature conservation and site management.

From the outset it was evident that there was a wider professional community in Wales interested in developing a robust method of assessing Welsh landscapes for multiple uses. Therefore, in 1994, CCW established the

---

BOX 12.1 WALES LANDSCAPE PARTNERSHIP GROUP

The Wales Landscape Partnership Group includes representatives of the following organisations:

- Cadw: Wales Historic Monuments
- Countryside Council for Wales (Chair and secretariat)
- Environment Agency Wales
- Forestry Commission Wales
- National Assembly for Wales: Agriculture and Rural Affairs Division and Highways Division
- National Trust
- Planning Officers Society Wales
- Wales Tourist Board
- Welsh Development Agency (WDA)
- Welsh Local Government Association
- A representative from Wales' five Areas of Outstanding Natural Beauty (AONBs)
- A representative from Wales' three National Park Authorities

---

Wales Landscape Partnership Group (WLPG) – a consortium of central and local government organizations concerned with various facets of the Welsh landscape (see Box 12.1). The initial purpose of the group was to devise, test and promote a single method for assessing the important components of landscape. Early work considered how 'landscape assessment information' is used for a wide variety of decision-making including the management of land and development. This was the impetus for *LANDMAP*.

The WLPG also provides a forum for discussing different approaches to landscape conservation and a mechanism for encouraging collaboration. In 1997 the Group collaborated on a policy document: *The Welsh Landscape* (CCW, 1997), which set out 48 policies to be achieved at national, county or local levels. Two of the most important aspects to emerge from this document were an agreed definition of the term 'landscape' and a commitment to establish a joint approach for assessment. The document's consultation version (CCW, 1996) outlined the method to contribute to the *'landscape assessment and decision-making process'* – hence the name *LANDMAP*.

The draft *LANDMAP* Handbook (CCW, 2001) refined the definition of landscape as follows:

> *the landscape consists not only of the objective reality of the rocks, plants, and buildings which make up the physical form, but also the environment perceived, predominantly visually, but also with all the other senses. Sight, smell, feel and sound therefore all contribute to landscape appreciation; as does our cultural background and personal and professional interests.*

An agreed definition of landscape was a starting point, but four other factors were influential in encouraging the WLPG to develop the *LANDMAP* method:

- Lessons learnt from the Countryside Character approach being developed in England, Northern Ireland and Scotland – information was freely exchanged through regular meetings of the countryside agency staff working on the these initiatives in the various parts of the UK.
- An awareness that certain landscape qualities were being lost – species and landscape diversity for instance. The WLPG wanted to establish a method that could not only be used to measure this change, but also provide an impetus for positive action.
- A belief that a method was needed that not only described the landscape, but also evaluated its qualities – to identify what's important, where and why.
- Advances in the use of Geographical Information Systems (GIS) as a way of handling complex data meant that the aim of developing a single method that combined both the landscape scale and more site specific data was technically possible.

HOW THE METHOD WAS DEVELOPED

CCW and the WLPG developed the *LANDMAP* methodology over a three-year period. An initial six-month pilot phase was run in 1997 to test the method. Four areas were chosen:

- The Llyn peninsula of Gwynedd – representing a coastal landscape of high visual value with important historical and biodiversity sites and an ancient farming pattern, much designated as AONB with a high percentage of Welsh speakers.
- Llanbrynmair-Mallwyd in Mid Wales – a mountainous rural area straddling the administrative areas of the Snowdonia National Park and the county of Powys.
- Rhymney Valley – an urban fringe area with social problems and under development pressure.
- South East Carmarthenshire – another area that already possessed a different kind of landscape assessment, as well as encompassing a diverse landscape with coastal, rural and industrialized areas.

The early results were, on the whole, encouraging; though it soon became apparent that resolving some of the technological difficulties was not going to be easy. Three of the pilots were paper-based and struggled to handle the amount of data systematically generated by *LANDMAP*. The fourth (Llanbrynmair area) study pioneered some of the technological issues of fusing landscape assessment techniques with the requirements of GIS. A consistent way had to be found for converting text information, such as 'this area contains rolling hills', into 'true' or 'false' answers. Data entry forms were devised which provided a template to adequately describe all the landscape types in that pilot area.

Following a seminar to evaluate the results of the pilots, four local authorities indicated their willingness to try the method out for real. Three, namely the Vale of Glamorgan, Cardiff and Newport were largely funded by the WDA. The fourth, Gwynedd outside the Snowdonia National Park, was grant aided by CCW. The Vale of Glamorgan study, which was the first *LANDMAP* study of a whole county to be undertaken, won a UK Landscape Institute (Landscape Planning) biennial Award (White Consultants, 1999). The jurors commented:

> *The study and its outcomes were well presented in considerable depth and at a variety of levels appropriate for the range of uses identified. It was also carefully designed to ensure use in conjunction with the statutory planning process and thus to have an effective impact upon decision-making. The jurors felt that the study's approach and outcomes have the potential to liberate landscape planning in the UK from a traditionally limited role in visual and character assessment, into a more substantial realm that fully connects with contemporary and real world issues of sustainability and quality of life. In this regard it outshone other entries and should rightfully* become a baseline for such studies and for the evolution of a more robust expertise in landscape and land-use planning *(emphasis added)* (Landscape Institute, 1999, pp24–25).

The Vale of Glamorgan study was subsequently chosen as one of two UK entries for the first Council of Europe Landscape Award, winning the regional or local authority category. This gave the development of *LANDMAP* in Wales a necessary boost, especially since the Vale of Glamorgan study was a paper-based prototype and subsequent studies have used GIS.

THE *LANDMAP* METHOD

The underlying objectives of *LANDMAP* are to:

* provide a single method of landscape assessment and evaluation that can be used for the widest possible range of landscape decisions;
* establish a method that is transparent by setting out clear justifications of why some parts of the landscape are more valuable than others;
* provide a rigorous methodology with clearly set out criteria and procedures – so that the results in one part of Wales can be compared with others; and to
* utilize GIS technology to ensure that landscape information can be easily stored, accessed, manipulated and updated.

LANDMAP starts from the premise of providing information that landscape decision-makers need in their every day work. It is therefore relevant, and somewhat obvious, first to consider exactly who those decision-makers are and then to examine their individual needs. Landscape decision-makers include: farmers, foresters, developers, planners, ecologists and historians. All of these professionals require different information about the landscape, but there are common elements. Generally, they all require information on: present uses; the nature and condition of important landscape qualities and their comparative value; how these qualities should be conserved/enhanced; and whether the value of the landscape would be reduced by certain developments. The requirements of landscape decision-makers will vary though, in that some will require detailed data – say an ecological survey of a particular habitat, whilst others will need more general and strategic information, for inclusion in a unitary development plan, for instance. There is a need therefore to collect and analyse information at different scales and complexities, but above all else to be able to present information about one discipline, say biodiversity, in a way that other professionals can understand. *LANDMAP* attempts, therefore, to collect information in a way that is relevant to different disciplines and then to convert it into a format that can be easily understood by all.

Before going through the method in more detail, let us first consider the range of landscapes and how different people perceive them. Contemplating the variety of Welsh landscapes would probably conjure up images as diverse as rocky mountains and deep glacial valleys, coastlines, expanses of moorland, rolling green hills and agricultural fields, woods, industrial plants, cities, market towns or small villages. But what makes one landscape different from another? Everyone, whether a professional engaged in a landscape assessment or a lay person, would be able to put forward a combination of factors, no doubt drawn from the underlying geology, the soil type, the agricultural practices and the impact of human development. The question is in some respects easy to tackle. But what makes one landscape more interesting or valuable than another? Each individual will respond differently based on their personal and professional interest, as well as knowledge, cultural background and so on. Clearly some landscapes are more valued by society, but 'better' or 'more valued' by whom? We immediately hit a stumbling block. The tourist will view the landscape in a different way from the poet, farmer or property developer. But, if we accept a definition of 'landscape' as being more than the aesthetic and agree that the term also encapsulates our appreciation of wildlife, history, geology and culture, then we can at least begin to establish some common vocabulary for describing the landscape and unravelling why some parts can be considered to be more appealing or worthy of conservation.

In order to protect the best or more sensitive parts of our landscape, society has devised not only a vast number of designations to cover each interest – from geology to visual quality – but also established a range of institutions with certain duties and powers. But the landscape is an integrated system, where action in one area affects other areas, and policies on, say, agriculture, for instance, affect the quality and quantity of biodiversity. It is clear, therefore, that there needs to be considerable dialogue between all those involved in managing the land or any of the recognized interests found there. *LANDMAP* attempts to foster such a dialogue.

There are two key stages in the core *LANDMAP* method, but it is worth stressing that *LANDMAP* is more than just a method of assessing and evaluating landscape – it aims to be an inclusive process that draws on a range of views.

Key Stage One: Orientation

Orientation is the word used in *LANDMAP* to describe two, related activities. The first is the activity of 'thinking about an area's landscape in order to take better decisions about its management' (CCW and WLPG, 2001, p6). The second is the activity of bringing together, and facilitating a dialogue between, the main groups interested in landscape management. The process of orientation is facilitated through 'Local Information User Groups'. Each local authority (or national park authority) involved with *LANDMAP* identifies a local *LANDMAP* manager who convenes this group. The interests who may form the local group will vary somewhat from area to area, but include the professional, statutory and voluntary sectors spanning development, conservation and land use (membership of a typical local information user group is illustrated in Box 12.2). These groups help to ensure wide ownership of the process and the ensuing data. The aim is that the groups will continue to function after the *LANDMAP* database has been established.

Key Stage Two: Data Capture

From the definition of landscape given above it is possible to desegregate the term into information on: landcover, geology and landscape habitats, current and historical uses, sensory and cultural qualities, as well as how different groups perceive the landscape. Information on the landscape can therefore be collected in a series of layers.

BOX 12.2 LOCAL INFORMATION USER GROUPS

A typical local information user group would consist of:

- Business and property development interests;
- Countryside Council for Wales;
- Environment Agency;
- The local authority and adjoining local authorities;
- Farming and landowing representatives (normally Country Land and Business Association);
- Forestry Commission;
- Local Archaeological Trusts;
- Local interest groups such as a Civic Society;
- National Assembly for Wales (Agriculture and Rural Affairs Division);
- National Farmers Union, Farmers Union of Wales;
- National Trust; and
- Welsh Development Agency.

Orientation should not be glossed over or treated as a formality. Important decisions need to be taken at the start of the process and it is vital that all the organizations involved become engaged right at the start. Each organization is asked what information they require and what information they already hold. An Information Coordinator is identified and appropriate specialists appointed to collect the data.

First, in order to gain a greater understanding of how the land is currently used, information is collected on the present *form* and *function* of the landscape. For example, the form may be a woodland and its function may be amenity. The local authority is usually the most appropriate organization to collect this information. A hierarchical scale enables information to be collected from a broad to a detailed perspective. So at 'level one', the task would be to divide the area according to the following classification:

- open space;
- built form;
- lines;
- woodland; and
- water.

In order to ensure consistency, a clear definition is used to tightly define each classification. At 'level two', *open space*, for instance, divides into:

- urban open space; and
- rural open space.

And at 'level three', *urban open space* divides into:

- urban parkland;
- recreational grounds; and
- derelict land.

The areas generated at each level are stored in a GIS format. A data entry form is used to standardize the data collected.

The above process is repeated for *landscape function*, the 'level one' classification being:

- agriculture;
- development;
- forestry;
- recreation; and
- other.

The result is a powerful GIS database, containing detailed information on land use and activities. The database might prove useful in answering a detailed query, relating to an individual site such as a planning application, but also at a broader scale. The use of hierarchical classifications enables the data to be used for more analytical purposes, such as generating a report on a local authority's open land, for instance.

So far the information collected has been purely descriptive. Data has been collected on what is there but nothing about 'what is of value' or 'what requires conservation'. The answers to such questions are shaped by a second set of information, which comes in the form of five separate disciplines *or evaluated aspects*:

- Geological landscape;
- Landscape habitats;
- Visual and sensory;
- Historical landscape; and
- Cultural landscape.

Information on these various 'aspects' is collected by an 'Aspect Specialist'. Such people are at the heart of the *LANDMAP* process; they are selected, trained and approved to generate the *LANDMAP* information. Their role is to provide information of a definitively comprehensive and accurate standard. This includes evaluating the landscape qualities and making recommendations for their management. Aspect Specialists should be 'expert in their aspect of landscape, with a wide-ranging knowledge and understanding of it. They will possess the expertise to justify their information as an expert witness' (CCW and WLPG, 2001, p6). *LANDMAP* requires that Aspect Specialists assess a wide array of information grouped into five broad themes (see Box 12.3).

The process described above provides information on 'what is there' (the identified qualities) and 'what is of value' (relative importance). But decision-makers will also require additional information. Other datasets may need to be examined alongside the information generated by *LANDMAP*. These may include:

BOX 12.3 ROLE OF THE ASPECT SPECIALIST

Classification divides the area into units of a similar nature or 'Aspect Areas' – a hierarchical scale is used starting from the broad and then working towards more detailed compartmentalization.

Description requires the Aspect Specialist to describe the qualities and features that distinguish one Aspect Area, or group of Aspect Areas, from another. The description process allows for the collation of subjective as well as objective information.

Evaluation is central to the *LANDMAP* process. It is assumed that in order to take any decision about landscape change it is necessary to assess each option against the nature of the values that exist within the landscape. The *LANDMAP* evaluation process is based on the principles of expert witness and transparency. The aim is to reach a judgement formed not on personal opinion but on a transparent, justified, rigorous assessment based on informed professional expertise and, in appropriate cases, consensus. There are three assessments under the broad heading of Evaluation. The first is an assessment of value (both intrinsic and extrinsic). Next is an evaluation of the Aspect Area's condition or current physical health. The final assessment is of trend or the predicted physical health of an Aspect Area.

Recommendation is concerned with eliciting a range of views on the current and future management of the Aspect Area. The aim is to provide decision-makers with initial information and recommendations from experts in their field in order to inform subsequent decisions.

Tolerance of change is an assessment by the Aspect Specialist of the tolerance of each of the Aspect Areas to certain pre-defined changes. This is an optional activity that involves the use of a simple check sheet.

- planning and nature conservation designations;
- listed buildings;
- water pollution levels;
- air quality;
- soil type and quality;
- forestry and wind farm potential;
- recreational opportunities;
- agricultural data;
- public perception; and
- economic and social data such as unemployment and deprivation, incomes, population distribution, employment opportunities and training needs.

When mapped, this information can be annexed to the *LANDMAP* database.

After the information has been quality assured by a national panel it is stored in a GIS. It can be accessed as individual layers or combined in a variety of ways, for instance a map showing all the landscape habitat areas that are of outstanding value and which require urgent management. More layers could then be added, such as the areas of outstanding visual and sensory importance. The scope for analysis and use of *LANDMAP* information for practical management is vast.

LANDMAP is usually undertaken at a county (unitary authority) scale. Whilst the aim is to compile a national dataset – the *LANDMAP Wales* information set – the approach is bottom-up rather than top-down. This contrasts to the national approach adopted in England (see Chapter 7). A national web site on which *LANDMAP Information* will be collated and accessed is being developed by CCW as part of a two-year European Union-backed project to demonstrate the use of *LANDMAP Information* in a variety of land management and development situations.

Characterization and Synthesis

The current *LANDMAP* manual (CCW and WLPG, 2001) outlines an optional way of deriving character areas, beyond the core Aspect Areas data. Production of these is not part of the published method because practice suggests that the five evaluated Aspects of *LANDMAP Information*, if analysed thoroughly, are sufficient for decision-making. The 'characterization process' is optional because CCW became sceptical of the usefulness of characterization due to the 'loss' of information and variability of the information content, and therefore 'character', within different character areas. This is a key distinguishing feature between *LANDMAP* and Countryside Character in England (see Chapter 7).

The *LANDMAP* method locates particular landscape qualities with precision, being particularly useful for examining the compatibility of geographically coincident ones. Moreover, both the visual and sensory and the historical landscapte aspects deploy and contain characterization *within* their assessments. Thus there is debate about the necessity, value, and indeed method, of undertaking this additional synthesized character areas routine. The final prognosis will become clearer as the Aspect Areas information is used more widely. CCW is currently undertaking research into the use of *LANDMAP Information* in decision-making which should help clarify the usefulness of the approach and the relative merits of characterization (see below).

Secondary Analysis and 'Products'

LANDMAP Information provides a base from which to develop a range of secondary products including landscape assessments and landscape strategies, and to support policy development.

A landscape assessment is a natural extension of the *LANDMAP* process and for some studies may be the end product. A landscape assessment is defined by CCW as (CCW and WLPG, 2001, p116):

> *an expert report on the state of the landscape that should:*
>
> - *Include information on the evolution of the landscape, its present condition and areas or features of particular interest.*
> - *Distil and communicate the particular character and personality of the landscape, dictated by the relationship between the extrinsic values of the different Aspects.*
> - *Include a summary of the public's perception of the landscape.*
> - *Note the forces for change which are operating within the study area and*
> - *Analyse the possible results of current landscape management trends and patterns.*

Management and Design Guidelines present the management recommendations for each Aspect Area, pointing up any potential conflict between the management objectives for individual (geographically overlapping) landscape qualities, and the scope for complementary management action. The area where a single set of Aspect Areas overlap is termed a landscape management unit. Each is broadly akin to a character area in concept. Further information is required to produce comprehensive design guidelines, but *LANDMAP Information* contributes basic information on the nature and spirit of places. It is an invaluable starting point for place analysis that will call on supplementary visual and cultural perception and information.

LANDMAP Information also helps to identify priority work to conserve or enhance the landscape qualities it has identified. It also reveals opportunities where development might be accommodated with relatively least harm to presently known landscape qualities. Such areas might be able to accept the creation of new landscape elements and qualities. This can be done by sieving out areas of low landscape importance, and having regard to the qualities of other Aspect Areas with which there is a visual or other relationship. In this way *LANDMAP* should aid the production of Unitary Development Plans, National Park Management Plans and a range of other policy documents (see Box 12.4). A key benefit is that the information can be viewed at different scales and that the same landscape information is being used by different organizations.

BOX 12.4 POTENTIAL USES OF *LANDMAP* INFORMATION

Countryside managers – aid to the production of countryside strategies, local biodiversity action plans, managing recreational sites, etc.

Developers – preparing economic development strategies, finding suitable locations for development, thus minimizing environmental damage and identifying opportunities for environmental gain.

Farmers and landowners – in managing their land and applying for agri-environment schemes.

Foresters – aid to the production of forest design plans.

Historians – in ensuring that important historical sites and those with strong cultural associations are conserved and where appropriate interpreted.

Planners – aid to the production of Unitary Development Plans or supplementary planning guidance. For example, through the systematic identification of special landscape areas.

Statutory undertakers – drawing up plans for the management of water resources, or improving the routes of transmission lines.

Managing the *LANDMAP Wales* database

The idea behind the *LANDMAP Information System* is to provide a universally accessible, up-to-date landscape database, rather than generate one-off, single-purpose reports. *LANDMAP Wales* has a management structure that unites the local *LANDMAP* study areas with one another in a national system. Partnership agreements are set to underpin the management and quality assurance of the data and feedback on its use. Local (Authority) *LANDMAP* managers will be able to convene meetings of their *LANDMAP Information* users' groups to review the use to which the information is, or is not, being put in their localities. The evidence from these meetings, together with an overview by the Wales Landscape Partnership Group, will help to inform any further refinements to the *LANDMAP Information System*.

WHERE NEXT – TOWARDS SUSTAINABILITY?

It is anticipated that all 22 unitary authorities in Wales and the three national park authorities will be participating in the *LANDMAP Information System* by the end of 2003. At the present level of resources, there should be geographical coverage of Wales to 'level three' data by Spring 2005. A national *LANDMAP* dataset will therefore:

- have the potential to be viewed at different scales, from national to regional, sub-regional and local;

- be used by a variety of landscape decision-makers in their every day activities;
- link data collection and policy formulation;
- encourage policy integration; and finally
- will be updated electronically and widely available.

Such a national data set will provide the basis for encouraging widespread understanding of how the landscape has been formed, the pressures upon it and how it should be managed for the benefit of both people and places. In short, it will provide the means for using the concept of landscape for integrating policy formulation in rural areas.

In the future, the *LANDMAP* methodology could be adopted to tackle specific locations, such as urban or coastal areas – providing additional detail on townscapes and seascapes, and CCW is already beginning to address these developments. However, the *LANDMAP* methodology will increase in value tremendously as the techniques for incorporating socio-economic data become more refined. A first attempt was made with the Monmouthshire *LANDMAP* data set to relate it to rural socio-economic information. This was done as two separate layers of information: data on economic opportunities and constraints, and a 'people' layer, capturing information on socio-economic characteristics: unemployment, skills and training needs, and so on.

This idea of collecting social and economic information in a comparable way to *LANDMAP*'s environmental information is also part of a two-year project that CCW has developed with EU funding to test the use of *LANDMAP* information in decision-making. This project examined the use of *LANDMAP* information in two pilot areas and through a range of different land management decisions. The overall aim has been to test *LANDMAP* as a tool for sustainable development. The opportunity has been taken to examine ways in which solutions to social and economic problems, or the realization of their opportunities, can be decided efficiently (using the various information) and yield results on the ground that are environmentally, socially and economically sustainable. This involves considering how development could take place in a way that minimizes harm to identified landscape qualities (across all the area and not just by avoiding designated sites). Also the data has been examined to generate innovative ways of using the landscape qualities to help create the right jobs in the right places. This will provide insights into how *LANDMAP* assessments could provide a tool for the pursuit of sustainable development. The results will be publicized through a *LANDMAP Information* web site.

The aim over time is to develop a national, integrated, spatial data set that incorporates environmental, economic and social information; fusing an understanding of the complexity of the link between people and places. In such a form, *LANDMAP* could form an important tool to deliver the National Assembly for Wales' legal duty to promote sustainable development.

REFERENCES

Countryside Council for Wales (CCW) (1993) *Threshold 21*, Countryside Council for Wales, Bangor

Countryside Council for Wales (CCW) (1996) *The Welsh Landscape; our inheritance and its future protection and enhancement: A consultation paper*, Countryside Council for Wales, Bangor

Countryside Council for Wales (CCW) (1997) *The Welsh Landscape: A policy document*, Countryside Council for Wales, Bangor

Countryside Council for Wales (CCW) (2001) Draft *LANDMAP Manual*, Countryside Council for Wales with the Wales Landscape Partnership Group, Bangor

Countryside Council for Wales (CCW) and Wales Landscape Partnership Group (WLPG) (2001) *The LANDMAP Information System*, Countryside Council for Wales with the Wales Landscape Partnership Group, Bangor

Landscape Institute (1999) 'Landscapes Working for the Vale of Glamorgan', Landscape Institute Planning Awards, *Landscape Design*, No 285, pp24—25

White Consultants (1999) *Landscapes Working for the Vale of Glamorgan*, Welsh Development Agency, Cardiff

Part 3

From Theory to Practice

Chapter 13

Applications of Landscape Character Assessment

Julie Martin

Landscape and Countryside Character Assessment have now been widely used throughout the UK and Ireland for approaching ten years. During that period there have been great advances in methodology and in the guidance available to practitioners, as described in Chapter 7. The extent of character assessment coverage has expanded dramatically, and the quality and detail of the assessments produced has continued to develop and improve. However, there is still considerable diversity of approach and output. There are variations in the content and style of presentation; and also in the ways in which the assessment data are subsequently used. While some assessments appear to 'sit on the shelf', others have been further developed, tailored and applied and have had a strong influence on decision-making in the fields of planning and land management. Increasingly people recognize that completion of an assessment is just the starting point: it is what comes afterwards that really matters.

This chapter examines how government agencies, local authorities, land managers, community groups and others are using Landscape Character Assessment (LCA). It focuses on England but also makes reference to experience from other parts of the UK. It begins with an overview of the range of uses for character assessment, their scope and potential. It then outlines, with case studies, some of the innovative methodological developments that have taken place around the country in the last few years. The final section comments on good practice and on the effectiveness of the different LCA applications.

RANGE OF APPLICATIONS

The range of potential LCA applications has already been touched upon in Chapter 7 and is summarized in Box 13.1. Broadly, applications of character

---

BOX 13.1 THE RANGE OF LANDSCAPE CHARACTER ASSESSMENT APPLICATIONS

Planning

Development plan policies
Landscape designations
Development capacity studies
Development briefs
Development control
Planning conditions
Countryside Design Summaries
Village Design Statements
Design guidance
Urban fringe, townscape and settlement
  analyses

Land management

Landscape management strategies
Landscape management plans
Monitoring landscape change
Agri-environmental scheme targeting
Forestry and woodland initiatives
Indicative forestry strategies
Forest design
Transport planning and appraisal
Environmental and economic
  regeneration
Marketing tourism and local produce

---

assessment fall into two categories, planning and land management. In terms of planning, LCA may contribute at a variety of levels to formulation of development plan policies; development capacity studies and strategies for particular forms of development; and development control and environmental impact assessment (EIA). In terms of land management, it may provide the basis for landscape management strategies and play an important role in a wide range of other initiatives including agri-environment schemes, woodland expansion, and strategies to tackle issues as diverse as transport planning, environmental and economic regeneration, and marketing of rural produce.

For each of these applications, there has been considerable innovation in recent years and there is a growing body of practical experience. One particular reservoir of experience can be found in the Countryside Character Network, an informal membership network established by the Countryside Agency. The Network aims to facilitate exchange of information and experience on countryside character applications among policy-makers, land managers and landscape practitioners through a regular newsletter and series of workshops on specific character assessment themes.

From involvement with the network it is clear that character assessment has huge potential to help us tackle some of the greatest environmental challenges that we face today, including fundamental issues such as how to accommodate the considerable need for new homes and how to revitalize the rural economy. However, the exact ways in which it can help are still being explored.

Hence in the field of development planning, many planning authorities have worked hard to translate landscape character into policy, but have used a number of different policy approaches. Studies of development capacity, a common follow-on from character assessment, are being undertaken across the country but some are location-led and others development-led, and as yet there is no clear consensus on how such studies should be undertaken. Landscape Character Assessment is being used in a variety of ways to guide development control and design. However, we still do not know if it is having

---

Box 13.2 Landscape policy in the Hart District Local Plan

Hart District Council bases its local plan on 15 local landscape character areas. Each landscape character area has a set of guidelines for landscape conservation, restoration or enhancement, which sit within the local plan's overall landscape policy:

> *Within the Landscape Character Areas, as indicated below and shown on the Proposals Map, development will be permitted if it does not significantly adversely affect the particular character of the landscape and is in accordance with other policies of this plan.*

The policy is not intended to be a restraint on development in the countryside. It aims to indicate landscape constraints and opportunities to be acknowledged by any development proposal; change for the positive is encouraged. The approach was tested through the local plan public inquiry. No significant objections were upheld. Many of the development proposals that were put before the inquiry took note of the Landscape Character Assessment and were supported by evidence to demonstrate that they were in accordance with local landscape character, hence raising the profile of landscape issues within the district.

In future, it is intended that specific development proposals will be tested against this policy. The Landscape Character Assessment provides an important reference source for assessing the suitability and impact of proposals, as well as the justification, where required, for negotiation of landscape conditions or refusal.

---

an effective influence on the quality of planning applications submitted, and there is some evidence that developers have difficulty with the concept. In the field of land management, there are issues of how to translate strategy recommendations into action, how to coordinate the activities of a diverse range of players, and how to monitor the effectiveness of the action that is taken. There is also a need for Landscape Character Assessment to achieve greater recognition by those working in agriculture, forestry, economic development and other related areas.

Character assessment and planning

Development Planning

Local authority LCAs are usually commissioned by the authority's planning department, the primary purpose often being to inform development plan policies. Traditionally, development plan landscape policies have tended to be restrictive, focusing on the protection of nationally and locally designated landscapes. More recently, with the introduction of Landscape Character Assessment, the balance has shifted away from policies for designated areas alone towards an emphasis on more positive policies aimed at maintaining the distinctive character of the whole countryside.

But what does that mean in practice? The most straightforward approach is to use a policy that simply requires that development is in keeping with the

---

BOX 13.3 LANDSCAPE POLICY IN THE STAFFORDSHIRE STRUCTURE PLAN

In reviewing their joint structure plan, Staffordshire County Council and Stoke-on-Trent City Council agreed to abandon their former use of local landscape designations in favour of a character-led approach.

The approach makes use of the concept of landscape quality (taken to mean landscape condition and integrity rather than scenic beauty or landscape value) and landscape sensitivity (meaning the degree to which a landscape can accommodate change without unacceptable adverse impacts on its character). Policy objectives have been formulated on the basis of five quality and three sensitivity classes, superimposed to give a map with 15 permutations, termed rural landscape policy objectives.

These are used in interpreting the structure plan's landscape policy NC1, which is that:

> *Development should be informed by and be sympathetic to landscape character and quality and should contribute, as appropriate, to the regeneration, restoration, enhancement, maintenance or active conservation of the landscape likely to be affected. Proposals with landscape and visual implications will be assessed having regard to the extent to which they would:*
>
> *(a) cause unacceptable visual harm;*
> *(b) introduce (or conversely remove) incongruous landscape elements;*
> *(c) cause the disturbance or loss of (or conversely help to maintain): landscape elements that contribute to local distinctiveness; historic elements which contribute significantly to landscape character and quality, such as field, settlement or road patterns; semi-natural vegetation which is characteristic of that landscape type; the visual condition of landscape elements; tranquillity.*

The approach was endorsed by the structure plan examination in public panel, which considered that developers' concerns that the whole countryside would in effect be covered by landscape designations were unfounded. The maps and landscape character descriptions have been adopted as supplementary planning guidance to the structure plan following public consultation. They are expected to influence the identification of new allocations when local plans are reviewed.

---

character of the landscape and maintains its distinctiveness. Such a policy must be accompanied by a character map, descriptions of landscape character types and areas, and guidelines for landscape change. An example of this approach is the policy adopted by Hart District Council in Hampshire (Box 13.2). The benefit of this type of policy is its simplicity; the possible disadvantage is that the landscape guidelines may be open to differing interpretations by the planning authority and developers. A more elaborate and prescriptive approach is to develop policies based on judgements about landscape quality and sensitivity. For example, in Staffordshire (Box 13.3), a policy for landscape protection and restoration is accompanied by a map indicating the policy objectives (regeneration, restoration, enhancement, maintenance, conservation) and also the degree of sensitivity to landscape change right across the county. One criticism that has been levelled at this approach, however, is that sensitivity is not an absolute matter and may vary according to the type of change that is being considered.

How well do such policies work? They certainly offer a more informed approach to landscape issues than in the past – particularly where the LCA is formally adopted as supplementary planning guidance and thereby becomes a material consideration in planning decisions. However, there is some evidence that planners are not finding the assessments as helpful or easy to use as they had hoped. For example, a study commissioned by Scottish Natural Heritage found that planners were looking for more material that could be transferred directly into draft policies within a development plan (Hughes, 1999). The study suggested that planners may need more guidance on how to utilize LCA in development plans, and need to be aware that further work such as studies of landscape capacity and the landscape implications of particular forms of development may often be required.

Other recent research (Turner and Alexander, 2001) has shown that despite the good character assessment coverage that now exists, levels of uptake and commitment to character-based policies within structure and local plans are still quite limited. This may reflect the fact that government Planning Policy Guidance (DETR, 1997) still does not fully endorse the character approach or advise on exactly how it should be translated into policy. Usefully, the research suggests a number of elements of good practice in formulating development plan landscape policy (Box 13.4).

Development Capacity

Increasingly, landscape capacity studies are being undertaken for various forms of development as a further input to development plan policy. Taking the Landscape Character Assessment as their starting point, these studies examine the specific capacity of individual landscapes to accommodate change and may focus on landscape constraints or opportunities or both. Potentially they can lead to policies that will highlight the specific landscape issues associated with a given form of development, thus complementing more general character-based landscape policies.

At a basic level, development capacity analysis may simply identify or map the key landscape features of a given area, such as distinctive landscape settings to settlements, key approaches, landmarks, viewpoints and prominent ridgelines. This list may also include key habitat and cultural landscape features. At a more detailed level, it may systematically examine the impacts of different forms of development in different locations, for example by looking at:

*   effects on the landscape resources, eg on the key physical features;
*   effects on the landscape experience, eg openness, enclosure, sound, etc;
*   visual effects, eg conspicuousness, intrusion into views;
*   effects on other important elements, eg cultural components of the landscape; and
*   possibilities for mitigation, eg by increasing landscape capacity through tree planting.

**BOX 13.4 GOOD PRACTICE IN FORMULATING DEVELOPMENT
PLAN LANDSCAPE POLICY**

Research undertaken at Liverpool John Moores University has examined the potential
benefits of the character approach for development plan landscape policies, concluding
that the character approach can provide a useful framework for landscape policies
across a whole local authority area. It can help integrate policies on a wide range of the
elements that make up landscape, from building design to wildlife habitats.

However, to be effective, requirements for the policy itself are:

- coverage of the whole plan area, with judgements about the varying quality or
  sensitivity of different character areas;
- inclusion of character area descriptions and landscape guidelines;
- reference to the full range of landscape elements, for example, habitats, historical
  features, built design features;
- positive encouragement of quality development and landscape enhancement;
- reference to the broader environment and to local social and economic needs.

Requirements for the explanatory memorandum and reasoned justification are:

- explanation of the character approach and its application;
- reference to the Landscape Character Assessment and related supplementary
  planning guidance;
- reference to the need for planning to work alongside other forms of land
  management ie policy integration;
- clear notes on implementation.

Source: Turner and Alexander, 2001.

Much of the recent work on landscape capacity for development has taken place
in Scotland, looking especially at capacity to accommodate new housing and
wind farm development. At national level, Scottish Natural Heritage has recently
completed a study of landscape sensitivity to wind farm development (Buchan,
2001), drawing on data from the national programme of LCA. This study has
identified seven inherent landscape characteristics that heighten sensitivity to
wind farm development (Box 13.5), and has used these to identify the degree of
landscape constraint at a strategic scale. It is an interesting example of how the
data from LCAs can be used in a rigorous, analytical way to help inform strategic
decisions on difficult landscape issues.

Work at local authority level has tended to focus on capacity rather than
sensitivity as local authorities strive to accommodate housing and other
development allocations. An interesting study in Argyll and Bute (David
Tyldesley and Associates, 2000) explored the benefits of a location-led approach
based on the identifying landscape constraints versus those of a development-
led approach based on identifying opportunities to meet particular landscape
criteria. It concluded that a development-led approach gave better results in
terms of informing the capacity evaluation, but that it was much more difficult
and time-consuming to carry out. As a compromise, a location-led approach
was used to evaluate development capacity in the key settlements while a
development-led approach was used elsewhere.

BOX 13.5 CRITERIA FOR ESTABLISHING LANDSCAPE SENSITIVITY TO WIND FARM DEVELOPMENT

Scottish Natural Heritage has identified seven landscape characteristics that have particular relevance to wind farm development. These are:

Landscape scale and openness. Generally larger-scale landscape can more easily accommodate bigger wind farms (unless the way in which the landscape is experienced results in a higher number of key viewpoints being affected).

Landform and shape. Sensitivity to wind farm development generally increased with increased complexity of landform; while different shapes (eg convex or concave hill, plateau, ridge, strath, glen) have varying sensitivities.

Settlement. Increased frequency and size of settlements (urban or rural) generally imply greater landscape sensitivity, partly due to space constraints. For this reason, dispersed settlements can make it difficult to accommodate a wind farm of any great size.

Landscape pattern and foci. This covers physical and cultural characteristics. For example, the tops of the Cairngorms lend a distinct physical focus to the landscape, which makes them vulnerable to development; while the crafting areas of Skye have a small-scale pattern that would be compromised by a wind farm.

Simplicity of visual composition. This refers both to built features such as field dykes, roads and power lines, and to features such as woods or tree belts. Increasing complexity generally means increased sensitivity.

Wild land and remote character. This identifies areas where a wind farm is likely to erode these characteristics and can be relevant even when other built elements and human activity are evident in the landscape.

Landscape rarity. This indicates that the intrinsic landscape characteristics are likely to be significantly affected, with resulting loss of a rare landscape resource.

Each group of similar landscape character units in Scotland was scored on a five-point scale for each of the seven landscape characteristics. The results were used to produce a strategic map of landscape sensitivity, indicating the scale of wind farm development that may be accommodated without significant adverse effects.

Source: Buchan, 2001.

The Countryside Agency's most recent planning advice to local planning authorities and the government (Countryside Agency, 2000) also suggests a policy approach that goes beyond landscape character and capacity to use positive objectives that take account of environmental, social and economic capital including the character and natural features of the countryside. The advice recommends that local plan policies should set out the criteria that a development must meet in the locality if it is to be 'good enough to approve', rather than 'bad enough to refuse'. Landscape Character Assessments are suggested as one practical way of setting these criteria locally. This approach is now being tested in South Hams District in Devon (Box 13.6), and may well lead to further innovation in development plan landscape policies.

**BOX 13.6 LOCATING NEW HOUSING DEVELOPMENT IN
SOUTH HAMS DISTRICT**

South Hams District in Devon is a rural district that contains nationally important and
sensitive landscapes including an Area of Outstanding Natural Beauty and part of
Dartmoor National Park, set within an attractive and distinctive wider countryside. One of
the key tasks within the District's local plan review is to identify how to accommodate
the structure plan housing allocation of 11,500 dwellings, around 6000 of which need to
be on greenfield sites.

Development on this scale is usually delivered by consortia of volume
housebuilders using standard house types. The challenge is to see whether such
development can be accommodated in a sustainable manner, responding to local
character and achieving community and environmental benefits. The project will test the
ideas presented in the Countryside Agency's policy statement *Planning for Tomorrow's
Countryside* (Countryside Agency, 2000).

Work to date has focused on understanding the characteristic relationships
between settlement, landscape setting and landscape features. Each of the areas of
search has been examined to see the extent to which these relationships could be
replicated in new development. This has helped to narrow the range of siting options
and has led to initial site concepts that will be the subject of community participation.
The reactions of landowners and developers will also be explored.

The key output of the project will be concept statements that have the status of
supplementary planning guidance and that will reflect the aspirations of local
communities, as well as providing greater advice and certainty for developers. The
results will need to be sufficiently robust to stand up to challenge at the local plan inquiry,
and to command the support of central government and the Planning Inspectorate.

Sources: Manning, 2000 and Robinson, 2001.

Development Control and Environmental Impact Assessment

Ideally, as a result of character assessment, an understanding of landscape
character should inform development control and the design of new
development. It should feed into site development briefs, indicating how key
landscape characteristics need to be maintained and how schemes should ensure
best fit with their landscape setting. Conditions attached to planning permissions
should assist in ensuring appropriate design to reflect landscape character. The
primary tools here are the landscape policy and the LCA itself. Experience
suggests that for effective development control the planning authority should
have a landscape architect or a planner with particular expertise in landscape
matters (Hughes, 1999).

In England two additional tools for development control may be available.
The Countryside Agency's Design in the Countryside Programme gives advice on
how to assess the character of the built environment and its relationship to the
landscape using Countryside Design Summaries (CDSs) and Village Design
Statements (VDSs) (Countryside Commission, 1996). CDSs are often prepared in
parallel with LCAs, using a common set of landscape character types and areas.
They focus on settlement pattern, structure, form and materials within the
landscape and set out the general design principles that should be used to maintain

---

BOX 13.7 COUNTRYSIDE DESIGN SUMMARY FOR WEST LINDSEY DISTRICT

In 1999, a Landscape Character Assessment was prepared for West Lindsey District in Lincolnshire. It was accompanied by a Countryside Design Summary (CDS). The CDS explored the relationship between settlements and their surrounding landscape and highlighted the key characteristics of the settlement pattern in each of the district's landscape character areas. It outlined design principles to ensure that new built development enhances local landscape character and sense of place.

As supplementary planning guidance, the CDS will play an important part in the development control process and in particular will be used to influence the following development issues:

- development on the fringes of settlements, which can cut towns and villages off from their landscape settings, block views and alter the relationship between field patterns and buildings;
- development of sensitive infill sites, which can affect street frontages, building scale and massing and urban vegetation;
- the character of open spaces within built up areas, which makes an important contribution to the quality of life and amenity of local residents;
- first impressions and the character of approaches to settlements, where gateway features such as avenues of trees and boundary walls may be vulnerable to change;
- conversion of farm buildings in rural areas, which requires careful attention not only to design issues but also to access, services, lighting, field boundaries, trees, skylines and views;
- future development and use of redundant air bases, whose redevelopment could have a wide visual impact; and
- the character of new planting in association with development.

Source: Environmental Resources Management, 1999.

---

and enhance the distinct and local character of each landscape unit (Box 13.7). At a local level, VDSs (and similar tools now being developed for use in market towns) provide an opportunity for the community to analyse settlement character and reach a consensus view on the changes that would and would not be desirable. As with LCAs, CDSs and VDSs need to be formally adopted as supplementary planning guidance if they are to have 'teeth' within the development control process.

Other potentially important and useful tools are urban fringe, townscape and settlement analyses, which may form part of a wider LCA. This field of assessment practice is still a relatively new one, with few LCAs yet providing an integrated view of character in the rural and urban context. Also, those assessments that have addressed urban issues have tended to do so in different ways.

For example, in Fareham Borough (Scott Wilson Resource Consultants, 1996), the LCA had a strong focus on built character and design within the urban area. The written descriptions of townscape character have subsequently been used to inform the development control process. In New Forest District (Environmental Resources Management, 2000), an approach based on mapping

---

BOX 13.8 THE HAMPSHIRE LANDSCAPE STRATEGY

The Hampshire landscape strategy is directed at those with a policy, advisory or design role and those who have an interest, influence or concern about the future of the landscape, including members of the public. The three aims of the strategy are:

Landscape character and diversity: to maintain and enhance the overall quality and diversity of landscape character across the whole county.

Biological diversity: to support and complement the aims of the Biodiversity Action Plan for Hampshire, enhancing biological diversity throughout the wider countryside.

Development: to support and complement planning polices by helping to ensure that new development respects and enhances character, sense of place and scarce and irreplaceable landscape resources.

The strategy has a particular role in coordinating objectives and actions in these three areas. It provides a summary description of each of the county's landscape character areas, highlighting particular landscape, nature conservation and recreational assets, as well as distinctive characteristics. It identifies county-wide landscape issues under topic areas of agriculture, woodland, etc, and notes which of these apply to which landscape character areas. Detailed guidelines are then provided, listing actions to tackle the issues in each of the topic areas and giving advice for each landscape character area on the principal characteristics to be maintained and enhanced.

Perhaps the most important section of the strategy deals with implementation. This details in matrix format the priority actions under each topic that need to be taken in each character area. It also sets out a framework for action, identifying the key players in each topic area and the main implementation mechanisms that they should use.

Source: Hampshire County Council, 2000.

---

the historical development of each of the district's principal settlements was used. The relationships between the town and its adjoining landscapes were then analysed, yielding pointers for future development and change within the urban fringe especially. At Winchester the environmental capital approach (a precursor of quality of life capital) was used to help identify the essential landscape/townscape attributes of the city and its setting and evaluate the contribution they make to its special character (Landscape Design Associates, 1998).

A key issue in relation to landscape character and development control is how useful LCA is to developers. A Countryside Character Network workshop (Environmental Resources Management, 2001) explored how LCA and quality of life capital can help in site planning and EIA of new development. In theory, both should be key tools for the developer, playing a vital role in site selection and in the evaluation of landscape and visual impacts. In practice, though, there appears to be a low level of awareness and a high level of scepticism about character among developers and their consultants.

BOX 13.9 IDENTIFYING PLANTING AREAS IN THE NATIONAL FOREST

The National Forest is set to transform some 200 square miles of the landscape in Leicestershire, Derbyshire and Staffordshire with a blend of wooded areas, open country, farmland and settlements. Eventually around 33 per cent of the area will be wooded, from a 6 per cent start, and a very special, multi-purpose woodland resource will be created.

Understanding the area's landscape character has been fundamental to the strategy for implementing the forest. A Landscape Character Assessment was one of a suite of specialist studies undertaken in the early 1990s (others examined the potential for forestry, farm diversification, recreation, nature conservation and heritage conservation). With all these data in place, an Indicative Forestry Strategy (IFS) was prepared, identifying broad 'preferred' and 'sensitive' areas. The preferred areas were those that offered most potential for extensive planting and hence landscape change; in the sensitive areas there were significant constraints.

The Landscape Character Assessment and the IFS were then used to identify indicative planning areas. Five categories of indicative planting were defined, namely urban forestry; recreation planting close to major towns and on derelict land; conservation planting in areas of nature conservation interest; commercial planting in open agricultural landscapes; and mixed commercial and recreational planting.

The map of indicative planting types very closely follows the map of landscape character types for the National Forest, demonstrating how strongly the landscape has influenced the forest strategy. Detailed planting design guidance by landscape character type helps to translate the strategy's landscape aims into action at the field level.

Source: Evans, 1999.

Developers argue that LCA coverage at district level is still not complete, consistent or helpful, with some authorities continuing to rely on landscape designations and others adopting character-based policies that are still restrictive in tone. Character tends not to be given much weight partly because it does not yet have a strong status in Planning Policy Guidance, but also because the developer's choice of site is strongly constrained by the ability to acquire land and by whether or not the site is allocated for development in the development plan. Moreover, developers question whether it is appropriate to rely on traditional forms of development in the 21st century, suggesting that new models should be explored instead.

From this perspective, forward-looking policies based on future aspirations or criteria (as in South Hams) as well as on existing landscape character, are likely to be most effective in achieving development that is in keeping with its landscape setting. Communities have a key role to play here, formulating strategies and visions for change that can inform planning policy. There may also be a role for competitions to identify the types of change and development that will best meet community aspirations and offer optimal benefits for the local environment.

CHARACTER ASSESSMENT AND LAND MANAGEMENT

Landscape Management Strategies

Particularly at county level, one of the main reasons for carrying out an LCA may be to inform and guide landscape change within the county at a strategic scale, highlighting the overall priorities for conservation, restoration and enhancement. The aim is to influence a whole range of different forms of land use change, not only those that fall within planning controls. There is often a particular link to biodiversity management. Typically the strategy will address land use issues including agriculture, woodlands, trees and forestry, hedgerows, biological diversity, historic landscapes and urban fringe issues, as well as planning and development issues including urban expansion, recreation and access, tourism, transport, mineral and waste and industry. In many ways, landscape management is a much more difficult area to tackle than landscape planning, because it cuts across so many different fields and effective action requires the coordination and involvement of a wide range of organizations and interests, each with its own agenda.

Two of the most recent and forward-looking county landscape strategies in England are those of Hampshire and Lancashire. The Hampshire landscape strategy (Box 13.8) builds on a huge and comprehensive programme of LCA within Hampshire at county and district level, the County Council providing strong coordination throughout. The County Council will take a lead in implementation of the strategy. During public consultation on the strategy, a number of organizations and agencies made commitments to contribute towards the strategy's aims; other key players are also being asked to make a commitment to incorporate the aims and guidelines of the strategy into their own programmes. Working groups will be set up and new partnerships established to carry forward the various courses of action required to implement particular guidelines. Direct action on the ground by farmers and landowners will also be encouraged. Some of the main priorities for action include landscape strategies at district level; detailed landscape management plans for Areas of Outstanding Natural Beauty and, in the longer term, for the whole of the county; and advice on landscape issues in relation to minerals and waste. In an effort to monitor landscape change, a separate study will identify locally relevant key indicators that can demonstrate trends over time.

In Lancashire, the landscape strategy (Lancashire County Council, 2000) has similar objectives but the output takes a rather different form. As well as providing an overview of forces for change and key landscape issues across the county, the strategy identifies for each landscape character type the local forces for change and their specific implications for key environmental features – effectively a mini-EIA of the landscape changes that may occur – and this is an extremely useful tool. The strategy then identifies strategies (conserve, restore, enhance) for specific features within the landscape type, and sets out recommendations for action. The key features are also suggested as potential indicators for monitoring landscape change, and a preferred direction of change (increase, maintain, decrease) is noted. Proposals for implementation, however, are perhaps less well-developed than in Hampshire. A partnership approach is recommended and a general indication is given of the bodies that need to be involved, but no specific responsibilities are indicated.

One of the difficulties with county landscape management strategies is their sheer complexity, which can make them difficult to understand and use. They need to look at broad issues and actions, but at the same time need to focus on the distinctive character of particular areas and the aspirations of local communities. Hence, the usefulness of the information and advice within a landscape management strategy very much depends on the way in which it is structured, presented and disseminated. Given the shared responsibility for implementation of landscape management strategies, communication becomes a critical issue, and this is one of the reasons that some authorities such as Durham County Council (subject of a Countryside Agency-sponsored LCA demonstration project) are experimenting with use of the web to present and access LCA and strategy material. If successful, this could open up many new opportunities for data exchange, cross-cutting analysis and partnership on landscape issues.

Agri-Environment and Forestry

Landscape Character Assessment has been applied to influence land use change through agri-environmental schemes for many years (Gough, 1999). The essence of such schemes – formerly administered in England by the Ministry of Agriculture Fisheries and Food and now by the Department for Environment, Agriculture and Rural Affairs (DEFRA) – is that farmers and land managers are offered payments to conserve and enhance land and features of environmental value through farming in an environmentally friendly fashion.

One of the earliest uses of LCA was in the Environmentally Sensitive Areas (ESAs), farmed landscapes of high landscape and wildlife value that were designated in the late 1980s. In the ESAs, an analysis of an area's landscape and nature conservation qualities is used to set tiered objectives and payments for retention, restoration and enhancement of important landscape and environmental features. Any suitable land within the designated area can be entered into the scheme.

Countryside Stewardship, by contrast, is a discretionary scheme that offers a wide menu of grants for land managers who are seeking to manage and enhance landscape, wildlife, amenity and historic features in the English countryside. The scheme has a fixed budget and so seeks to prioritize applications to select those that will offer the greatest environmental benefit and address the key features of an area. To assist in the appraisal of applications, target areas and target objectives are identified for each county. This is a collaborative process whereby views on the current condition and management needs of key environmental features and their priority for action are sought from a wide range of organizations with relevant interests. The Countryside Character Areas, with their clear descriptions of key landscape features and conditions, have provided the strategic framework within which to develop targets and analyse uptake, and have worked well for this purpose.

However, a new project, the Countryside Character Database, will soon provide a more detailed framework (Cornwell, 1999). This project, led by the Countryside Agency with sponsorship from project partners DEFRA, English Heritage, English Nature and the Centre for Environment and Hydrology, builds on the Countryside Character Areas, incorporating additional information from county LCAs and other sources. It includes a generic national landscape typology, based on specific combinations of physiographic, land cover and cultural attributes. In future the database will be the framework for recording how landscape characteristics are changing over time, identifying the important benefits each characteristic provides and recording the management recommendations that will conserve and enhance these benefits. Intended initially to inform the process of developing Countryside Stewardship Scheme targets, in the longer term the database should help to improve efficiency and reduce the costs of scheme targeting, management and monitoring, which are relatively high. The project is now being taken to a second phase to develop national landscape indicators of change in countryside character and quality. The database and indicators should eventually be powerful tools to assist with all sorts of strategic decision-making on a wide range of landscape issues in England.

In the forestry sector, the use of LCA is still rather less developed than for agriculture. The Forestry Strategy for England (Forestry Commission, 1999) makes particular mention of the role of landscape character in helping to guide decisions about the location and design of new woodland, but as yet no new tools have been developed for this purpose at a strategic scale. At an intermediate scale, new forestry and woodland initiatives such as the National Forest (Box 13.9), the Community Forests and the Cumbria Woodland Forum have made significant use of LCA to indicate where there is greatest potential for woodland planting and where expansion is undesirable in terms of landscape character. At a detailed local level, LCA also has had an important role in guiding the design and management of woodlands and forestry (Forestry Commission, 1994).

Although the application of LCA to forestry initiatives has often been successful, sometimes landscape character input to forestry has been perceived as being too elitist, restrictive or lacking in vision. For example, in Dumfries and Galloway there was considerable debate over the LCA input to the local forestry framework (Howe, 1999). This may be partly due to the fact that that tree planting involves very dramatic landscape and habitat changes as well as significant changes in the local economy, land ownership and access. This demonstrates that the use of an approach based primarily on landscape issues is particularly inappropriate in relation to forestry, where wider studies and engagement with stakeholders are especially valuable.

CHARACTER ASSESSMENT AND OTHER STRATEGIC INITIATIVES

Finally it may be useful to touch upon the variety of other strategies and initiatives for which LCA is being used. Some of these are in the relatively early stages of development; others have been ongoing for many years.

Box 13.10 Traffic Appraisal and Impact Monitoring System (TAIMS)

TAIMS sets out a new approach to understanding and reconciling the widespread impacts of road traffic on the countryside and its communities, to address the insidious, cumulative impacts of traffic growth in rural areas, which may undermine countryside character and rural quality of life. TAIMS aims to assess the full range of traffic impacts on rural areas and to help identify solutions to those impacts.

The key steps in the appraisal process are to:

- identify the range of potential traffic impacts in an area;
- establish the sensitivity of the area and its characteristic elements to traffic;
- define thresholds above which the impact of traffic will result in unacceptable impacts;
- identify the likely key impacts that are expected to occur;
- study network capacity to accommodate these impacts; and
- identify solutions to address capacity problems.

The process is informed by character assessment and environmental capital concepts and information. Local stakeholder involvement is a crucial part of the process, providing local knowledge, input to the evaluation of impact thresholds, and advice on how solutions can address local needs.

Source: James, 2000.

In the field of transport planning, the Countryside Agency has recently embarked upon pilot projects to develop a practical methodology, called the Traffic Appraisal and Impact Monitoring System (TAIMS) (Robertson, 2000), to measure and manage the impact of road traffic on the countryside and its communities (Box 13.10). It works from a baseline assessment of any chosen area's countryside character. The methodology, which is being piloted at county level in Durham and at regional level in the West Midlands, uses a matrix analysis systematically to identify the multiple traffic impacts (visual intrusion, severance, pollution, nuisance, noise and vibration) that affect local or regional assets (landscape, ecology, cultural features, community, natural resources and economic well-being).

TAIMS is seen as a long-term management tool that will assess traffic impacts on the landscape; help define the thresholds above which further traffic cannot be sustained without unacceptable impact; and identify a range of solution to address capacity problems. Stakeholder participation is being built into the developing TAIMS methodology, especially the identification of impact thresholds and potential solutions. TAIMS is intended mainly for use by highways authorities, complementing the government's trunk road appraisal systems (DETR, 1999a, 1999b), of which countryside character is already a key component. It is too early to say how useful TAIMS will prove to be. A key test will be whether it is understood and accepted by transport planners, who are likely to be the main users.

In the fields of environmental and economic regeneration, LCA has long been recognized as having a key role. Where an assessment indicates that a

---

BOX 13.11 LANDSCAPES WORKING FOR THE
VALE OF GLAMORGAN

This project, carried out by White Consultants for Vale of Glamorgan Council, the Welsh Development Agency and the Countryside Council for Wales, is an excellent example of how Landscape Character Assessment can be used to foster environmental and economic regeneration. The brief was to prepare a comprehensive assessment of and strategy for the Vale's landscapes using the *LANDMAP* process, including:

- a clear vision for the landscape character areas;
- design guidelines that could be used if required as supplementary planning guidance;
- a landscape framework for the Eastern Vale;
- development and management briefs for proposed development areas and road corridors;
- landscape assessment and management frameworks for two country parks;
- an action programme for implementing works on the ground; and
- sustainable proposals for management and maintenance.

The Landscape Character Assessment was thorough, robust and used good visuals to help the reader understand the Vale's character and the key landscape issues. The design guidelines set out a palette of built forms and materials that would help to counteract adverse change; and exciting design ideas for new landscapes were also presented. The study won a Landscape Institute Planning Award. It was particularly commended for its combination of planning, landscape and urban design skills, and for embracing the creation of new landscapes as well as the conservation and enhancement of existing landscapes.

Source: Landscape Institute, 1999.

---

strategy of enhancement is appropriate for a particular landscape character type or area, this signals scope for significant positive change in the landscape – often by creation of a new landscape to suit a new function. This may improve the local environment; enhance people's quality of life; and at the same time contribute to economic success. The relevance of character assessment to this process is recognized by development agencies and others (for example, the Welsh Development Agency, 1995 and English Partnerships, 2000) and has been applied successfully in areas such as the Vale of Glamorgan (Box 13.11) and the Thames Gateway. However, some would argue that existing LCA guidance, with its emphasis on landscape conservation, restoration and enhancement, does not adequately address the creation of landscapes. Such comments may reflect a lack of communication and synergy between planners and designers within the landscape profession, and misunderstanding of how LCA can be used creatively.

A Countryside Agency project, called Eat the View, reinforces the message that landscape has a monetary value. This fact has been underlined dramatically by the impact on local tourism and economies in rural areas by the outbreak of Foot and Mouth Disease in 2001 (Countryside Agency, 2001). Conscious that trends in agriculture have worked against local economies, local products and traditional farming methods, and that they have helped to erode diversity in the farmed landscape, the Agency is encouraging farmers' markets, farm retailers and regional food groups to develop marketing and awareness of regional farm products and their value to a sustainable rural economy. By helping consumers to see the link between buying the product and enhancing the character of the local landscape, it is hoped that farmers, local communities and visitors to the countryside will all see benefits. The Agency is working closely with the English Tourism Council to develop similar initiatives that demonstrate how the relationship between the landscape, local economy and tourism opportunities can be enhanced and sustained.

TOWARDS GOOD PRACTICE

As we have seen, there is now a great wealth and variety of LCA applications. The case studies reveal that government agencies, planning authorities and others have all invested considerable time and effort in applying the findings of character assessments; and that character is beginning to have a real and positive influence on many spheres of planning and land management. This has involved the development of new methodological tools. Like all such tools, they have strengths and weaknesses. In the next few years attention must shift to comparison and appraisal of their effectiveness, and to preparation of advice, particularly from central government, on how they should be used.

In the planning arena, more work is needed to develop and test the effectiveness of landscape policies based on character. Further research, endorsement from government and guidance for planning authorities are essential. One particular area that needs to be examined is whether policies should focus on character alone or adopt a more prescriptive approach based on judgements about landscape quality and sensitivity. Some would argue that the latter approach is not very different from an approach based on designations, and also that sensitivity varies depending on the type of change that is being considered. In formulating policies for specific types of development, development capacity studies and a criteria-based approach have much to offer, but again need further research, development and good practice guidance. There is also a growing range of character assessment tools for use in development control. While these may be helpful to planners, it is apparent that they still need to win the support of developers, who tend to seek simpler, more clear-cut advice.

In land management too, there are new challenges. Landscape management strategies are increasingly thorough and complex; but may present a mammoth task in terms of communication, coordination and implementation. It is hoped that new web-based systems will open up opportunities for effective involvement and action by a wide range of interested parties. Landscape Character Assessment is now well established and tested for use in agri-environmental schemes, but still needs to gain wider acceptance in relation to forestry, where there is a greater requirement for consensus-building on landscape change. It is encouraging to see that LCA is being used for a wide set of other purposes, and is gradually being integrated into all aspects of our thinking on landscape management. One of the key hurdles is to convince farmers, foresters, transport planners, economists, politicians and the general public that character is relevant and useful. This process has begun but has still some way to go.

REFERENCES

Buchan, N (2001) 'Strategic Wind Farm Sensitivity Mapping', *Countryside Character Newsletter*, Issue 5

Cornwell, S (1999) 'A New Countryside Character Database for Agri-Environment', *Countryside Character Newsletter*, Issue 2

Countryside Agency (2000) *Planning Tomorrow's Countryside*, Countryside Agency, Cheltenham

Countryside Agency (2001) *Foot and Mouth Disease: The State of the Countryside*, Countryside Agency, Cheltenham

Countryside Commission (1993) *Landscape Assessment Guidance*, Countryside Commission, Cheltenham

Countryside Commission (1996) *Countryside Design Summaries*, Countryside Commission, Cheltenham

Countryside Commission (1996) *Village Design*, Countryside Commission, Cheltenham

David Tyldesley and Associates (2000) 'A Study to Inform Area Capacity Evaluations in Argyll and Bute', unpublished report to Argyll and Bute Council and Scottish Natural Heritage, Scottish Natural Heritage, Edinburgh.

Department of the Environment Transport and the Regions (DETR) (1997) *Planning Policy Guidance Note 7: The Countryside – Environmental Quality and Economic and Social Development*, Department of the Environment Transport and the Regions, London

Department of the Environment Transport and the Regions (DETR) (1999a) *New Approach to Trunk Road Appraisal*, Department of the Environment, Transport and the Regions, London

Department of the Environment Transport and the Regions (DETR) (1999b) *Guidance Note on Methodology for Multi-Modal Studies*, Department of the Environment, Transport and the Regions, London

English Partnerships (2000) *Space for Growth Handbook*, English Partnerships, London

Environmental Resources Management (1999) 'West Lindsey Countryside Design Summary', unpublished report to West Lindsey District Council, Environmental Resources Management, London

Environmental Resources Management (2000) 'New Forest District Landscape Character Assessment, Main Report and Supplementary Annexes', unpublished report to New Forest District Council and others, Environmental Resources Management, London

Environmental Resources Management (ed) (2001) *Accommodating Development in the Landscape*, Proceedings of a Countryside Agency Workshop held in London on 13 June 2001, Countryside Agency, Cheltenham

Evans, S (1999) 'Creating Landscape Change: The National Forest Experience', *Countryside Character Newsletter*, Issue 2

Forestry Commission (1994) *Forest Landscape Design Guidelines*, HMSO, London

Forestry Commission (1999) *A New Focus for England's Woodlands: Strategic Priorities and Programmes*, Forestry Commission, Cambridge

Gough, F (1999) 'Countryside Character and Agri-Environment', *Countryside Character Newsletter*, Issue 2

Hampshire County Council (2000) *The Hampshire Landscape: A Strategy for the Future*, Hampshire County Council, Winchester

Howe, R (1999) 'Landscape Character and Forestry in Dumfries and Galloway', in Environmental Resources Management (ed) *Managing Change in the Countryside: The Role of Countryside Character*, Proceedings of a Countryside Agency Workshop held in London on 3 December 1999, Countryside Agency, Cheltenham

Hughes, R (1999) 'Landscape Character Assessment and Development Plans', *Countryside Character Newsletter*, Issue 1

James, A (2000) 'Participation, Character Assessment and Transport Planning in County Durham', in Environmental Resources Management (ed) *Stakeholder Participation in Countryside Character Assessment*, Proceedings of a Countryside Agency Workshop held in Birmingham on 22 November 2000, Countryside Agency, Cheltenham

Lancashire County Council (2000) *A Landscape Strategy for Lancashire*, Lancashire County Council, Preston

Landscape Design Associates (1998) 'Winchester City and Its Setting', unpublished report to Hampshire County Council, Landscape Design Associates, Peterborough

Landscape Institute (1999) 'Landscapes Working for the Vale of Glamorgan', Landscape Institute Planning Awards, *Landscape Design*, No 285, pp24–25

Landscape Institute and Institute of Environmental Assessment (1994) *Guidelines for Landscape and Visual Impact Assessment*, E & FN Spon, London

Manning, S (2000) 'Planning for Quality of Life in a Sensitive Landscape', *Countryside Character Newsletter*, Issue 4

Robertson, K (2000) 'The Character of Road Traffic', *Countryside Character Newsletter*, Issue 4

Robinson, A (2001) 'Accommodating the Structure Plan Housing Allocation in a Sensitive Landscape – Lessons from South Hams', in Environmental Resources Management (ed) *Accommodating Development in the Landscape*, Proceedings of a Countryside Agency Workshop held in London on 13 June 2001, Environmental Resources Management, London

Scott Wilson Resource Consultants (1996) 'Fareham Borough Landscape Assessment', unpublished report to Fareham Borough Council, Scott Wilson Resource Consultants

Turner, S and Alexander, D (2001) 'Landscape Character and Development Plans', *Countryside Character Newsletter*, Issue 6

Welsh Development Agency (1995) *Landscapes – Working for Wales*, Welsh Development Agency, Cardiff

Chapter 14

The Link Between Landscape, Biodiversity and Development Plans: A Move Towards 'Positive Planning'?

Kevin Bishop and Richard Bate

This chapter assesses the extent to which the development of local biodiversity action plans (LBAPs) and the requirements of Article 10 of the Habitats Directive are moving us towards 'positive planning'. The term 'positive planning' is used to describe policies in statutory development plans that promote enhancement, management and habitat creation, ie policies that go beyond control and protection. The chapter is based on a survey of local planning authorities in England, Scotland and Wales that:

*   reviewed the existing range of development plan policies designed to encourage the management of features in the landscape; and
*   explored the links between LBAPs and statutory development plans.

THE POLICY CONTEXT FOR POSITIVE PLANNING

The preparation of LBAPs and the implementation of the Habitats Directive provide contrasting approaches to the development of 'positive planning'. The LBAP approach is voluntary, based on concepts of partnership and local empowerment (Local Government Management Board and UK Biodiversity Group, undated) (see Chapter 2) whilst the Habitats Directive represents a legalistic approach that is effectively top-down (see Chapter 3). Nevertheless, both view the statutory town and country planning system as a potential implementation mechanism for delivery of BAP targets and conservation and enhancement of Natura 2000.

Article 10 of the Habitats Directive states that: 'Member States shall endeavour, where they consider it necessary, in their land use planning and development policies and, in particular, with a view to improving the ecological coherence of the Natura 2000 network, to encourage the management of features of the landscape which are of major importance for wild flora and fauna'. This has been introduced into UK legislation through the Conservation (Natural Habitats &c.) Regulations 1994 (the Habitats Regulations), which, in part, passes the implementation of the directive to the town and country planning legislation. Regulation 37 'Nature conservation policy in planning contexts' states:

> *For the purposes of the planning enactments mentioned below [Town and Country Planning Act 1990 and Town and Country Planning (Scotland) Act 1991], policies in respect of conservation of the natural beauty and amenity of the land shall be taken to include policies encouraging the management of features of the landscape which are of major importance for wild flora and fauna.*

The Habitats Directive as a whole is binding on member states and must be implemented in domestic legislation in such a way as to give effect to the text and purpose of the directive. However, the obligation to give effect to Article 10 is a relatively weak, as this is couched in the terms 'where they consider it necessary'. Thus member states can decide not to transpose this aspect of the directive. The UK government has taken the view that implementation is indeed necessary, and introduced Regulation 37 for that purpose. Having accepted the principle, the steps taken should be capable of achieving the purpose of Article 10, namely 'to encourage the management of features of the landscape'.

Regulation 37 states the 'enactments' through which it will be applied. These are the provisions in the Town and Country Planning Act 1990 for the preparation of unitary development plans, structure plans and local plans. The 1990 Act states that these plans shall contain policies in respect of the development and use of land. These in turn 'shall ... include policies in respect of – (a) the conservation of the natural beauty and amenity of the land:' (emphasis added), and Regulation 37 directs that this provision 'should be taken to include policies encouraging the management of features of the landscape'. Thus policies 'encouraging management' *must* be included in development plans, but are still seen as a type of 'development and land use' policy.

The effect of Regulation 37 is to expand the ambit of what were traditionally 'development and land use' policies under the planning system. It is also clear from the phraseology that, to be lawful, a plan *must* include a policy of the type referred to, though the law does not define or constrain the nature or extent of such a policy. A local planning authority could not properly refuse altogether to include such a policy, nor could it delegate the formulation and operation of it to a non-statutory mechanism outside the formal plan process.

Development plan policies must give effect to the requirements of Regulation 37. As the notion of 'management' of a landscape feature conveys a sense of continuing obligation, it would have to form the subject matter of either a planning condition or a legal obligation (such as an agreement under section 106 of the 1990 Act). Policies to give effect to Regulation 37 would be likely to presume against the granting of planning permission where there are landscape features to be 'managed', unless suitable agreements are put in place to undertake the necessary 'management'. This falls just short of an absolute requirement to enter into a section 106 agreement to secure ongoing management, which would be unlawful.

In contrast to the statutory approach of the Habitats Directive, LBAPs are non-statutory though they are increasingly the subject of the national planning policy guidance. For example, in Scotland *National Planning Policy Guidance 14* on the Natural Heritage (Scottish Office, 1998) states that 'Planning Authorities can make an important contribution to the achievement of biodiversity targets by adopting policies which promote and afford protection to species and habitats identified as priorities in LBAPs' (para 18).

RESEARCH METHOD

The overarching aim of the research reported in this chapter was to assess the extent to which local planning authorities (LPAs) were promoting positive planning. As noted, positive planning was defined in terms of Regulation 37 policies and the degree of integration between LBAPs and development plan policies (focusing on enhancement and management rather than just protection).

A postal questionnaire was sent to every LPA in Great Britain (county, district and unitary authorities including national park authorities). This enabled an overview to be drawn of the development of Regulation 37 and LBAP related development plan policies across the country. The results of the questionnaire survey were then used to select a sample of LPAs for more in-depth study via telephone interviews and participation in a roundtable workshop (Bate and Bishop, 2000). A total of 20 LPAs were selected for the follow-up research. These were chosen to represent a range of differing approaches to Regulation 37 policies.

The postal questionnaire to LPAs yielded a total of 172 usable responses. Of these 157 were from local planning authorities in England; 5 from Scotland; and 10 from Wales. The survey covered a total of 359 development plans. Of these, 201 were adopted and 158 'emerging' plans. Most of the completed questionnaires were returned by district councils.

DEVELOPMENT OF REGULATION 37 POLICIES

LPAs were asked to state, for each plan that their authority was (or had been) responsible for preparing, whether it currently included a reference to 'management of features of the landscape which are important for wild flora and fauna' (the question cross referenced them to explanatory notes outlining the requirements of the Habitats Directive and the Habitat Regulations 1994).

In total, 133 local planning authorities stated that they had a 'Regulation 37' policy on the management of landscape. These policies were mainly in 'emerging' development plans (85 per cent of all of the emerging development plans analysed in the survey were said to include 'Regulation 37' policies, compared with 51 per cent of all adopted development plans).

Table 14.1 *Factors influencing the decision to include a Regulation 37 policy in development plans*

	Number of respondents stating this was 'Very important'	Number of respondents stating this was 'A factor'	Number of respondents stating this was 'Not important'
Natural Area profile (England)	5	25	52
Countryside Character profile (England)	6	22	55
LANDMAP (Wales)	1	3	4
National Heritage zone/unit (Scotland	16	19	56
Local Biodiversity action plan	16	19	56
Government planning guidance	77	32	11

Respondents were asked to indicate the reasons that influenced their decision to include a Regulation 37 policy. They were given a list of potential reasons and the opportunity to indicate a range of 'other' factors, and asked to indicate the importance of these on a sliding scale of 1 to 3 (with 1 indicating a very important factor and 3 no influence on the decision). As illustrated in Table 14.1, central government planning guidance was the main factor cited for inclusion of a 'Regulation 37 policy' with advice (from statutory conservation agencies, in-house experts, etc) an important 'secondary' consideration. The new countryside planning tools discussed in Part 2 of this book, such as natural area profiles, *LANDMAP*, countryside character and natural heritage futures, had had little influence, at the time of the survey, on the formulation of Regulation 37 policies. This is probably a reflection of the time delay between new approaches being developed and subsequently adopted in plan preparation. LBAPs were cited a 'very important' factor in influencing the decision to include a Regulation 37 policy by 16 local planning authorities though the survey of LBAP coordinators (see below) suggested that there was little material in existing/evolving LBAPs on the management of landscape features of major importance for wild flora and fauna. Three planning authorities stated that they had included a Regulation 37 policy on the 'recommendation of the local plan inspector'.

The main reason cited for not including a Regulation 37 policy was 'timing': 35 local planning authorities stated that the plan pre-dated the Habitat Regulations and/or relevant government planning guidance (see Table 14.2). Those authorities stating that the requirements of Regulation 37 were covered by other initiatives cited such examples as: 'countryside management service', 'nature conservation strategy', 'existing local plan policies' and 'Community Forest Plans'.

Each LPA was asked to append their 'Regulation 37' policy(s) to the questionnaire and these were analysed in detail. The results show considerable variation in how LPAs and others have interpreted the law and planning guidance on Regulation 37 policies.

Table 14.2 *Factors influencing the decision not to include a Regulation 37 policy in development plans*

Factors	Number of respondents stating this was 'Very important'	Number of respondents stating this was 'A factor'
Covered by other initiatives	10	3
Objections from consultees	2	0
Doubts over implementation	5	5
Lack of external expertise	1	3
Lack of in-house expertise	3	19
Pre-dates Habitat Regulations and/or government planning advice	35	3
Never thought of it/Not a priority/ Not requested	9	16

Confused interpretation

Despite the statutory requirement for Regulation 37 policies being in place for over six years, the questionnaire demonstrated widespread confusion and considerable variation in the format and wording of the policies that were cited as examples of 'Regulation 37' policies. Many LPAs cited as their Regulation 37 policy(s) policies on:

- wildlife corridors (protection, creation and enhancement of);
- tree and woodland protection;
- site protection (especially those concerned with Local Nature Reserves);
- mitigation/compensation;
- landscaping of development sites; and/or
- general landscape protection.

Box 14.1 provides an example of the difficulty in defining what constitutes a 'Regulation 37' policy. Policy LN10 in the Adopted West Lancashire Local Plan is an example of a corridor and open space policy linked, in part, to the Habitats Directive. The reasoned justification for Policy LN10 refers to the Habitats Directive, and the thinking it enshrines, on the importance of landscape features as stepping stones and/or corridors but there is no reference to management and the policy is ambiguous in its reference to landscape features.

Even when the LPA demonstrated an understanding of the requirements of Regulation 37 there was often ambiguity in the wording of the policy. For example, many of the policies were general statements of intent, unrelated to development proposals and with no explanation of how the policy was to be implemented. Also, even when the requirements of Regulation 37 were cited, no examples, or definitions, of 'landscape features of major importance for wild flora and fauna' were given.

We estimate that less than 10 per cent of those stating that they had a Regulation 37 policy actually operated a policy which met the following criteria/definition of such a policy:

BOX 14.1 WEST LANCASHIRE LOCAL PLAN (ADOPTED) 1999

POLICY LN10

Development will not be permitted which would destroy or significantly impair the integrity of the Green Spaces and Corridors shown on the Proposals Map, by:

- resulting in the loss of the undeveloped open character of the area;
- reducing the width or causing direct or indirect severance of a corridor;
- restricting the potential for lateral movement of wildlife;
- restricting public access to a Green Space or Corridor;
- causing degradation of the visual, ecological and historical functions of the area; or
- directly or indirectly damaging or severing links between Green Spaces, corridors and the open countryside.

Development may be permitted where it will provide a substantial environmental gain to include the visual, ecological or appropriate recreational functions of the Green Space or corridor.

Justification

The Green Spaces and Corridors identified on the Proposals Map are those areas of open land which provide or have the potential to provide one or more of the following:

- opportunities for informal outdoor recreation;
- an important visual contribution to the landscape or townscape character;
- habitats for wildlife;
- corridors for the movement of wildlife; and/or
- historical, cultural or geological features.

These spaces and corridors perform important functions and contribute to the quality of the environment in West Lancashire. PPG9 (Nature Conservation) and the EC Birds and Habitats Directives recognize the importance of landscape features which, because of their linear and continuous structure or their function as 'stepping stones', are essential for migration, dispersal and genetic exchange. Linear biological features can act as 'corridors' along which wildlife can move and live. Continuity is an important factor for many species; an isolated site is restricted in the range of species able to colonize it. Corridors can be damaged or rendered unviable by a reduction in their width or complete severance. Direct or indirect severance can be caused by the introduction of roads, pathways, landforms, services and other constructions and by way of changes in vegetation management within the Corridor. Restrictions of the lateral movements of wildlife or in the accessibility and safe use of the site by the public should be avoided wherever possible. This can be achieved by retaining any adjoining or nearby corridors and avoiding the introduction of fencing or other barriers on one or both sides of the corridor. Any development which reduces any of these functions will be resisted by the Council. In line with government advice and Regional Guidance the Council will also protect Green Spaces and corridors and the open countryside in order to encourage wildlife into urban areas and to allow public access between town and country.

- A reference to Regulation 37 (or Article 10 of the Habitats Directive) within the policy or supporting text.
- A statement defining the landscape features in the development plan area that are of major importance for wild fauna and flora.

- An explanation of how the policy will become operational (eg 'planning permission will not be granted for development or land use changes in places where there are landscape features of major importance...') and a statement of how the management will be secured (eg through the use of planning conditions, planning obligations or other means).

Disjointed and contradictory messages from government

The research revealed various interpretations of the requirements of Regulation 37 between different levels of government (central and regional) and within the Planning Inspectorate.

The wording of Policy C15/16 in the Devon Structure Plan First Review (see Box 14.2) was heavily influenced by the advice of the Government Office for the South West which objected to a more specific policy in the Structure Plan because of difficulties in achieving 'clearly focused policies which provide clarity and certainty for decision-makers and those affected'. The Government Office for the South West identified three particular concerns. First was the issue of mapping landscape features of major importance for wildlife on proposals maps. They argued that government guidance required any sites, features or areas to which local plan policies apply to be shown site-specifically on the Proposals Map (or Inset Map) (DoE, 1992, para 7.14). The second concern related to importance, scale and number. They anticipated that most of these important features would be large enough to plot on an Ordnance Survey map at scale 1:50,000 to 1:10,000. As the Habitats Directive calls them features of 'major importance in the context of the Natura 2000 network', the Government Office deemed that there would not be a large number of them in any one LPA area and thus there would be no problem in plotting them on a Proposals Map. The third concern related to the relevance of the policy to planning decisions. Whilst accepting the novelty of the management in a land use planning context, the Government Office argued that the policy should seek to protect these features and thus only come into play where they were affected by physical development. They noted that because agriculture and forestry operations are excluded from the definition of development contained in the planning acts, such policies would be limited in how effective they were in achieving appropriate management.

The interpretation of PPG 9 (DoE, 1994) and the requirements of the Habitat Regulations by the Government Office for the South West point towards confusion within central government over the meaning and implementation of its own policies. Equating 'major importance' with 'relative scarcity' is not in fact indicated in PPG 9, nor in the Habitat Regulations, nor the original Directive. Indeed, the opposite could be argued: such features are of major importance because of their frequency and/or continuous nature.

Somerset County Council also reported conflict with the Government Office for the South West when attempting to include a Regulation 37 policy in the Structure Plan Review Deposit Draft. A reference to '... enhancement and management of special landscape features' was deleted at the instigation of the Government Office which stressed that the management of land was not a land use planning consideration and should not, therefore, be incorporated into

---

BOX 14.2 DEVON STRUCTURE PLAN FIRST REVIEW 1995–2011 (ADOPTED) 1999

Another element of the Devon environment which is of particular nature conservation significance is addressed by Policy C15/16. This is the complex network of landscape features that make up a web of wildlife habitat around the county. These features are those which, because of their linear or continuous structure or their function as stepping stones, are essential for migration, dispersal and genetic exchange and play a critical role in the conservation and enhancement of the biodiversity across Devon. Such features include rivers and their immediate corridors, traditional field boundaries – such as hedgerows and Devon banks, small woodlands and ponds.

The Natural Habitats (&c) Regulations require local authorities to adopt policies encouraging the beneficial management of features of the landscape which are of major importance for wild flora and fauna. Policy C15/16 indicates that such features should be defined within Local Plans.

POLICY C15/16

In addition to sites included within the terms of Policy C14, Local Plans should define sites and features of nature conservation importance, including landscape features which provide wildlife corridors, links or stepping stones between habitats.

---

strategic or local plan policies. Epping Forest District Council also reported that proposed policies inspired by Regulation 37 had met resistance from the Government Office for the Eastern Region because the policies were considered insufficiently tied to development control.

The apparent confusion and inconsistency of approach between and within government offices for the regions was mirrored by the inconsistency of approach between planning inspectors. The research revealed instances where local plan inspectors had recommended that Regulation 37 policies be edited or removed and other examples where they had recommended the insertion of such policies. At the Wealden Local Plan Inquiry the Inspector recommended that all 'promotional' policies (ie those which 'promote', 'encourage' or 'support' actions) should be removed because they were statements of intent rather than land use policies. The Inspector at the North West Leicestershire Local Plan Inquiry determined that existing site protection policies were sufficient to meet the requirements of the Habitats Directive, thus ignoring the management requirement. The Inspector also determined that the list of features that English Nature had identified as being of 'major' importance (and which were consistent with guidance from the Royal Town Planning Institute (1999)) would lead to 'over-elaborate plan making and thus be contrary to government guidance'. In contrast, at the Shrewsbury and Atcham Borough Local Plan Inquiry, the Inspector supported an amendment to a policy on protection of the natural heritage to include provision for management of features of the landscape which are of major importance for wild flora and fauna.

Uncertainty and reluctance to address a novel issue

The requirements of the Habitat Regulations are novel and the research revealed some reluctance amongst planning authorities to respond positively to these requirements and think beyond traditional site protection.

Local authorities are under little pressure from the relevant government department/devolved administrations to take the necessary steps to implement Regulation 37 policies effectively. This provides little incentive to develop policies in a new and innovative area, especially when there is a counter pressure to produce slimmer and swifter development plans. It also provides a weak basis from which to enter negotiations with developers on the management of landscape features, particularly when implementation is likely to involve a section 106 agreement and take additional time and effort (time which authorities feel disinclined to afford as they are under considerable pressure to improve application handling times, and effort which they are disinclined to apply due to widespread under-staffing in planning departments). The feeling of many respondents to the follow-up telephone survey was that this was in effect a discretionary policy area and one where progress was more often dependent upon personal interest. Interviewees also noted a lack of member interest in this subject area (as reported by planning officers).

The telephone interviews revealed a belief amongst planners that developers were reluctant to embrace innovative conditions on planning permissions or to enter into legal agreements concerning the management of landscape/wildlife features. To some extent this is a general resistance to 'further regulation', but there also is concern that it could be an unequal burden borne by selected developers – or perhaps only by the first to agree to it! The problem, as expressed by more than one respondent, was to persuade developers that habitat enhancement was an opportunity that would add to the value of the development rather than another planning hurdle.

Inadequate application of ecological expertise

The authorities in our survey which had made most progress with introducing Regulation 37 policies were those which employed ecologists on their staff or had access to adequate ecological expertise by other means, such as consultants or expert voluntary organizations. Furthermore, ecological expertise must be available for the function of development control and not simply for plan preparation: evidence at the workshop clearly demonstrated that at least a modest level of ecological competence was necessary (either through training of development control staff or by bringing in expert advice) to implement Regulation 37 policies in practice. This applied even where efforts had been made to identify the relevant landscape features in advance: expertise was still needed in terms of the practical management required.

Even where authorities were in principle willing to promote Regulation 37 policies and practices, a dearth of ecological expertise could still result in weak implementation of policy. For example, in Rutland County Council it is unclear how a policy introduced in response to pressure from English Nature and the RSPB will be followed through in practice, whilst Wealden District Council reported inadequate support from the voluntary sector when a decision based on a Regulation 37 policy, which had been included in response to lobbying by the voluntary sector, came to be defended at a planning appeal.

Corporate weaknesses

Finally, there is some evidence of inadequate corporate management in local authorities in handling Regulation 37 issues and applying ecological expertise effectively. This can arise between departments, in which there are conflicting objectives for land management (eg between a Parks Department and a Planning Department). Moreover policies in the development plan may be prepared with due consideration for wildlife, but because of poor internal communications development control staff are insufficiently aware of how they are expected to implement policy and forward planning staff are insufficiently aware of the success or otherwise of policies. Monitoring information, if there is any, all too often does not find its way back into policy evaluation, especially in policy areas that are often deemed 'discretionary' (see above).

POLICIES PROMOTING/ENHANCING BIODIVERSITY

The questionnaire survey asked LPAs to state whether plans for which their authority was (or had been) responsible, included references/policies to 'promoting/enhancing biodiversity (habitats or species)'. The explanatory text, which accompanied the questionnaire, emphasized that we were interested in policies that went beyond control and protection, and that we were specifically interested in development plan policies promoting (or referring) to land use planning – related LBAP targets and objectives. In total, 101 local planning authorities stated that their development plan included such policies. Of these respondents, 88 were in England, 5 in Scotland and 8 in Wales. Perhaps surprisingly, there was no discernible bias towards such policies being in 'emerging' development plans: the split between adopted and emerging development plans was relatively even across the three countries.

There was considerable variation in the wording of 'promotion/ enhancement' policies. Many LPAs provided a list of policies in response to this question and such policies often covered 'traditional' site conservation as well as more positive measures. Most examples were of general policies that included the words 'promote' and or 'enhancement' as opposed to being specifically related to LBAPs or clearly focused on 'positive planning'. They were often related to mitigation measures. Environment Policy 3 in the Leicestershire, Leicester and Rutland Structure Plan 1991–2011 (Consultation Draft) (see Box 14.3) is an example of such a policy. There was also often a close link between Regulation 37 policies and promotion/enhancement policies with many LPAs citing the same policy.

In some instances, the 'promotion and enhancement of biodiversity' have been included as overarching aims of the development plan as well as, or instead of, including a specific policy in the relevant chapter. The Dumfries and Galloway Structure Plan is built around the guiding principle: 'to encourage the growth and development of sustainable communities in Dumfries and Galloway'. To achieve this, the following aims were set:

BOX 14.3 LEICESTERSHIRE, LEICESTER AND RUTLAND STRUCTURE PLAN 1991–2011

Environment Policy 3: Ecology

Measures will be taken to promote natural biodiversity, protect and conserve sites of ecological significance and protected species and their habitats, and enhance the wider ecological value of the environment.

Development will only be acceptable where it would not adversely affect any protected species or its habitat, or any proposed or designated National Nature Reserve, Special Protection Area, Special Area of Conservation, Ramsar Site, or Site of Special Scientific Interest designated because of its ecological interest, unless an overriding national need for the development can be shown to outweigh the ecological interest and there is no other site for that development.

Development will only be acceptable where it would not adversely affect any Site of Importance for Nature Conservation, Local Nature Reserve, landscape feature of importance for wildlife by reason of its continuous nature or function as a stepping stone between habitats, unless an overriding national or local need can be shown to outweigh the ecological interest.

In the exceptional circumstance where development is allowed which would adversely affect any site of ecological significance, conditions will be imposed to:

- minimize disturbance;
- conserve its ecological interest as far as possible; and
- provide new or replacement habitats where damage is unavoidable so that the total ecological resource remains at least at its current level.

- to support development of the local economy;
- to support urban and rural communities;
- to support and protect the natural and built environment;
- to make best use of services and facilities.

These then link to a series of 'Strategy Statements', including one on the Quality of Life which refers to '… caring for the natural and built environment' and includes reference (within the supporting text) to 'protecting and enhancing the most valued elements of the environment …', and 'maintaining and enhancing the area's biodiversity'.

Policies linking or attempting to link LBAPs to development planning policy frameworks were rare. Most of the examples of LBAP policies uncovered in the development plan survey related to policies indicating the LPAs' support for the preparation of an LBAP. In other examples, such as the Deposit Bournemouth District Wide Local Plan (1999), there is a discussion of the BAP process covering the UK, regional and local levels, but this does not relate specifically to any one policy. A question arises as to whether policies such as those illustrated are actually land use policies (as defined by government guidance) and thus appropriate for inclusion in development plans at all. Surprisingly, the survey did not reveal any examples of development plan policies that were specifically related to LBAP targets.

Table 14.3 *Implementation mechanisms for positive planning policies*

Implementation mechanism	Number of LPAs stating that they use this mechanism to implement:	
	Regulation 37 policies	Promotion/enhancement of biodiversity policies
Issues treated as a material planning consideration (based on government policies)	98	79
Issues treated as a material planning consideration (based on LBAP policies)	31	31
Planning conditions	77	73
Planning obligations	68	63
Development briefs	67	60
Supplementary planning guidance	46	23
Design guidance	27	14
Article IV directions	6	6
'Cleaning up order'	4	4
Damage mitigation measures identified through an ES	7	3

IMPLEMENTING POSITIVE PLANNING POLICIES

Respondents were asked a series of questions relating to the implementation of Regulation 37 and promotion and/or enhancement of biodiversity policies. It is clear from the responses to these questions that the main implementation mechanisms for both categories of policy are planning conditions, planning agreements/obligations and development briefs (see Table 14.3). Whilst most LPAs stated that they were treating these issues as material considerations, it was mainly on the basis of government policy rather than development plan policies. No LPA (in either the postal survey or telephone interviews) provided any examples of how such issues had been treated as a material planning consideration in a development control decision, making it difficult to assess the validity of these claims.

A significant number of LPAs are using development briefs to implement such policies. The examples provided tended to instruct potential developers that a detailed ecological survey of the area would be required or highlighted sensitive locations within development sites (eg wildlife corridors based on streams or woodland blocks). Only five LPAs stated that they had adopted the LBAP for their area as supplementary planning guidance. There is some evidence that the requirements of Regulation 37 are being incorporated into design guidance (27 LPAs stated that they were using design guidance to implement such policies). A good example of this is the Design Guide for North Cornwall. Very few LPAs indicated that they used more interventionist planning powers (such as Article IV Directions) to implement either Regulation 37 or promotion/enhancement of biodiversity policies.

The follow-up telephone interviews revealed a clear implementation deficit. Many of those interviewed reported that they were so hard-pressed for time to deal with planning applications that policies which are not easy to implement may not be given much attention: this can apply to Regulation 37 policies if, for example, the landscape features to be managed are not clearly identified or if section 106 agreements are needed to achieve that management. They were also concerned that so-called 'positive planning' policies were not sufficiently well-established to survive challenge at planning appeals. There is also some resistance from developers to Regulation 37 policies on grounds of expense (whether or not this is justified, and some respondents considered it was not) and novelty: the lack of understanding of the issues suggests a need for greater explanation and communication to developers. The low political profile of biodiversity was also cited as a problem in terms of implementation: members are often unwilling to support officers' recommendations for refusal or the imposition of planning conditions on biodiversity grounds, unless related to a designated protected area (national or local wildlife site).

CONCLUSIONS

There is a clear legal obligation on local planning authorities to include in their development plans policies to give effect to Article 10 of the EC Habitats Directive (as implemented in the UK through Regulation 37 of the Habitats Regulations). The effect of the legislation is to establish more explicitly than before the role of the town and country planning system as including the management of landscape features. As such it represents an important broadening of the role of the planning system away from site protection and towards consideration of the wider countryside and linkages between protected areas.

This emphasis on the whole countryside is also reflected in the content of most LBAPs. As with the Habitats Directive, LBAPs often identify the planning system as a key implementation mechanism and not just in terms of site protection. Indeed, in a separate survey of LBAP coordinators, 88 per cent of those responding stated that planning had an important role to play in encouraging positive management and enhancement of biodiversity (Bate and Bishop, 2000).

Notwithstanding the regulatory requirements of the Habitat Regulations and the non-statutory, partnership-based ethos of LBAPs, the research reported in this chapter highlights an important implementation deficit. Whilst previous research has indicated an improvement in the terms of local authority planning for nature conservation (Marshall and Smith, 1999) this improvement would appear to be focused on policies for site-based protection with little evidence of development plans reflecting the new focus on the wider countryside and joining-up protected areas. Although there is an inevitable time lag between new policy advice/requirements coming into force and development plans reflecting this advice, the implementation deficit identified by this research would appear to have more to do with inadequate central government guidance, lack of official pressure, uncertainty amongst LPAs about how to address novel policy issues and a lack of ecological expertise at the local authority level.

The process of policy transfer and adoption could be aided by more detailed planning guidance that went beyond mere advocacy to explain how such policies should be structured. Indeed, there would appear to be a strong case for model policies. They avoid duplication of effort (each LPA having to research individually the requirements of Regulation 37) and can provide for a standard approach, open to local variation. They would, moreover need to be promoted as a template rather than a rigid national policy to be replicated locally. Model policies would help to break the cycle of non-implementation of Regulation 37 but would need to be supplemented by:

- better corporate management (ensuring development control staff have an active role in policy formulation and development plan staff were properly informed about implementation);
- ready availability of ecological advice/expertise either through in-house professionals or a more active partnership role for the relevant statutory agency or local wildlife trust); and
- evidence that Regulation 37 policies were being upheld at appeal.

The model policy approach would also appear likely to help the link between the land use objectives of LBAPs and development plans. At present the relevant planning guidance either pre-dates the emergence of LBAPs (England) (DoE, 1994) or refers to the importance of development plans in helping to achieve LBAP targets but fails to explain how they should do this (Scotland and Wales)(Scottish Office, 1998; Welsh Assembly Government, 2002; Welsh Office, 1996). Even informal advice from the Local Government Management Board and UK Biodiversity Group (undated) and Royal Town Planning Institute (1999) fails to explain how development plans can help implement LBAP policies.

In conclusion, the statutory planning system has a key role to play in site protection but there is little evidence yet, based on the results discussed above, of a widening of this approach to embrace 'positive planning' in the countryside at large.

REFERENCES

Bate, R and Bishop, K (2000) Positive Planning, unpublished research report to the Royal Society for the Protection of Birds, Royal Society for the Protection of Birds, Sandy

Department of the Environment (DoE) (1992) *Planning Policy Guidance Note 12: Development Plans and Regional Planning Guidance*, Her Majesty's Stationery Office, London

Department of the Environment (DoE) (1994) *Planning Policy Guidance Note 9: Nature Conservation*, Her Majesty's Stationery Office, London

Local Government Management Board and UK Biodiversity Group (undated) *Guidance for Local Biodiversity Action Plans: An Introduction*, Local Government Management Board and UK Biodiversity Group, London

Marshall, R and Smith, C (1999) 'Planning for Nature Conservation: The role and performance of English district local authorities in the 1990s', *Journal of Environmental Planning and Management*, vol 42(5), pp691–706.

Royal Town Planning Institute (RTPI) (1999) *Planning for Biodiversity*, RTPI, London

Scottish Office (1998) *National Planning Policy Guidelines 14: Natural Heritage*, Scottish Office, Edinburgh

Welsh Assembly Government (2002) *Planning Policy Wales*, National Assembly for Wales, Cardiff

Welsh Office (1996) *Planning Guidance (Wales) Technical Advice Note (Wales) 5: Nature Conservation and Planning*, Welsh Office, Cardiff

Chapter 15

A New Way of Valuing Land in the Countryside: Are We Lost Without a Map?

Jo Milling

Mendip is a small rural district in north-east Somerset. It lies a few miles south of Bath and Bristol but has its own distinctive rural character. It covers 285 square miles and has a population of around 100,000. It includes some of Somerset's most varied and attractive landscapes, from the limestone plateau of the Mendip Hills to the rich farmlands of the Frome valley and the Somerset levels and moors. The environment is recognized as one of the district's main assets and designations for historic, wildlife and landscape interest are numerous. The district includes 27 Sites of Special Scientific Interest (SSSIs), 250 County Wildlife Sites, 2,700 listed buildings and 220 Scheduled Ancient Monuments. It also includes part of two Areas of Outstanding Natural Beauty (AONBs), and the attractiveness of the rest of the countryside is widely recognized.

Each of Mendip's five market towns (Frome, Glastonbury, Shepton Mallet, Street and Wells) has its own distinctive character, but all are well connected to larger centres such as Bath, Bristol, Taunton and Yeovil. There are more than 60 smaller villages. Around 40 per cent of the district's population live outside the towns.

Mendip District Council recognizes the value of its high quality environment through many of its plans and strategies, and has sought new ways of valuing the countryside which add to these. The district has tried several new techniques for valuing and managing the countryside within its Local Agenda 21 (LA21) programme and in conjunction with the preparation of the Local Plan (Mendip District Council, 1998). The new techniques which have been tried include the following:

- *Landscape characterization*: a landscape assessment of the district was carried out, which identifies character areas. A description of the elements which make up the character of each area is included, and highlights those aspects of the landscape which are most valuable. The exercise was carried out as part of the preparation of the Local Plan and is linked to policies for the protection of the landscape. The landscape assessment is intended as a tool to be used in Development Control, enabling a judgement to be made on the effect of a proposal the landscape.

- *Biodiversity Action Plan (BAP)*: in 1995, Mendip was the first UK District authority to produce a BAP (Mendip District Council, 1995). It included action plans for five priority habitats and ten priority species and identified Prime Biodiversity Areas. The plan made recommendations for actions to address biodiversity priorities and for the development of a scheme for community-based recording and monitoring of wildlife.
- *Village Design Statements (VDSs)*: Mendip has worked with parish councils to produce VDSs, setting out the valued features of the village and providing guidelines for the design of future development. VDSs will be adopted as Supplementary Planning Guidance, and given further weight through policies in the Local Plan.

The Council has employed these new techniques as it has sought new and better ways to protect its high quality environment. The Council is also strongly committed to its LA21 programme and has focused on initiatives which allow the participation of local communities both in the systems of local governance and in valuing the environment. The purpose of this chapter is to evaluate critically the success of each of the new techniques and to highlight some of the problems common to them.

LINKS TO THE STATUTORY LAND USE PLANNING SYSTEM

The statutory development plan sets out policies for the development and use of land in the countryside. Landscape characterization and VDSs also fit within the land use planning system. Thus, while the local plan establishes a policy framework which has statutory backing, the landscape characterization and VDSs can be adopted as supplementary guidance, providing tools for the more detailed assessment of proposals needing planning permission. Also both have a wider role in focusing community debate and generating participation, in the planning system and more generally in valuing the local environment. Both these tools allow local people to make an input into decisions about development in a more systematic, long-term and productive way than the traditional objection to a planning application.

The *Mendip Biodiversity Action Plan* (BAP) (Mendip District Council, 1995) guides the management of wildlife resources in the district and was prepared as part of the Council's LA21 programme. It focuses more on issues outside planning control but still has strong links to the planning and development arena.

EFFECTIVENESS OF THE NEW APPROACHES

Landscape Characterization

A landscape assessment of the district was carried out (Chris Blandford Associates, 1997), partly within the Council's LA21 programme and partly to inform the local plan preparation process. The Council's State of the Environment Report (Mendip District Council, 1994) highlighted a lack of information on the district's landscape. A landscape assessment of the Mendip Hills, centred on the AONB, was under preparation by the Countryside Commission at about this time and provided encouragement to the Council to commission an assessment of the character of the whole district (Countryside Commission, 1996a).

The primary use to which the assessment has been put is as a tool in the development control process. It is linked to policies in the local plan for the protection of the countryside, controlling the impact of development on the landscape. The type of development and its location are strictly controlled by the plan's settlement strategy. Where development is permitted outside the towns and villages, its design, siting, location and layout must be such that the scenic quality and local character of the landscape, as set out in the characterization, are protected. The characterization provides a series of thumbnail sketches of the character of each area. These have been summarized and included as an appendix to the local plan to provide a ready reference. An extract from this appendix is shown in Box 15.1.

The assessment followed guidance in the Countryside Commission's *Landscape Assessment Guidance* (Countryside Commission, 1993) and included the following stages:

BOX 15.1 LANDSCAPE CHARACTER AREA DESCRIPTIONS

The East Mendip Hills

Cranmore Ridge and Slopes: Prominent ridge, conifer plantations, rectilinear fields on ridge, ridgeline barrows, wide views, gentle sideslopes, irregular fields on slopes, frequent trees on slopes, abandoned quarries.

Sheppey Valley: Attractive stone villages, steep sided valley opening out to the west, disused mills and evidence of cloth industry, parkland character, tree cover, frequent woodland.

Northern and Eastern Farmlands: Very gentle slopes, well-tended hedgerows, openness, scattered hedgerow trees, major parklands, irregular field pattern, local area of drystone walling, large post-medieval farms, frequent arable land use.

Somer Valley: Contrasting field pattern, neglected urban fringe patches, attractive village cores, sprawling settlement.

Source: Chris Blandford Associates, 1997

- literature review;
- familiarization visits;
- desk study of main physical features;
- identification of preliminary landscape areas using a desk study;
- field work to identify and record main features of the landscape, using record sheets, photographs and annotated maps;
- identification of landscape types based on landform, geology, vegetation and visual qualities;
- identification of recurrent features of the landscape which have an impact on character, such as boundary treatment, watercourses or woodland; and
- identification of landscape character areas.

Previous development plans had recognized the value of the district's countryside through a 'Special Landscape Area' (SLA) designation. This is a county-level designation based on the quality of the landscape (Somerset County Council, 1993). It shows some parts of the countryside as being of greater value than others, deserving additional protection. In Mendip more than 80 per cent of the land was designated as either SLA or as nationally important AONB (Somerset County Council, 1993). The designation did not, however, differentiate between the wide variety of landscapes within the SLA and gave no indication as to what was valuable about them. Judgements about what was valuable about each stretch of countryside and how a proposed development would impact on it had to be made from scratch on each occasion, without any agreed guidance from the development plan.

The landscape characterization acknowledges that all of the district's countryside is valuable (even the 20 per cent previously undesignated) and that each part has a character of its own. It also provides an agreed basis against which judgement on the impact of development proposals can be made. The characterization has more weight, having been prepared as part of the statutory development plan process rather the ad hoc judgements on which development control previously relied.

Some difficulties do however remain in using the landscape character approach. Whilst the character assessment divides the district into some 58 areas, the descriptions of each can give no more than a summary of the character of the landscape. The scale and number of the character areas means that the descriptions are often too general to be helpful in judging the impact of a development in its immediate context. For example, the description of 'Cranmore Ridge and Slopes' in Box 15.1 indicates that the prominent ridge would not be a suitable location for development, and that anything affecting the ridgeline barrows, wide open views or tree cover would be likely to be inappropriate. However, it is not sufficiently detailed to inform judgements on the effect, for instance, of a single dwelling on the edge of one of the small settlements on the lower ground within the character area. VDSs should, to some extent, help to address this and are discussed later in the chapter.

The character area approach has often been widely misunderstood, both by professionals and local people, as demonstrated by objections to the local plan. Some have interpreted the characterization as an additional layer of restraint, asking for specific sites to be excluded from it. Others have interpreted it as the removal of protection from the landscape, as some areas are no longer regarded as 'special'. The character approach does not seek to extend or reduce the protection afforded to the landscape, but it provides an agreed context within which to judge development proposals. As such, it does not provide the security of defined areas which are protected from development, or within which development can take place, but it is more sensitive to the individual character of landscapes and thus is ultimately more useful as a tool in the planning process.

Biodiversity Action Plan

The Mendip BAP (Mendip District Council, 1995) has been used principally as a tool by Mendip District Council and key partners such as the Somerset Wildlife Trust in identifying priority habitats, species and areas, and encouraging implementation of actions and the targeting of resources towards them.

As a planning tool, the BAP has, until recently, been difficult to use and to relate to development decisions. There are no established mechanisms within the planning system to seek improvements for BAP priority habitats or species, unless they can be directly related to a specific development requiring planning permission. Moreover, so-called 'planning gain' must be reasonably necessary for the development in order to be legitimate. In the majority of instances, improvements which would meet the aims of the BAP have not been viewed as legitimate planning gain. The next step for the Council, and one of its actions under the BAP, is to develop and adopt supplementary planning guidance for biodiversity, to strengthen the consideration of biodiversity issues within the planning process. It is hoped that the process of preparing such guidance will help clarify the relationship between the BAP and the statutory planning system.

Mendip District Council plays a coordinating role in the ongoing BAP process, through the Council's Wildlife Officer. Partners in this process are consulted and involved in this work in three ways: through a Steering Group (which meets annually); through a Working Group; and via direct liaison with the Council's Wildlife Officer. Decisions are made through the Steering Group, who oversee the ongoing development and implementation of the BAP, and actions derived from it. Its members include lead partner organizations (eg Somerset Wildlife Trust, English Nature) as well as representatives from the landowning/farming sector. All stakeholders are encouraged to take part in Working Group meetings (these are held throughout the year) and include representatives from community groups, individual enthusiasts, farmers and specialists (as well as members of the Steering Group). The Working Group addresses issues such as agreeing priorities, making commitments to actions which contribute to the overall plan, and sharing ideas and good practice. An example of the Group's work is the development of a farmers' questionnaire seeking views on biodiversity issues. The results from this have been used in the development of a 'Mendip Farm BAP' – an 'issue-based' BAP – targeted specifically at supporting farmers to help biodiversity, the broad elements of which will underpin the broader Mendip BAP. Finally, direct liaison with the

Council's wildlife officer provides an opportunity to address issues which relate only to individual partners' contributions to the BAP process, and is a means for partners to become involved who find it difficult to attend group meetings.

Outside of this formal structure efforts are made to involve the wider public, especially young people, as their support is seen as crucial to the success of the BAP process. Community projects (which may often be developed through parish and town councils or local community groups), talks, walks, practical events and initiatives such as 'Wildcheck' (a community wildlife recording and activities scheme run by the Council), all contribute to this. The Council is also developing a BAP web site to promote biodiversity more widely through schools and to the public.

Village Design Statements

As part of the local plan process, a series of village planning days were held, covering all the villages in the district. Local residents were invited to identify their aspirations for the future of their village (see below for the techniques used). At around the same time, the Countryside Commission published its *Village Design Guidance to Local Communities* (Countryside Commission, 1996b) and started to promote the production of village design guides by Parish Councils. The concept of community-driven design guides which could be adopted as supplementary planning guidance, and would add value to the development control process fitted well with the Council's LA21 programme. An officer was therefore employed within the Planning Department's conservation section to promote the production of VDSs and to give assistance to Parish Councils in their production.

This process was started in 1997. However, by 2002 only two VDSs had been adopted as supplementary planning guidance; a third was in preparation. The overwhelming impression given by Parish Councils in Mendip District is that they are reluctant to embark on a project of this scale and that they are intimidated by the need to engage with the formal planning system further than the traditional consultations on planning applications. Evidence from the two VDSs that have been adopted as supplementary planning guidance suggests that the communities rely heavily on Council support and that VDSs will not be produced without that. Because of this limited interest and funding constraints, the Council suspended the post dedicated to supporting the production of VDSs, declaring it to be an 'extra service' that it was not mandated to provide.

However, the two VDSs that have been produced and adopted as supplementary planning guidance have proved valuable, guiding decisions on planning applications in these communities, but, some problems have also become evident (see Box 15.2).

Problems with the preparation of VDSs have been encountered when the inclusive, democratic processes suggested in the Countryside Commission scheme of 1996 have not been followed. In Wookey, the Parish Council decided to undertake a VDS and delegated two members of the community to carry out the appraisal (Wookey Parish Council, 1998). Unfortunately the process was not well publicized within the village and a document was produced which did not

---

BOX 15.2 VILLAGE DESIGN STATEMENT FOR LEIGH ON MENDIP

A VDSs for Leigh on Mendip was produced with the support of the Countryside Commission. The design guide (Leigh on Mendip Village Design Group, 1998) identifies the main features of the village as being:

* the strong linear pattern, with Leigh Street (the only thoroughfare) acting as the focus of the village;
* substantial stretches of the street with views onto open countryside;
* traditional building styles with two-storey construction and roofs between 40 and 45 degrees;
* use of rubble limestone and clay tiles for construction;
* small front gardens with low limestone walls fronting Leigh Street.

Some of the more recent developments though pre-date the VDS and do not always respect the characteristics identified in the VDS. The most recent of these, at 'The Hedgerows' is pictured in Figure 15.1 (see Plate section). The design guide acknowledges that this development is linear in nature, continuing the pattern along Leigh Street. However, the materials and layout result in a development which does not blend well with the character of its surroundings.

Now adopted, the design guide has been used within the development control process, to improve the design and layout of development in its local context. A good example is at Townsend Farm where an application was made for four houses. Here, the houses have been laid out on the site so as to respect the historic pattern of development. The houses have a unified frontage to the road, with small front gardens and low walls. Vehicle access is to the rear of the development (see Figure 15.2 in Plate section).

However, the Leigh on Mendip VDS also identifies local limestone as the traditional building material, which has raised expectations that it will be used for the construction of new developments. But Leigh is an area where local stone is no longer quarried for building. It is generally difficult to acquire, expensive and usually only available through recycling. The Council believed that it was unrealistic to insist on recycled natural stone, notwithstanding the VDS. Nor did it consider that harm would be done to the character of the village through the use of carefully chosen alternative materials. Thus, planning permission was granted for development at Townsend Farm using reconstituted stone and render. This decision created local opposition, with many in the village believing that the Council had undermined the VDS. From the Council's perspective the VDS had raised an expectation that could not be realized through the planning process.

---

have the backing of large sections of the community. The document is largely concerned with the protection of the heritage of the village and does not take into account the needs and aspirations of other parts of the community for local facilities and affordable housing. It could be argued that the document reflects elitism amongst a section of the community with a particular interest in the heritage of the village. The District Council has now become involved and is trying to broker agreement between the competing sections of the community. It is currently unwilling to adopt the VDS as supplementary planning guidance because of its contested nature.

Barriers to Effective Use of the New Approaches

Each of the new approaches to valuing the countryside, which have been 'tested' by Mendip District Council, has much to recommend it. However, they all share some common problems.

Lack of understanding

There is a lack of understanding of the character-based approaches which have been taken in assessing and valuing countryside capital. This includes professionals and local people and there is a need to promote a wider understanding of the characterization concept. Whilst the concept is more useful than the quality-based assessments it replaces, it is more difficult to understand and use. It does not provide a black and white 'line on the map' within which certain types of development will be allowed. It requires a more thoughtful and balanced assessment of the qualities of an area.

Lack of resources

The projects using character-based approaches to valuing the countryside which have been undertaken at Mendip are regarded as non-statutory activities of the Council (with the exception of the Mendip BAP which is seen as a quasi-statutory requirement). Each of the strategies feeds directly into a statutory process and enhances that process. However, the limited allocation of resources to them reflects their non-statutory status.

Lack of tools for implementation

The characterization approach can raise issues that the Council does not have the tools to tackle. For example, many of the threats identified by the BAP require direct investment or action by parties other than the Council. Whilst the Somerset Wildlife Trust has targeted its investment towards protecting and enhancing priority habitats its resources are limited and the real solution lies in changes to the Common Agricultural Policy – something the Council has little, if any, influence over. The process of producing VDSs often raises issues outside the planning arena or outside the remit of the Council altogether, such as the cleanliness of streets, the provision of services such as playgroups, schools and post offices or the behaviour of motorists. In some cases the only tool which has been available to tackle the issues raised has been the Local Plan. However, this can relate only to land use planning issues and is part of a formal system of regulation and control, whilst many of the issues raised by the new methods of valuing the countryside can be solved only through the pro-active actions of the community. The formalities associated with the Local Plan mean that it is not a good tool for achieving this type of action. The Community Strategy has the potential to provide a more effective tool to tackle these issues, but is not yet well advanced.

Integration of the new approaches

There is generally a lack of coordination between strategies and disciplines. Whilst individual officers are aware of the interrelationships between issues, timescales and committee structures often do not allow different strategies to advance together. There is also still a culture of competition between some departments. The council is seeking ways of changing this culture by restructuring both its committees and departments, seeking a more corporate approach to service delivery with shared responsibility for major projects and a greater emphasis on partnership working.

Multi-purpose decision-making

Because strategies are not always well coordinated, there is no overall mechanism which ensures that opportunities for multi-purpose projects are taken. Though opportunities often arise to serve several interests through one project, this requires that individual officers recognize opportunities to achieve the aims of other department's strategies, with which they may not be familiar. There is a need, therefore, for an overall mechanism which ensures that the connections between strategies are made.

Setting priorities

Currently, there is no mechanism in place for determining priorities between competing interests. The consideration of environmental, economic and social issues together is becoming more accepted within Council structures. However, setting priorities within these broad categories is more difficult, particularly when different types of environmental capital need to be prioritized. All of the new approaches to valuing the countryside which have been tried at Mendip concentrate on a specific type of environmental capital, such as biodiversity or built heritage. Where these come into conflict with each other and no means can be found to serve all identified interests, there is no means to allow priorities to be established. Even the Local Plan, which sets out to provide guidance on a wide range of land use planning issues, does not provide a means of choosing between competing policies. This is currently done by the development control system, in the circumstances of an individual development proposal.

Global interests versus local interests

Global issues rarely impinge directly on local people's quality of life in the immediate way that local issues can. They often lack champions in the local community and are simply easier to ignore in the short term. Therefore, in the absence of systems to integrate and prioritize topics, local quality of life issues (such as the appearance of the landscape or local heritage) tend to be emphasized at the expense of wider 'global survival' issues (such as generation of greenhouse gases and transport patterns).

This has been evident in the response of the local community to the proposed allocation of greenfield sites for housing in the Local Plan. The Local Plan has sought to allocate those sites most likely to generate sustainable travel patterns, encourage modes of transport other than the private car and reinforce local services and facilities: several sites combining housing and employment uses were suggested. In some cases this would result in a local environmental loss, usually in the appearance of the landscape, and it is this which has given rise to most objections. Sites which are less sustainable overall, but which have less local impact on the landscape, have proved to be more popular.

COMMUNITY INVOLVEMENT

Each of the strategies for valuing the countryside that has been tried by Mendip District Council has been produced with maximum community involvement, in the context of the Council's LA21 Strategy. The Local Plan provides a good example of the techniques which have been used.

Initially the techniques employed for public involvement were quite traditional, with leaflets, press coverage and exhibitions. Exhibitions were held in local supermarkets as well as town halls and libraries. These were particularly successful in raising awareness of the exercise.

As this phase of consultation progressed, local pressure groups began to emerge. The local groups worked with the Council to understand the planning situation and were able to generate a level of awareness and degree of consensus amongst the local community that the Council would have found difficult to achieve. They gained press coverage unavailable to the Council, produced a series of leaflets and questionnaires that were extremely well supported and held a public meeting, to which the Council was invited, along with other interests. Because the groups were seen to be independent from the Council local people were more ready to listen, to consider the issues and to enter into debate. A high degree of consensus was achieved as a result of the exercise.

As well as working with communities in the towns, the Council held a series of 'Visioning Days' in local villages. These events were used to get a picture of local residents' aspirations for their village, prior to a draft of the Local Plan being drawn up. The events were publicized with the help of the Parish Councils and often covered two or three related villages; this helped to get a wider consensus on key issues. A series of 'stations' were set up, at which residents were asked to respond to a variety of questions. The answers were posted onto boards or written on feedback sheets. Answers were visible for others to read but non-attributable. Questions included:

- What would you like your village to be like in 2011?
- What do you like about your village? What do you dislike about your village? What would you like to change? (The Good, The Bad and The Ugly).
- What makes your village special?
- What are the priorities for change?

Finally a large-scale map was provided and residents were invited to highlight problems, areas where development could take place and areas which were highly valued.

A permanent record of each event was made and circulated in the villages. It continues to be used as a tool in the District and Parish Council's work (Mendip District Council, 1997).

The 'Visioning Days' were well attended and provided an interactive and open forum for residents to express their views on the future of the village. Discussion was frequently generated between residents as well as with Council staff. People stayed on average for about an hour and often revisited stations as new issues were raised. Comments indicated that people generally found the events thought provoking.

The events generated a great deal of useful information, which has been used in Local Plan preparation and by other sections of the Council. The issues which raised the most universal concern were traffic and access, and work is underway to address these problems. The open and interactive format was widely welcomed, helping to show how the Council was listening and responsive to local views. It also allowed people who would not otherwise have become involved in the Local Plan process to participate. The events started the process of generating a consensus among local residents as to what the future of their village should be. In some instances this has developed into an interest in producing a VDS.

These new methods of community involvement have engaged sections of the community who have previously been reluctant to become involved with local government. They attempt to make the issues relevant and to involve local communities on their own terms. However, some problems have been encountered in sustaining long-term and meaningful community participation.

Short-term involvement

Public involvement has sometimes been short lived and has taken place in response to a perceived threat (such as the allocation of new housing sites in the Local Plan). The initial level of involvement has been difficult to sustain, particularly where the timescale for the production of a document, such as the Local Plan, extends to several years. Local groups have remained involved but active participation has decreased to the stalwart few. Similarly, as indicated above, initial interest in VDSs generated by village visioning days has rarely resulted in the production of a VDS. Considerable additional input has been required from both the district and parish councils in order to produce such a document, and even then the results have been disappointing overall.

Elitism

Community participation processes still suffer from a degree of elitism, both because professionals lead the process and because relatively few members of the community have the interest and motivation to remain actively involved. The process for preparing the VDS for Wookey (see above) is a good example of some of the problems that can occur when a small group is seen to have 'captured' a process, leaving the rest of the village feeling alienated and disenfranchised. The new techniques for participation used in producing the local plan go a long way towards making sure that a representative section of the community is involved, but are by no means foolproof.

Leadership

The problems highlighted above demonstrate the need for effective leadership from an established organization, such as the local authority, to ensure that the community is able to organize itself and that participation is representative. Leadership is also needed to ensure that the output from a community exercise such as a VDS is useable and fulfils the requirement for adoption as supplementary planning guidance. However, it is not leadership in the traditional sense of expecting everybody to follow but rather a more subtle form of leadership that empowers and enables communities to assume greater responsibility for what happens to their environment.

CONCLUSIONS

The new techniques for valuing the countryside which have been tried at Mendip have been a great step forward. They allow for a more meaningful assessment of the value of countryside features and have been combined with a real attempt at engendering local participation in the planning process. However, they can be more difficult to use and understand, and they require more sustained input both from the local authority and the local community.

In particular, there is a need for wider understanding of characterization as an approach to valuing the countryside. Problems include a lack of resources for implementation of the new approaches, which are often not regarded as part of the statutory function of the Council. Moreover, in some cases the tools do not yet exist to tackle the issues which were raised by the strategies. Furthermore, the Council's structure works against true integration of work from different departments and disciplines and there is no means of prioritizing between issues, particularly where one type of environmental capital is unavoidably in competition with another. Local authorities are well placed to ensure that participation in valuing the countryside is representative and that the tools produced are appropriate and useable but it demands a new and more sensitive approach to leadership, which recognizes and encourages the potential in the community.

REFERENCES

Chris Blandford Associates (1997) *Landscape Assessment of Mendip District,* Mendip District Council, Somerset

Countryside Commission (1993) *Landscape Assessment Guidance,* Countryside Commission, Cheltenham

Countryside Commission (1996a) *Landscape Assessment of the Mendip Hills,* Countryside Commission, Cheltenham

Countryside Commission (1996b) *Village Design, Making Local Character Count in New Development,* Countryside Commission, Cheltenham

Leigh on Mendip Village Design Group (1998) *Leigh on Mendip Village Design Statement,* Leigh on Mendip Village Design Group, Leigh on Mendip

Mendip District Council (1994) *Mendip Environment,* Mendip District Council, Shepton Mallet

Mendip District Council (1995) *Mendip Biodiversity Action Plan,* Mendip District Council, Shepton Mallet

Mendip District Council (1997) Reports of Village Planning Days, unpublished report, Mendip District Council, Shepton Mallet

Mendip District Council (1998) *Mendip District Local Plan: Deposit Draft,* Mendip District Council, Shepton Mallet

Somerset County Council (1993) *Somerset Structure Plan, Alteration Number 2*, Somerset County Council, Taunton

Wookey Parish Council (1998) Wookey Village Appraisal and Conservation Plan, unpublished working document

Chapter 16

Community Involvement in Countryside Planning in Practice

Diane Warburton

Formal town and country planning processes incorporate public participatory steps in the creation of development plans, and these provide valuable opportunities for certain interest groups to input their view. Development control procedures do allow for objections from the public and from other interested bodies. And there is a whole range of consultative mechanisms that are used by some local authorities to open up discussion of specific development proposals with local communities.

Yet the growing acceptance of the benefits and importance of community involvement in countryside planning is usually still more apparent in the rhetoric than in reality. Thus, while almost every new piece of planning legislation or guidance purports to address the need for community involvement, the extent to which mainstream countryside planning processes currently involve communities remains minimal. Even though there are examples of good practice (for example, RTPI, 1996; Bishop et al, 1994) these tend to be exceptions rather than the norm.

This chapter examines community involvement in countryside planning in practice. It does this by: identifying some basic frameworks for analysing community involvement; describing two innovative approaches to community involvement in countryside planning from outside the mainstream land use planning system (parish appraisals and Village Design Statements); and by drawing out some general lessons and issues from these examples and elsewhere. The perspective adopted here towards countryside planning is that of a potentially positive activity, even though land use planning in the UK has become almost entirely negative, at least in the public mind. It is usually seen as preventing development rather than as encouraging good, sustainable development (TCPA, 1999). This chapter, both in the examples identified and the conclusions drawn from them, attempts to investigate how community involvement can contribute to the kind of positive countryside planning which can benefit the entire nation.

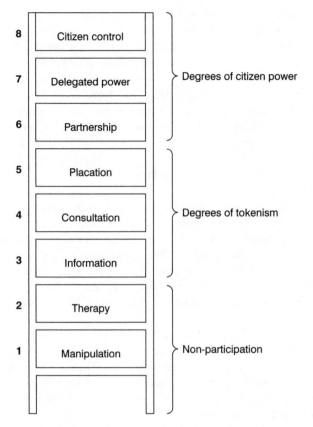

Figure 16.1 *Arnstein's ladder of participation*

FRAMEWORKS FOR ANALYSING LEVELS OF COMMUNITY INVOLVEMENT

A number of frameworks have been used in recent years to analyse and assess community involvement in planning processes, but the best known remains Arnstein's ladder of participation (Arnstein, 1969). Originally published in 1969 in the *Journal of the American Institute of Planners* (and reprinted in 1971 in the *Journal of the Royal Town Planning Association*, vol 57, pp176–182), this model remains valid and is much used to analyse power relationships in participatory working. It is often amended to meet specific circumstances, but the original is illustrated in Figure 16.1.

This analysis can be extended and simplified further into three simple 'positions' which could be adopted by an organization in designing and managing processes of community involvement:

(i) *We will do it alone.* In these circumstances there is *no* community involvement. In principle, these circumstances are likely to be rare but could arise. For example, emergency action may need to be taken, allowing no time for involvement (e.g. urgent closure of a dangerous or polluting facility to prevent further damage). Even the circumstances would require consideration of the local community, if only to provide information.

(ii) *We want to work with others.* In this case, the organization cannot achieve its objectives entirely alone and needs contributions from others. Arnstein's ladder fits neatly into this 'position' and approaches can range widely. At one end, the organization seeking involvement remains responsible for any decisions and outcomes, but seeks information or other resources from others. At the other end, the organization may negotiate to set up new partnerships with shared objectives because it recognizes that its objectives are also the responsibility and interest of other bodies, and it needs their support to succeed.

(iii) *We want to help others do things which meet our objectives.* This position recognizes that the most effective strategy can be to support existing and potential activities by other interests. These interests could be community groups, businesses and other public bodies who are seeking to meet their own objectives for their own reasons but which also meet the sponsoring organization's objectives. Support may take the form of grants and advice, fast track permission for activities, provision of land or buildings, etc.

These three 'positions' are not mutually exclusive, and an organization may use all three approaches at the same time on different issues, or one may follow another in a developmental process on one site, project or programme. Organizations using this approach as a framework should be clear how much involvement they are actually seeking, and what the implications are for their own decision-making processes.

However, it is not enough to use these frameworks alone in analysing community involvement in planning, because they are deficient in three ways:

- First, neither framework takes account of the importance of community protest, in triggering a community involvement initiative. Many organizations start to consider designing effective community involvement processes only when they are faced with a major protest, and only then do they begin to learn that there are more productive and positive ways for decision-makers and communities to relate to each other. Protest and demand for involvement can be valid and effective strategies for communities and other stakeholders to adopt to get their views heard, and may often be used in conjunction with engaging in dialogue (Craig et al, 2001).
- Second, neither framework takes the community's perspective: they are all 'top-down' analyses. The 'highest' levels of participation in Arnstein's ladder are explained in terms of 'delegating' decisions, with an assumption that decision-making is in the gift of the institution seeking involvement. The three 'positions' all adopt the perspective of the organization seeking involvement. Both frameworks are therefore open to the challenge that power, and the capacity to make decisions, is assumed to lie solely in the hands of the institution seeking involvement (which can 'empower' others), and do not recognize that power may also lie elsewhere.

• Third, both frameworks focus on decision-making rather than action (although this criticism applies more to Arnstein's ladder than the 'positions' framework). Neither fully takes into account the possibility that communities may already be active in a whole variety of ways, including on policy issues such as countryside planning, quite outside the sphere of activity controlled by the institution seeking community involvement. The extensive range and scale of activities occurring 'below the radar', as well as those expressed through established voluntary and community organizations in rural communities, can surprise those in public institutions and local government.

EXAMPLES OF COMMUNITY INVOLVEMENT IN COUNTRYSIDE PLANNING

As already noted, there are many examples of good practice in community involvement in countryside planning that have been led by local authorities, both as part of the mainstream planning process and as a result of specific initiatives such as LA21 (see Chapter 5). Some of these activities have been designed to feed results from grassroots visioning activities into the planning process at very early stages. More commonly though, they have had the more limited aim of attempting to gain community involvement at later stages in the process – such as responding to draft plans – by which time the agenda and parameters have largely been set.

In addition to the good work being achieved by some local authorities, several initiatives have been led by government agencies, notably the Countryside Agency and the Environment Agency, and by voluntary organizations, which have taken positive planning further forward.

In England, the Countryside Agency was formed from a merger of the Countryside Commission and the Rural Development Commission (RDC) in 2000. It is the statutory government agency responsible for conserving and enhancing the countryside; promoting social equity and economic opportunity for the people who live there; and helping everyone, wherever they live, to enjoy the countryside as a national asset (Countryside Agency, 2000). At the time of its establishment, the new agency undertook a major exercise, travelling around the country holding meetings, to debate its draft Prospectus, thus bringing participation into the formulation of its own national policy at a critical time.

The Countryside Agency inherited this approach from its predecessors, as both the Countryside Commission and the RDC had long championed community involvement. The RDC had supported rural community development for many years, notably through its core funding for the 38 county rural community councils (RCCs) – see below. For its part, the Countryside Commission had piloted a range of highly innovative community action projects in the mid- to late 1980s (BDOR, 1991). Both agencies were involved in the national Rural Action for the Environment programme (in which they were joined by English Nature). Rural Action promoted and supported community action in rural areas through support, advice and grants, and by links to national voluntary organizations including BTCV (British Trust for Conservation Volunteers), ACRE, The Wildlife Trusts and NVCO (National Council for Voluntary Organisations) Environment Support Team (NEST). Grants were administered through the county-based RCCs. County networks were established to deliver support to local groups and projects, and to help the agencies shape their own programmes, including training, to meet emerging needs identified at the local level (Warburton, 1998a).

Rural Action was closed down as a national programme in 1999, but the success of that programme fed into new developments at the agency, particularly the Community Service Grant scheme (see below). The Agency has also funded various other programmes to promote community involvement, including:

- the Millennium Greens programme (followed by Doorstep Greens in 2001) which funded community ownership and management of open spaces;
- experimental village action plans (funding for them became available nationally in 2001 under the Parish Plans Scheme, see below);
- several initiatives around rural design and heritage which brought together ideas of local distinctiveness and local history;
- the Countryside Character programme to strengthen awareness and action on local landscape distinctiveness and character;
- the Community Forests programme, dating back to the 1980s, to stimulate community involvement in the creation and management of woodland on unused land around a dozen towns and cities; and
- the Local Heritage Initiative, a ten-year programme, financed by the Heritage Lottery Fund, running from February 2000 to provide grants to help local groups to investigate, explain and care for their local landscape, landmarks, traditions and culture.

In April 2001, the agency launched four new schemes 'that will let local people decide what their communities need – then help turn those aspirations into realities' (Countryside Agency, 2001, p4). These initiatives are:

- a three-year £15 million Parish Transport Fund for small-scale community transport projects (grants up to £10,000);
- a Rural Transport Partnership to continue larger-scale transport projects (grants up to £250,000);
- a three-year, £15 million Community Service Grant scheme (grants £500 to £25,000) for a wide range of rural projects such as reopening shops or pubs, childcare facilities or training schemes; and
- a Parish Plans Scheme, which makes £5 million available to parish and town councils to produce action plans that find solutions to locally-identified problems which could include housing, transport or other services.

The Chief Executive of the Countryside Agency summed up his organization's new approach as follows:

> *In all these schemes, the emphasis will be on what I have been calling 'discovery not direction' – in other words through the new grant schemes the Countryside Agency, rather than seeking to direct solutions, helps communities discover that they do have many of the answers locally* (Wakeford, 2001).

Wakeford has also made it clear that the agency 'can't achieve any of our goals on our own ... [and we are] looking forward to working with government, business and communities for a high quality countryside – beautiful, prosperous and a good place for those who live there and those who visit' (Countryside Agency, 2000, p6). One of the agency's goals is 'prosperous and inclusive communities', which are described in the following terms:

> *The countryside is the people who live there as much as it is landscape and industry. Communities are important. Sustaining vital and viable communities requires access for people to good quality jobs, opportunities to thrive, accessible services and affordable housing... Part of the solution is to encourage a stronger sense of community. People need to take an active interest in the problems of their locality* (ibid).

Indeed putting communities in control of their own futures is one of the key priorities in the Countryside Agency's strategy (Countryside Agency, 2001).

The Environment Agency, which operates in England and Wales, has also begun to articulate its commitment to community involvement throughout its areas of responsibility, which include river catchment and water resource management, pollution regulation and control, and contaminated and derelict land. The Agency's policy in this field was set out in *An Environmental Vision* (Environment Agency, 2001) as part of its contribution to sustainable development.

Although the nine themes for future work established within the Vision relate directly to the Agency's core mission of environmental protection and management, the wording emphasizes the need for public involvement if the vision is to be realized. For example, the targets include (emphasis added):

- people having 'peace of mind from knowing they live in a healthier environment';
- 'everyone will understand the importance of safeguarding biodiversity';
- 'uses [of coastal and inland waters] needed by a thriving and healthy community';
- greener business will 'secure trust in the wider community';
- other bodies and individuals 'will minimise the waste they produce', reuse and recycle material more and make more efficient use of energy and materials;
- 'the role of wetlands in reducing flood risks will be recognised'.

In terms of delivery on these issues, the Vision stresses themes like finding new ways of measuring progress, prevention rather than cure, working with others to create shared solutions, consulting widely and delivering results.

All these statements make it clear that the Agency recognizes that it cannot achieve its goals alone and thus require it to engage in a mixture of education, awareness-raising, participation and partnerships with public, private, voluntary and community sector organizations, and with the public.

The Vision also sets out the need for imaginative new approaches if these themes and roles are to be fulfilled. It lists four of these in particular: changing attitudes and behaviour; growing collaborative partnerships; exploiting technological innovation; developing social awareness. Once more, the focus is on action with and through others. Its initiatives to increase local community involvement have included participatory exercises in preparing the Local Environment Agency Plans (LEAPs), which are built around river catchment areas. As many as 130 LEAPs have been produced, covering all of England and Wales and involving around 30,000 local organizations including environmental organizations, voluntary bodies, local authorities, trade associations and industry (Environment Agency, 2000a). Although there has been some deeper involvement in a limited number of LEAPs, levels of involvement have primarily focused on information giving and consultation – Arnstein's levels 3 and 4. The Environment Agency has also experimented with extending community involvement in several other areas, such as pollution regulation and control, the licensing of waste facilities, the regulation of the nuclear power stations and major industries, flood defence projects, recreation projects and navigation programmes, and a programme (undertaken with RSPB, English Nature and others, on the wise use of floodplains) (Cuff, 2001). More recently, work around Catchment Flood Management Plans (CFMPs), Catchment Abstraction Management Schemes (CAMS), and plans to implement the EC-led Water Framework Directive, have increased the Agency's experience of community and stakeholder engagement. The commitment to participation has been taken to the heart of the Agency's work: its Annual General Meeting in 2000 was structured as a public debate on environmental equality, involving a panel of senior Agency representatives and others (Environment Agency, 2000b).

These examples serve to illustrate the overall directions towards much greater community involvement being pursued by two of the major government agencies working in the English countryside. The policy drivers which underlie these approaches have already been outlined (see Chapter 5), but there are two other factors which may also have encouraged moves towards greater community involvement: resources and public accountability.

Although the two agencies differ greatly in size, the nature of their responsibilities and focus, they both face continuing pressure to do more, as environmental and planning issues – roads, development, pollution, flooding, etc – move up the public agenda. As more attention focuses on rural regeneration and economic development, and landscape and biodiversity, so there is a demand for better quality regulation, and more monitoring and enforcement. Recognizing that few of the goals they have been set can be met by going it alone, government agencies are being forced to work more closely with others – and to draw on these additional resources as well. This has benefits all round: the agencies can achieve more for their investment, and their partners find they have greater influence over the use of resources – and sometimes can get direct access to the resources.

In a climate of greater openness and transparency in decision-making within agencies, attitudes to public and community involvement are undergoing important changes. Thus in recent years, the corporate sector and public agencies have both been held much more to account for their social and environmental performance. This is part of a wider movement towards greater public accountability, and sense of corporate social responsibility, on the part of bodies that have an impact on society and the environment.

As a result, there are now numerous examples of deep community involvement in a whole range of countryside planning activities. Two of these are described below: parish appraisals, promoted by ACRE, a national voluntary organization operating in England; and village design statements, promoted by the Countryside Agency, also throughout England.

Parish Appraisals

Parish appraisals are essentially questionnaire surveys of, by and for the local community to identify local characteristics, problems, needs, threats, strengths and opportunities (Moseley, 1999). Although there is no definitive information on how many parish appraisals have been completed following the first one in Stocksfield, Northumberland in 1971–1972, it has been estimated that around 400 had been completed by the late 1980s and over 2000 by March 1999 (Moseley, 1999).

Intended as a means of taking stock of the community and creating a sound foundation of awareness and understanding on which to base future action, parish appraisals have been DIY exercises for local communities in community appraisal and development. They were intended both as a process of community development and as a means of collecting data and presenting it in a formal report. In some cases, these reports were accompanied by exhibitions in village halls to ensure the widest possible dissemination of the outcomes and commitment to the recommendations. Exhibitions were also used to display the creativity released through parish mapping, ranging from formal maps to tapestries and other art works (Greeves, 1987).

Guidance and promotional materials were prepared and disseminated by ACRE, the rural communities charity and umbrella body for England's Rural Community Councils. RCCs are key voluntary and community sector agencies in rural areas; they usually provide services and support to a wide range of voluntary and community groups within their areas, with a particular focus on social welfare but increasingly on environmental and economic issues as well (Warburton, 1994).

A detailed study of the nature of parish appraisals (Moseley et al, 1996), based on a sample of 44 appraisals, suggested that the appraisals were often managed by a parish appraisal committee with between 6 and 17 members, generally drawn from existing activists involved with the parish council, Women's Institute and other groups and organizations. Each appraisal in this study took an average of 10 months to complete, although many took over a year. Four factors seemed to be present in all appraisals:

- a sense that all was not well in the parish;
- a trigger event, such as an announcement of the preparation of a draft local plan which was perceived as potentially leading to proposals for development;
- an offer of support, usually from an RCC;
- the subsequent willingness of a number of volunteers to take on the task.

As national guidance was provided by ACRE, including software packages for organizing and analysing the data collected, there was fairly uniform coverage of issues which included housing, transport, local environment, crime, recreation and the local council. The study found that most recommendations related to traffic, including parking and speeding, followed by the need for low-cost housing for local people. Calls to restrict speculative housing development came next (Moseley et al, 1996), then environmental issues (local improvement, clean ups, tree planting), though recycling and litter were also important. Overall, however, the researchers concluded that the dominant and widespread concern was against excessive speculative housing development.

Moseley (1997) identified eight main stages in devising a parish appraisal:

1   establishing local support;
2   forming a steering group to decide 'what' and 'how'; planning the survey and drawing up the questionnaire;
3   collecting the information from the parish's households and/or individuals; analysing the information;
4   drafting an appraisal report including any recommendations;
5   distributing it locally;
6   local discussions to get a mandate for action;
7   follow up action; and
8   monitoring and evaluation.

All this work was carried out by the community itself, with support primarily from the RCC, but the scope and coverage, the exact methods, and the recommendations varied greatly from place to place.

The 1996 study also found that about half the recommendations and action points in the 44 appraisals they examined were addressed to the community themselves, and the other half to other agencies and authorities. One-third of the recommendations and action points had been completely or substantially carried out, one-third partially achieved, but nothing done about the remaining third. Although the activities and achievements may not always be a result of the appraisal, two things are fairly clear: the appraisal gave local people a chance to articulate their priorities and draw up an agenda for action (both for themselves and others); and that, without the appraisal exercise, these priorities were unlikely to have been articulated in this way. So the appraisal process appears to have contributed to policy debates on planning and helped to identify local priorities for community action.

The benefits of parish appraisals could be summarized as follows:

- Providing valuable information on local needs, resources and priorities. These would probably not have come to light through conventional methods: professionally organized social surveys would have been too expensive, and would probably have failed to access the special local knowledge which surveys run by and for local people can tap into.
- Providing a stimulus to self-help and community action, especially where these initiatives could be achieved by communities themselves, on projects such as information provision through parish newsletters, renovated village halls, community transport, good neighbour schemes, neighbourhood watch, footpaths, playgrounds, small-scale practical environmental action, and recycling.
- Conferring legitimacy on decisions: when action was in line with community views as revealed by the appraisals, it was more readily understood and accepted.
- Taking community involvement beyond the 'usual suspects' and those with axes to grind: response rates were typically over 50 per cent; the 1996 study found average response rates of 74 per cent (but see below for caveats).
- Contributing to community development and capacity building: 'the process is the product with the value of enhanced local skills, awareness and confidence' (Moseley et al 1996, p312).
- Improving relationships within communities, and between communities and local authorities; local planners especially were often contacted for help and advice, as well as receiving the information collected.

There are downsides too: 25 per cent of local communities (at least) did not respond (according to the 1996 study), and possibly more elsewhere, and this group is likely to be made up disproportionately of disadvantaged and traditionally excluded groups (eg people living in poverty or housebound.). However, this shortcoming has been recognized in evaluations of the scheme, and the current emphasis of the government (and the Countryside Agency) on tackling social exclusion should encourage communities to be more inclusive in future appraisals of this kind. Two other dangers have also been identified. First, some communities may have feared that their priorities could be hijacked by agencies with their own agendas. Second, there is also a risk that local volunteers may feel disillusioned, thinking they are simply cheap labour, collecting data for public bodies. In practice, though, most communities managed to avoid this danger.

The various evaluations also suggest, implicitly rather than directly, the importance of resources. Resources are obviously needed to carry out the appraisals and take action on the recommendations. Rural Action was an important source of funding while it was operational, and funding became much more scarce after it was wound up, even though the new schemes announced by the Countryside Agency in 2001, especially the Parish Plans Scheme, are intended to support future initiatives of this kind (Countryside Commission, 2001).

The lasting test in community development terms of the success of parish appraisals is that community involvement lasts beyond the initial phase. So it is to be welcomed that some parishes have set up action groups, and others intend to repeat the research to test progress and update data (eg after five or ten years) (Moseley, 1997). Such follow-up actions are 'helping to devolve to local people a significant share of the task of caring for their immediate community and environment' (Moseley, 1997, p327).

Village Design Statements and Countryside Design Summaries

Village Design Statements (VDSs) and Countryside Design Summaries (CDSs) were promoted by the Countryside Commission as a means to move good design in new developments in the countryside up the public and political agenda, and particularly to reverse the erosion of local distinctiveness. Both aimed to encourage local communities in rural areas, together with planning authorities, to define the character of their villages and assess the type of design that would be appropriate for new development in and around them. VDSs are local appraisals led mainly by the local community and intended to complement the CDSs. CDSs are area-wide appraisals carried out by planning authorities.

The Countryside Commission's work on rural design drew on a number of other initiatives. The Commission itself had, for some time, supported work by Common Ground on local distinctiveness, which drew attention to the unique local characteristics of place which contributed to a sense of belonging (Clifford and King, 1993). The loss of local distinctiveness has been described as leading to 'an increasingly standardised form of development essentially suburban in character' (Owen, 1998). The work on local distinctiveness also linked to the Commission's community action pilot projects (BDOR, 1991) and other research which suggested the importance of local community involvement in maintaining and restoring local distinctiveness. Both VDS and CDS work also contributed to wider national government thinking and priorities on improving the quality of design in new developments (DoE, 1994).

The first step for the Commission was a statement of proposals published as Design in the Countryside (Countryside Commission, 1993). Four pilot VDSs (plus another one later) and three pilot CDS schemes were then initiated. These pilots were the subject of three separate evaluations: the first focused on the means by which local communities could influence decisions about their own localities (Countryside Commission, 1994); the second assessed the effects of the VDS on the design of new development; and the third assessed how far VDSs had been useful in guiding development and improving design standards (Countryside and Community Research Unit, 1997). A further evaluation and monitoring report covered subsequent experience (Countryside Commission/W S Atkins, 1998). In this chapter, we review findings on a key hope for the VDS mechanism – that there would be a high degree of community involvement in the process (Owen, 1998).

The first evaluation concluded that VDSs provided a sound basis for improving the design of new development through the involvement of the local community (Countryside Commission, 1994). It suggested that the pilots had also 'shown that design discussion need not be restricted to a professional elite' (ibid, p24) and that:

local communities can become fully involved, with great enthusiasm, and contribute considerable skill. Local people can produce articulate, logical and clearly presented ideas on managing change in their local environment. Neither the size nor the development context of a village appears to affect local enthusiasm for participation. Those who participate will value the opportunity, and build a strong sense of local 'ownership' of the VDS and its messages (ibid, p26).

The Commission's formal guidance on VDS was based on the experience in the pilots. This proposed that an effective VDS should be developed, researched, written and edited by local people, needed to be representative of the views of the village as a whole, and should be 'entirely community-based' (Countryside Commission, 1996, Part 1). Local people were considered best placed to do it given their unique appreciation and understanding of the place in which they lived.

The processes in the five pilot villages were very different, with varying levels of joint working between local resident and the planning authorities, ranging from complete community control and no direct contact with planning authorities, to VDS production being controlled by the district council with only limited community involvement. The relationship with the local planning authority is a vital strand in the process. It was found that the VDS could be adopted relatively easily as Supplementary Planning Guidance (SPG), which meant that it carried much more weight in the formal planning process and could therefore directly affect the nature of new development. The evaluation report concluded that, although a community-based VDS can help to guide local design even if it does not acquire SPG status, it would be more likely to deliver the Commission's objectives if it was fully integrated with the statutory planning system, probably as SPG (Countryside Commission, 1994, p29).

Like parish appraisals (see above), the benefits of VDS activity were believed to go beyond the immediate practical production of the VDS document itself. The evaluation report suggests that, with careful management, VDS activity can generate improved relationships within the local community, and between the local community and others including developers, architects and planners. In addition, groups of local people involved will be well-placed to influence subsequent development proposals. The report suggests that 'The maximum flexibility, and the most added value, comes when as much attention is paid to the process by which the summaries or statements are generated, as to the products themselves' (ibid).

Following the pilots, and the publication of guidance by the Commission, VDS and CDS initiatives were conducted throughout England. Each Countryside Commission region had a budget to promote a number of exemplar VDS, intended to act as catalysts for other nearby villages. By 1998, it was estimated that around 27 CDSs had been prepared or were in preparation, although around 40 authorities had been involved and so it was likely that others were at earlier stages of discussion; an estimated 167 VDSs had been prepared or were in preparation, with at least 170 villages taking part (Countryside Commission, 1998). Feedback from the planning authorities was generally favourable: the summaries had helped to guide design and support policies in the local plan. The major problem identified by them was a lack of resources, although the evaluators suggested that this could actually be a question of task prioritization (ibid, piv).

The evaluation concluded that 'there are numerous individual examples where VDS has improved design, sometimes even before completion of the statement' (ibid, pvii). Additional indirect benefits were also identified, including that the VDS process contributed to raising awareness of design issues at all levels, from government through to local residents. The VDS process has also helped to improve relationships, for example between planning officers and the local community, and has contributed to community development.

Success, however, was not always easily achieved. Conflicts arose between some Village Design Groups and parish councils during the pilots, and in some cases the 'ownership' of the statement was felt to have been taken over by the planning authority (Owen, 1998, p372). Owen suggests that further guidance and support were needed for communities and planning authorities on dealing with these conflicts. Nevertheless, he concludes that: 'VDSs demonstrate significant potential, and some tangible achievements, in encouraging greater community involvement in local decision-making' (ibid, p377). He further suggests that 'it would be fruitful to pursue linkages between VDSs and other instruments within or related to the statutory planning system such as design briefs for individual sites, village appraisals, individual village plans, conservation area statements and statutory local plans'. In this way, it should be possible to encompass aspects of a locally responsive approach that were not addressed by the VDS, particularly in relation to local social and economic needs and greater localized economic activity (although neither of these two factors were intended to be included in a VDS). In summary, Owen concludes that 'VDSs do provide a means whereby aspects of a locally responsive approach to village planning and design can be both encouraged and implemented to varying degrees' (ibid, p379).

Issues Arising from these Examples

Despite the success of community involvement, many government bodies and agencies (including local and regional government, the Environment Agency and the Countryside Agency) continue to use conventional professional approaches, based on technical knowledge and long-established networks. But the rhetoric is clearly changing rapidly, and practice is following on. What lessons can be learnt from recent experience as community involvement is adopted ever more widely in future?

First, many of these areas of activity would in the past have been considered the territory of local government. The growing role now given to the voluntary and community sectors, as well as to business, extends into some major areas of public service and delivery, including planning, housing and transport. The implications for local authorities and voluntary organizations are not yet fully understood. In particular, the role of the voluntary sector in providing mainstream public services is being increasingly questioned. There are doubts on grounds of both in reliability and ethics. For example, volunteers may be perceived as 'cheap labour', voluntary organizations traditionally go through peaks and troughs of effective activity and, more fundamentally, a service delivery role can undermine the independence of those organizations and their ability to comment and campaign on public policy (Craig et al, 2001). Beyond that, there may be deeper questions about the significance of such initiatives for the traditional structures of representative democracy and the role of voluntary and community organizations in civil society..

Second, many of these initiatives depend on time-limited grant schemes. Rural Action ran for a number of years and was considered highly successful, but even so it was closed down. There was then a hiatus while new initiatives were designed to cover some of the same ground. Agencies can put such influential initiatives into place which affect local conditions, but can then just as easily terminate, or re-direct the initiatives, leaving community organizations without the support they had come to rely on.

Third, the rhetoric about principles of increasing community involvement (to get closer to citizens' needs and wants), and increasing self-determination for local communities is one thing. But the practice can be something rather different. Tight management of funding, for example, places much tougher expectations on voluntary bodies. Thus, the Countryside Agency has for some years been operating a system of funding for RCCs, based on service level agreements (SLAs) which state the specific services the Agency is expecting for the funding they give. This is very different from the previous core grant aid and has implications for those organizations: they cannot easily experiment with innovative solutions outside those issues covered by the SLAs, and they may feel inhibited about biting the hand that feeds them by criticizing policy and spending priorities.

Fourth, parish appraisals are intended to provide data on local needs and desires, which can provide useful background information for the formal local planning processes. VDSs have been adopted as SPG, which gives them more influence. There remains a 'perceived difficulty that even when neighbourhood plans and village design statements are adopted as SPG, they do not carry the same weight as the development plan in development control decisions' (Local Government Association, 2000). Both these initiatives have left local people much better informed about their own shared priorities and about design and development issues. They have also developed better relationships with the planning authorities. This equips the community to engage in productive discussions with planning authorities about specific development proposals and about wider planning priorities. However, the essentially 'voluntary' (rather than statutory) status of the outputs of these processes remains a limitation.

Fifth, evaluations of both parish appraisals and VDSs repeatedly assert that they are as important for their processes as for their products. The processes contribute to capacity building (eg individual confidence, skills, awareness) and community development (eg new relationships, action groups, experience in articulating community concerns). As the information in the appraisals and statements inevitably dates over time, the development of these skills and experience should allow those rural communities that have participated in these initiatives to move on to collect new data and find new solutions appropriate to changing circumstances. It has been noted elsewhere that 'the process of bringing a community together to participate in its own development is often valuable in itself above any other measurable targets. An initial process can then be a catalyst for future action' (Allies et al, 1999, p33).

And finally, both the examples chosen illustrate potential approaches to positive planning. There remains a sense in government that rural communities are inherently anti-development and that any attempts to gain community involvement will simply be hijacked by NIMBYs (people who cry 'not in my back yard') who want to stop all development, and preserve their current levels of amenity, at any costs. But the outputs of the village appraisals and the focus of the VDS process suggest otherwise. Thus, the appraisals showed that the need for affordable housing was placed just as high on local priorities as any concerns over inappropriate speculative housing development; and the VDS showed an enthusiasm for better design of appropriate new development. It does not seem from these findings that rural villages are anti-development but rather are against creeping suburbanization, both in terms of the design and target clientele of new housing. The enthusiasm and effort that has been put into these exercises, both of which are essentially focused on change, suggest that rural communities are not so intent on preserving the status quo, but are actually bubbling with ideas about how to actually initiate and support development that improve quality of life in rural areas.

OVERALL STRANDS AND THEMES

Many of the public policy drivers for increasing community involvement in planning were outlined in Chapter 5: public demand for a greater say in what happens to the local environment, a stronger NGO sector, and the need for ways to increase government and public sector legitimacy and accountability at a time when support for representative democracy appears to be in decline. This chapter has added to this list: resource constraints and greater public accountability for public agencies. But other more general trends may also be at work.

There are many signs that the public is more risk averse and less trustful of science than it was a few decades ago. People are notably less willing to accept 'official' information based on what might previously have been seen as 'objective' scientific analysis. The disquiet over GM foods and crops, BSE, the MMR vaccine are all cases in point. It was the emergence of this trend that led the Royal Commission on Environmental Pollution (RCEP) to devote such a large part of their report on *Setting Environmental Standards* (RCEP, 1998) to the need to work more closely with the public. The RCEP called for a wider and deeper debate about the social and environmental values that underpin public policy, and it proposed much greater investment in deliberative methods of community and public involvement so that controversial issues could be considered in a calmer atmosphere.

The nature of complex contemporary problems has been characterized elsewhere as 'wicked issues', which are defined as a special class of policy problem:

one without an obvious or established (or even common sense) solution, defying normal understanding – and often not sitting conveniently within the responsibilities of any one organization (Clarke and Stewart, 1997). Examples of such wicked issues include environmental topics and aspirations for sustainable development, crime and the desire for safe communities, and discrimination and the wish for an equitable society. Tackling such issues calls for holistic thinking, thinking and working across organizational boundaries, and involving the public in developing responses. Again, this is not a matter of collecting existing public opinions about simple issues, but rather a need for proper dialogue between professional, technical and 'lay' sources of knowledge.

However, while the emphasis is now clearly on increasing community involvement in all elements of public policy, including countryside planning, there remain issues to be resolved. Tensions remain between top-down professional techniques and bottom-up initiatives. But experience suggests that neither 'top-down' nor 'bottom-up' is the 'right' answer: both are needed and mechanisms should allow the strengths of both to be brought into play. This is not to gloss over the conflicts, which exist between different interest groups, nor to downplay the importance of differing levels of power, control and resources. Indeed, it has been suggested that the conflict at the heart of the current debate on rural development is:

> *between a tradition of central state-managed normative and procedurally dominated universalist public policy, and the growing need for a more differentiated, locally generated, project-oriented and partnership-based rural development policy that takes this diversity into account and builds upon it* (Baldock et al, 2001, p36).

While things are changing in rural development formulation and implementation, and 'the prevailing ethos on the rural development debate is that partnership between official agencies and between them and a wider range of social actors should be one of the foundations for all policy' (ibid, p37), new partners (especially local people) are still not fully accepted. Lack of transparency in developing recent rural policy initiatives is a failing noted by many stakeholders. While partnerships are relevant to finding the solution, they are:

> *seen as a challenge often putting stress on bureaucratic systems used to more autocratic procedures. There is a widespread sense that a new agenda and change in style requires more institutional adaptation than has yet taken place. Institutional reengineering is seen as critical by many of the actors most committed to a more integrated and sustainable rural policy* (ibid, p37).

In this analysis, future stakeholder involvement must be properly resourced, the lessons extracted and learned, and projects, programmes and even institutions themselves will have to change to accommodate the needs, priorities and knowledge of the community.

Too many participatory exercises have been initiated afresh with each new public policy initiative. Few of these laudable initiatives, including parish appraisals and VDSs, have been properly tied into wider planning and implementation procedures. Community involvement therefore, needs to extend over longer time scales and to be better integrated with other decision-making processes. As Allies et al (1999) note, the challenge is for the expectations that are engendered by community participation to be married up with those of others, such as the funding agencies, and to be consistent with strategic objectives. Until there is better integration of all these varying initiatives and participatory mechanisms, the public, communities and other stakeholders, as well as those working in public institutions, will find participatory working a constant struggle.

There remain, too, concerns about the legitimacy of some participatory exercises. Those in public institutions deplore the influence exerted by the 'usual suspects' and NIMBY organizations, which they often see as concerned to protect only their own patch – although that should come as no surprise since that is why many such bodies exist. This may have been one of the prompts for the introduction of initiatives which attempt to 'leapfrog' established organizations and consult directly with the less experienced and often un-organized 'public'. But while there are important issues about representativeness, legitimacy, and accountability of pressure groups and campaigns, many voluntary and community organizations share that concern and are themselves making considerable efforts to ensure they can answer these criticisms fully (Craig et al, 2001).

In any case, very few supporters of increasing community involvement in public policy and services would want participatory democracy to undermine, let alone replace, representative democracy. As Donnison (1993) argues, there is no magic about community – routine tasks of government still have to be performed. What is needed is more sensitive and effective civic leadership, not less of it, from democratically accountable public authorities.

It is often asserted that community involvement privileges the local and the parochial. While there are circumstances where the local needs to take priority, there is also growing understanding that local circumstances have to be set within a broader context that needs to be taken into account in shaping public policy. Community organizations are in a double bind here: they gain their legitimacy from their grassroots connections, but they are expected to take a broader view when engaged in partnerships covering wider issues. LA21 has helped by encouraging wider understanding of the interconnections between different spatial levels, particularly between global environmental problems and local policy choices. More practically, linkages are beginning to be developed between community strategies, regional plans and national priorities. Whatever changes are made to the planning system in future need to recognize that the unwillingness of some communities to accept the development of certain unpopular facilities in their neighbourhood is as valid as the desire of certain other interest groups to increase the provision of these facilities. Involvement in oppositional campaigns is not something people enter into lightly, and such protests are usually evidence of great public disquiet. It would therefore seem to be a more effective strategy to consider alternative proposals to meet the particular problem rather than simply seeing local people as an inconvenient barrier. The questions this raises for the relationship between community involvement and national representative democracy are likely to rumble on for some time.

We still lack much hard evidence about the effectiveness and costs of participatory working in comparison to coventional methods of planning and management. New approaches are being developed to evaluate the effects of participation (eg InterAct, 2001; Frewer et al, 2000; Cuff, 2001). But at present the evidence is largely anecdotal (personal experiences of specific schemes) and/or ethical (it is the 'right' way to do things and people have a 'right' to be involved). One study which provides practical details of the costs and benefits of participatory working, the World Bank (1994) study (and offers evidence of overall cost savings), is an internal working paper and not easy to access – and its focus on rural villages in developing countries allow its conclusions to be dismissed by some as irrelevant to the UK context. This situation will change as formal evaluation becomes more widespread, but it will take time, and a considerable investment of resources, and in the meantime participatory initiatives will continue to be established with less than rigorous assessments of their 'success' or achievements.

Finally there is a debate about techniques, which is coloured by the way that certain methodologies have been promoted by certain organizations. Thus the Neighbourhood Initiatives Foundation has encouraged Planning for Real; and the New Economics Foundation has promoted visioning, Future Search and others. Such 'tools' can be useful and may be warmly welcomed by professionals coming face to face with the public for the first time; they seek a technical fix which will deliver results while avoiding difficulties and conflict. One bad experience at a public meeting – and few traditional public meetings are really good events – and the planner or public institution will reach for the 'toolkit' of techniques.

However, the concept of a toolkit is being challenged (Cowell and Owens, 2001; Owens and Cowell, 2001). It often fails to address the complexity of the kind of 'wicked' issues discussed above. Nor does it do justice to the basic questions that must be addressed, such as: what are the objectives of the exercise? Is the approach really to support a community-led initiative or is it intended that matters will stay firmly in the control of the agency or institution? Which stakeholders or constituencies have an interest in the issue? or how will traditionally excluded groups be encouraged to take part? 'We should abandon the "toolkit" metaphor, with its implied linear relationship between process and outcome, and accept that techniques and procedures become inseparable from (contested) interpretations of sustainable development. The reality is less elegant and considerably less tidy than the metaphor... The challenge now lies not so much in the refinement of "tools" (though that has its place), but in showing how different approaches actually function in the political project of reorienting social and economic development' (Cowell and Owens, 2001, p12–14). A toolkit may be useful for a one-off event, but it is not adequate to the task of involving the community in helping to reorient development so that it is sustainable.

CONCLUSIONS

This broad review of some of the social and political complexities of community involvement in countryside planning has identified some key questions. They relate to the legitimacy and effectiveness of participatory working, and the difficulties of 'doing' community involvement in ways which do not do a disservice to the potential for radical and positive change.

It is clear that the process of community involvement is as important as the product of countryside planning: it is a learning experience, and a journey of discovery, for all involved. That means it can be messy and difficult. It is equally clear that there is a need to assess whether the process, as well as the product, has been a success. Only then will community involvement be done better in future.

The subject is so difficult to pin down because it works in a context of the ever-changing values of society, against a background of the ever-greater complexities of the modern world. In such a state of flux, there can be no underlying consensus that can be reached if only we can find the right technique. Rather, the challenge is to find processes that allow society to struggle with the conflicts and uncertainties, and establish areas of agreement that will serve for the time being. Community involvement is one of those processes – its appeal is likely to grow as more people experience the satisfaction of being part of decisions about their own futures.

REFERENCES

Allies, P, Cuff, J and Mills, J (1999) *Working Together. Communities, Conservation and Rural Economies*, Royal Society for the Protection of Birds, Countryside Agency, Cheltenham and Gloucester College of Higher Education, Cheltenham

Arnstein, S (1969) 'A Ladder of Citizen Participation in the USA', *Journal of the American Institute of Planners*, vol 35(4), pp216–224

Baldock, D, Dwyer, J, Lowe, P, Petersen, J and Ward, N (2001) *The Nature of Rural Development: Towards a Sustainable Integrated Rural Policy in Europe. A Ten Nation Scoping Study*, Synthesis Report, WWF UK, Godalming

BDOR (1991) *Countryside Community Action: An Appraisal*, Countryside Commission, Cheltenham

Bishop, J, Davison, D, Hickling, D, Kean, J, Rose, J and Silson, R (1994) *Community Involvement in Planning and Development Processes*, Her Majesty's Stationery Office, London

Clarke, M and Stewart, J (1997) *Handling the Wicked Issues – A Challenge for Government*, School of Public Policy, University of Birmingham, Birmingham

Clifford, S and King, A (eds) (1993) *Local Distinctiveness*, Common Ground, London

Cowell, R and Owens, S (2001) 'Going Crisply to Damnation? Challenging the metaphor of the "toolkit"', *EG Magazine*, vol 7(8), pp12–14

Countryside Agency (2000) *Tomorrow's Countryside – 2020 Vision. The Future of the Countryside and the Countryside Agency's Role in Shaping It*, Countryside Agency, Cheltenham

Countryside Agency (2001) *Countryside Focus*, April/May 2001

Countryside and Community Research Unit (1997) 'Assessment of Village Design Statements', unpublished research report to the Countryside Commission, Countryside and Community Research Unit, Cheltenham

Countryside Commission (1993) *Design in the Countryside*, Countryside Commission Cheltenham

Countryside Commission (1994) *Design in the Countryside Experiments: Report of a Programme to Pilot Countryside Design Summaries and Village Design Statements*, Countryside Commission, Cheltenham

Countryside Commission (1996) *Village Design. Making Local Character Count in New Development. Parts 1 and 2*, Countryside Commission, Cheltenham

Countryside Commission/W S Atkins (1998) *Design in the Countryside. Monitoring Countryside Design Summaries and Village Design Statements (Final Report)*, W S Atkins, Cambridge

Craig, G, Monro, S, Taylor, M, Warburton, D and Wilkinson, M (2001) *Willing Partners? Voluntary and Community Organisations in the Democratic Process: Interim Research Report*, University of Brighton and University of Hull, Brighton

Cuff, J (2001) 'Participatory Processes: A tool to assist the wise use of floodplains', unpublished draft report for the EU LIFE funded Wise Use of Floodplains project; see also www.floodplains.org.uk

Department of the Environment (DOE) (1994) *Quality in Town and Country*, Department of the Environment, London

Donnison, D (1993) 'Society: Fair City – Listen to the voice of the community', *Guardian*, 10 November 1993

Environment Agency (2000a) *Environment Agency Annual Report 1999–2000*, Environment Agency, Bristol

Environment Agency (2000b) *Achieving Environmental Equality*, Environment Agency AGM Debate Highlights, 5 September 2000, Environment Agency, Bristol

Environment Agency (2001) *An Environmental Vision*, Environment Agency, Bristol

Frewer, L, Rowe, G, Marsh, R and Reynolds, C (2000) *Public Participation Methods: Evolving and Operationalising an Evaluation Framework*, Institute of Food Research, Norwich (supported by the Department of Health; see www.doh.gov.uk/risk.htm)

Greeves, T (1987) *Parish Maps*, Common Ground, London

InterAct (2001) *Evaluating Participatory, Deliberative and Co-operative Ways of Working*, InterAct Working Paper, London

Local Government Association (LGA) (2000) *Reforming Local Planning: Planning for Communities*, Local Government Association, London

Moseley, M (1997) 'Parish Appraisals as a Tool of Rural Community Development: An assessment of the British experience', *Planning Practice and Research*, vol 12(3), pp197–212

Moseley, M (1999) *Innovation and Rural Development – Inaugural Lecture*, Countryside and Community Research Unit, Cheltenham

Moseley, M, Derounian, J, Allies, P (1996) 'Parish Appraisals – A spur to local action?', *Town Planning Review*, vol 67(3), pp309–329

Owen, S (1998) 'The Role of Village Design Statements in Fostering a Locally Responsive Approach to Village Planning and Design in the UK', *Journal of Urban Design*, vol 3(3), pp359–380

Owens, S and Cowell, R (2001) 'Planning for Sustainability – New orthodoxy or radical challenge?', *Town and Country Planning*, vol 70(6), pp170–172

Royal Commission on Environmental Pollution (RCEP) (1998) *Setting Environmental Standards, Royal Commission on Environmental Pollution 21st Report*, Her Majesty's Stationery Office, London

Royal Town Planning Institute (RTPI) (1996) *The Local Delivery of Planning Services*, Royal Town Planning Institute, London

Town and Country Planning Association (TCPA) (1999) *Your Place and Mine: Reinventing Planning*, Town and Country Planning Association, London

Wakeford, R (2001) 'The Parish Discovery Trail', *Town and Country Planning*, vol 70(1), p17

Warburton, D (1994) *Supporting Environmental Action: Providing Support for Environmental Action by Community and Voluntary Groups*, National Council for Voluntary Organsiations, London

Warburton, D (1997) *Participatory Action in the Countryside – A Literature Review*, Countryside Commission, Cheltenham

Warburton, D (1998a) 'The Achievements and Effectiveness of Rural Action', unpublished research report for the Rural Action steering group, Countryside Commission, Cheltenham

Warburton, D (1998b) 'A Passionate Dialogue: community and sustainable development', in Warburton, D (ed) *Community and Sustainable Development. Participation in the Future*, Earthscan, London, pp1–39

World Bank (1994) *The World Bank and Participation*, report of the World Bank Learning Group on Participatory Development, World Bank, Washington, DC

Index

access 53, 73, 95, 96, 163, 181
accountability 76, 95, 257, 266
ACRE *see* Action with Communities in
    Rural England
action
  communities 68–71, 259
  defining 183, 185
  emergency 252
  plans 19–36, 95, 180
  positive 22–24
  rural 253–254
  see also biodiversity action plans
Action with Communities in Rural
    England (ACRE) 258
aesthetic sensitivity 149–150
afforestation 146
agri-environmental aspects 4, 6–7, 45,
    215–216
AONBs *see* Areas of Outstanding
    Natural Beauty
appraisal approaches 127–128, 257–260
archaeological work 156, 163
Areas of Outstanding Natural Beauty
    (AONBs) 51, 110
Argyll, Scotland 208–209
Arnstein's ladder of participation 251–252
arrangement 147, 148
aspect specialists 195
assessment of character *see* historic
    aspects; landscape character
    assessment, countryside character
attitudes 49–51, 185
audits 25–26, 75
awareness
  Category V approach 57
  Eat the View project 218
  landscapes 62, 126, 127–128, 129, 139,
    190
  Natural Areas 98
  public involvement 246, 248, 257
  VDS 262

BAPs *see* biodiversity action plans
Biodiversity: The UK Action Plan 26–28
biodiversity *see* Convention on Biological
    Diversity
biodiversity action plans (BAPs)
  development 19–36
  local 222–236, 238, 241–242
  UK 9–10, 94–95, 101
  see also action plans
*Biodiversity Challenge: An Agenda for
    Conservation in the UK* 25–28
*Biodiversity Counts: Delivering a Better
    Quality of Life* 30, 32
biogeographic frameworks 11, 91–108
Birds Directive 10, 33, 37–48, 95
bottom-up approaches 13, 74, 158–159,
    161, 196, 265
boundary issues 92, 101, 105, 161–162,
    181
Brundtland Report 71
Bute, Scotland 208–209

Caithness, Scotland 178
CAP *see* Common Agricultural Policy
capacity 79, 119, 207–210, 259
categorization 56–57, 62–63
CBD *see* Convention on Biological
    Diversity
CCW *see* Countryside Council for Wales
CDS *see* Countryside Design Summaries
change
  baselines 175
  diversity 171
  forestry 216
  historic 156, 164, 165
  landscapes 125, 144–145, 151–152, 214
  monitoring 120–121
  tolerance 195
  see also development; sensitivity
character assessment *see* countryside
    character; historic aspects; landscape
    character assessment

Character Map of England 115, 157
Chilterns Natural Area 92, 93
Circular 27/87, Department of the
    Environment 44
classification 148, 150, 173–174, 194, 195
CLRAE *see* Congress of Local and
    Regional Authorities
coastal dynamics 181
COE *see* Council of Europe
collaboration 99, 177–182, 183–184, 189,
    215
commercial viability 151
Common Agricultural Policy (CAP) 4, 7,
    45–46, 63
community level
    historic landscapes 164
    participation 6, 8, 10, 14, 246–248,
        250–270
    policy 68–87, 80, 213
    VDSs 211, 242–243
    vegetation 102
    see also local level
conflicts 32–33, 228–229, 265
confused interpretation 226–228
Congress of Local and Regional
    Authorities (CLRAE), Europe 59
Conservation of Natural Habitats and of
    Wild Fauna and Flora *see* Habitats
    Directive
consultation
    BAPs 241–242
    focus group meetings 149
    Natural Areas 98, 99
    public 214–215, 246
    specialist 160
contact communities 102
containment planning 4–5
control 210–213, 212, 239, 243, 250, 255
Convention on Biological Diversity
    (CBD) 9–10, 19–22, 33
Convention Concerning the Protection
    of the World Cultural and Natural
    Heritage 10, 54–55, 62
cooperation 61, 138
coordination 131, 212, 241–242,
    244–245
Cornwall 157–158, 164
corporate strategies 180, 181–182, 231
corridors *see* ecological corridors
costs 267
Council of Europe (COE) 58–60
Countryside Agency 204, 253–255

countryside character 11–12, 82, 99–100,
    204, 216, 225
    see also historic aspects; landscape
    character assessment
Countryside Commission 99, 110, 111,
    113, 114–115
Countryside Council for Wales (CCW)
    188–200
Countryside Design Summaries (CDSs)
    121–122, 210–211, 260–262
Countryside and Rights of Way Act 2000
    29–30
Countryside Stewardship 215, 216
County Clare, Ireland 129–136, 161
County Cork, Ireland 150–151, 152
county level character assessment 112,
    129–136, 150–151, 152, 161, 214
County Limerick, Ireland 161
cultural aspects 49–51, 54–55, 57, 62,
    138, 155

databases 193–196, 216
decision-making
    character assessment 116–123,
        163–164
    heritage awareness 127
    LANDMAP 199
    multi-purpose 245
    participation 81, 246, 247, 251–253
    stakeholders 191–192
    see also management
definitions 2, 56, 125–126, 189
democracy 76, 83, 266
descriptive aspects 194–195
design 121, 146–151, 197, 260–262
    see also Countryside Design Summaries;
        Village Design Statements
designation 54–55, 110, 240
deterioration of habitats 39
development
    biodiversity 222–236
    capacity 207–210
    community 69–70, 259
    containment planning 4–5
    control procedures 151–152, 210–213,
        239, 243, 250
    LANDMAP 197, 198, 199
    planning 121, 127, 204, 205–207, 238
    policy 137–138
    public participation 250–270
    rural 73
    SPAs 41

technology 13
 see also change; sustainable
  development
devolution 8–9, 75
Devon, England 228, 229
distinctiveness 260
district level character assessment 112, 213
Dobris Assessment 59
domestic drivers 6
Dumfries and Galloway Structure Plan
 231–232
dynamic landscapes 129

Eat the View project 219
ecological corridors 94, 226, 227
economic aspects 105, 182, 218–219, 267
EIA *see* environmental impact
  assessments
ELC *see* European Landscape
  Convention
elitism 243, 247
emergency action 252
English Nature 11, 91–108, 113–115
enhancement 122, 231–235
Environment 2010: Our Future, Our Choice
 72
Environment Agency 255–256
environmental impact assessments (EIA)
 210–213
Environmentally Sensitive Areas (ESAs)
 215
Epping Forest District Council 229
ESAs *see* Environmentally Sensitive
  Areas
EU *see* European Union
European Landscape Convention (ELC)
 10, 58–61, 63, 64–65
European Union (EU)
 directives 10, 33, 37–48, 72, 94–95,
  183, 222–224
 landscape characterization 61–62, 138
Europeanization 10, 73
evaluated aspects 194–195
evaluation 75, 260–262, 263–264
experiential learning 83–84, 130
expertise 65, 135–136, 160, 195, 230–231

Fareham Borough, England 211–212
farm level 4–5, 29, 157
fenlands 92, 93
FIPS *see* Forest Inventory and Planning
  System

flood defence 40
focus group meetings 149
Forest Inventory and Planning System
 (FIPS) 146–150
forests 4–5, 131, 146–150, 164, 213, 216
 see also woodland
forward-looking policies 213
fragmentation 94, 104, 170, 171, 175
functional divergence 5–6
fundamentalism 4
funding 254, 263
Futures Programme, Natural Heritage
 171–187

geographic frameworks *see* biogeographic
  frameworks
Geographical Information Systems
 (GIS) 131, 132, 134, 135, 153, 165,
 166, 190
 FIPS 148
Germany 40
GIS *see* Geographical Information
  Systems
globalization 9
good communities 80
'good enough to approve' approach
 209–210
good practice 208, 219–220, 253
governments
 action plans 24, 25, 29, 34
 guidance 207, 228–229, 234–235
 perceptions 75–76
 policy 77–78, 130–131, 138
 Regulation 37 225
 roles 4, 262–263
 targets 101–102
Green Spaces and Corridors 227
guidance
 development 141–154, 151
 government 234–235
 management and design 197
 parish appraisals 258
 planning 163, 225, 228, 261, 262
 use 207

Habitat Regulations 223, 234
 see also Regulation 37
Habitat Restoration Project 102–103,
 104
Habitats Directive, EU 10, 33, 37–48, 95,
 222–224
Hampshire, England 212, 214

Hart District, Hampshire 205, 206
heathland 102–103, 164
heritage 11–12, 115–116, 125–140, 155, 170–187
Heritage Council 11–12
heritage, *see also* historical aspects
high sensitivity 148
hills 178–179
historical aspects
    community involvement 68–71
    land-use influence 12, 118, 133
    LCA 113, 155–169
    perceptions 49–50, 52
    see also relicts
Hobhouse Committee, 1947 5–6
horizontal integration 33
housing development 210
Human Rights Act 1998 72
Huxley Committee, 1947 5–6

idealized communities 78, 79
IFS *see* Indicative Forestry Strategy
image assessment 143, 144
IMAGINE Expert Classifier 136
implementation
    action plans 32, 95, 234
    community involvement 84
    Habitats Directive 223–224
    lack of tools 244
    management strategies 214–215
    national level 40–41, 42–44
    positive planning 233–234
importance variable 145
incentives 215, 230
inconsistency 228–229
Indicative Forestry Strategy (IFS) 213
indicators 38, 120–121, 174, 216
information
    Futures Programme 180
    LANDMAP 196–197
    participation 193, 252, 259
    sharing 96, 138, 190
    see also knowledge
integrated approaches
    action plans 12, 13–14, 32, 33–34
    Heritage Council 128
    Lifescapes 103–105
    Natural Areas 92–94
    new 244–245
    policies 53–54, 137–138, 139, 180, 181
    Scotland 170–187
integration, *see also* partnerships

international level 10, 49–67, 72–73
interpretation 226–228, 228–229
involvement *see* participation
Ireland 11, 12, 125–140, 141–154, 161
    see also Northern Ireland
Irish Heritage Council 125–140
issue-based BAPs 241
IUCN *see* World Conservation Union

Joint Map *see* Character Map of England
judgements 116–119, 206, 219, 240

knowledge 57, 65, 135–136
    see also information

LA21 *see* Local Agenda 21
Lancashire, England 214–215
Land Parcel Information System (LPIS) 133
Land Utilisation Maps 96
LANDMAP, Wales 12, 13, 188–200, 225
Landscape Character Assessment (LCA)
    applications 203–221
    forestry 146–148
    guidelines 11–12, 141–154
    historic 155–169
    LANDMAP 188–200
    local 13, 237–241
    national 109–124, 117, 142–144, 174–175
    Natural Areas 102
    policy 125–140
    subjectivity 51
landscapes
    biodiversity 8, 10, 46, 222–236
    divisions 96–97
    integration 103–105
    partnerships 189
    perspectives 49–67, 190, 192
    sensitivity 142, 144–146, 148–150, 151–153
Lappel Bank case 41
layered approaches 105–106, 193–194
LCA *see* Landscape Character Assessment
leadership 247–248
LEAPs *see* Local Environment Agency Plans
legislation 40–41, 43, 58, 138, 155, 223
legitimacy 76–77, 83, 241, 259, 266
Leicestershire, Leicester and Rutland Structure Plan 1991–2011 231, 232

Leigh on Mendip, England 243
Leybucht Dykes case, Germany 40
Lifescapes 103–105
limestone 243
Local Agenda 21 (LA21) 65, 73–74, 266
Local Environment Agency Plans
    (LEAPs) 256
local level
    BAPs 28–29, 222–236
    distinctiveness 260
    global interests 245
    historic characterization 159–160
    information user groups 193
    internal collaboration 184
    Natural Areas 98
    participation 73
    partnerships 179–180
    perspectives 176
    planning authorities 224–236
    policy 205–207
    sensitivity 208–210
    see also communities
location 147, 148
LPIS *see* Land Parcel Information System

management
    biogeographic frameworks 97–98
    characterization 164, 197, 198
    conservation and enhancement
        121–122
    corporate 231
    land 214–215, 220
    positive planning 223–224
    protected areas 56
    QoL 120
    sensitivity 149
    see also decision-making
mapping
    actions 185
    community involvement 246
    development of 96–103, 114–115, 150
    government guidance 228
    historic 157–158, 161–162
    image units 144
    LANDMAP 193–196
    overlay 132, 135
marshland 40–41
Meeting the Rio Challenge 28
Mendip, England 237–249
Midvale Ridge Natural Area, England
    92, 93
model policy approaches 235

monitoring 26, 95–96, 120–121, 260
moors 178–179
mudflats 41
multidisciplinarity 50

National Biodiversity Network (NBN)
    96, 106
National Development Plan 2000–2006,
    Ireland 127
National Heritage, Scotland 225
national level
    action plans 25–28
    applications 112, 113–116, 213
    conservation strategies 21, 22
    databases 196, 198–199
    directive implementation 40–41,
        42–44
    historic aspects 158–161, 163, 164
    indicators 216
    internal collaboration 184
    Natural Areas 98, 99, 100
    partnerships 61, 179
    Rural Action 253–254
    Scotland 175–176
National Parks and Access to the
    Countryside Act 1949 5, 6
National Trust 58, 66
Natura 2000 10, 38, 42
Natural Areas, English Nature 11,
    91–108, 114, 225
NBN *see* National Biodiversity Network
networks 92–93, 96, 106
New Forest, England 212
New Map of England 99, 114
NGOs *see* non-governmental
    organizations
non-governmental organizations
    (NGOs) 25
North West Leicestershire Local Plan
    Inquiry 229
Northern Ireland 161

objective-led approaches 23–24, 25, 29,
    34
    see also targets
Ordnance Survey 133
organizational aspects 97–98, 180,
    181–184, 231
orientation 193
outcomes *see* targets, objective-led
    approaches
overlay mapping 132, 135

ownership 68, 98, 171–172, 184, 193, 262
Oxford Landscape Declaration 64–65

Pan-European Biological and Landscape Diversity Strategy (PEBLDS) 46, 59
parish appraisals 257–260
participation
  BAPs 32–33
  community 8, 10, 14, 68–87, 246–248, 250–270
  landscape 153
  stakeholders 137
partnerships
  agri-environmental schemes 101–102
  BAPs 30, 32, 241–242
  Futures Programme 177–179
  historic characterization 158
  Ireland 137
  LA21 74, 75
  LANDMAP 189, 198
  management strategies 214–215
  participation 265, 266
  see also integration
Partnerships in Rural Integrated Development 75
peatlands 178
PEBLDS *see* Pan-European Biological and Landscape Diversity Strategy
perceptions
  communities 77–82
  government 75–76
  landscape 52, 53, 129, 192
  public 264
period characterization maps 165
perspectives 49–67, 176, 252
physical assessment 143, 146
pilot projects 129–136, 146, 190, 217, 260–261
Planning Policy Guidance Note 9 (PPG9) 44–45
policy context
  agriculture 6–7
  biodiversity 231–233
  collaboration 189
  communities 68–87, 77, 80
  development 121, 205–207
  historic 164
  impacts 44–45
  integration 32, 33, 180, 181
  international 10, 49–54
  Ireland 125–140

positive planning 222–231
  social capital and trust 81
polygon mapping 144
positive planning 222–236, 264
power 76, 77, 251
PPG9 *see* Planning Policy Guidance Note 9
predictive modelling 165
prescriptive approaches *see* judgements
preservation 22–24
priorities
  Biodiversity Challenge 26
  conservation 23
  landscapes 125–140
  Natural Areas 100
  parish appraisals 258, 259
  setting 245, 263
  see also visions
product approaches 10, 197
profile documents 100
promotion 231–235
protected areas
  boundaries 181
  categorization 62–63
  European Directives 38–42
  landscape character 241
  positive action 22–23, 234
  Scotland 171
  site-specific conservation 5, 7
  World Heritage 54–58
  see also Natura 2000; site-based aspects; Special Areas of Conservation; Special Protection Areas
protest 68, 252
public participation *see* participation

QoL *see* Quality of Life Capital
quality of landscape 118, 196, 206
Quality of Life Capital (QoL) 109, 119–120, 145
quantification 51
questionnaire surveys 224–236, 257

RCCs *see* Rural Community Councils
recommendations 195
Red Data Birds in Britain 23–24
regeneration programmes 70–71, 217–219
regional level 29, 52, 112
  see also European Union
registration 160–161
Regulation 37 223–231, 233–234

see also Habitat Regulations; Town and Country Planning Acts
relationships 165–166, 251, 259, 261, 262, 263
relicts 159, 161, 162
see also historical aspects
Report on Land Utilization in Rural Areas 3–4
representativeness 266
research 163, 165
resources
  BAPs 30, 31
  lack of 244, 248
  parish appraisals 259
  partnerships 256–257
  SNH 182–183
responsibility 60, 256–257
river catchment areas 256
road traffic 217–218
roles 4, 76, 184, 262–263
Royal Society for the Protection of Birds (RSPB) 23–24, 33
RSPB *see* Royal Society for the Protection of Birds
Rural Action for the Environment programme 253–254
Rural Community Councils (RCCs) 257
Rural Development Commission 253
Rural White Paper 'Our countryside: the future' 2000 75
Rutland County Council 230

SACs *see* Special Areas of Conservation
Santona Marshes case, Spain 40–41
scale 53, 101, 112–113, 147, 148, 153, 182
Scotland 11, 12, 115–116, 159–160, 170–187, 208–209, 231–232
Scott Committee 3–4
Scottish Natural Heritage (SNH) 115–116, 170–187
sense of place 94, 125, 144, 164
sensitivity
  landscape 142, 144–145, 148–150, 151, 152, 206
  see also change
service level agreements 263
SEU *see* Social Exclusion Unit
Shrewsbury and Atcham Borough Local Plan Inquiry 229
Sites of Special Scientific Interest (SSSIs), Natural Areas 91, 102

site-based aspects 5, 7, 42–43, 45, 47, 156
  see also protected areas
sites and monuments records (SMRs) 165–166
Sites of Special Scientific Interest (SSSIs) 43, 63
Sixth European Environmental Action Programme 61
Skeffington Committee on Public Participation in Planning 69–70
SLA *see* Special Landscape Area
SMRs *see* sites and monuments records
SNH *see* Scottish Natural Heritage
social aspects 79, 81, 105, 110, 182, 259
Social Exclusion Unit (SEU) 79
socio-economic aspects 104, 199
soils 133
Somerset County Council, England 228–229
South Hams District, England 210
Spain 40–41
SPAs *see* Special Protection Areas
Special Areas for Conservation (SACs) 10, 38, 42
Special Landscape Area (SLA) 148, 240
Special Protection Areas (SPAs) 10, 38, 39–42
species centred views 30, 31
SPG *see* Supplementary Planning Guidance
SSSIs *see* Sites of Special Scientific Interest
Staffordshire County Council, England 206
stakeholders 81, 113, 137, 177–182, 191–192
standardization 159, 235
statutory plans 238
Stoke-on-Trent, England 206
strategic documents 181–182
subjectivity 50–51
Sunderland, Scotland 178
Supplementary Planning Guidance (SPG) 261
support 74, 179, 252, 253–255, 263
surveys 224–236
sustainable communities 80, 83, 84
sustainable development
  Habitats Directive 41
  LA21 73–74
  LANDMAP 199

landscapes 53–54, 165
participation 71
planning 7
SNH 180
*Sustaining the Variety of Life: Five Years of
the UK Biodiversity Action Plan* 30, 32
synthesis 196–197

TAIMS *see* traffic appraisal and impact
monitoring system
targets
BAPs 30
Biodiversity Challenge 26
Countryside Character Database 216
defining 183
Environment Agency 255
governments 25, 29, 34
Natural Areas 95, 96, 100, 101–103
see also objective-led approaches
technical aspects 131–132, 267
technology development 13
time-limited grant schemes 263
toolkit of techniques 3, 267
top-down approaches 159–160, 161, 265
Town and Country Planning Acts 4, 69,
223
townland boundaries 161–162
traffic appraisal and impact monitoring
system (TAIMS) 217–218
transport planning 217–218
trust 76, 81, 83, 264
type maps 157–158

UK *see* United Kingdom
UNCED *see* United Nations Conference
on Environment and Development
uncertainty 230
UNCHE *see* United Nations Conference
on the Human Environment
UNEP *see* United Nations Environment
Programme
United Kingdom (UK) 21, 41, 62–66,
223–224
United Nations
Conference on Environment and
Development (UNCED) 21, 72
Conference on the Human
Environment (UNCHE) 72
Convention on Biological Diversity
(CBD) 9–10, 19–22
Environment Programme (UNEP) 20,
62–63

United States of America (USA) 78
urban areas 211–212
USA *see* United States of America

Vale of Glamorgan, Wales 191, 218
value 118–119, 123, 145, 149, 192,
237–249
values-led government 77
VDS *see* Village Design Statements
vegetation communities 102
vertical integration 34
Village Design Statements (VDSs) 109,
121, 210–211, 238, 242–243, 260–262
visions
communities 80, 83, 213, 246–247
Environment Agency 255–256
Ireland 128–129, 139
Natural Areas 102, 103
Scotland 173, 178–179, 185
see also priorities
visual assessment 143–144
voluntary sector 22–23, 51, 74, 253–254,
257, 262–263

Wales 12, 13, 160–161, 188–200, 218
WCMC *see* World Conservation
Monitoring Centre
WCPA *see* World Commission on
Protected Areas
Wealdon, England 229, 230–231
West Lancashire 227
West Lindsey District, England 211
wicked issues 264–265, 267
Winchester, England 212
wind farms 150–151, 152, 208, 209
woodland 157, 164
see also forests
World Commission on Protected Areas
(WCPA) 63
World Conservation Monitoring Centre
(WCMC), UNEP 62–63
World Conservation Union (IUCN)
56–57, 63
World Heritage Convention *see*
Convention Concerning the
Protection of the World Cultural
and Natural Heritage

Yorkshire Dales Natural Areas 94

zonal approaches 157–158, 172, 174